About the Authors

Richard Kozul-Wright is a senior economist at the United Nations Conference on Trade and Development (UNCTAD) in Geneva. He received his Ph.D. in economics from Cambridge University, from where he went to work at the United Nations, first in New York on the *World Economic and Social Survey* and subsequently in Geneva on the *World Investment Report,* the *Trade and Development Report* and the *Economic Development in Africa Report.* He has published articles on a broad range of issues in economic development and economic history in the *Economic Journal,* the *Cambridge Journal of Economics,* the *Oxford Review of Economic Policy* and the *Journal of Development Studies.*

Paul Rayment studied economics at Magdalen College, Oxford and spent several years on the research staff of the National Institute of Economic and Social Research in London before joining the United Nations. He worked first in the United Nations Conference on Trade and Development (UNCTAD) and then moved to the UN's Economic Commission for Europe, where he became Director of Economic Analysis. In addition to a large output published under the UN imprint, he has written papers on economic development, transition economies and international trade that have appeared in a number of academic journals and collective works.

D0223006

The Resistible Rise of Market Fundamentalism:
Rethinking Development Policy
in an Unbalanced World

Richard Kozul-Wright and *Paul Rayment*

TWN
Third World Network
Penang, Malaysia

Zed Books
London and New York

The Resistible Rise of Market Fundamentalism:
Rethinking Development Policy in an Unbalanced World
is published by
Zed Books Ltd,
7 Cynthia Street, London N1 9JF, UK and
Room 400, 175 Fifth Avenue, New York, NY 10010, USA
and
Third World Network,
131 Jalan Macalister, 10400 Penang, Malaysia

Distributed exclusively in the USA on behalf of Zed Books
by Palgrave Macmillan,
a division of St Martin's Press, LLC
175 Fifth Avenue,
New York, NY 10010, USA

Printed by Jutaprint,
2 Solok Sungai Pinang 3,
11600 Penang, Malaysia

ISBN: 978 1 84277 636 0 hb (Zed Books)
ISBN: 978 1 84277 637 7 pb (Zed Books)
ISBN: 978 983 2729 07 5 (TWN)

A catalogue record for this book is available from the British Library
US CIP data is available from the Library of Congress

Contents

For

Zeljka and Carolyn

Preface and Acknowledgements

A CENTRAL premise of this book, echoing the work of Amartya Sen, Joseph Stiglitz and others, is that the general values of open, participatory systems can have a significant influence in strengthening the prospects for more rapid rates of economic development. Democracy is such a system, and one of its major strengths is that it is generally better at solving problems than other forms of government. This is because it encourages free and open debate and inquiry, it nurtures experimentation and new ways of thinking, and it does not imprison or exterminate those who hold dissident or otherwise controversial views or who reach conclusions that are objectionable to those in power. The rise of more democratic forms of government in recent years is therefore a welcome development. We are well aware, however, that their roots are still often shallow and that they may prove as vulnerable to authoritarian temptations as were the democracies of Western Europe between the two World Wars. We are also aware that many, although by no means all, of the countries that have lifted themselves out of poverty in the last 50 years have not always adhered to democratic forms of government, at least not in their western denomination. Nevertheless, in most of these cases, traditional mechanisms for consultation and discussion helped to create a popular consensus for change.

It is all the more worrying therefore that this democratic trend has coincided with an increasingly triumphalist tone among economic policy makers in some of the western democracies, which intensified after the collapse of communism, and a resurgent fundamentalism on what constitutes the right path to economic salvation. Perhaps more troublesome still, such fundamentalism appears to be gaining ground across an ever-wider range of scientific and social issues. These developments have contributed to a sharp polarisation of debates over many of the key questions in both domestic and world politics. Criticism of official views is met with rapid rebuttal, using all the means of modern communications technology, and legitimate differences of opinion and judgement are frequently dismissed with disdain and derision. In such an environment, policy debate tends to degenerate into the rhetoric of extremes: good versus evil, progressive versus reactionary, cosmopolitan versus provincial, outward-looking versus protectionist, the right-thinking versus the wrong-headed, and so on and so on. Such polarisation is not a healthy trend, particularly in fledgling democracies.

This is especially true of the variegated phenomenon known as globalisation, disagreement on which constitutes one of the major faultlines in contemporary world politics. On the one hand, many proponents and supporters of globalisation insist that their agenda for liberalisation on a global scale is the only way to eliminate poverty and ensure a prosperous economic future for rich and poor alike – identifying globalisation as a "win-win" process. At the other end of the scale are various groups from both developed and developing countries who see globalisation as a western corporate conspiracy against the poor and who see market-friendly policies simply as a means of perpetuating privilege – identifying globalisation as a "winner takes all" process. At neither extreme does there appear to be any willingness to acknowledge the fact that at any one time the market economy exists in many varieties and that over time it has shown, in contrast to the former centrally planned economies of the Soviet Union and its satellites, considerable flexibility in adapting to changing circumstances and, not least, in responding to the demands of democratic politics.

Somewhere between these polar positions as to where the world economy is moving, are most of the developing countries, still struggling to lift large sections of their populations out of poverty and seeking ways to create the foundations of sustainable development and to catch up with the income levels of the west. In most of these countries, admiration for the achievements of the western democracies is heavily qualified by two major considerations. The first is that western liberalism, whether in its earlier self-presentation of bearing "civilisation" to the rest of the world or, as now, creating opportunities for the poor to "trade their way out of poverty", is widely regarded in the developing world as narrowly self-serving. The "win-win" neo-liberal economic agenda, the major "selling point" of market fundamentalism, has certainly produced gains for some (particularly in rich countries), but it has come with heavy costs (including for communities in rich countries) and has also led to large numbers of losers (particularly in developing countries where there are few if any social safety nets). This distrust, and the increasing resistance to the opportunistic bias of the major western powers, is a major sticking point in the current Doha Round of World Trade Organisation (WTO) negotiations.

The second qualification is that the actual success stories of recent decades, particularly those in East Asia, do not appear to have followed the neo-liberal script. Their growth seems to undermine the insistence of the western democracies, and the international financial institutions they control, that if developing countries are to accelerate their development, there is no alternative to liberalising trade and foreign capital flows, and to hosting large, mainly western transnational corporations. Indeed, both economic theory and the results of empirical analysis are much more ambiguous and uncertain about the strength and causal direction of such relationships than is commonly assumed. As we hope to show in this book, the strong policy recommendations of the neo-liberal agenda rest on weak foundations.

A basic problem with the neo-liberal agenda is that it forces proposals for systemic and institutional change on countries with little regard for local conditions, preferences and traditions. This is both foolish and dangerous. Foolish, because it ignores the fact that the traditional cultures in developing countries already contain many of the values and institutional elements on which modern democratic polities can be constructed; and dangerous, because in arrogantly sweeping aside or ignoring such values, it adds to the resentment generated by economic deprivation and increases the attraction of political or religious fundamentalist movements which seek to anchor their own legitimacy in the same values but with very different objectives. Thus, those we regard as market fundamentalists undermine their own professed objective of a more liberal, prosperous and peaceful world.

Another worrying characteristic of the neo-liberal revival since the 1980s is its insistence that economic challenges can only be effectively tackled through a pro-business culture. This means much more than acknowledging a central role for private investment in sustaining economic growth: it also involves a proselytising role for business leadership and the promotion of business skills and values in finding the quickest and most efficient solutions to a wide range of contemporary policy issues, from healthcare provision through urban renewal to climate change. This mindset is dominated by the rhetoric of targets, partnerships, synergies and other platitudes that drain policy discussion of all substance, and inevitably tends to ignore or gloss over the difficult trade-offs that face political leaders in democratic societies. The result is a string of ready-made economic fixes for poorer countries, from privatisation to currency boards to micro-credit. A central argument of this book, however, is that there is no fast or ready-paved road to sustainable development and it is a dangerous delusion to suppose otherwise. This is a criticism, we would add, that also extends to many of the critics of market fundamentalism. Debt relief, increased foreign assistance, improved market access in a fairer international trading system can all be achieved relatively quickly, provided (and this is no small proviso) there is sufficient political will on the part of the leading powers, and all are almost certainly worth having – indeed, for some countries they are probably necessary, but not sufficient, for getting the development process started. But countries must ultimately rely on their own efforts to mobilise the energies of their populations and, especially, to raise their levels of domestic capital investment and technological know-how.

To do that, however, they need to have the widest possible room in which to experiment in order to discover what works in their particular conditions, and not to be subject to a constant narrowing of their policy space by the WTO and other international institutions. Moreover, the developed world needs to show not only more humility in lecturing developing countries on how they should solve their problems but also more tolerance in accepting the possibility of different economic and social arrangements from those prevailing in the west: the fact that the populations of most developing countries are generally in favour of democracy and effective market economies does not necessarily imply that they want to be facsimiles of Western Europe or the United States. Instead, they want to evolve in their own way, and if the western democracies remain true to their own principles they should not find it too difficult to live with such differences. Edmund Burke's warning to Lord North and George III in 1775, that the peace of their empire rested on "a unity of spirit, though in a diversity of operations", was ignored and the War of Independence had to be fought in order for Americans to be able to conduct their own affairs in the light of their own preferences and interests. In the longer run the western democracies will anyway have to accept such differences of operation in the rest of the world and so it would be as well to start now by considering less dogmatic approaches to the problems of under-development. As we see it, this should be central to any strategy that purports to be seeking a more just, liberal and stable world order.

In writing this study, both of us have drawn on our work as members of research teams within the United Nations: the United Nations Conference on Trade and Development (UNCTAD) and the United Nations Economic Commission for Europe (UNECE), respectively. Inevitably, we have drawn on the work of our colleagues and although they may not always agree with our use and our interpretation of it, our debt to them is considerable. In particular, we want to acknowledge the considerable contribution of Yilmaz Akyüz, who, with Shahen Abrahamian, was largely responsible for turning UNCTAD's *Trade and Development Report* into a valuable international source for the analysis of development trends and policy issues. We have greatly benefited from the analysis that has appeared in successive *Reports*. In particular, we want to acknowledge our intellectual debts to Andrew Cornford, Charles Gore, Jan Kregel, Jörg Mayer and John Toye in UNCTAD, as well as to Ha-Joon Chang, Gabriel Palma and Bob Rowthorn in Cambridge (UK) and to Will Milberg at the New School in New York who, at various times, have all worked closely with the UNCTAD team in Geneva. For insights into the transition and development issues facing the former centrally planned economies of Central and Eastern Europe, we are indebted to the work of Rumen Dobrinsky, Dieter Hesse, Handan del Pozzo, Vitalija Gaucaite-Wittich, Joe Smolik and Claus Wittich of the UNECE. It goes without saying that any errors of fact or interpretation fall entirely on our shoulders. We are also grateful to Martin Khor of Third World Network and to Robert Molteno of Zed Books for encouraging us to write this book. Two people who were an inspiration and support to us over many years and to whom we often turned for advice and critical comment – not to mention lunch and a glass of wine – are no longer with us: Shahen Abrahamian, Acting Director of UNCTAD's Global Interdependence Division, who died in 1995, and Professor Paul Bairoch of the University of Geneva, who died in early 2000. We would like this book to be a modest tribute to their memory.

R.K.-W.
P.B.W.R.

Abbreviations

BIS		Bank for International Settlements
FAO		Food and Agriculture Organisation
FDI		foreign direct investment
GATS		General Agreement on Trade in Services
GDP		gross domestic product
GNI		gross national income
G7		Group of Seven developed economies (France, Germany, Italy, UK, Canada, USA, Japan)
G77		the 132 developing-country members of the "Group of 77" in the United Nations
IFIs		international financial institutions
ILO		International Labour Organisation
IMF		International Monetary Fund
NIEs		newly industrialising economies
	First tier	Rep. of Korea; Taiwan, P.C.; Hong Kong; Singapore
	Second tier	Indonesia; Malaysia; Thailand; Philippines
NIEO		New International Economic Order
ODA		official development assistance
OECD		Organisation for Economic Cooperation and Development
SSA		Sub-Saharan Africa
TNCs		transnational corporations
TRIMs		Trade-Related Investment Measures
TRIPS		Trade-Related Aspects of Intellectual Property Rights
UNCTAD		United Nations Conference on Trade and Development
UNDESA		United Nations Department of Economic and Social Affairs
UNDP		United Nations Development Programme
UNECA		United Nations Economic Commission for Africa
UNECE		United Nations Economic Commission for Europe
UN-HABITAT		United Nations Human Settlements Programme
UNIDO		United Nations Industrial Development Organisation
WTO		World Trade Organisation

Chapter 1

The Rise of Market Fundamentalism

A.   Globalisation: What's in a name?

ALTHOUGH it is often forgotten in the hard-edged debates on current economic realities, globalisation is a child of the 1960s. The phrase "global village" first appeared in the early 1960s to describe the ability of new communications technologies to transmit news and ideas around the world in real time, and to suggest, as a result, that a profound restructuring in the organisation of social and personal life was under way. At much the same time, the call to "think globally and act locally" anticipated a broadening of the political agenda as new constituencies began to break down longstanding ideological boundaries. Economics eventually caught on to this new trend; towards the end of the decade renewed labour struggles in the advanced countries pushed distributional issues to the front of policy discussions and at much the same time the growing assertiveness of the developing world gave rise to talk of a New International Economic Order (NIEO) to bring about a fairer distribution of global resources.

As it turned out, international economic relations took a different turn, beginning in the late 1970s with a policy backlash in the rich industrial countries against growing economic instability. The initial response by policy makers in these countries to the breakdown of the Bretton Woods system, two oil shocks, rising labour militancy, a loss of control over inflation and, to some extent, government budget deficits had been a series of ad hoc adjustments that aimed to contain the threat of "stagflation", i.e., a simultaneous acceleration of inflation and deceleration of output growth (Bruno and Sachs, 1985). However, as ruling elites and democratically elected governments increasingly saw monetary disorder as the root of a wider socio-political malaise, moves to control the money supply, liberalise financial flows, cut welfare provision and use unemployment as a policy tool crystallised into an alternative policy paradigm which aimed to shift the distribution of income back towards profits, through a "withdrawal of the state" from the economy and the dismantling of the post-war political and social compromise (Mazower, 1998:332-66). Ronald Reagan's refusal in 1981 to give any credence to the Report of the Brandt Commission at a meeting in Cancún effectively ended any lingering hopes of negotiating an NIEO and signalled that the new policy agenda would not be limited to the national arena.[1]

The ongoing revolution in communications and information technology was quickly detached from issues of social justice and tuned to increasing the reach and profitability of market opportunities by lowering transaction and coordination costs. Transnational corporations (TNCs) took advantage of these factors to extend and coordinate their activities across large swathes of the globe, and to control a growing share of international trade and fixed investment. The same technologies also helped to convert monetary assets into international commodities, instantaneously tradeable on global markets by ever-larger and ever-more-undifferentiated financial institutions. In the minds of many policy makers, averting the threat of "capital flight" was a far more pressing challenge than that posed by disgruntled trades unions.[2] As these trends intensified they also

---

[1] A special session of the UN General Assembly in 1974 adopted the "Declaration on the Establishment of a New International Economic Order" which covered a wide range of issues from improving commodity terms of trade to obtaining a more equitable transfer of technology. The thrust of the initiative was to break the binding international constraints on growth in poorer countries. Somewhat ironically, negotiations evolved over a decade when per capita growth in developing countries was actually faster than in the advanced countries (largely due to the sharp slowdown in the latter), although its unevenness would be an important factor in weakening the political cohesion of "the South" that had been key to the initiative in the first place. On the intellectual origins of the NIEO, see Arndt (1987:140-45), and for an assessment of its achievements and limitations, see Toye and Toye (2004:254-57).

[2] The experience of the Mitterrand government in France in 1980-81 is frequently seen as symptomatic of the trend and as the last gasp of Keynesian expansionary policies. The episode is often presented in rather simplistic terms but see Petit (1986) for a more balanced account. It is also worth recalling that, after the Volcker shock, which lasted from 1979 to 1982, US monetary and fiscal policy switched to a more expansionary stance for the remainder of the decade. Such a stance, at the same time, was deemed irresponsible when adopted by developing countries, an early sign of the double standards of market fundamentalists.

became intertwined, stock-market valuations becoming the measure of good corporate governance, mergers and acquisitions becoming the dominant component of foreign direct investment (FDI) and the dividing line between international production and international finance becoming blurred.

These same developments in turn helped to accelerate and amplify the progressive liberalisation of trade, under way since World War II. Indeed, with the Uruguay Round (1986-94), multilateral trade negotiations which had previously done little more than codify the underlying structural pressures towards greater integration among the rich countries (Rose, 2002) not only gave an independent stimulus to trade liberalisation but extended the liberalisation agenda to many new areas that had previously been regarded as the preserve of national policy, such as industrial development and intellectual property law. Once again, in areas such as banking and insurance, the lines between trade, production and finance became increasingly difficult to draw.

Against this backdrop, public intellectuals, politicians and business leaders have increasingly drawn attention to what they see as the unprecedented speed and endless complexity of the changes deriving from an ever-deeper interaction between local and global forces. Traditional borders between nations, disciplines and occupations are seen as the vestiges of a passing era and obstacles to modern efficient structures. The call invariably is to cast aside old institutions and loyalties and to embrace the new challenges and opportunities of a globalising world. By the end of the 20th century, "globalisation" had become a catch-all term to describe this new and encompassing reality. Discussions of a wide range of subjects, from crime to culture, from migration to the environment, from terrorist atrocities to health scares, now rarely proceed for long without reference to the role of globalisation in some form or another.[3]

Running through most of these discussions is a general sense that globalisation is somehow akin to an irresistible force, driven by countless invisible hands and by a permanent technological revolution, and beyond the control of governments. Indeed, many believe that

---

[3]   Using citations from the *New York Times*, Stanley Fischer (2003) found that globalisation was absent from most commentary in the 1970s, became more frequently used in the 1980s but only came to dominate discussions in the 1990s.

only property-owning households and firms can make the right economic choices in this new world, that states should adapt by relinquishing economic sovereignty to mobile capital, and that efforts to direct it are futile and resistance will only result in marginalisation, or perhaps worse.[4] The impersonal and inevitable nature of this globalising power, relentlessly eroding national independence, is captured by a series of over-worked – and overstretched – metaphors invoking some force of nature such as the weather, gravitational pull, or butterflies beating their wings in the Amazon jungle. For those still unsure about where things were going, British Prime Minister Tony Blair spelt out the implications at the 2005 Labour Party Conference:

> I hear people say we have to stop and debate globalisation. You might as well debate whether autumn should follow summer. They're not debating it in China and India. They are seizing its possibilities in a way that will transform their lives and ours…In the era of rapid globalisation, there is no mystery about what works – an open liberal economy, prepared constantly to change to remain competitive. The new world rewards those who are open to it. Foreign investment improves our economy.

Economic life, we shall argue, is a good deal more complicated and mysterious than such fundamentalist proselytising would have us believe. Nor do recent trends add up to a "new world" and certainly

---

[4]   In an article deploring the slow progress in the Doha Round of trade negotiations, the *Financial Times* journalist Martin Wolf described French President Chirac's scepticism as to the virtues of unlimited free trade as "foolish, even depraved", since if the negotiations "should fail, disorder alone should triumph" (Martin Wolf, "The world has everything to lose if trade liberalisation fails", *Financial Times,* London, 2 November 2005). It is not clear why a failure to extend the rules of the global trading system should lead to the collapse of those already agreed and embodied in the WTO, unless of course the leading powers, in a fit of irresponsibility, were to abandon them in retaliation for not getting their way. Such verbal overkill usually appears whenever international trade negotiations run into difficulty, but it clearly illustrates the passions aroused in the globalisation debate.

not a brave one.[5] The economic and political consequences of the intertwining of nations, the rise of new technologies and the breakdown of traditional ways of life have been a recurring source of policy debate and dispute since at least the French Revolution (Stedman Jones, 2004). And, *pace* Mr Blair, the world is likely to be better off for having such debate; there is certainly a good deal of it on these matters in both India and China.

History never simply repeats itself. Still, parallels with the past abound. The increasing interdependence of peoples, businesses and territories in the four decades leading up to World War I was also marked by a rush of new intellectual currents grappling with the transition to modernity, with both secular and religious underpinnings (Bayly, 2004:Part III). Then, as now, talk of "new worlds" was all too often driven by the enthusiasm of innovators and by the vested interests of those who judged themselves to be ahead of the curve or who simply saw an opportunity for preserving or expanding their political and economic power by changing the existing structures of rules and institutions. Then, as now, it was assumed that the dominance of the international economy had put an end to state power. Then, as now, those at the bottom of the social hierarchy saw (and experienced) the workings of the global economy in a very different light from those at the top. Radical movements in the late 19th century looking to promote the rights of workers, women and citizens were quick to connect the internationalisation of economic activity, abuses of power at home and abroad and widening social differences.[6]

---

[5]   As Saul (2005:196) has rightly pointed out, the ideology of globalism, "which declared itself the force of capitalism and risk, was spoken for largely by tenured professors of economics and management while being led by technocrats – that is private sector bureaucrats – working for large joint stock companies that were rarely owned by blocs of active shareholders. And most of the changes they sought were aimed at reducing competition".

[6]   For a classic account of the challenges to liberalism in the late 19th century, see Dangerfield (1970) and also Hobsbawm (1994), whose particular brand of Marxist historiography has always been sensitive to both the global dimension of economic development and the richness of the "superstructure". Bayly (op. cit.) offers an excellent discussion of the varying intellectual currents promoting and opposing "globalisation" in the second half of the 19th century. Although his views are apparently unworthy of Mr Blair's ear, to a poor Jamaican banana farmer today "globalisation seems like a system where the man with power uses a big stick to put the man without power in his place", and with scant improvement in his lot and that of his family (quoted by Younge, 2005).

It is perhaps not surprising therefore that the blanket use of a single term to describe the contemporary era has led to confusion about the nature of global economic interdependence and the issues involved. There is confusion at times, often deliberate, as to whether the term "globalisation" is being used to refer to an actually existing state of international relations or to a projection of their future development. There is also a good deal of confusion about the leading forces driving the process, whether consumer tastes, business behaviour, technological progress, political ideology, cultural homogenisation, or, indeed, all of these. There is also confusion about whether this future is inevitable or simply preferred by a coalition of special interests and idealists. The interests certainly include TNCs, international banks and other suppliers of financial services, who see greater opportunities for their own expansion if national rules and other restrictions on their activities can be swept away or, at least, harmonised; but they also include new political constituencies that see the processes of globalisation as creating the opportunity to replace national sovereignties with some form of supranational authority or coalition, at regional or global levels, and which they believe will improve the prospects for peace, prosperity and security. According to one frustrated observer of the debates, "the very term globalisation has become so slippery, so ambiguous, so subject to misunderstanding and political manipulation, that it should be banned from further use" (Helleiner, 2000:1).

The view of an irresistible and inevitable global *zeitgeist* derives from a heightened sense of the role of economic forces. This is the point where the debate on globalisation becomes caught up in a whirl of numbers: the volume of world trade has increased more than five-fold since the late 1970s, 12-fold for high-technology goods and over 20-fold for developing countries; FDI rose almost 30-fold between the late 1970s and the late 1990s, with that in developing countries increasing 25-fold; the daily turnover of foreign exchange was just $15 billion in the mid-1970s but today stands at $1.9 trillion. These sound like very large amounts, and in some respects they are, although, as we shall try to show in later chapters, taken out of context they often hide more than they reveal. However, "the universal interdependence of nations" resulting from the perpetual ebb and flow

of cross-border flows of goods, services and factors of production –
still as good a definition of globalisation as is currently available –
does not in itself describe a new trend and there is plenty of room for
discussing just how far recent developments have gone, what role
policies have played in shaping them and whether or not there are
limits to their expansion.[7] Rather, "globalisation", as the term is
commonly used, is best understood as a political project aimed both
at extending the sway of free markets on a global scale through a
singular set of economic policies to be adopted by all countries
regardless of their circumstances (Gray, 1998) and at ceding direction
over an increasing area of policy-making (and the public realm more
generally) to business leadership and the values of the marketplace
(Saul, 2005).

As such, the current globalisation agenda, while retaining some
of the utopian spirit from which it sprang in the 1960s, is much more
the product of bitter crisis conditions in the rich countries in the late
1970s and, in particular, of the turn to neo-liberal policies in the United
States and the United Kingdom in the early 1980s which spread,
somewhat fitfully, to other OECD countries during the rest of that
decade (Glyn, 2006:24-49). The deflationary macroeconomic policies
that ushered in that turn also provoked a debt crisis in many parts of the
developing world in the early 1980s as the combination of higher oil
prices, rising interest rates and declining export revenues made for an
unmanageable external position (UNCTAD, 1988:92-94). That crisis,
in turn, provided the opportunity to promote a similar policy agenda
in many developing countries, usually as a condition of debt
restructuring and for obtaining assistance from the international
financial institutions. The worldwide trend towards liberalisation,
privatisation and deregulation essentially dates from this period.

---

[7] The definition comes from Marx and Engels. The literature defining and tracking
    globalisation is vast and repetitive and it is not our intention to review it here; for
    useful discussions, see Milberg (1998), Hirst and Thompson (1999), and Glyn
    (2004).

B.   The neo-liberal revival

Neo-liberalism, in its early guise of monetarism, began modestly as a critique of Keynesian macroeconomic policy and a call for a simpler rule-based approach to economic policy-making.[8] The revival of a broader and more radical agenda coincided with the election of the Reagan and Thatcher governments in the US and the UK. Their policies owed less to the technocratic economics of Chicago and much more to the political arguments of public choice theorists such as James Buchanan, and to the Austrian economist Friedrich Hayek, whose more overtly philosophical defence of free markets rested on the virtues of unregulated competition, entrepreneurial talent and consumer choice. In this sense, neo-liberalism is a fusion of sound money principles and radical individualism wrapped around a far-reaching agenda of economic and political restructuring which aims at privileging trade and finance over labour and production.[9] On this basis, a universal set of policy prescriptions, which includes restrictive fiscal and monetary measures, rapid liberalisation, the dismantling of restrictions on corporate activity and the privatisation of state services and assets, was advanced to liberate the market and correct the alleged economic distortions inherited from the "Keynesian welfare era" (Armstrong et al., 1984:405-23).

Neo-liberalism has been tempered in the advanced economies by practical and social constraints on policy-making; to take a simple measure, the share of public spending in GDP for most OECD countries over the past 25 years has remained remarkably stable, and

---

[8]   This call combined the idea of "adaptive expectations" (which placed strict limits on the potential impact of active macroeconomic policies) with a target for the money supply, a proposition promoted by Milton Friedman, but which he subsequently rejected.

[9]   See Gamble (2001) for a clear introduction to neo-liberalism. Tomlinson (1990) offers an excellent introduction to the contribution of Hayek. It should be added that Reagan and Thatcher were not the originators of the neo-liberal shift in their respective countries. In both cases moves in this direction had begun under previous (Democratic and Labour) governments. For a good introduction to the Thatcherite experiment and related cases in New Zealand and Mexico, see the discussion in Gray (1998). In the case of Western Europe, where there was a good deal more scepticism at the national level about this neo-liberal revival, its diffusion was closely connected to the moves in the European Union towards a single market, the introduction of the Stability and Growth Pact, and the creation of the European Central Bank.

in the case of social spending has been on a rising trend (Glyn, 2006:166). But, as has often been the case, when policies devised for the developed countries were "sold" to poorer countries, they were applied more crudely. The key ideas that have been transferred to the field of development policy include the following: that the more competitive an economy the better; that there should be no obstacles to the free play of market forces, domestic or international; that property rights must be clearly defined and protected by law; and that government intervention in the economy should be minimised. "Stabilise, privatise and liberalise" became the policy mantra for all developing countries facing the shocks of the early 1980s and, later, for the transition economies of Eastern Europe. This was not just an approach of technocrat economists: according to John Williamson (2002), the mission (in the guise of what he had earlier dubbed the "Washington Consensus") was to abolish a state of "global apartheid" which had banished developing countries to a nether world of state-led development and economic marginalisation. It is in this insistence on a single path for developing countries, one that requires a rapid opening of their economies to global market forces and TNCs, regardless of their institutional and industrial state, that we see the kernel of a fundamentalist way of thinking.

In its more technocratic guise, neo-liberalism can, of course, call upon a highly respected body of partial and general equilibrium theorising, and is careful to profess its neutrality by sticking to the "positive" (as opposed to the "normative") side of the epistemological divide. The line, however, is difficult to maintain. Indeed, the two become closely intertwined through the prediction-cum-promises of a "win-win" logic whereby all-round welfare gains can be maximised if only market forces are left alone to guide self-motivated firms and individuals in the allocation of their time and assets, on whether or not to spend their income and, if so, on what. Such logic confirms the claim, running across much of the debate on globalisation, that the world economy is (and should be) heading towards a future where firms and financial institutions operate transnationally, i.e., outside the confines of national boundaries, where factors of production and financial assets are almost perfect substitutes everywhere and where it will no longer be possible to consider states as distinct economic entities with autonomous decision-making powers in the pursuit of national objectives.

In this truly global market economy the prices of goods, factors of production, equities and interest rates in different (national) markets would indeed converge, income differences between different locations would disappear and policies in individual countries would be designed as if they were part of the same political unit. Indeed, the promise of global convergence is the apotheosis of the "win-win" logic whereby core economic institutions conform to a standard pattern compatible with the demands of unhindered market competition. Standard neo-classical growth models have long predicted the arrival of just such a "flat world", although the historical record has not treated this prediction kindly. Nevertheless, mixing old and new theories of trade and growth and relying principally on cross-country regression analysis, "conditional convergence" in per capita incomes has been claimed for a globalising world (Sala-i-Martin, 1996), with success for poorer countries contingent on their embracing liberal economic policies (Sachs and Warner, 1995).[10] This finding has become something of a touchstone for subsequent research on globalisation and has been given wide publicity by the multilateral economic institutions. It is also the basis on which economic alternatives are ruled out of court.

This promise of convergence is intellectually rooted in the theory of "comparative advantage" which is endowed with canonical status among professional economists. It is, of course, no accident, as Saul (2005:40-44) has recently documented, that the original case for free trade in Britain in the 1840s was seen by its proponents as a "religious question" and couched in Biblical language. According to Richard Cobden, "A Law which prevents free trade is a law which interferes with the wisdom of the Divine Providence, and substitutes the law of

---

[10] Convergence occurs when there is an inverse relationship between the initial value of a given variable, usually per capita income, and its subsequent growth. Of course, it is the case that even if a poorer country grows faster, the absolute income gap with a richer country can still be widening. The initial approaches to convergence in early growth models assumed this to be an automatic tendency, assuming that the savings rate and technology in the two countries are identical. Conditional convergence assumes that this is only a potential outcome, contingent on a range of conditions, including the right policies. For references, see Chapter 3, footnote 26.

wicked men for the law of nature." Market fundamentalism has deep roots. We shall examine some of its more earthly and empirical shortcomings in later chapters. However, for those worshipping at the contemporary altar of globalisation, trade liberalisation does not carry quite the same ardent conviction: after all, it had been an integral part of the Keynesian era. Similarly, while advances in telecommunications over the last two decades are important, they too can be situated at the upper end of a long logistic curve.[11]

The new factor that appeared in the 1970s was the massive increase in capital mobility, especially of finance capital, that followed the collapse of the Bretton Woods system of fixed exchange rates and the dismantling of capital controls in advanced countries. In contrast to the progressive trade liberalisation of the past four decades or so, this marked a much more radical break with the international policy framework that was established at the end of World War II (Camdessus, 1997). Of course, in the mind of the market fundamentalist, given that international trade is itself only a second-best solution in a world of restricted or limited factor movement, increased capital mobility should only strengthen the convergence pressures released by liberating market forces. Financial liberalisation should induce greater financial deepening, inter alia increasing the availability of credit to local consumers and enterprises, improve the mobilisation and intermediation of domestic savings and generally spur investment.[12] Free movements of international capital should also mean that capital investment in a developing country will no

---

[11] The real revolution in global communication occurred in the 19th century. In 1775 it took the British cabinet some five-and-a-half weeks to discover that its smouldering American conflict had erupted into open warfare at Lexington and Concord (Steele Gordon, 2005:153). In 1790, an Australian woman wrote that the loss of a ship off the coast of Brazil had left her community "without any direct intelligence from Europe for twelve months. We firmly believed that a revolution or some national calamity had befallen Great Britain" (Niall and Thompson (eds.), 1999). But when Krakatoa erupted in 1883, killing some 36,000 people, the calamity was known around the world within hours thanks to the submarine cable (Winchester, 2003).

[12] Despite this, there is a good deal of reluctance even among globalisation enthusiasts to endorse financial liberalisation. This, as we shall see in a later chapter, has given rise to issues about the "sequencing" of reforms. However, this is an (uncharacteristically) ad hoc construction which fails to save the notion of a fully liberalised economy from its historical abstraction.

longer be limited by the level of domestic savings but can be enhanced by foreign capital that will also bring better technology and management skills to raise productivity and incomes.

In reality, and no less than with trade liberalisation, the gains from liberalising capital flows are not simply there for the taking; instead, they are contingent on the presence of a range of institutional and supply-side conditions. When these background conditions are incomplete or missing, liberalisation is as likely to crush nascent entrepreneurialism and infant industries as to stimulate them, and thus weaken rather than improve the developing country's prospects for productive integration with the global economy. Moreover, the belief that liberalisation (improved access for developing-country exports in developed markets and vice versa) will automatically boost economic growth glosses over the question of the direction of causality. How far output is determined by supply or demand factors is a crucial and difficult question for those trying to design effective policies for growth and development. Their relative importance is most likely to vary with the level of development (and with the level of aggregation – the national economy, industry or firm) but for many developing countries the priority is likely to be the creation of supply capacities. In other words, the expansion of domestic output is more likely to lead to faster export growth rather than vice versa, but, once the process is under way, demand (and demand expectations) will play a larger role and the challenge is to ensure that this develops into a virtuous circle of higher output, increased productivity and the further expansion of exports.[13]

Thus, while trade and output growth are becoming more interrelated and mutually reinforcing, this is not a process conventional economic thinking finds easy to handle. While these "endlessly spinning cobwebs" are key to unlocking the development process,

---

[13] Trade, as we shall see in later chapters, is not the only variable that is likely to have a circular and cumulative relationship with output. In analysing the loss of England's lead in technology to the US in the late 19th century, Habbakuk concluded that "the abundance of entrepreneurial talent in the USA was the consequence rather than the cause of a high rate of growth; and it was the slow expansion of English industry which accounted for the performance of English entrepreneurs...not the reverse" (Habbakuk, 1962:213).

they are "the nightmare of equilibrium economics" (Hirschman, 1958:65-66). Instead, they take us back to Allyn Young's (1928) famous reworking of Adam Smith and to Gunnar Myrdal's notion of "circular causation". This requires more than recognising that markets can fail, although doing so is a necessary step away from fundamentalist thinking; it also means giving a much more prominent role to the interplay of economic, political and social forces that lie behind institutional development. It also means emphasising the role of industrialisation and of fixed investment in the growth process, particularly in the early stages of development when capital markets are imperfect and the influence of government policy is very important. That is why, in our search for alternative approaches, we shall give special emphasis to strengthening the accumulation dynamic including its relation to exports and domestic savings (Chapters 6 and 7).

C.   From neo-liberalism to market fundamentalism

One of the major flaws of neo-liberalism, as noted in the last section, is the practice of abstracting the economy from its political and social context. This is usually defended on epistemological grounds, although mistakenly in our opinion, as an initial simplification en route to a more complex analysis. However, it is particularly dangerous when economic policy makers adopt the same approach. The working assumptions of the theorist then too easily become the wishful thinking of the politician, a danger that Keynes had in mind when he famously warned that "Madmen in authority, who hear voices in the air, are distilling their frenzy from some academic scribblers a few years back" (Keynes, 1936:383).

When applied to the global economy, the tendency has been to ignore the political checks and balances that have historically allowed markets to function as sources of growth and development and to downplay the diversity that, as a consequence, has marked the successful evolution of market-based societies. In recent years, the tendency has been instead for those in authority to give overriding importance to the pursuit of economic efficiency and to regard political and social demands to influence the level or content of economic growth as an irrational and unwarranted interference with the free market which, left to itself, can be relied upon to generate the best of all possible outcomes for all members of society. It is this proposition that we take to be the touchstone of market fundamentalism. When combined with the claim of a single path to successful development, it gives rise to a "one-size-fits-all" approach to policy design which, in turn, can be seen as the outgrowth of a political project which seeks to make social relations conform to the dictates of a rarefied market logic.[14] Thus, neo-liberals and conservative politicians like to stress the ineluctability of market forces and to insist that "there is no alternative" to their key proposals. As we shall argue in Chapter 6, this confidence in the correctness of the chosen policy line rests on a mixture of implicit or hidden assumptions, myths about the history of their own countries' economic development, and special interests camouflaged in the rhetoric of the general good. It also leads to an effective denial of democratic politics, which is quintessentially about weighing alternatives and choosing between them. These attitudes in our view are not only a major source of policy errors and misjudgement but ultimately pose a threat to the longer-term viability of the market economy itself.

Unlike the textbook world of pure competition, the free-market system in practice leads to considerable concentrations of private and corporate economic power. This need not be antithetical to growth but it can certainly generate economic and political tensions and can lead to a clash with larger public and social interests. In 1926, in his essay on *The End of Laissez-Faire*, Keynes warned that resolving this conflict was crucial for the survival of the free-market system: if the private pursuit of economic efficiency could not be reconciled with a socially acceptable distribution of its benefits, the entire system would be under threat from authoritarian alternatives from the extreme right or the extreme left. For some three decades after World War II this conflict was resolved, especially in Western Europe, by various degrees of government intervention to ensure a balance between the

---

[14] A project famously reflected in the alleged assertion of the former UK Prime Minister Margaret Thatcher that "There is no such thing as society."

need for market-driven efficiency and the requirements of social justice.[15] For developing countries, however, the problem for policy is not only balancing economic and social objectives in a more globalised world but whether the pursuit of economic efficiency by private actors in the developed market economies is compatible with the pursuit of catch-up growth and structural transformation at lower levels of development. It is a principal theme of this book that, contrary to the prevailing "win-win" rhetoric of neo-liberalism, such a collision is highly likely and, for that reason, developing countries should be allowed a much larger policy space – a wider choice of policy goals and instruments – than is currently sanctioned by the rules and practices of the international economic organisations, by the conditionality attached to western provision of economic assistance and bilateral agreements of various kinds and by the ideological stranglehold of conventional economic wisdom.

There is broad agreement that the combination of freer trade, technological progress and increased mobility of capital has increased the interdependence of national economies to the point where no policy maker or firm can ignore the influence of events and policies in other parts of the world or the reaction of others to their own actions.[16] However, as we shall see in later chapters, there is plenty of room for discussion of just how far this process has actually gone and how best it should be managed. Whether they are global or national or local, market forces are always shaped and controlled by policy choices and the institutional frameworks in which they are

---

[15] This social-democratic version of the market economy proved far superior to the pre-war model of *laissez-faire* in delivering both economic growth and greater equity. It is also true that Keynesianism also proved less adept at managing some of the conflictual consequences of that success, thereby providing an opening for the neo-liberal revival. Still, in those European countries which have moved back towards the more liberal model since the early 1980s, economic and social performance has been less successful than in the 30 "golden" post-war years; in contrast, those that have stayed with the social-democratic approach, notably the Scandinavian countries, have continued to maintain a strong economic performance without sacrificing their social objectives.

[16] Again, it should not be forgotten that it was the recognition of such interdependence, and the need to avoid a repetition of the beggar-my-neighbour policies that had worsened the depression of the 1930s, that lay behind the creation of the Bretton Woods system in the first place.

made and implemented. Increased interdependence, both within and among countries, is thus the joint outcome of private agents pursuing their economic interests, including across national borders, *and* the degree to which governments constrain and promote those interests. Certainly, for the more advanced countries, globalisation *à la carte* has been the practice to date, as it has been for successful developing countries over the last 20 years.

The various policies and processes that are currently grouped together under the term "globalisation" are largely a consequence of the dynamics of the capitalist economies of North America and Western Europe and in many important respects are organised to perpetuate their continued dominance.[17] Indeed, it seems to us that the idea of one-policy-to-fit-all is very much part of an effort to consolidate that economic dominance, or what Ha-Joon Chang (2002), recalling Friedrich List, dubs "kicking away the ladder". The one-size-fits-all approach to development policy has, for the most part, been conducted by or through the Bretton Woods institutions – the World Bank and the International Monetary Fund (IMF) – and, belatedly, the World Trade Organisation (WTO), whose surveillance and influence over domestic policy makers was considerably extended, and their authority to impose disciplinary measures strengthened, following the debt crisis of the 1980s. Consequently, the power of these institutions over the poorer countries greatly increased just as their influence on the developed countries was disappearing. Thus, countries seeking financial aid or debt rescheduling from the Bank or the IMF must now not only adopt approved macroeconomic stability programmes but also agree to "structural" and political reforms which extend the influence of markets – via liberalisation, privatisation, deregulation, etc. – and

---

[17] In his important contribution to the globalisation debate John Gray (1998) has identified one of us as part of a "sceptical" school of thinking on globalisation which sees nothing new in the current era. This he attributes to our being too eager to find parallels between current trends and the period before 1914, and, as a consequence, downplaying the unprecedented degree of instability and anarchy that has resulted from allowing markets to become so dominant in the current era. We would plead not guilty to the first of these positions, as will become clear in the next chapter. But while we do acknowledge the damaging degree of instability in the current era our own emphasis on the unevenness of economic interdependence suggests that market forces give rise to systemic biases and asymmetries that favour some countries and communities over others.

reduce the economic role of the state. Similarly, the Uruguay Round of trade negotiations extended the authority of the WTO to embrace services, agriculture, intellectual property and trade-related investment measures, thereby, although to varying degrees, restricting the policy space available to developing countries to manage their integration into the global economy (UNCTAD, 2006a). WTO members who fail to align their domestic laws and arrangements with WTO agreements may be subject to sanctions on their exports. These institutions, and to a lesser extent the Organisation for Economic Cooperation and Development (OECD), have become the principal vectors for diffusing neo-liberal economic policies.[18] They are also institutions where the dominant influence over their activities remains with the governments of the leading developed market economies.

Emphasising the role of policy, and of the international economic institutions in promoting one set of policies rather than another, is an important correction to the view that globalisation is an autonomous, irresistible and irreversible process driven by the impersonal forces of the market and technical progress. Such forces are undoubtedly important, but essentially they are instigated by specific policy choices and shaped by existing institutions which provide incentives for countries that cooperate and impose penalties on those that choose to go their own way. It is a dangerous delusion to think of the global economy as some sort of "natural" system with a logic of its own. It is, and always has been, the outcome of a complex interaction of economic and political relations in which one or a few major powers have been dominant, punctuated by intermittent challenges from newly emergent industrial nations.

---

[18] The new policy course had its antecedents in the work of a generation of more liberally minded development economists who had resisted the turn to dirigisme after World War II. This was particularly true for trade economists working in the World Bank (Toye, 1993). More recently, these policies have been developed and diffused under the rubric of the "Washington Consensus", which was initially designed to correct specific economic imbalances in Latin America after the debt crisis. While some contest the link, it is difficult to separate the debate over the "rights" and "wrongs" of this approach from the wider globalisation discussion (Stiglitz, 2002). As we have suggested, the intellectual heritage is direct. The influence of the advanced countries, and particularly the most powerful, in recasting development policy, including through their grip over the Bretton Woods institutions, was frankly acknowledged by the former United States Secretary of State, Dr Henry Kissinger, when he observed that "what is called globalisation is really another name for the dominant role of the United States" (Kissinger, 1999).

Contrary to the myriad voices heralding the emergence of a seamless global market economy, we shall argue (in Chapters 3 and 4) that the principal variables behind the globalisation process, international trade, FDI and portfolio investment, are still largely concentrated on the developed market economies. This is not to say that trade in manufactures and foreign investments in the developing world have not risen significantly since the 1980s, or that the capital flows entering developing countries cannot be a very disruptive influence on their development prospects, only that their importance relative to global flows remains quite small, and that these are heavily concentrated in just a handful of countries. It is also possible, indeed likely, that this relative concentration of trade and foreign investment in the developed market economies will diminish with the rapid growth of India, Brazil, China and other countries in South-East Asia, although neither the pace nor wider impact of these developments is easy to predict. We shall also suggest (Chapters 3 and 4) that there are powerful forces working for the regional concentration of trade and investment, especially among countries where industrialisation has taken off.

The more important point that we wish to underscore here is that because these forces of "external integration" cannot be divorced from trends in capital formation, technological upgrading and structural change, i.e., "internal integration", the picture of the contemporary global economy is much more uneven than proponents and opponents of globalisation tend to assume.

The normative case for globalisation as a policy objective is based on the argument that the removal of obstacles to the international flows of goods, services and capital, combined with liberalisation of domestic markets, will stimulate the forces of entrepreneurship and economic growth in the poorer countries of the world and thus enable them to catch up with the levels of income per head prevailing in the economically more advanced countries. Our review of the evidence (Chapter 5) suggests that since the 1980s economic growth has not only been weakened in most of the developing countries undergoing rapid liberalisation and become more volatile, but the investment climate has also deteriorated along with premature deindustrialisation and a significant rise in informal economic activity. Moreover, income inequalities within and between countries have not narrowed and in many cases have continued to widen.

The principal exceptions to this generally poor performance are the economies of East Asia, which have industrialised at a rapid pace and have been closing the income gap between themselves and the market economies of North America and Western Europe. In all these cases, market forces have been harnessed to a dynamic economic transformation. This might suggest that wholehearted adoption of the neo-liberal agenda is the recipe for success but in fact the opposite is the case: instead of following the neo-liberal advice of the developed countries, the East Asian countries adopted the kind of pragmatic policy approach actually followed by the United States and Western Europe (not excepting the United Kingdom) when they were starting to industrialise in the 18th and 19th centuries (see Chapter 2). Paul Bairoch (1993:168-69) neatly summarised these experiences as "those who don't obey the rules win". The two emerging powerhouses of China and India suggest that this maxim remains true today. On closer inspection, local policy heresies nevertheless share a number of common features: they often include measures to stimulate the growth of infant industries, including incentives to export and invest; they also include expanding the supply of local inputs, including through research and development and training; they also include state-owned enterprises and extensive public infrastructure support. Still, in all these respects, institutional and policy details show a good deal of subtle variation.

In contrast, many Latin American and African countries followed faithfully the advice of the IMF and the World Bank after the debt crisis of the 1980s to open up their economies and liberalise, but their performance in the 1990s was no better and often worse than before the crisis (see Chapter 5). Faced with increasing evidence that neo-liberal policies have failed to create an economic environment that can sustain faster rates of growth of output and productivity in developing countries, a change in direction might have been expected. A growing body of academic research has certainly helped to shift attention to the importance of institution-building as a prerequisite of liberalisation, and the terms of the policy discussion are moving away from one-size-fits-all to matters of feasibility, sequencing and diversity (Rodrik, 2003; World Bank, 2005a). But, with a few qualified exceptions[19], policy makers in the developed market economies and in the international financial institutions still cling tenaciously to the core neo-liberal agenda. The blame for failure is often, and perhaps increasingly, placed on domestic conditions such as weak institutions, corruption and so on, but most of these were present during the earlier periods of more rapid expansion and can be just as easily found among the success stories. It is this refusal to admit to doubts about the agenda and to alter course that more than anything else characterises market fundamentalism.[20]

Fundamentalists, whether religious or secular, are usually distinguished by a conservative and limpet-like attachment to a basic set of beliefs and to linear models of causation which, given their assumptions, provide a simplified and coherent account of how the world works. This in turn encourages a Manichean view of the world inhabited by those who are either for or against the pronounced truth.[21]

---

[19] The UK government has stated that developing countries should not be forced to liberalise as a condition for receiving assistance: they should do so only at their own pace and in the light of their specific situations. In the Doha Round of trade negotiations, however, the EU and the United States are pressing hard on developing countries to liberalise significantly their markets for industrial goods and services. The EU's Trade Commissioner, Peter Mandelson, only discovered the desirability of gradual liberalisation for the EU after imports of Chinese textiles rose rapidly following the abolition of the quota system on 1 January 2005.

[20] A typical example of a convinced fundamentalist is Gustavo Franco, President of the Central Bank of Brazil until the crisis of 1999, who once described his policy objective as "to undo forty years of stupidity" and declared that the only alternatives in Latin America were "to be neo-liberal or neo-idiotic" (according to an interview in *Veja*, 15 November 1996). Another is the UK Conservative Party's former spokesman on education who, at the time of the 2005 general election, declared that the market "is the engine of progress and achievement and higher standards in every field of human activity" (remarks of Mr Tim Collins, as reported in the *Financial Times*, London, 28 April 2005, p. 4). In a similar vein, Jacquelyn Brechtel Clarkson, a New Orleans city councillor, saw "nothing better than free enterprise and the free market to decide how this city is rebuilt" following the devastating flooding there (quoted in the *Financial Times*, "Mayor urged to let market forces reshape New Orleans", 10 January 2006).

[21] Polarisation tends to be a common trait of neo-liberals, neo-conservatives and football fans. One notable fan of neo-liberal populism is Thomas L. Friedman, who posits a "flat world" where liberty and everything that makes for a civilised and benign society arises from the untrammelled workings of free markets (Friedman, 2005). Paradoxically, neo-liberals such as Friedman resemble vulgar Marxists in accepting that political and social factors are subordinate to and shaped by the irresistible forces of the market and technology.

This "retreat from complexity" (May, 2005:23) is all the more entrenched when myths and streamlined ideologies provide, or are supported by, general precepts for individual conduct.[22] For early-19th-century liberals the combination of private property rights and competition, with the associated elements of personal initiative and voluntary contract, not only underpinned the market economy but also reinforced the private virtues of hard work, honest dealing, self-reliance and personal responsibility, virtues also sanctioned by religion and seen as underpinning family life and the moral fabric of society at large. Given the coalescence of an economic model with private virtue and public religion, it is no surprise that 19th-century liberals were confident that the truths of the liberal economy would be proselytised "by impersonal missionaries more powerful than those of Christianity and Islam" and that the result would eventually be a world where "national differences would disappear" (Hobsbawm, 1977:83). It is not very difficult to see parallels here with the approach to development since the 1980s and with predictions that globalisation will make the nation state redundant.

---

[22] The fundamentalist mentality is by no means confined to those with a particular view of the workings of the world economy. The President of the Royal Society in London warned in November 2005 that the core values of the Enlightenment and thus of scientific endeavour – "free, open, unprejudiced, uninhibited questioning and enquiry; individual liberty; separation of church and state – are under serious threat from resurgent fundamentalism, West and East". This combination of stringent ideology and the denial of facts and complexity "can make it impossible for a democracy to fashion real-world solutions to otherwise intractable problems" (May, 2005). His remarks echo closely our concerns in this book at the contrast between the ambiguous and contingent answers to problems provided by theoretical and empirical economics (much more so than those provided by the natural sciences) and the certainty with which neo-liberals propose policies for the real world, a certainty that, by encouraging a deep and troubling disdain for alternative viewpoints and for the value of policy experimentation, is inimical to vibrant democratic values.

D.   The greatly exaggerated death of the nation state

A major flaw in the scenario of a world without borders is that it ignores both the resilience of the nation state[23] and the fact that the economy is not an entity *sui generis* but a component of a larger political and social reality, a reality from which the market economy draws its legitimacy rather than the reverse. A long line of social thinkers, including Adam Smith, have emphasised the importance of a framework of shared values, of moral sentiments, that underpin the formal and conventional rules of behaviour that lead to a successful market economy. That framework does not arise exclusively from within the market economy but from the modes of cooperation that are created within the political and social culture of the nation state. The idea that free markets are self-regulating provided that a few clear and well-enforced rules of the game are in place is a chimera: regulated markets are the norm. Indeed, on sound Smithian principles, the very idea of a global market is utopian. On similar grounds, the idea of the rootless global corporation is also largely a myth: most TNCs retain strong national identities and their "most strategically significant operations...continue to vary systematically along national lines" (Doremus et al., 1998), and, as we shall show in Chapter 4, most TNCs still largely respond to economic circumstances rather than acting as catalysts for structural change. There are still important issues concerning the relations between nation states and TNCs, as we shall discuss in greater detail in that chapter, but these are more the perennial questions of corporate power and its influence over policy.

This is not to deny that there has been an erosion of state capacities in many countries, thanks in part to the heightened power of mobile capital and the misguided policy advice of market fundamentalists. In some regions, notably in Africa and parts of the former Communist bloc, this has been particularly damaging (Mkandawire, 2001). The nation state, however, still remains the basic unit of legitimacy and accountability, and it is still the focus of political

---

[23] Claims that the nation state is an anachronism can be found among Habsburg political thinkers and British imperial theorists at the beginning of the 20th century (Mazower, 1998:44-45).

loyalties and social cohesion. Nevertheless, what appears to us to be a prominent (and pernicious) trend of the past 25 years, albeit to varying degrees in different countries and regions, is a relentless pressure to "soften" state power by the steady transfer of public values to the marketplace and with the subordination of political leadership to the management practices and narrow focus of the business community.[24] The process is often presented in terms of a rhetoric of public-private cooperation or partnership but in practice it blurs the distinction between the private and public realms and, thus, between private interests and a broader public good. The pretence that there is no conflict between the two – what is good for the company must be good for the country – obscures or buries the public debate over their respective roles and behaviour that should be a necessary element of a healthy democracy.[25] At the same time, this means that the often difficult trade-offs and choices that should be the subject of democratic debate and compromise are handed over to be resolved by the market or whatever corporate interest has the most influence over the issue in question. This is a dangerous development: not only does it undermine democratic politics but in the longer run it also risks undermining the legitimacy of the market itself by increasing the risks of a destabilising backlash from those who consider themselves neglected or unheard by their elected leaders and their interests crushed by impersonal market forces.

When, in recent years, states have disintegrated, it has not been due so much to their failure to adapt to the "forces of globalisation" as to a volatile mixture of economic shocks, ethnic tensions and the re-assertion of national identities previously submerged in an unbalanced federation or suppressed by a foreign hegemony: the

---

[24] As Hywel Williams (2006) has suggested, the rise of unregulated finance capital is intimately associated with the softening of the state. With respect to the British context, he notes that unlike previous periods when the City of London had to compete and coexist with other forms of elite power, the capture of the state by financial elites has meant that "Britain's once self-regulating professional elites have had the heart ripped out of them by the benchmarking, target-focused state and by a bogus consumerism, with its empty jargoneering about 'customer-shaped service delivery'."

[25] This development is not restricted to nation states. Ever eager to follow the latest fashions, international economic organisations have introduced public-private partnerships with the aim of encouraging TNCs to be more sensitive and socially responsible about the impact of their activities in developing countries.

break-up of Yugoslavia typifies this combination. Indeed, the welcome given by Western Europe to the emergence (or rather, re-emergence) of new nation states in Central Europe after 1989 was accompanied by considerable anxiety, not about the revival of a redundant institution, but as to whether the balance of relations among the existing nation states would be upset. This was still a Westphalian world and the principal response was to enfold the newcomers as quickly as possible into the political, economic and security structures created by the western powers. The new states welcomed this but the price to be paid was a significant narrowing of their policy options particularly with regard to their economic development.

In this there are some disturbing echoes of the 1920s; then, as now, welfare cuts, labour-market flexibility and restrictive monetary policies were the promised route to competitive economies and sustainable growth (Mazower, 1998:112-13). As in that earlier period, those who today blithely trumpet the virtues of unrestricted market forces and predict the disappearance of the nation state do not appear to have any coherent idea as to what should replace it other than vague calls for new political alliances or some sort of global or regional technocratic authority, inspired, as we shall see in the next chapter, by a mythical view of the international gold standard.

Something like the European Central Bank writ large is hardly a plausible (or a desirable) substitute for the present political communities that sustain the nation state or for the citizenship that it confers. A sense of citizenship is a major element of the process in which people find and define their identity, not always perhaps for the best of reasons or with the best of results, but the reality is that it is deeply embedded in national political cultures and to deny or defy such identities is to risk serious instability (Anderson, 1991; Berlin, 1990:Chap. 8). Democracy, in particular, requires a well-defined political domain in which to function effectively and for that purpose nothing so far has proved superior to the nation state. Democratic institutions need to remain in close touch with their constituencies if they are to thrive, but this becomes increasingly difficult if the distance between electorates and their governments is stretched too far. It is therefore by no means clear why, when challenged by global market forces, the nation state should always be expected to yield. Predictions of its demise also overlook the fact that it has already been long subject to global forces and has responded by creating fairly dense networks of international cooperation to deal with problems that cannot be solved by individual countries acting alone. We are in no doubt that, in recent years, the persistent bending of multilateralism to the actions of narrow vested interests has obvious parallels with, and connections to, the softening of the national state. Indeed, correcting this bias is essential if there is to be a return to a more balanced global order. Accordingly, facing up to the challenges of the developmental and democratic state is a central theme of our search for alternatives to market fundamentalism, at both national and international levels.

The fact that this search must take place against the backdrop of an interdependent world necessarily complicates policy choices. However, the simple dichotomy perpetuated by market fundamentalists, between the global economy and the nation state, is a false one. In reality, rehabilitating and hardening the state will follow diverse paths reflecting historical legacies, cultural traditions and choices about the kind of capitalist development to be followed (Jacques, 2005). And there remains a considerable array of international institutions that provide structures for intergovernmental cooperation on issues ranging from postal services and telecommunications to health, meteorology, a large number of technical standards, international trade, intellectual property rights, atomic energy, nuclear and biological weapons control, and so on and so forth.[26] Some of these activities attempt to deal with the negative effects of economic activity (trans-boundary air and water pollution, for example), while many are focused on market-extending measures such as the harmonisation of technical standards and bureaucratic practices that hinder international economic transactions. Others manage truly global public goods such as the distribution of radio frequencies or environmental commons. In all these domains national governments surrender a measure of sovereignty in order to maintain or strengthen their capacities to attain their national objectives and meet the needs and interests of their electorates.[27] Their degree of

---

[26] The International Telegraph Union was founded in 1865 and the Universal Postal Union in 1874, so, again, we are discussing not so much a new phenomenon as one that has greatly accelerated since World War II.

[27] For an account of how cooperation within the European Union "saved" the nation states of Europe, see Milward (1992).

commitment varies from entering into formal treaty obligations backed by sanctions on defaulters through conventions to informal agreements to observe certain "best practices", but in all the many varieties of multilateral cooperation the nation state remains the basic unit for action and the source of legitimacy.[28] In this framework of international cooperation the nation state is not so much defending its autonomy as strengthening its ability to act on behalf of its citizens.

A great many of the activities involve highly technical and abstruse discussions and negotiations among government officials from specialised ministries, and as a result they usually lack visibility and rarely attract much attention from the news media until the results are announced. This raises a number of problems. When technical standards are involved, national officials are often accompanied or advised by representatives of the private sector most directly affected, a practice that may be useful for assessing the likely consequences of particular actions but which raises the obvious danger of public goods being "captured" by special interests. Effective participation in these activities also presupposes that countries are equipped with an adequate supply of well-trained civil servants, a requirement that is likely to put many developing countries at a significant disadvantage in negotiations over what is essentially the creation of international rule-systems. One of the most damaging consequences of the demonising of the state in the developing world, particularly in regions such as Sub-Saharan Africa, has been to leave the public sector denuded of capacities to deal effectively with these matters (Mkandawire, 2001).

A more general problem is the risk of a backlash if the results of such intergovernmental cooperation prove unpopular or too costly, collide with too many national interests or appear to be an unnecessary interference with customary rules and practice. When that happens, electorates may lose confidence in their government's ability to look after their personal and collective interests and this in turn can further weaken confidence in political institutions. The consequence is more likely to be a resurgence of inward-looking nationalism than increased

---

[28] For an original analysis of specialised intergovernmental networks as global governance, see Slaughter (2004).

enthusiasm for supranational institutions. Governments are thus always faced with the need to balance perceived national interests and sensitivities against the necessity to participate in multilateral frameworks. When the balance between the national and multinational forces is upset, the odds are generally in favour of it falling on the side of increased nationalism unless greater transparency and democratic accountability can be introduced into the activities of intergovernmental networks.[29]

Market liberalisation and the free flow of information may help to weaken certain authoritarian regimes, but it is difficult to see how the instability of global financial markets can encourage the growth of democracy: if anything, the financial crises in Asia and Russia in 1997-98 were counter-productive. Equally, it seems unlikely that the steady rise of the informal economy and attendant uncertainties in working conditions will help to create an informed citizenry and extend political participation. Nor is it at all obvious that the multinational company is a force for democracy and individual liberty: like officers of the police and the customs, the record of TNCs suggests they can adapt to any regime as long as their property rights are secure and they remain free to repatriate their profits. Democratic institutions, just like those required for the market economy, cannot be imposed on a country by outsiders, be they foreign governments, bureaucrats or companies: they can only evolve from the choices made, usually over a long period, by a population in its particular social, political and historical context.

One of our key concerns in this book is to support the claim to primacy of democratic politics over technocratic determinism. International bureaucrats often regard national politicians as a hindrance to the introduction of "sensible" policies to which "there is no alternative". But, even ignoring the very poor track record of these experts, questions about the direction of economic development, the level of government spending and its composition, the level and incidence of taxation, whether or not to privatise the water-supply

---

[29] Helleiner (2000) suggests a road map of where this might go. The current crisis of the European Union, following the popular rejection of the draft constitution in 2005, can also be seen in terms of such an imbalance.

industry, and so on, are all essentially political decisions and are properly the responsibility of domestic politicians, not technicians from the IMF. National constituencies have every right to be affronted when key decisions concerning them are imposed by foreign governments or the international financial institutions. The latter justify their action with the argument that liberalisation will automatically benefit all and claim that there is no misalignment between the interests of the developed and the developing countries, but these are little more than ideological assumptions. The great danger is that such interference will generate a national backlash that will damage the prospects of a transition to both democracy and the market economy and thus possibly hinder the pursuit of broader objectives such as international peace and security. Domestic politics may not always produce the right answer to domestic problems, but that is the responsibility of local political leaders who, unlike international bureaucrats, are, or face the possibility of becoming, accountable to their domestic constituencies.

E.   Entry points

The focus of this book is very much on the economic dimension of globalisation and, more specifically, on the ways in which recent economic trends have helped or hindered prospects for growth in the poorer countries of the world. This is not to deny the importance and significance of matters such as the environment, security, public health or cultural diversity. Nor is it to suggest that the challenges only lie in the developing world – far from it. Our focus is partly dictated by the limits of our own professional capacities as well as the need to keep the text within manageable proportions; but it also reflects our belief that the damage from market fundamentalism has been greatest in the economies of the developing world and that resistance to market fundamentalism and the search for more just and democratic alternatives needs to begin by finding ways to renew and re-balance their economic and political structures.

There are many different interpretations of the nature of globalisation and a diversity of critics and opponents of both the present structure of the world economy and the policies that are believed to have created it and those that are required to sustain it. Since some of these critics reject entirely the market economy and economic integration – and since some of the more fundamentalist defenders of market-driven globalisation try to place all of its critics in this extreme category – it will be useful at this point if we briefly set out the broad lines of our critique and the alternative approach to development policy that we shall try to elaborate in subsequent chapters.

Firstly, the potential benefits of increased trade and foreign investment, and of greater integration with the world economy in general, are recognised, but the actual experience of the last two to three decades suggests that they will not be realised by simply unleashing market forces on the developing economies. In part, this is because many of these economies lack the institutional and productive capacities to respond quickly to the opportunities created by greater openness to world markets and to cope with competition from the more developed economies. But it is also because one-dimensional and technocratic approaches to the design of market-friendly development strategies fail to prepare policy makers for the difficult choices and trade-offs facing most developing-country governments in a more interdependent world.

Secondly, while there is no disputing that international trade and factor movements have increased considerably in the wake of liberalisation over the last two decades, there can be no presumption that the trend is synonymous with a less distorted economic environment facing developing countries. In fact, the process has been highly selective and has progressed on terms dictated by the developed countries: international trade in goods has been greatly liberalised but the exceptions (agriculture and food products, textiles, clothing and a range of labour-intensive products) favour vested interests in the developed countries; international financial markets are liberalised but the free movement of labour is greatly restricted; and the agenda for further liberalisation, covering a wide range of trade-related matters in the WTO for example, is again largely driven by developed-country interests.

Thirdly, given the existing biases and asymmetries in international economic relations, moves towards a more open and integrated economic space are just as likely to reinforce as they are to diminish the gaps between developed and developing countries. In particular, the capacity to respond to liberalisation favours the already-developed countries, which, because of first-mover advantages, economies of scale and learning capabilities, are able to acquire and reinforce dominant positions in developing-country markets. Implicit in our approach is the idea that economies are subject to processes of cumulative and circular causation: whether global market forces establish a virtuous circle where domestic economic growth and integration into the global economy reinforce one another, or a vicious one where the exposed economy falls further behind, will depend on the initial conditions at the time of exposure and the effective design and implementation of policies to manage the integration process. In the presence of cumulative processes of growth, there can no longer be any presumption that free trade and capital will automatically benefit all participating countries.

Fourthly, and following from the previous points, in a world where growth and development prospects hinge on an uncertain mixture of (unbalanced) global forces and (uneven) local productive capacities and experience, institutional diversity and policy experimentation will be key to establishing a more effectual combination of economic forces. Achieving this in a more interdependent world is likely to be a more demanding task than in the past. Building the institutional structures that are necessary to encourage productive investment, manage structural change and facilitate integration with the global economy will still require a strong national dimension in which the state, far from being minimised, has a major role to play. This is not to defend the many misguided interventions by governments in the past or to downplay the need for competent, honest and effective government and administration, but it does mean the transformation of the institutions of the state in order for it to play a key role in the development and integration process, not the marginal one envisaged by neo-liberals.

Finally, it needs to be stressed repeatedly that there is little consensus among economists and economic historians as to the key determinants of economic growth, why development takes off in some countries and fails in others. The confidence of neo-liberals that they have all the answers is simply misplaced, as Nobel laureate John Hicks very clearly recognised nearly 50 years ago:

It is all very well for us to have *theories* of economic
phenomena which constantly repeat themselves – like the
formation of prices, the balancing of international
payments, even the rise and decline of particular industries.
But the long-run growth of an economy is not a thing that
repeats itself; it does not repeat itself in different nations;
their growth is all part of a single world story. One cannot
argue from what did happen in the United States in a certain
period so as to establish laws of economic development.
All we can hope to get from our analysis is a better
understanding of what did happen in the United States at
that time (Hicks, 1960:132).[30]

In other words, there are no easy solutions, no quick fixes and no
escape from complexity for developing countries seeking a path to
sustained growth and ways to integrate with the global economy on terms
that do not perpetuate their unequal status vis-à-vis the present developed
market economies. They therefore need to experiment in order to discover
what will work, not just in their particular economic circumstances but
also in the light of their prevailing social and political conditions and
their national histories. This is why we argue that developing countries
must be allowed a much larger policy space than is currently permitted
when they are forced to seek assistance from the international financial
institutions or the major developed economies, or wish to be admitted to
international bodies such as the WTO. A distinguished American scholar
of economic development, certainly no opponent of the market economy,
on the basis of both European and Asian economic history, reached the
"inescapable conclusion…that had the neo-liberal Washington Consensus
been enforced on the East Asian miracle countries during the fifties, sixties
and early seventies, there would not have been an East Asian miracle"
(Adelman, 2000). Or, to adapt a remark by the social historian R.H.
Tawney, if today's economic minnows are to create their own growth
miracles, they must find ways to escape the neo-liberal pikes.

---

[30] Paradoxically, where economics and econometrics *are* capable of providing
reliable, evidence-based advice for policy, such as raising taxes on tobacco and
alcohol in order to reduce consumption, many western governments tend to ignore
it in favour of less effective, non-market measures which are more acceptable to
corporate interests in the two industries.

Chapter 2

Back to the Future?
Globalisation in Historical Perspective

A.   Introduction

IN the previous chapter we suggested that the prediction and the promise that income convergence would follow from the opening up of economies to global market forces and downsizing the state is a *leitmotif* of market fundamentalism. This promise, which implies a much brighter future for the world's poorest communities and countries, usually comes with claims of endorsement by such intellectual economic heavyweights as Adam Smith, David Ricardo, Alfred Marshall, Joseph Schumpeter, Bertil Ohlin and Milton Friedman. With a certain sense of ironic satisfaction, globalisation enthusiasts have also called on Karl Marx and Friedrich Engels in support of their cause:

> The bourgeoisie, by the rapid improvement of all instruments of production, by the immensely facilitated means of communication, draws all, even the most barbarian, nations into civilisation. The cheap prices of its commodities are the heavy artillery with which it batters down all Chinese walls, with which it forces the barbarians' intensely obstinate hatred of foreigners to capitulate. It compels all nations, on pain of extinction, to adopt the bourgeois mode of production; it compels them to introduce what it calls civilisation into their midst, i.e., to become bourgeois themselves. In one word, it creates a world after its own image (Marx and Engels, 1967 [1888]:84).

Whether the rhetorical excesses of *The Communist Manifesto* really mark the pinnacle of Marx and Engel's thinking on the "universal interdependence of nations" is, of course, a debatable point.

Still, their anticipation of a borderless world provides an historical signpost pointing at economic developments in the half-century before 1914 as a first test of the claim that rapid liberalisation, by "drawing almost all regions of the world into arrangements of open trade and harmonised economic institutions", i.e., levelling the economic playing field, will bring about faster growth in the poorest countries.[1]

In this chapter, without, we hope, unduly taxing the patience of the reader more interested in contemporary trends and developments, we shall follow this historical detour, asking some basic questions about the forces that shaped economic performance before 1914 and which we believe have resonance in current policy debates: (i) was liberalisation the driving force behind trade expansion before 1914?; (ii) were the gains from trade reinforced and amplified by capital flows to the advantage of poorer countries?; (iii) did technological transfers from richer to poorer countries help to spread the growth dynamic?; and (iv) was downsizing the state the way by which losers became winners in this earlier episode of globalisation?

B. Through the looking glass: Economic integration before World War I

1. *The structure and geography of global trade*

There is certainly no disputing the rapid expansion of international trade between 1870 and 1913: it grew on average by 3.4 per cent per annum, and with output growing at an annual rate of 2.1 per cent the share of trade in global output – the simplest measure of openness – rose steadily to between 15 and 16 per cent by the end of the period (Table 2.1).[2] There was, of course, a good deal of country variation, with a group of smaller, "super-trading" economies, such as Belgium, the Netherlands and Switzerland, all reaching much

---

[1] Sachs and Warner (1995:62-63). See Wolf (2003) for a pithy, liberal-nostalgic account of the pre-1914 era.

[2] Mitchie and Kitson (1995:Table 1.1) offer slightly higher figures. As we shall see later, measurement of the concept of openness abounds with problems. Using constant or current prices can make a significant difference to the measure, as can the choice of an appropriate numerator. For a discussion of these issues in an historical context, see Held (ed.) (2000).

Table 2.1
Merchandise exports as a percentage of GDP, 1870 and 1913, and growth in the volume of exports, 1870-1913 (per cent per annum)

	1870	1913	1870-1913
World	4.6	7.9	3.4
Western Europe	8.8	14.1	3.2
Eastern Europe	1.6	2.5	3.4
Western Offshoots	3.3	4.7	4.7
Latin America	9.7	9.0	3.3
Asia	1.7	3.4	2.8
Africa	5.8	20.0	4.4

Source: Maddison (2001), Tables 3.2a and 3.2b.

higher degrees of openness than larger economies such as France, Italy, Japan and the United States.[3]

Despite its dynamism, the underlying structure of the trading system did not change much during this period. In the first place, international trade remained a predominantly European affair; its share of world trade fell slightly from 67 to 62 per cent between the mid-1870s and 1913, while the share of "North Atlantic" trade (Europe plus North America) was essentially unchanged throughout the period, accounting for three-quarters of the world total (Kenwood and Lougheed, 1994:80-81). Secondly, the bulk of trade remained in raw materials. The share of primary products peaked in the late 1890s, when it accounted for 68 per cent of total world trade; it fell back slightly by 1913 but was still higher than in the late 1870s (Kenwood and Lougheed, 1994:83).

Primary goods were of course a particularly large component of exports from countries which now make up the developing world, accounting for over 90 per cent of the total, almost all of which went to the industrialising core. Nevertheless, countries in the North Atlantic bloc accounted for 62 per cent of primary exports in the late 1870s and over 63 per cent in 1913, i.e., a good deal of intra-Northern trade was in primary

---

[3] This small group of export-oriented, newly industrialising economies bears some comparison with today's NIEs in East Asia. For further parallels, see Chang and Kozul-Wright (1994).

products. Indeed, as Bairoch (1993:59-70) has shown, taking the European economies as a bloc, it enjoyed a surprisingly high degree of self-sufficiency in the key raw materials – including metal ores, energy and even textile fibres – needed for industrial development. There were, however, signs of a changing geography of trade with the spread of industrialisation. The dominant position of Britain was under threat; its share of world manufactured exports fell sharply, from 38 per cent in the late 1870s to 25 per cent in 1913, while the shares of the United States, Germany and Japan were rising. Still, this trade was also very much about exchanges among the industrial countries, their intra-trade accounting for 54 per cent of world trade in manufactures (Maizels, 1963:89).[4]

More significant for contemporary debates is whether or not the expansion of trade in this earlier period was the result of sustained liberalisation policies. Contrary to conventional wisdom, the answer is quite clearly not. In the first half of the 19th century, free trade, both in theory and in practice, was a predominantly British preoccupation, reflecting its own early rise to industrial pre-eminence.[5] Declining trade barriers did become a more general trend from around 1860 following the Anglo-French trade treaty, which spawned a series of copycat treaties between France and many other countries, and led to tariff disarmament in Continental Europe, mostly as a result of the inclusion of the most-

---

[4]   Intra-*industry* trade was already an element of intra-industrial-country trade at this time although it would become an increasingly significant feature of the modern trading system after 1945; see Rayment (1983).

[5]   As Chang (2002:19-24) documents, that rise was itself based on protectionist measures in support of domestic industry. The extent to which mercantilism contributed to the rise of British industry is an ongoing debate among economic historians. The rise and fall of the Dutch economy – also based on mercantilist policies – does suggest, however, that commercial success alone was not sufficient to bring about a truly modern economy; see Greenfeld (2000). It should also be remembered that Britain's colonial policy was a highly effective form of protection that was maintained well after it adopted free trade at home. In the 18th century, Britain's protectionist policies had been largely directed at keeping out Indian textiles in order to develop Lancashire's infant textile industry which would become the centre of the machine revolution. There was nevertheless a longstanding mercantilist fear, articulated among others by Robert Torrens in the 1820s, but dating from before then and persisting well into the 20th century, that the development of manufacturing industries in the colonies would undermine Britain's industrial pre-eminence. It is probably true to say that in the latter part of the 19th century Britain was more concerned with meeting this potential threat from its colonies than with promoting free trade in Europe.

favoured-nation clause (Kenwood and Lougheed, 1994:64-66)[6]. However, this interlude lasted less than two decades and was confined to Europe (Bairoch, 1989). Coinciding with the start of European liberalisation, and accelerating after the North's victory in the Civil War, the United States' economy began its period of catch-up growth behind rising tariff barriers; from 1866 to 1883 import duties averaged 45 per cent for manufactured goods, with individual rates ranging from about 25 per cent to around 60 per cent.

Table 2.2
Incidence of protection, 1875 and 1913

	Average levels of duties on manufactured goods		All products
	1875	1913	1913
Austria-Hungary	15-20	18-20	18-23
Belgium	9-10	9	6-14
Denmark	15-20	14	9
France	12-15	20-21	18-24
Germany	4-6	13	12-17
Italy	8-10	18-20	17-25
Netherlands	3-5	4	3
Russia	15-20	84	73
Spain	15-20	34-41	37
Sweden	3-5	20-25	16-28
Switzerland	4-6	8-9	7-11
United Kingdom	0	0	0
United States	40-50	44[a]	33[b]

[a]   After 9 October 1913, 25 per cent.
[b]   After 9 October 1913, 16 per cent.

Source: Bairoch (1993), Tables 2.2, 2.3 and 3.2; and Bairoch (1989), p. 144.

---

[6]   The most-favoured-nation clause in international trade agreements binds the contracting parties to grant each other treatment as favourable as they give to any other country regarding import and export duties and other trade measures.

During the three decades up to World War I, protectionism was the dominant policy trend across the developed world[7], becoming particularly pronounced from the early 1890s although there were some signs of easing in the years just prior to 1914. By the time war broke out, all the larger industrialising countries were protectionist (Table 2.2) and even some of the smaller European economies, such as Sweden, had moved decisively in this direction.[8] After regaining its autonomy over tariff policy in the late 1890s, Japan also provided tariff protection for its infant industries.

This protectionist trend was weaker in most developing regions, particularly where trade was organised under colonial rule. Most colonies were forced to accept the free entry of goods regardless of origin, although disguised measures were often used to favour imports from the "motherland". And in the nominally independent states of Latin America, the Middle East and East Asia, Western pressure in the first half of the 19th century imposed on most of them treaties (mainly with Britain) which entailed the elimination of customs duties.[9] Generally, it was the "5 per cent rule" that applied, that is, a tariff regulation under which no duty could rise above 5 per cent of the import value of the good in question. At the same time various non-tariff measures denied local trading interests access to information, mercantile techniques, capital and insurance, while the strategic use of health and safety standards on ships made it all the more difficult for local merchants to compete. All such treaties and actions opened up markets to British and European manufactured goods (Bayly, 2004:137-38). However, the lower-tariff story is not a universal one. For political reasons, the self-governing colonies (such as Canada, Australia and New Zealand) were not forced to open up, and they used their independence to protect infant industries, even as they benefited from

---

[7] Although tariffs rose only gradually up to the early 1890s, because most new duties were based on specific quantities and were not *ad valorem*, and because this was a period of falling prices, the significance of tariff protection was greater than the nominal figures might suggest.

[8] It should be noted that for the smaller and more open economies, average tariff figures hide the fact that many industries received no protection (because there was nothing to protect), while specific industries received much higher levels of protection.

[9] China's treaty with Britain signed in 1842 was typical of the pattern in the Asian region, although some countries such as Siam opened up "voluntarily" in response to gunboat diplomacy elsewhere; see Clemens and Williamson (2002:7).

access to "Northern" markets which helped to stimulate export-led growth. Moreover, while low tariff rates persisted in the Middle East, Africa and Asia for most of the period up to 1914, in Latin America tariffs rose steeply in the second half of the 19th century. Indeed, Clemens and Williamson (2002) estimate that by 1914 it was among the most protected regions, with tariffs averaging between four and five times those in Asia, and higher still in some countries, such as Colombia, Brazil and Uruguay which ended the period with the highest levels of protection.[10]

While liberalisation was clearly not the driving force behind international trade before 1914, efficiency gains in line with comparative advantage might still offer the best explanation for its expansion and thus a principal force for income convergence during this period (Irwin, 2001). It is possible that protectionism was just a desperate response to increased competitive pressures released by ubiquitous technological advances such as those linked to new means of communication. Broadly speaking, the resource-endowments story would suggest that land-rich poorer countries would export primary commodities to the richer industrial world, importing the latter's manufactured products. If the United Kingdom – the leading trading nation throughout this period – is taken as the exemplar, it might indeed be justified to see the global trading system in terms of an exchange of "Northern" manufactures for "Southern" primary commodities (Krugman, 1995), but in this respect the United Kingdom was the exception rather than the rule (Table 2.3).

It is also important to remember, when examining trade flows during this period, that many of the leading primary exporters were not low-income economies; on the contrary, in 1870 some of the world's richest economies were primary-commodity exporters. These included wool producers such as Australia and New Zealand, timber producers such as Canada, as well as a number of agricultural exporters, including Argentina, Denmark, Uruguay and the United States. Many of these countries benefited from growing demand as industrialisation took off elsewhere. Trends in the terms of trade suggest a mildly positive movement in favour of primary exporting countries in the period before 1914, particularly for

---

[10] Between 1870 and 1890, a number of Latin American countries, notably Brazil, turned to more protectionist policies as a means to promote industrialisation. The first Brazilian tariff of 1879 was the result of a trade mission to Europe to study trade liberalisation, the outcome of which was to convert it to infant-industry protection (Bandeira de Mello, 1935).

Table 2.3

Commodity and geographical composition of exports, 1913

(percentage shares)

	Share of world exports	Trade with the North	Exports of manufactures as share of total exports	Exports to other industrial economies as share of total manufacturing exports
United Kingdom	22.8	37.9	76.6	31.8
France	12.1	68.2	57.9	63.8
Germany	21.4	53.4	71.7	53.5
Other Western European	15.0	70.3	49.4	62
United States	22.1	74.5	34.1	63.2

Source: Maizels (1963), Tables A1 and A3.

Table 2.4: Index of manufactures output per capita, selected countries, 1913

(USA = 100)

UK	90
Belgium	73
Germany	64
Switzerland	64
Sweden	50
France	46
Italy	20
Spain	15
Russia	9
Canada	84
Australia	75
New Zealand	66
Argentina	23
Japan	6
Brazil	2

Source: Kenwood and Lougheed (1994).

the high-income raw-material exporters who had successfully moved into processing.[11] Indeed, as a result of such a shift, some of these countries had by 1913 reached higher levels of industrial output per head than the newly industrialising economies of Europe (Table 2.4). By contrast, there were already signs that a failure to diversify into industrial products could leave even relatively wealthy economies vulnerable to terms-of-trade shocks and unfavourable technological trends.

O'Rourke and Williamson (1999a:5-28) have recognised that a conventional North-South story does not properly describe trade patterns before 1914, arguing that the real pressures of globalisation were manifest in narrowing wage differences between a labour-abundant, low-wage Europe and the labour-scarce, high-wage New World, and within the latter between new arrivals, such as Argentina and Canada, and the more established economies of Australia and the United States. But even here the convergence tendency does not appear as strong as they suggest; wages in the European industrial core (Belgium, France, Great Britain, Netherlands and Switzerland) failed to converge on those in the United States, for example, and catch-up on the European periphery was confined to the newly industrialising Scandinavian economies.[12]

In any event, what seems certain is that trends before 1914 are poorly described by a world moving to "open trade and harmonised economic institutions". Even more troubling for the fundamentalist cause, the protectionist drift did not have the expected adverse effect on economic growth and, if anything, seems to have stimulated it. Thus, the period of trade openness during 1860-79 coincided with a slowdown in the growth of both output and exports. Just as significantly, the subsequent move towards protectionism coincided with a period of more rapid rates of growth of both output and trade: during the 20 years following the reintroduction of protectionism, output increased by more than 100 per cent and the volume of exports by more than 35 per cent. This pattern is

---

[11] See Bairoch (1993) and Hadass and Williamson (2001). According to Bairoch, earlier findings of a downward trend in developing-country terms of trade during this period reflected an excessive reliance on British and Latin American price data. However, he also notes that sugar was a clear exception to the mildly positive trend in the terms of trade.

[12] In their summary of this experience, O'Rourke and Williamson (1999a:278-83) do conclude, however, that trade was not a consistent factor in the convergence story and that labour migration was the major force pushing in this direction.

Table 2.5
The pattern of trade policy reform, exports and growth in selected European countries
(annual growth rates based on three-year annual average)[a]

	Date of policy change	Ten-year period preceding protectionist move		Periods following protectionist move			
				First 10 years		Second 10 years	
		Exports	GNP	Exports	GNP	Exports	GNP
Belgium	1887	4.9	1.2	2.3	2.0	2.7	2.8
Denmark	1889	1.4	3.3	4.3	3.8	4.1	3.0
France	1892	2.1	1.2	1.9	1.3	2.7	1.5
Germany	1885	3.0	1.3	2.4	3.1	5.2	2.9
Italy	1887	0.4	0.7	1.7	0.5	4.5	2.7
Sweden	1888	3.4	1.5	2.8	3.5	2.4	3.3
Switzerland	1887	0.4	...	-0.6	...	3.8	...
Continental Europe	1889	3.0	1.1	2.6	2.3	3.7	2.3

a Average of three years preceding the period, including the year when the policy change was made.

Source: Bairoch (1993).

reflected at the level of individual countries (Table 2.5), and much the same experience is found in the periphery. Thus, much like in the European and North American core, high tariffs coincided with relatively strong rates of economic growth in Latin America, both in comparison with its own previous period of openness and with the more open economies of Asia. However, within Latin America the countries with the highest tariffs were not necessarily the fastest growing, although the region's economic powerhouse, Argentina, maintained a relatively high tariff rate, albeit one largely geared to revenue generation rather than strategic industrial support.

It would be wrong to jump to simple causal explanations on the basis of these coincident trends.[13] However, they do destroy the myth

---

[13] The description of this experience by Clemens and Williamson (2001) as a "paradox" is not satisfying either, implying as it does that there is a singular notion of "normal" capitalist development.

of a liberal cosmopolitan trade order before 1914 and open the way to a central contention of this book, namely, that far greater attention must be given to the particular mix of policies and institutions that help countries to combine successfully the forces of economic nationalism and international integration. The closely related issue of policy space and how it is used, misused or abused will be taken up in later chapters, but there should be little doubt as to its relevance to understanding the examples of successful development in this earlier period of globalisation.

2. On and off the rails: Capital markets in the late 19th century

While Sachs and Warner (1995) blazed a trail back to the pre-World War I era in a search for virtuous linkages between trade openness, economic growth and income convergence, economic historians quickly shifted attention to the role of financial flows in shaping the global economic order that emerged after 1870.[14] Since capital mobility is a defining feature of the contemporary globalisation process, there is a particularly attentive audience seeking lessons from this earlier period.

There is no doubting the impressive scale of international capital flows before World War I. Between 1870 and 1913 their growth exceeded that of trade and output, and by 1913 their volume had reached 5 per cent of the GNP of the capital-exporting countries (Bairoch, 1976:99). Western Europe was the major source. In 1874, the combined outflow from Britain, Germany and France was some $6 billion; by 1914, it had risen to $33bn, three-quarters of the world total. Among these leading financial powers, Britain was unquestionably the single largest overseas investor, accounting for over two-fifths of the total; between 1870 and 1914, the average annual outflow of capital was around 4 per cent of its national income, and it reached a staggering 9 per cent towards the end of the period.

Equally impressive was the size of inflows to some of the recipient countries. Using current account data to measure net capital inflows and outflows, an average annual figure of nearly 4 per cent of national income in the major borrowing countries in the period 1890-1913 represents the

---

[14] Stanley Fischer (1995:101), commenting on the Sachs and Warner paper, was already pointing to finance as the more powerful force shaping global interdependence before 1914.

historical peak (World Bank, 1999:Table 6.1), while figures for individual countries were even larger, by as much as a factor of four (Baldwin and Martin, 1999:Table 5). Moreover, the available evidence – whether from the correlation between domestic investment and savings or interest rate differentials – points to a significant degree of integration of international financial markets during this period.[15]

Whether or not this earlier movement of capital was on a greater scale than contemporary trends continues to divide economic historians. However, the more important question is whether international market forces, linked to the increasing mobility of capital, improved the international allocation of resources in a way that brought about income convergence. Conventional economic logic suggests that this should be the case. Allowing savings to be pooled and allocated in response to the best investment opportunities should improve global efficiency, with capital flowing from richer countries to the poorer South where capital scarcity offered higher returns to Northern savers. For many a market fundamentalist looking back to the late 19th century, the gold standard's combination of monetary discipline and exchange-rate predictability seems to describe precisely the kind of ideal neo-liberal international monetary system best suited to liberating the forces of convergence in a global economy (Wolf, 2003:405). The evidence, however, does not seem to point in this direction. Indeed, if anything, capital flows were a powerful force for divergence in the world economy before 1914 (O'Rourke and Williamson, 1999a:245).

The gold standard has been the object of affection and nostalgia ever since its demise (Kindleberger and Lindert, 1978:391), but as with trade policy, many of the myths surrounding international finance stem from leadership bias, i.e., an undue focus on Britain's role in the world economy. Again, this is not altogether surprising given that Britain's early industrial start triggered a series of copycat monetary models which helped the formation of an international system.[16] It is also true that the role of

---

[15] For useful broad-brush historical accounts of the significance of capital flows in this period, see Zevin (1988); Taylor (1996); Obstfeld and Taylor (1997); and for a somewhat dissenting view, see Eichengreen and Bordo (2002).

[16] Whether Britain also financed the development of potential rivals, at what appear to have been relatively low rates of return, is also a contentious issue among economic historians.

sterling and the dense network of institutions that made up the London capital markets were pivotal both to the efficient workings of the evolving international trade and financial system (Eichengreen, 1996) and in developing new and innovative techniques to better manage the risks generated by that system (World Bank, 1999).

This system, however, had been a long time in the making. Britain had stumbled onto its gold standard in the early 18th century, taking well over a century to perfect the system, during which time its financial institutions acquired an enviable degree of sophistication, in large part tuned to the needs of financing a growing public debt (Weiss and Hobson, 1995:117-19). It was only after Germany's adoption of a gold standard in the early 1870s that this system can be said to have begun to take on more of an international dimension, and only with the adoption of a full gold standard by the United States in 1900 that an international system had truly arrived. Even then it would be something of an exaggeration to describe it as a global system. Indeed, as Panić (1992:114-16) has pointed out, just 12 permanent members – six European capital-exporting countries, four capital-importing Scandinavian economies and North America, which began as a capital importer but became an exporter towards the end of the period – comprised the core of the system. Moreover, all of these, with the possible exception of Canada, had joined the gold standard *after* a period of sustained growth.[17] This suggests not only that the system was rather short-lived but also that there was a good deal more to successful economic development than simply joining the gold standard. The very uneven spread of capital flows in the late 19th and early 20th centuries would seem to confirm this conclusion. While half of all lending went to Asia, Latin America, Oceania and Africa, half went to other advanced countries, and one-quarter to North America alone,

---

[17]   Eichengreen (1996:21) classifies just four countries as maintaining pure gold standards throughout the period – England, Germany, France and the US – although he describes France as a "limping" member for retaining silver as legal tender. Panić (1992) adds Canada, the Netherlands, Switzerland, Belgium and the Scandinavian economies to the "core" membership. Other countries (Austria-Hungary, Russia and Japan) were late arrivals, others were in and out (Argentina, Italy, Mexico, Portugal and Bulgaria) or never joined at all (China, Brazil and Spain).

by then the wealthiest region of the world economy (Table 2.6).[18]
Moreover, flows were also unevenly distributed within regions; during
the 1880s, just two countries – Argentina and Uruguay – were responsible
for over 60 per cent (of the value) of all loans negotiated in Latin America
(Marichal, 1989:127); and within Africa, 60 per cent of the total went to
South Africa (Kenwood and Lougheed, 1994:28). Taking a closer look
at the receiving countries confirms that in the period before 1914, capital
flowed to those that were already relatively developed.[19]

Capital flows during this period were certainly longer-term in
structure. However, it is a myth that the gold standard was finely tuned to
the needs of budding entrepreneurs (Eichengreen and Bordo, 2002). Less

Table 2.6
Main international lenders and borrowers, 1913
(percentage of total)

Lenders			Borrowers		
	Total overseas investment	FDI	Region	Total overseas investment	FDI
Britain	41	45.5	Europe	27	17.7
France	20	12.2	Latin America	19	32.7
Germany	13	10.5	North America	24	16
United States	8	18.5	Asia	14	20.9
Others	18	13.3	Africa-Oceania	16	12.6

Source: Kregel (1994), p. 23; Dunning (1984).

---

[18] Between 1870 and 1914, British investors acquired a more diversified portfolio;
the share of British foreign investments going to Europe and the United States
halved, from 52 per cent to 26 per cent of the total, while the share of Latin
America and the British Dominions rose from 23 per cent to 55 per cent of the
total (Kenwood and Lougheed, 1994:30). Still, according to the figures in
Eichengreen and Bordo (2002:Table 3), the top 10 recipients of British capital
during 1865-1914 accounted for over 70 per cent of the total, and the top five
(United States, Canada, Argentina, Australia and India) for over 55 per cent.

[19] See Twomby (1998); Clemens and Williamson (2004). There was also a large
urban bias in the destination of these flows. Indeed, as Eichengreen and Bordo
(2002:10) have noted, even in the largest recipients "wide swathes of their
economies remained virtually untouched by foreign capital".

than 10 per cent of British investment abroad was directly put to use on farms, in mines or through firms. The bulk was for infrastructure development. Securities markets were also a minor part of the story. Bond issues predominated over other debt instruments, with the flotation of new issues dominating the trading of second-hand debt. Although a fairly significant proportion of these flows did bring together developing-country issuers of long-term liabilities with private individuals and financial institutions in developed countries (Kregel, 1994), and increasingly so as the era progressed (Clemens and Williamson, 2004:329), the fact that the bulk of foreign lending went into railways, utilities and public works meant that one of the most important features of international capital markets at this time was the influence of government borrowing. In 1914, as much as 70 per cent of outstanding British and French foreign investments consisted of government and railway bonds, and nine out of every 10 pounds sterling of British overseas investment went into railroads and government bonds in the white settler colonies.[20] Even where the government was not the principal borrower, the success of these projects often depended on strong government support through land grants, subsidies or loan guarantees.[21]

The claim that under the gold standard external balances took precedence over internal balances – the supposed hallmark of its adjustment mechanism – is also a partial truth. In a period of persistent trade surpluses and deficits in core member countries, stability can hardly be said to have been guaranteed by automatic changes in monetary conditions and corresponding price adjustments. It has long been recognised that gold flows were never on a scale to alter incomes,

---

[20] See Bloomfield (1968:4). The scale and significance of railway construction in successful late developers is difficult to exaggerate; for its centrality to American economic development from the mid-19th century see Steele Gordon (2005:191-282). Only military ventures offered lending opportunities on the same scale, and were themselves often triggers of development.

[21] The longer-term nature of capital flows during this period appears to reflect a combination of factors – a fear of equity investment because of weak domestic financial structures in emerging markets and the absence of international financial institutions (Bordo et al., 1999), and a willingness to hold longer-maturing bonds because railroads and public utilities were transparent and easy to monitor (World Bank, 1999), or because these offered the biggest returns (de Long, 1999) – to which the gold standard gave its seal of approval but was not the instigator (Clemens and Williamson, 2004:333).

prices and the balance of payments through their effect on the money supply. Rather, the sustainability of long-term flows was made possible and strengthened by attractive lending opportunities thanks to rapid (industrial) growth, which made it possible to pursue national interests without jeopardising membership.

The gold standard is thus best described as a "socially constructed" monetary arrangement which promoted a network of close financial ties among a "club" of favoured members. Certainly, these members shared a common political philosophy that resisted legal restrictions on cross-border flows, professed sufficient confidence in the system to give it a certain amount of self-reinforcing stability, and accepted strong leadership from the dominant economy, Britain, which was willing to keep its borders open (even when others did not reciprocate) and to let the rest of the membership hold growing amounts of its ready liquidities (which they of course were willing to do). That consensus was further consolidated by a close-knit rentier class, which was in a position to build international economic solidarity across the system and play a pivotal role in ensuring stability particularly in response to crises (Eichengreen, 1996:32-35). What is less often recognised is the degree of policy space it allowed its members in providing both incentives for factor movements and support for industrial development, including the complementary system of managed trade discussed in the previous section.[22] Moreover, and despite capital flows occurring among a small group of countries with a considerable degree of economic complementarity, governments played a critical role in providing incentives for capital and labour to move in the desired direction (Panić, 1992:81-117).

The bias towards long-term capital flows, however, did not mean an absence of volatility, and economic crises linked to sharp fluctuations in international capital flows were an endemic feature of the period. There were 32 financial crises in 21 industrial and emerging economies between 1880 and 1914 (Eichengreen and Bordo, 2002).

---

[22] It is important to recognise that these financial arrangements were built on local class alliances. It is telling in this regard that the adoption of the gold standard in the US was part of a complex political compromise between Eastern and Western states, and between financial, farming and industrial interests; see Eichengreen (1996:21-22).

These were predominantly banking crises and were costly affairs, on average taking around 10 percentage points off cumulative growth. But they could be even more damaging, particularly when a currency crisis was involved, as in the United States in 1893 and 1907, and Argentina in 1890. Behind these crises, the interaction of herd mentalities, asymmetric information, speculative risk-taking and corruption featured prominently in the workings of the international capital markets (de Long, 1999), and even long-term productive investments, such as railway construction, were susceptible to "fraud, bankruptcy and debt default" (Bordo et al., 1999: 29). Moreover, the boom conditions created by initial inflows could often trigger an increase in credit-fuelled consumption, whether for public or private spending (including real estate), which was accompanied by falling domestic savings and a deteriorating current account. The fact that these cycles stayed within manageable limits under the gold standard, unlike the period after 1918, appears to have had less to do with the innate sophistication of market forces and much more with the absence of countervailing pressures to shape economic outcomes, i.e., essentially thanks to the limited reach of the democratic process and the weakness of labour movements.

Geography, as well as politics, also mattered for the workings of this system. A prominent asymmetry concerned the much greater vulnerability of peripheral countries, including the richest, to financial shocks and crises. Not only were their banking systems weak and their commitment to the gold standard less secure, but their specialisation in a narrow range of primary products left many of them vulnerable to external shocks. Under these conditions, financial and trade shocks could become mutually reinforcing and, particularly when banking and currency crises were combined, the impact in terms of lost output was all the greater and their resolution took much longer than crises in the core countries (Eichengreen and Bordo, 2002:24-29). Moreover, while problems on the periphery rarely threatened systemic stability, shifting monetary conditions in the creditor countries could, and did, trigger crises on the periphery.[23]

---

[23] Eichengreen and Bordo (2002:18-20) see this asymmetry as partly an automatic outcome of the financial arrangements. There could still be contagion effects in the North, however, when crisis hit an emerging market, as was the case most famously during Argentina's financial crisis in 1890.

3. Production matters

The key to catch-up growth during the period 1870-1913 was industrialisation. During that time, manufacturing output rose four-fold at an annual growth rate of a little over 3.5 per cent (League of Nations, 1945:Table 1), more rapidly than both total world trade and trade in manufactures. It was in this period that Britain ceased to be the only truly industrial power, and by 1913 both the United States and Germany were contributing a larger share of world output. Just as striking, while no country had achieved a level of industrial output per head equivalent to half that of the United Kingdom in 1870, by 1913 the levels in eight economies (the United Kingdom, Belgium, Switzerland, Germany, Sweden, Canada, Australia and New Zealand) were more than half that of the United States. Moreover, as Table 2.4 suggests, some of the most industrialised economies (on a per capita basis) were those that had moved from exporting crude raw materials to processing them.

Nevertheless, a very small group of economies still dominated world industry. Indeed, while the three leading industrial powers produced a little over a third of total output in 1860, by 1913 their share was a little under two-thirds of a much larger total. Experiences were very different outside this core group. Industrialisation in much of Southern and Eastern Europe was confined to enclaves and its growth was erratic. This was the case for Italy, Russia and Austria-Hungary, each of which had pockets of advanced industrial development by 1913, but failed to achieve and sustain the very rapid rates of growth of other newly industrialising economies. A favourable set of economic and political circumstances towards the end of the period did enable Japan to begin to build on its handicraft industries and to export low-skilled manufactures (Bayly, 2004:179-84).

Even more telling than the pattern of uneven industrial development among the more advanced countries was the widening gulf between these countries and the developing world. Both in absolute terms and as a share of world manufacturing output, the position of the latter declined sharply between 1830 and 1860 (Table 2.7) and continued to do so for the rest of the century, by which time the developing-country share of world manufacturing production had declined from over one-third to under a tenth (Bairoch, 1982).

Table 2.7
Distribution of the world's manufacturing production
(per cent)

	United States	United Kingdom	Germany	France	Russia	Other developed	Other
1830	2.4	9.5	3.5	5.2	5.6	13.3	60.5
1860	7.2	19.9	4.9	7.9	7.8	15.7	36.6
1913	32.0	13.6	14.8	6.1	8.2	17.8	7.5

Source: Bairoch (1982).

This "deindustrialisation" trend was the result of massive imports of European manufactured goods, particularly of textiles and clothing, but also of other products such as steel and ships: free trade exposed local artisans and craft producers to an onslaught from more capital-intensive, high-productivity "Northern" producers. The destruction of the Indian textile industry provides the best-known example of this process, but similar cases can be found across Africa, Latin America, the Middle East and China.[24] One of the stated aims of Britain's colonial policy was to suppress "any emerging industrial activity which might threaten the traditional complementarities between the metropolitan's export of manufactures and the colony's exports of primary products" (Rayment, 1983). This, of course, had been a factor leading to the revolt of the American colonies, but the policy, an early form of involuntary export restraint, was still being pursued in Egypt at the end of the 19th century and the start of the 20th by the imperial proconsul, Lord Cromer (Owen, 2004).[25]

---

[24] See Kennedy (1988:28-45); Batou (1990); Bayly (2004:177-86).

[25] Cromer opposed the establishment of a cotton mill in Cairo in 1895 because of its probable consequences on the state's finances, from the loss of import revenue, and because protests would "most certainly be forthcoming from Lancashire". Like most imperialists, past and present, Cromer was "unwilling to admit that there could be any basic contradiction between the interests of Britain and those of its colonies" (Owen, 2004:313). Cromer's policies provide much of the political background to Ahdaf Soueif's excellent novel *The Map of Love:* "...it was the Lord's policy of combating any nascent industry that led directly to the bankruptcy of the Basha's textile factory. Other friends, who had invested in the tobacco and sugar industries, were in similar difficulties" (Soueif, 2000:397).

This destruction of nascent industrial capacities in the South appears to have largely stopped around 1900 and, in some instances, was followed by quite rapid bursts of growth, often with advanced industrial techniques linked to FDI. However, the legacy of colonialism was a fragmented and often highly irrational political geography in which stunted urban development and small populations usually made for limited markets and a weak fiscal base. Some countries, such as Argentina, Mexico and Chile, were left with pockets of industrial development similar to those in Eastern Europe (see Table 2.4), but in no case was a basis for sustainable industrial growth laid down in the developing world.

Falling behind in the industrialisation process was all the more damaging because the period before World War I was one of rapid technological change. Inevitably, only a few countries occupied a leadership role. Indeed, at the beginning of the globalisation era, only in the United Kingdom had industry been visibly affected by the new technologies; for the developed countries as a whole, less than one-fifth of industrial production was produced with them. This situation had changed dramatically by the end of the period (Table 2.8), as part of a cumulative and dynamic shift towards more high-technology industries (such as chemicals and engineering products), which were also among the most rapidly expanding areas of international trade (Maizels, 1963:Chap. 7). New sources of power, new modes of transportation, new materials and new consumer products were associated in turn with institutional changes at the enterprise level and in the organisation and location of industry, all of which were integral parts of a new notion of modernity and progress. Thus, successful catching-up for most countries depended upon their gaining access to new technologies and ensuring that these played a role in enhancing the competitiveness of their industries through sustained productivity growth.

While technological progress was an important component of sustained growth, it was not an exogenous one. Success depended on the presence of two other elements. Firstly, strong states became much more active in managing technological change and in guaranteeing markets. This was particularly the case with the organisation of national transportation and telecommunication networks, which were not only technological leaders in their own right but also had extensive links to other new industries, such as steel and engineering. In addition, there was also growing state involvement in technological progress through

Table 2.8
The share of new technology industries[a]
in the total manufacturing output by region, 1830-1913
(percentage)

	United Kingdom	Other developed countries	Third World (including Japan)	World
1830	32-40	6-10	0-1	4-6
1860	60-70	18-24	0-1	17-23
1880	62-74	30-38	1-3	30-38
1900	68-78	49-57	4-9	49-56
1913	72-80	55-65	10-19	54-62

[a] The concept of "new technologies" is inevitably rather rough. The estimate of their importance in each region and period is based on distinctions made not only between sectors, but also within sectors. In the case of cotton, for example, a different "new technology" weighting factor has been used for each region and in each period for spinning and for the rest of the operations of the sector. Although these percentages have been derived from a huge mass of direct and indirect information, they are of course only approximations. Still, because of the emergence of new sectors within traditional industries, it is likely that the figures are biased in favour of the first industrialisers.

Source: Bairoch (1982), p. 288.

the creation of demand for new military hardware (Hobsbawm, 1994:308; Bayly, 2004), as well as through the more direct funding of technical education and research (Freeman, 1989a&b).

Secondly, since then, as now, much technological change is embodied in new equipment and depends on advancing complementary skills, there is a particularly close link between technological progress and the investment process. Indeed, nurturing these linkages has been seen as key to the productivity growth miracles behind most success stories (Baumol et al., 1991). There seems to be little doubt that capital accumulation accelerated at the end of the 19th century in line with the needs of late industrialisation (Gerschenkron, 1962). The United Kingdom's industrial leadership had been established with a rate of capital formation that never exceeded 10 per cent of national income, and was supported by a financial system that had evolved very slowly (Pollard, 1964; Studart,

1995). In contrast, rates of capital formation in the late-industrialising countries rarely fell below 10 per cent and in some cases exceeded 20 per cent (Panić, 1992:Table 3.1).

This more demanding investment regime in turn led to institutional changes. The rise of new forms of corporate governance and managerial structures was integral to the successful evolution of larger-scale, more standardised and more geographically dispersed industrial activity. The public domain was also reshaped around the provision of a communications infrastructure and the management of urban centres. In addition, closer links between finance and industry were central to the growth of late-industrialising countries, links that were frequently supported by the close involvement of government (Schumpeter, 1935:178). The rise of universal banking in Germany typifies this trend (Kregel, 1996b), but there were similar developments in Sweden (Chang and Kozul-Wright, 1994), one of the most successful late-industrialising economies of the late 19th century, and in Japan, where "large banks were increasingly important in financing both the initial and the continued development of large-scale enterprise, based on high indebtedness and stable interest rates" (Studart, 1995:73).

Increased economic concentration in turn led to new responsibilities for the state, as coordinator, monitor and regulator of economic activity. Drawing on her own extensive historical work (with Cynthia Morris) in *Comparative Patterns of Economic Development*, Irma Adelman (2000:58-59) has provided a definitive summary of the role of the state in 19th-century industrial development which is worth recalling here in the light of neo-liberal accounts of the period:

> What we learn from nineteenth century development is that the state played a pervasive role in the initiation of development in all countries, particularly the late-comers to the Industrial Revolution. It used a large number of instruments, both direct and indirect, targeted and un-targeted. It intervened most directly in the least developed late-comers, by financing investment itself, by targeting these investments to branches of industry it wanted to develop for a mix of economic and political reasons, by

substituting for missing factors and underdeveloped institutions and by working to increase their domestic supply. We also learn that the process took time and required continued commitment. That administratively capable governments were needed, and that they required a certain degree of autonomy in setting policies and designing interventions. Finally we learn that the state's influence on the economy depended critically on who controlled the state. Government controlled by feudal landed elites could only achieve narrow-based growth without development.

The combination of growing firm size and a more active state was also the progenitor of new patterns of international economic relations. While industrial development was very uneven during this period, the presence of FDI, as well as the intra-firm and intra-industry trade noted earlier, is a reminder of the growing internationalisation of production. Foreign direct investment grew rapidly, accounting for as much as one-third of overseas investment. Indeed, the stock of FDI reached over 9 per cent of world output in 1913, a figure not surpassed until the early 1990s (Bairoch and Kozul-Wright, 1996). The role of FDI in the development process will be examined in greater detail in Chapter 4 but, like other capital flows, FDI before 1914 was very heavily concentrated in a small number of locations and activities, with a little over half of it going directly to the primary sector (Dunning, 1984:89).[26] It is unlikely that FDI was a major source of technology transfer during this period. Indeed, given the concentration of FDI in the primary sector and related services, a good deal of international production in developing countries was confined to enclaves with limited spillovers and linkages to the rest of the economy (Singer, 1950).

---

[26] A relatively larger share of intra-European flows of FDI (where Germany and France were the major source countries) was in manufacturing, with Russia a major destination. It seems likely that FDI in this sector was a substitute for trade which was inhibited by rising tariff barriers (Kenwood and Lougheed, 1994:35).

C. Global divergence

A rapid pace of integration with the world economy was undoubtedly a factor accounting for high rates of growth in some of Western Europe's best-performing economies in the period before 1914, as well as in some primary exporting countries. However, as we have seen, there was nothing automatic in this process. The difference between success and failure during this earlier period of globalisation rested on a series of domestic institutional reforms, including the strengthening of property rights and commercial laws, improvements in education, the creation of more efficient and nationally integrated markets, and new patterns of corporate governance and financial intermediation, which together helped to nurture an industrial entrepreneurial class willing to commit resources to ever larger and riskier investment projects over longer time spans. In most successful late-industrialising economies, these institutional reforms were carried out by a "hard" modernising state, with sufficient fiscal and policy space to implement its own growth and development agenda, and to manage integration with the global economy.[27]

Moreover, as O'Rourke and Williamson (1999a:282) have recognised, the different international factor markets provided very different kinds of impulses, with financial (negatively) and labour (positively) flows the major influences on convergence and trade playing only a marginal role. These contained the potential for interdependent and cumulative development. A sustained industrial take-off was the basis for successful entry into the international economy in a way that reinforced growth and development. Industrial growth not only drove trade, it also helped to attract the foreign capital needed to finance growing import requirements and large-scale infrastructure development, and to obtain access to modern technologies. Furthermore, it made it possible for such countries to

---

[27]   On the concept of hard versus soft states, see Myrdal (1968), and Weiss and Hobson (1995), who show that Britain's early success was premised on the emergence of a strong state. Bayly (2004:279) has recently argued that the mythology of the "night-watchman" state is based on a partial if not altogether misleading reading of Anglo-Saxon experience, where state power was in practice used both overtly and covertly to promote economic integration and industrial development, well before the protectionist wave at the end of the 19th century; see also Supple (1974) and Kozul-Wright (1995).

join and remain on the gold standard which, in turn, facilitated capital inflows and strengthened the outlook for investment. Successful integration in turn provided larger markets for industry and cheaper sources of finance for investment. Success begot further success.

Elsewhere in the world economy, the impact of international trade and factor flows was very different. In some land-rich economies, mobile factors chased each other into the primary sector, sometimes generating spectacular spurts of growth, as in Argentina and Mexico, and also, towards the end of the period, in Russia. But in these cases, a class of strong industrial entrepreneurs failed to emerge, capital remained footloose, and speculative investment was widespread, fuelling more unstable growth.[28] This was particularly the case in Latin America, where unsustainable financial flows could quickly give way to deflationary pressures, debt crises, falling imports, particularly of capital goods, and a significant slowdown in growth rates (Marichal, 1989:169-70). Finally, in countries under direct colonial rule industrial growth was consciously suppressed. Instead, dependence on raw-material exports was often associated with enclave economies dominated by food products, which constituted the least dynamic and most volatile sector of world trade. At the same time, these economies became markets for manufactures from the industrial core and, although these markets were small by world standards, imports could prevent the emergence of domestic industries or, worse, could lead to deindustrialisation. This was far from being a converging global economy: before 1914, divergence was in fact the dominant trend (Chart 2.1).

D.   Conclusions

Market fundamentalists have looked to the period before 1914 for confirmation of their belief that well-functioning markets are latent in all socio-economic circumstances and will emerge if only governments get out of the way. We see little evidence for this in the history of that period. Perhaps this should not be surprising.

---

[28]   See Kenwood and Lougheed (1994:137-40), and Senghaas (1985:Chap. 3); on Argentina and Mexico in this period, see Marichal (1989).

Chart 2.1: Income convergence and divergence among countries in 1870-1913

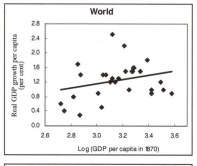

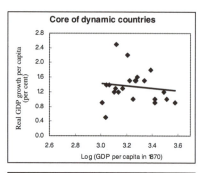

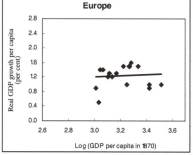

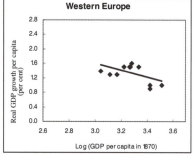

Source: UNCTAD secretariat calculations, based on Maddison (1995).
Note: Growth rates of GDP per capita are annual averages for the period. The country groupings are as follows:
Western Europe: Austria, Belgium, Denmark, Finland, France, Germany, Italy, Netherlands, Norway, Sweden, Switzerland, United Kingdom.
Europe: Western Europe plus Czechoslovakia, Hungary, Ireland, Portugal, Russia, Spain.
Core of dynamic countries: Europe plus Argentina, Australia, Canada, New Zealand, United States.
World: core dynamic countries plus Brazil, China, India, Indonesia, Japan, Mexico.

Conventional economics has long resorted to myths in an effort to protect its own brand of "intelligent design" from messier and less certain processes of industrial growth and capital accumulation which unfold in historical time (Bairoch, 1993).

This chapter has argued that harnessing international economic forces for sustained growth in the period prior to 1914 depended on a successful industrial take-off. This was achieved by only a small number of "hard" states that were able to forge an ideology of economic nationalism to help challenge the early lead of the first industrialisers and to better manage their integration with the international economy. The different ways in which profit-making opportunities emerged and were supported in more dynamic sectors explain why national development paths exhibited considerable diversity in the late 19th and early 20th centuries. There was no one model for every occasion, and while growing export opportunities were certainly an important part of most success stories, albeit to varying degrees, the trade stimulus did not come from a policy of liberalisation. Indeed, the fact that successful development reflected a mixture of market forces, collective action and institutional deepening seems to us to rule out any uniform pattern of "late" economic development for others to blindly follow. The idea that the gold standard provided a standardised institutional setting in which capital flows brought about convergence is also mythical. Not only did the banking systems of successful member countries exhibit considerable differences but foreign capital flows before 1914 appear to have been a particularly powerful source of divergence, flowing to countries that were growing rapidly or had already achieved high levels of income per head.

We also find little support for the idea that globalisation came to an abrupt end in 1914 thanks to the triumphant rise of closed bureaucratic nationalism over liberal market cosmopolitanism.[29] Such a conclusion, as we shall see in subsequent chapters, has permeated much current thinking about the possible dangers facing our own globalising world. This earlier globalising era was not a world of all boats rising but one where international economic forces supported increasing prosperity in a small core of countries while others were left behind or were forcibly pushed back. As such, openness to international markets did not in itself provide an automatic trigger for extending prosperity. Indeed, as Polanyi (1944:231-36) pointed out in his classic study of the inter-war period, designing economic policies exclusively around the notion of a self-regulating market was the hallmark of the 1920s when policy makers attempted to return

---

[29] This account of the "end of globalisation" can be found in Wolf (op. cit.) and has been more extensively developed in James (2001).

to "economic normalcy" after the dislocations of World War I.[30] The resulting insistence on a standard set of policy measures and, above all, on lower wages to help engineer a return to the gold standard was an early, and deeply damaging, manifestation of market fundamentalism. As Eichengreen and Temin (1997:38) have rightly noted:

> Its rhetoric dominated discussion of public policy in the years before the Great Depression, and it sustained central bankers and political leaders as they imposed ever greater costs on ordinary people. The *mentalité* of the gold standard proved resistant to change even under the most pressing of economic circumstances. "What is astonishing," Basil Blackett observed in 1932, "is the extraordinary hold which what is called the gold mentality has obtained, especially among high authorities of the world's Central Banks. The gold standard has become a religion for some of the Boards of Central Banks in Continental Europe, believed in with emotional fervour which makes them incapable of an unprejudiced and objective examination of possible alternatives."

The consequences of this quasi-religious rhetoric were very harmful for many European economies in the 1920s and were even more disastrous for the world economy in the 1930s. Unfortunately, as we suggested in the previous chapter, the propensity of fundamentalists to keep faith in simple models, to persist with them despite evidence that they are failing to produce the predicted results and to deny possible alternatives has not been confined to the inter-war years. The next chapter will take a closer look at some of the consequences of the revival of market fundamentalism for developing countries in our own time.

---

[30] Perhaps ironically, given current talk at the WTO, Polanyi referred to this as a "Geneva" consensus.

Chapter 3

Engines of Growth?
Trade and Financial Flows in an Open World

A.   Introduction

A SYSTEM of unrestricted international flows of goods, services and factors of production has always been one of the principal aims of economic liberalism and since the late 1970s has been regarded by many as the essence of globalisation. In part, recent arguments in its favour have harked back to the "classical" liberal theme linking commercial activity to personal liberty through constraints on the potential abuse of state power.[1] However, it has principally drawn on the standard neo-classical theory of international trade whereby specialising according to their comparative advantage allows countries to reap efficiency gains from moving to a production and trading profile that uses their relatively abundant resources to the full and importing goods that embody otherwise relatively scarce resources. Thus, countries with plentiful supplies of unskilled labour and little land will produce and export basic manufactures, while importing capital goods and primary inputs from countries with the appropriate structure of endowments. Even countries which are lagging behind in all sectors can benefit by following this path. This "win-win" logic has been described as "the deepest and most beautiful result in all of economics" (Findlay, 1991:99).

Starting in the early 1980s, and fully exploiting the economic shocks that hit much of the developing world at that time, an eager band of international economists set about correcting what they saw as years of economic distortion from high levels of protection, state

---

[1]   The reference point for this is usually Adam Smith, who today's globalisers adopt as the patron saint of the cause. This is usually based, however, on a superficial reading of Smith's analysis of the links between commerce, liberty and justice; see Winch (1978:70-102).

subsidies and overvalued exchange rates by providing the right set of incentives for competitive firms and farms. One of that band, Anne Krueger (1997), had no doubt that the blame for past failures rested firmly on the shoulders of the early generation of post-war development economists for "deviating so far from the basic principles of international trade". More often than not, the alleged failures of managed trade were seen as just part of the more widespread damage caused by the spread of excessive state intervention and rampant rent-seeking behaviour (Bhagwati, 2003). The liberal economists' case for unleashing global market forces provided the perfect antidote, bolstered by the unnerving precision with which they claimed to be able to pinpoint the gains from trade liberalisation (Cline, 2005).

Because the biggest gains are expected in poorer countries, not only as a result of their abandoning entrenched protectionist traditions but also because the removal of remaining trade barriers in the richer countries should further unlock the suppressed economic potential of countries endowed with plentiful supplies of cheap, unskilled labour, the resulting burst of growth should automatically trigger global income convergence. Moreover, in this new liberal international economic order, political leaders, however mischievous or misguided their nationalist ambitions, will not for long lead a country down the wrong path, as the optimal allocation of resources is quickly restored through the actions of consumers with access to the global marketplace and through the exposure of domestic enterprises to unrestrained global competition. In essence, what was being offered was the realisation, at long last, of a self-regulating market order. In the case of developing countries, the Bretton Woods institutions have been in the forefront of efforts to promote this vision as a guide to "getting prices right", a programme that subsequently became known as the "Washington Consensus" (Williamson, 1990).

While the underlying model is much admired for its mathematical elegance, it rests on a set of severely restrictive assumptions whose distance from reality has troubled generations of leading economists beginning with Adam Smith, no less, who insisted that a universal system of free international trade was more a utopian ideal than a coherent blueprint for policy and that the costs of adjusting to it required that it be done "only by slow gradations, and with a good deal of reserve and circumspection" (cited in Panić, 1988:124). For others, the implausibility of a world populated by small firms, with perfect information about consumer tastes and available production technologies, where learning or scale economies are absent, and immobile factors of production fully employed, has long cast a cautionary shadow over recommendations for rapid trade liberalisation (Panić, 1988:121-39). Indeed, both Smith and David Ricardo were fully aware of how, in the event these assumptions proved invalid, freer trade might very well lead to widening income gaps, i.e., to economic divergence rather than convergence (Darity and Davis, 2005). Although the case for free trade still courses through the veins of every economics student, leading members of the profession have kept at least one sceptical eye on its "win-win" logic, as testified by Paul Samuelson's (2004:142) recent acknowledgement that "genuine harm" can result for some countries from "the roulette wheel of evolving comparative advantage".[2]

Introducing factor mobility offers one way to move the model closer to reality. In principle, this should not be a difficult step. As one established international economics textbook puts it: "The principles of international factor movement do not differ in their essentials from those underlying international trade in goods" (Krugman and Obstfeld, 1997:159); countries with significant productive investment opportunities relative to existing capacity will offer higher returns (real interest rates) on those investments than in countries where such opportunities are not available, triggering cross-border capital flows. Thus, assuming that foreign investment is as good as domestic investment – increasing both incomes and employment and enlarging the capacities for future growth – leaving markets to allocate financial resources and determine interest rates should mean not only an increased willingness of households to save and hold financial assets, but also that the scarce resources will be employed by the most productive firms regardless of their location. Financial liberalisation (like trade liberalisation) should not only remove the distortions arising from an artificially repressed financial

---

[2]   Empirical doubts among economists began in the early 1950s with Leontief's paradoxical discovery that US exports were more labour-intensive than its imports. More recently Trefler (1995:1029) has pointed out that the factor endowment theory "predicts the direction of factor service trade about 50 percent of the time, a success rate that is matched by a coin toss".

sector but also strengthen the traded-goods sectors and ease external payment constraints by channelling global savings to the most profitable investments in the capital-scarce, poorer countries of the world. Indeed, with new technologies allowing money markets to stay permanently open and making financial assets even more globally tradeable than real goods, the logic of efficient financial markets appears to reinforce the case for linking openness and economic convergence (Bekaert et al., 2001).

Nevertheless, economists have been reluctant financial liberalisers. Even as he was penning a case for freer trade, David Ricardo was warning against removing restrictions on capital exports, in the belief that the greater mobility of capital would take England dangerously close to its "stationary state" (cited by Panić, 1988:134). More generally, the idea that capital should be treated just like any other good has had to contend with a history of "manias, panics and crashes" in international financial markets which have all too often led to considerable damage to the real economy (Kindleberger, 1984). A long and eminent line of economists, again going back to Smith but including Fisher, Wicksell, Keynes and Stiglitz, have analysed the damaging effects of financial-market failure, suggested remedial policies and recommended regulatory action (Toporowski, 2005).

Many of today's ardent free-traders remain sceptical about liberalising finance in developing countries (Bhagwati, 1998), calling for a careful "sequencing" of the reform agenda which would discriminate between good and bad types of capital flows. But however sensible, such calls sacrifice the rigour and elegance on which the free-trade argument has built its reputation, without providing any clear guidance on how to set priorities in what by implication must be a "second-best" world. Instead, proponents of rapid liberalisation have added muscle to their case by quietly setting aside the "static" Harberger-type gains[3] from liberalisation (which anyway fall woefully short of the promised benefits from opening up), emphasising instead the "dynamic" gains from trade. These include scale economies from enlarging the potential market through exports and from increasing the diversity of intermediate inputs, spillovers and learning effects

---

[3]   These gains from trade essentially derive from the different impact on consumer and producer surpluses coming from one-off price shifts as an economy moves from autarky to an open regime.

that come with importing goods and hosting FDI, and a much faster pace of capital formation from easing an otherwise binding savings constraint (Bhagwati and Srinivasan, 1999:31-32). From this perspective, trade liberalisation mixed with measures to attract the right kind of capital is expected to act as a catalyst for productivity growth (Edwards, 1998), including through institutional improvements and better governance (Winters, 2004).[4]

Again, this is not necessarily a happy state of affairs for the pure at heart, because it usually means that core principles have to be strongly qualified. In practice, the task of measuring the impact of liberalisation through these various channels is not easy and most statistical exercises resort to an ad hoc mixture of partial and general equilibrium modelling, combining traditional assumptions with more modern insights. Alan Winters (2004) acknowledges as much in his frequently cited review of the links between trade liberalisation and economic performance, bringing in investment as a likely catalyst for why openness works in successful cases. As we shall see in the next chapter, however, for market fundamentalists that usually means attracting FDI.

More generally, as core principles are left behind, a good deal of the case for rapid liberalisation appears to rest less and less on grand theory and more and more on specific episodes of growth and integration, particularly in East Asia (Krueger, 1997:17).[5] Bhagwati and Srinivasan (1999:32), in response to a growing body of literature

---

[4] These dynamic arguments for trade openness owe a lasting (though all too often unacknowledged) debt to the classical tradition and in particular to a seminal paper by Allyn Young (1928); see Rayment (1983) and Ocampo (1993). It is worth noting that there is a similar dynamic interpretation of the effects of liberalising capital flows, drawing on the Schumpeterian notion of "creative destruction"; for a review see Rajan and Zingales (2001).

[5] According to Bhagwati (2003:42), and despite professing his own analytical agnosticism, the "preponderant evidence on the issue (in the post-war period) suggests that freer trade tends to lead to greater growth after all". Not surprisingly, references to the "preponderant evidence" in support of trade liberalisation are not restricted to the more academically inclined supporters of free trade. In an indignant response to an article in *The Guardian* newspaper (24 May 2003) by Stephen Byers, who led the UK delegation to the WTO Ministerial meeting in Seattle in 1999 but had subsequently come round to realising that in a world where the trade rules were rigged in favour of the richest players further moves towards liberalisation would almost certainly damage some developing countries, Patricia Hewitt and Valerie Amos (then UK Secretaries of State for Trade and Industry and International Development respectively) berated him for ignoring "the bulk of evidence" showing free trade was good for the poor.

suggesting that the East Asian miracle was more investment-led than trade-led, have insisted that "investment rates cannot be divorced from the trade policy these countries pursued". Accordingly, much of the discussion of trade and financial liberalisation turns to the establishment of an "investment-export nexus" involving a positive and cumulative interaction between the two, with exports (imports) and fixed investment (saving, both domestic and foreign) on a rising trend, both absolutely and in relation to GDP. In this chapter we shall consider whether or not the market fundamentalists have actually made a convincing case for invigorating this nexus in poorer countries by rapidly opening their economies to international market forces.

B.   Trade liberalisation takes charge

General and rapid trade liberalisation in the developing countries began in the mid-1980s (Chart 3.1), largely under the tutelage of the Bretton Woods institutions. The rhetoric supporting this trend emphasised "global interests" and the prospect of positive-sum outcomes.[6] It also promised to put an end to the kind of deep economic crisis that had hit many developing countries in the early 1980s. Still, it was hardly a coincidence that such moves occurred as the industrialised market economies were entering a phase of much slower growth and as their firms were beginning to look for new markets to support flagging profits. This identification of wider efficiency gains with narrower corporate interests in the advanced countries is a recurring feature of market fundamentalism. It also helps to explain why three-quarters or so of the World Bank's Structural Adjustment

---

[6]   See World Bank (1987, 1991). This approach was supported, for example, by a seven-volume study by the World Bank, which concluded that the benefits of open trading had been "sufficiently demonstrated and described, by economic historians and analysts" (Papageorgiou et al. (eds.), 1991). In a careful review of this study, which carries considerable weight as the author is one of the leading analysts of international trade, David Greenaway argued that the demonstration was in fact far from sufficient and that the considerable diversity of developing-country experience did not support the "extravagant" claims made for the generality of the study's conclusions (Greenaway, 1993). As we shall see later, this has not stopped similar claims resurfacing.

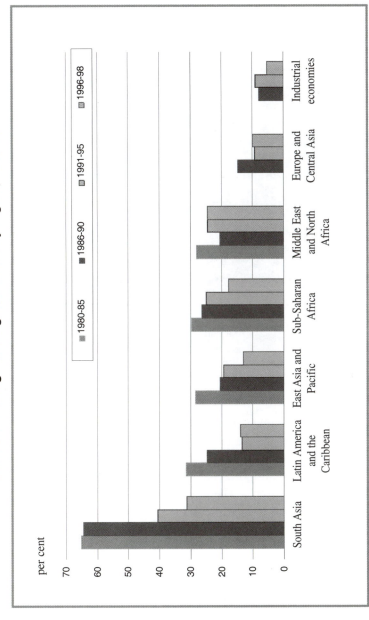

Chart 3.1: Average unweighted tariffs by region, 1980-98

Sources: World Bank and World Trade Organisation.

Note: Europe and Central Asia essentially refers to the transition economies of the former Soviet bloc, for which the data were not applicable for 1980-85.

Chart 3.2

Change in the volume of world merchandise exports and real GDP, 1971-2002

(per cent change over previous year)

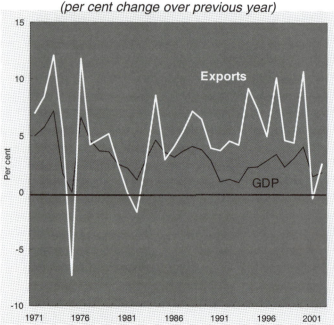

Source: UNCTAD *Trade and Development Report 2003*, from WTO, *International Trade Statistics, 2002.*

Loans (SALs) included demands for trade-policy reform, and why similar conditions were attached to IMF stabilisation programmes.[7] This pressure on developing countries to liberalise trade has almost certainly been more important than that exercised through multilateral or regional negotiations. The latter, however, particularly during the early 1990s, helped to keep trade liberalisation on track towards the signing of the Uruguay Round agreements at Marrakech in 1994.

---

[7]   According to Stewart (1995:9), half of IMF programmes in the early 1980s included trade-liberalisation measures and this was an essential part of its "mission creep" to embrace development issues. The importance of trade liberalisation in adjustment lending was to some extent eclipsed in the 1990s by the proliferation of governance-related conditions. For a discussion of the evolution of conditionality in multilateral lending, see Buira (2003).

Indeed, some qualitatively new elements to the liberalisation process were added en route, notably the inclusion of services and trade-related intellectual property issues, both of which had very strong corporate backing in advanced countries (Shukla, 2002).

The accelerating pace of liberalisation coincided with international trade growing more rapidly than output, both globally and for developing countries (Chart 3.2). In the latter, merchandise exports grew on average by over 10 per cent per annum between 1985 and 2000, before slowing down at the turn of the millennium.[8] After declining in the 1980s, the share of developing countries in world trade rose sharply in the 1990s to reach 32 per cent by 2000. Trade among themselves also became more important, rising from just over 20 per cent in the mid-1970s to over 40 per cent by the end of the century. This growth in developing-country exports was accompanied by significant changes in their structure (Chart 3.3). The share of agricultural products in the total halved, from about 20 per cent at the end of the 1970s, and that of minerals and oil also fell, although with greater fluctuations due to the instability of prices (especially of oil). The significant change from the point of view of longer-run development prospects has been the considerable rise in the importance of manufactures, from one-fifth in the decade or so to the early 1980s to around two-thirds by the beginning of 2000. Moreover, this trend occurred in all the major developing regions, albeit with Africa, where a little under one-third of exports are manufactured goods, lagging some way behind.

By implication there has been a sharp rise in the number of low-skilled workers participating in the trading system, reflecting to a large extent the increased entry of highly populated low-income countries, most notably China. On one estimate, their number rose by some 400 million between 1985 and 2000 (UNCTAD, 2002a:125-26); others have suggested a much larger increase in the "global labour pool", perhaps as much as a doubling since the collapse of the Soviet bloc (Freeman, 2005). Whatever the exact number, the global capital-labour

---

[8] Growth in trade exceeded output for every year between 1985 and 2000, and by as much as 7 percentage points in some years (UNCTAD, 2003a:45); this was reversed in 2001 when trade actually contracted, but a positive, if somewhat smaller, difference has since been re-established. It should be recalled that this was not a new trend: there was a similar pattern in the 1960s and early 1970s.

Chart 3.3
**Composition of merchandise exports from developing
countries, by major product group, 1973-2002**

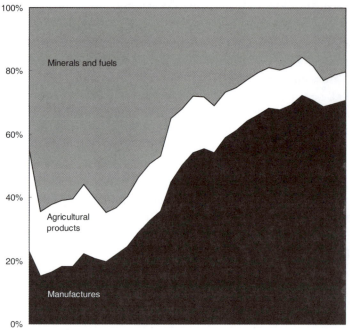

Source: United Nations *Monthly Bulletin of Statistics* database, 2000-02; UNCTAD *Handbook of Statistics 2004.*

ratio has shifted decisively in favour of the former, placing considerable strains on labour markets worldwide.[9]

The rapid growth of trade in developing-country manufactures has also been closely linked to the integration of many more countries into the international production networks of TNCs, within which parts of the same final product may cross and re-cross national boundaries more than once, contributing to the expansion of intra-

---

[9]   As we shall see later, the increasingly frantic nature of the competition among this growing body of workers to work with the available stock of capital also reflects a sharp slowdown in capital formation since the early 1980s, particularly in the advanced countries.

industry trade and somewhat inflating the gross value of global trade (Krugman, 1995). There also appear to have been positive results insofar as the shares of medium- and high-skill and technology-intensive products in developing countries' exports have risen sharply – from just under 20 per cent in 1980 to nearly 50 per cent by 1998, their share of world exports of the same product categories rising from under 47 per cent to nearly 60 per cent. As a result, developing countries appear to have succeeded in moving into some of the most dynamic product categories in world trade, notably computing and office equipment; telecommunications; audio and video equipment; semi-conductors; and clothing.[10]

On the face of it, rapid trade liberalisation since the mid-1980s does seem to have strengthened a number of the elements widely regarded as essential for sustained catch-up growth. Such trends underpin confidence in the "win-win" logic of free trade, as producers in the North benefit from expanding markets for their higher-technology goods while their consumers enjoy more competitively priced imports. The *Financial Times* journalist Martin Wolf puts this development at the heart of his case for a new liberal internationalist world order of peace and unbounded economic prosperity which, he claims, has finally broken down the barriers erected by inter-state power games after more than two centuries of intellectual and political struggle (Wolf, 2005). The much-repeated claim that this ascendant global market economy has also led to declining levels of inequality among participating countries has, for market fundamentalists, sealed the case in favour of this new economic order.[11]

A closer look at what lies behind these aggregate trends, however, reveals a more confused and less encouraging picture. First, there are many countries, especially in Africa, that are still heavily dependent on primary commodities for their export revenue. Over the past two

---

[10] UNCTAD (2002a:Chap. III). For the medium skill and technology categories the shares in developing-country exports were 8.2 and 16.8 per cent in the same two end-years, and of world exports 26.4 and 29.6 per cent. For the high skill and technology categories the shares were 11.6 and 31 per cent and 20.2 and 30.2 per cent, respectively.

[11] Trends in global income distribution have also been taken as a definitive riposte to the anti-globalisation movement; see *The Economist*, London, 13-19 March 2004. We discuss these findings later in this chapter and also in Chapter 5.

decades, these countries, with some exceptions, have had to contend
with relatively stagnant export markets, a persistently high level of
price volatility and generally declining terms of trade; as a result,
they are being increasingly marginalised in world trade despite their
maintaining some of the highest levels of openness, at least as
conventionally measured by the trade-to-GDP ratio.[12] On one estimate,
unfavourable movements in the terms of trade alone have cost Sub-
Saharan Africa (SSA) one-and-a-half percentage points of its annual
growth rate since 1980 and six percentage points on its share of
investment in GDP (UNCTAD, 2002b). Failure to control for countries
that are dependent on primary commodities greatly exaggerates the
positive association between liberalisation and growth. According to
one estimate, simply adding a "commodity dependence" variable to
the relevant regression equations reduces the apparent effect of the
openness variable on economic growth by one-half (Birdsall and
Hamoudi, 2002). The vulnerable position of commodity producers in
the international division of labour is probably the principal reason
why even the World Bank predicts only marginal gains from extensive
trade liberalisation for SSA (World Bank, 2002a); and given that these
predictions tend to ignore the potential downside risks from trade
liberalisation, through import surges, lost fiscal revenues and various
adjustment costs, factoring these into the picture would further
decouple trade liberalisation and strong growth performance.[13] But
such risks are not confined to the poorest countries. In some middle-
income countries too, particularly in Latin America, where the terms
of trade deteriorated very sharply in the 1980s before recovering
modestly in the 1990s, trade liberalisation appears to have slowed the

---

[12] For discussions of these trends see Cashin and McDermott (2002); UNCTAD
(2003b); UNDP (2003).
[13] The FAO (2004) has reported a widespread increase in import surges since 1984
as a result of trade liberalisation. According to the UN Economic Commission for
Africa, the countries of SSA have seen their trade-related fiscal revenues, which
account for close to one-third of the total, fall sharply since the mid-1990s, posing
considerable macroeconomic problems (UNECA, 2004). A recent study, focusing
on the balance of trade effects of rapid liberalisation, estimates that this has cost
SSA some 12 per cent of GDP since the mid-1980s because of a persistent tendency
for imports to exceed exports (Kraev, 2005). The same study also reports similar
losses for the poorest countries in Asia and Latin America, in some cases larger
than in SSA.

shift away from commodity exports (Table 3.1) and in some cases has stalled the process of structural diversification that began in the 1960s.[14]

A second feature which emerges from a closer look at the aggregate trends is that the number of successful manufacturing exporters is small and geographically concentrated. Thus seven of the top 10 manufacturing exporters from the developing world in the 1990s were East Asian, accounting for almost three-quarters of the developing-country total; and of the 17.7-percentage-point increase in the developing-country share of world manufacturing exports between 1985 and 2000, some three-quarters (12.8 percentage points) were the result of increased exports from these same countries.[15] Indeed, China alone has increased its share of world manufactured exports from under 1 per cent in 1980 to over 7 per cent in 2003. As is also clear from Table 3.1, East Asian countries have (albeit to varying degrees) been successful in moving into more sophisticated export goods over time. There is no doubt that this success with manufacturing exports, beginning with Japan's rapid post-war growth, demonstrates the potential of outward-oriented catch-up strategies built on the expansion of manufacturing capacity.[16] Indeed, in many of these cases,

---

[14] Whether natural resources help or hinder economic growth remains a controversial issue; for contrasting views see Sachs and Warner (1995) and Mayer (1997). Murshed (2004) offers a good summary of the debate and a more nuanced assessment of why developing countries with large mineral reserves have tended to grow slowly since the 1970s. Still, there are success stories to point to, including among today's developed countries, as well as more recent cases, such as the second-tier Asian NIEs, Botswana and Chile. However, even in these the mobilisation of natural resources to spur growth was never a simple matter of opening up to the world economy.

[15] Those countries are Hong Kong, Singapore, Korea, Taiwan, Malaysia, Philippines and China.

[16] It is important to stress at the outset that openness, the removal of all restrictions on international trade, and outward orientation are not the same although they are often equated. "Outward orientation" usually describes a strategy that stresses the importance of world markets for domestic producers but which is often accompanied by significant and selective restrictions on imports. Much of the evidence that is quoted to support a causal link running from trade liberalisation to rising shares of exports and imports in national output and rapid rates of economic growth is heavily influenced by the inclusion of the East Asian NIEs, which did not in fact adopt the standard set of liberal trade policies as part of their industrialisation strategies.

Table 3.1: Commodity structure of exports from selected developing economies, 1980-2000
(percentage of total non-oil exports)

Commodity group	Argentina 1980	1990	2000	Brazil 1980	1990	2000	Chile 1980	1990	2000	Colombia 1980	1990	2000	Mexico 1980	1990	2000
Group I	76.0	68.2	59.9	60.3	46.3	39.8	91.4	89.7	83.8	79.6	59.8	43.0	40.6	30.3	7.5
Food	51.7	42.7	39.9	40.2	21.8	17.4	17.0	23.2	21.9	73.5	51.7	32.2	21.2	16.6	4.3
Non-ferrous metals	1.8	2.4	1.9	0.5	4.8	3.3	51.8	44.2	29.9	0.1	0.2	0.7	6.3	5.2	0.9
Other primary commodities	22.6	23.1	18.1	19.6	19.7	19.0	22.6	22.3	32.1	6.1	7.9	10.1	13.1	8.6	2.3
Group II	8.7	10.0	8.8	9.4	12.7	12.9	1.8	3.7	5.2	13.2	26.0	22.1	8.7	7.8	12.8
Group III	3.1	8.1	4.9	6.4	13.5	8.6	2.0	1.4	1.4	1.3	5.1	6.2	2.2	7.5	4.5
Group IV	5.4	5.4	14.9	15.0	15.6	19.3	0.9	0.9	3.0	2.5	2.5	8.6	19.4	35.8	43.6
Group V	6.7	5.8	11.1	8.3	11.0	18.8	4.0	3.9	6.3	2.8	5.6	18.7	24.9	16.5	29.3

Commodity group	Côte d'Ivoire 1980	1990	2000	Morocco 1980	1990	2000	Turkey 1980	1990	2000	Egypt 1980	1990	2000	Ghana 1980	1990	2000
Group I	93.3	87.2	81.6	75.3	45.8	33.5	70.6	30.6	16.9	69.6	39.8	36.3	98.4	94.9	84.0
Food	60.8	59.7	61.5	28.2	25.9	22.1	41.4	18.2	10.7	18.4	13.1	13.5	78.3	73.3	49.5
Non-ferrous metals	0.0	0.0	0.0	2.1	1.8	1.5	0.6	1.8	1.4	2.1	12.3	5.8	14.0	4.2	15.6
Other primary commodities	32.5	27.5	20.1	45.0	18.2	9.9	28.7	10.6	4.8	49.1	14.4	17.0	6.2	17.5	18.9
Group II	3.2	9.9	8.8	12.8	27.2	39.8	22.2	42.0	44.2	26.5	44.8	36.9	0.6	2.4	9.0
Group III	0.5	0.7	1.4	0.2	0.9	1.0	1.4	13.6	9.9	1.9	6.7	5.3	0.2	1.7	1.1
Group IV	1.6	0.6	2.6	0.6	2.6	4.7	3.0	4.9	16.4	0.1	1.2	5.5	0.2	0.3	4.3
Group V	1.4	1.5	5.2	10.8	23.0	20.4	2.4	8.0	10.3	1.7	7.0	13.1	0.5	0.3	1.3

Commodity group	Republic of Korea 1980	1990	2000	Taiwan Prov. of China 1980	1990	2000	Malaysia 1980	1990	2000	China 1980	1990	2000	India 1980	1990	2000
Group I	9.9	5.5	4.0	10.7	6.7	3.6	74.9	33.7	10.3	..	20.4	8.7	40.9	26.6	18.9
Food	6.7	3.1	1.5	8.7	4.0	1.2	4.8	5.3	1.9	..	12.1	5.1	25.2	14.7	12.9
Non-ferrous metals	0.5	0.6	1.2	0.3	0.9	1.1	12.0	1.9	1.0	..	1.1	1.4	0.2	0.5	0.7
Other primary commodities	2.7	1.7	1.3	1.8	1.7	1.3	58.1	26.5	7.3	..	7.3	2.2	15.5	11.4	5.3
Group II	42.5	33.3	14.8	40.6	28.3	14.1	6.7	12.3	9.3	..	38.9	33.2	38.5	51.1	52.6
Group III	19.1	14.7	11.5	8.6	10.3	10.5	0.7	3.2	1.9	..	5.9	8.4	5.7	4.8	6.6
Group IV	8.2	13.3	21.5	12.3	18.7	19.5	3.0	8.5	10.9	..	13.7	15.7	7.0	6.6	6.6
Group V	16.8	27.9	46.3	18.6	27.5	48.2	14.3	39.0	66.1	..	14.8	26.2	5.1	9.3	11.7

Source: UNCTAD secretariat calculations, based on United Nations Commodity Trade Statistics tapes and estimates by the United Nations Statistical Office.
Note: Total non-oil exports refer to SITC sections 0-8, less section 3. *Group I* refers to primary commodities: *Group II* to labour-intensive and resource-

Table 3.2: Growth of fixed capital stock (per cent per year changes)				
	Japan	**Korea**	**China**	**India**	**Brazil**
1960s	12.5	8.9	1.9	4.5	5.8
1970s	8.5	14.6	7.2	4.1	9.6
1980s	6.1	11.2	8.4	4.9	4.1
1990s	4	9.6	10.9	6.2	2.2

Source: Glyn (2006), Table 4.2.

given their small domestic markets and the unavoidably heavy demand for imports of intermediate and capital goods, exporting was crucial in creating a virtuous interdependence between structural change, investment and market expansion. Particularly in the early stages of industrialisation, a "vent for surplus" allowed these countries to meet growing import demand without threatening domestic output growth and, subsequently, to achieve scale economies as they sought to compete internationally, less on the basis of low wages and more through product diversification and rising productivity.[17] In all cases, a very rapid rate of capital formation helped to raise and sustain the rate of economic growth, including in the earliest stages of their development (Table 3.2). It was the establishment of this "export-investment nexus", not the simple logic of comparative advantage, that underpinned success. Trends in China over the past 25 years appear to confirm this conclusion.[18]

As we shall insist throughout this book, economic development can never be seen as a simple act of imitation. Specific country features,

---

[17] "Vent for surplus" differs from conventional trade theory, which assumes full employment of resources, by emphasising the role of international trade in providing an outlet for domestic productive capacities that would otherwise remain underutilised. This was one of the elements in Adam Smith's attempt to explore the relationship between trade and development; its relevance to the problems of developing countries was first explored in Myint (1958).

[18] There is a good deal of econometric evidence supporting the idea that the positive impact of exports on growth is conditional on a strong investment performance; see for example Levine and Renelt (1992); Bosworth and Collins (2004).

including natural-resource endowments, market size, institutions and geographical location, have all shaped, and will continue to shape, the pattern and speed of structural change and the way in which the investment-export nexus evolves at the country level. In addition, the changing international context, including geo-political factors, also has a strong bearing on development prospects.[19] In this respect, there seems little doubt that China's emergence as a major economic power is rapidly rearranging the external environment facing other developing countries, with little consensus on the likely winners and losers.[20] It should be remembered, however, that China's export boom is not unprecedented; for example, the combined share of Korea and Taiwan in world exports of manufactures rose from just 0.6 per cent in the late 1960s to 5.5 per cent by the late 1980s (UNCTAD, 2005a:Table 2.9).[21]

Recalling these experiences highlights a third feature of the new trading system which tends to be neglected by many of today's enthusiasts for globalisation: unlike in the first three decades after World War II, when Japan, the Western European periphery and the first generation of East Asian NIEs emerged as successful manufacturing exporters, most of the large markets for labour-intensive manufactures have since been growing much more slowly, while at the same time, the remaining producers of such goods in the North

---

[19] There can be little doubting the importance of geo-political circumstances, for example, in influencing the generosity of richer countries with respect to aid flows and market access in the 1950s and 1960s. Korea and Taiwan, in particular, were beneficiaries of this generosity. Many have argued this precludes drawing any lessons from their experiences. We consider this to be too strong a conclusion.

[20] See Glyn (2006:18-24) and UNCTAD (2005a). Rowthorn (2006) discusses the possible impacts on advanced economies.

[21] However, as the figures on the expanding size of the global labour force suggest, this is exceptional for a country of China's size and level of development. Most observers accept that if China continues to grow at current rates it will still need to continue expanding exports to pay for its rising import bill. Where there is still a good deal of uncertainty is the extent and the pace at which this is likely to occur. In part, this will depend on whether wages continue to lag behind productivity growth to the extent they have in the past. If wages do begin to accelerate rapidly, China will have to resort increasingly to internal sources of growth. Eichengreen (2004:27-28) has suggested that export-led growth in East Asia may have reached its limit, and, if so, these countries will have to shift their policy orientation to search for domestic sources of growth in the coming years.

have been a good deal more reluctant to see further declines in their output.[22] If this situation persists, rapid export growth will only be possible for an individual country if it can increase its share of world markets, but this will be increasingly difficult against a backdrop of persistent trade barriers including quotas, tariff peaks[23], high rates of tariff escalation or effective protection, anti-dumping actions and other forms of contingent protection, as well as a variety of barriers relating to labour and environmental standards.[24]

While such action by rich countries has often (and rightly) been taken to reflect double standards in their approach to the multilateral trading system, perhaps more importantly it points to a reversal of principle from the original intentions of multilateralism. While the post-war arrangements were founded on the belief that adverse influences emanating from trade, finance and debt should be countered with measures that preserved growth and development, under present arrangements and policies developing countries almost invariably find themselves obliged to adjust to international imbalances through domestic retrenchment. In direct contrast to the arrangements originally considered necessary to support the international trading system, current arrangements have moved international trade towards a single-tier system of rights and obligations in which developing countries have generally the same level of obligations as the developed countries. The recognition that full employment was to be an integral

---

[22] It is no accident that the most rapid decline in the low-skill industries in the North occurred during the 1960s and early 1970s when full employment was underpinned by rapid rates of investment and structural change. This made it easier for Japan, the European periphery and the first-tier NIEs to expand in these sectors. Just how much of the subsequent decline in manufacturing employment can be attributed to trade with developing countries is a matter of dispute among economists. Most balanced assessments suggest it has been a non-negligible but secondary factor; see UNCTAD (1995) and Rowthorn (2005).

[23] These are rates above 15 per cent for imports defined at the six-digit level of the Harmonised System.

[24] Since the early 1980s, products such as textiles, clothing, footwear, leather and leather goods, and travel goods, where developing countries have a comparative advantage, have faced such restrictions: on one estimate, made at the end of the Uruguay Round, the protection of just one "sunset" industry in the North, clothing, was costing developing countries up to $200bn per year in lost export revenues and the total figure was perhaps as much as $700bn (UNCTAD, 1996:149-50). No great improvement emerged from the Uruguay Round; see Finger and Nogues (2001).

part of a successful free trade system has been weakened. Indeed, trade liberalisation has been given priority over economic growth and full employment. This resetting of priorities does not, as many market fundamentalists suggest, mean the end of a managed trade system: far from it. What it does mean is a very different regulatory style in which private means (which are by definition distributed very unevenly across the world) take precedence over public ends and, by implication, where almost any activity that might carry detectable consequences that cross borders, from employment to health to culture, can, in principle, be made subject and accountable to liberal trade rules and disciplines.

C.   The exaggerations and limits of "win-win" arguments

The metaphors of choice for market fundamentalists describing the workings of the international trading system are those of "growth engine", "levelling the playing field" and "delivering global public goods" (Lamy, 2006). These figures of speech do not shed much light on the workings of the system. On the contrary, their repeated use colours the discussion of trade liberalisation as an act of "fairness" that promises large gains for developing countries, while obscuring both the persistently uneven outcomes and the growing weight of private power which characterise today's more interdependent trading system. This is familiar from the exaggerated claims that emerge from trade simulation exercises which seem to multiply whenever multilateral or regional trade negotiations are under way (Freeman, 2003). In this imaginary world of ubiquitous market clearing and permanently full employment, a lower tariff option is pre-programmed to deliver an outcome that is superior to current arrangements, while the convenient techniques of comparative statics brush aside any troubling adjustment costs that might arise during the transition to the new and improved equilibrium. The result is usually a headline-grabbing multi-billion-dollar figure of the gains from trade liberalisation ostensibly being denied to the world's poorest communities by its wealthier citizens who are being swayed by "protectionist", "nationalist" or "luddite" thinking. The fact that on closer examination the promised gains in such exercises are disproportionately enjoyed by richer countries, making trade liberalisation a source of income *divergence*, is usually glossed over, as is the vulnerability of the size of gains to minor adjustments in the models' parameters.[25]

The intimidating technique associated with computable general equilibrium modelling introduces a veneer of technical authority in the debates on the costs and benefits of openness. However, more robust empirical support for the "win-win" logic of a globalising world has turned instead to estimating cross-country regression equations. These follow a standard format of measuring the size and significance of the coefficients on a set of country-specific variables related to a dependent variable, usually per capita income growth but sometimes the level of income, and where a positive coefficient on the openness variable, variously defined, is taken as sufficient to support rapid trade liberalisation. The World Bank was quick out of the blocks with this type of analysis in its *World Development Report* in 1987, which classified 41 developing countries according to their openness to trade since the 1960s, reporting the highest growth in income per capita in the strongly outward-looking economies and the lowest in the strongly inward-looking ones. A subsequent slew of more academic studies followed, all reporting similar findings.[26] The IMF (1997:84) was soon promoting these as evidence that "policies toward foreign trade are among the more important factors promoting economic growth and convergence in developing countries". The WTO (1998:45) was close

---

[25]   The tendency to exaggerate the gains from further liberalisation seems to have begun with debates about Northern trade agreements, such as the Canada-US free trade agreement and the single European market, but it became commonplace during the Uruguay Round and reached new heights in the run-up to the 4th WTO Ministerial meeting in Doha when free-traders fell over themselves to promote the new Round as a panacea, post-9/11, for a whole range of conditions from global stagnation to terrorism. In its *Global Economic Prospects 2002*, p.xiii, the World Bank was predicting between $1.5 and $7.5 trillion of additional cumulative income to developing countries from the liberalisation of goods and services. Significantly, in the run-up to the Hong Kong Ministerial meeting in December 2005, the World Bank markedly scaled back its predictions of the likely benefits of significant tariff cuts and other liberalising measures to below $100bn and accepted that most of the gains would accrue to the richer countries. For a review of why the kinds of model used in these exercises have a serial tendency to exaggerate the benefits and downplay the costs, see Dorman (1997), Ackerman (2005) and Akyüz (2005).

[26]   Particularly influential studies include Sachs and Warner (1995), Edwards (1998), Frankel and Romer (1999), and Dollar and Kraay (2001).

behind, drawing on much the same body of evidence to identify a "virtuous circle" between trade liberalisation and growth: "Periods of high growth seem to provide an impetus for more open markets (presumably because it alleviates adjustment problems and reduces resistance to change), and more open markets in turn are conducive to growth." Again drawing from the same body of literature, the World Bank (2002b:1) concluded that "Globalisation generally reduces poverty because more integrated economies tend to grow faster and this growth is usually widely diffused."

Despite the repeated assertion by market fundamentalists, there are plenty of familiar methodological pitfalls in trying to capture a process as complex as economic convergence in a simple econometric equation: the vague definition of openness and the failure to separate episodes of export promotion from those of import liberalisation can easily lead to the misrepresentation of trade regimes, making it difficult to draw meaningful cross-country comparisons and interpret the findings; cross-sectional averages hide country-specific differences and breaks in the series; the failure to present an explicit counterfactual, together with biases in country selection, raise further doubts about the robustness of the results; and the general inability of such approaches to analyse non-linear historical processes greatly diminishes their value for guiding policy. Findings from one study examining six common measures of trade policy found that countries can be very differently ranked according to the measures employed, with few significant cross-country correlations between these measures, raising obvious questions about the reliability of the various indicators used to measure trade policy, and about the empirical results derived therefrom (Pritchett, 1996). Other studies have found that the results reporting a strong link between openness and growth are sensitive to additional variables (Levine and Renelt, 1992), to cyclical factors (Harrison, 1996) and to periodisation (Wacziarg and Welch, 2003). Having carefully reviewed the leading econometric studies reporting a strong causal link between lower policy-induced trade barriers and faster growth, Rodriguez and Rodrik (1999) conclude that "There is a significant gap between the message that the consumers of this literature have derived and the facts that the literature has actually demonstrated" and that "the relationship between trade policy and economic growth remains very much an open question. We are sceptical that there is a general, unambiguous relationship between trade openness and growth waiting to be discovered".

Moreover, even assuming that a positive statistical association between trade liberalisation and economic growth is established, this still leaves open the direction of causation, with plenty of reasons to suppose that the direction may run from domestic success in raising productivity to increased trade rather than the reverse. Indeed, a good number of studies report precisely this direction of causation.[27] It also needs to be stressed that even if there is a close general statistical association between trade liberalisation and growth or some other variable, it does not necessarily imply that liberalisation will produce the same effect in a specific country: a high coefficient of determination (R^2) says nothing about the individual case even if it might suggest a broad tendency. In fact, and as is occasionally acknowledged, linear regression models are particularly ill-equipped to link up the many "significant" factors in a plausible, or even consistent, growth story. Despite these basic limitations, such exercises continue to flourish.

This is not, it should be said, how classical economists approached the links between trade and development. Adam Smith certainly believed that by erasing the remaining vestiges of the feudal and mercantilist worlds and stimulating international trade, a process of cumulative expansion could be triggered, to the benefit of all nations. But Smith's starting point was an uneven world of underutilised resources in which laggard regions were usually victims of geography, policy or demography.[28] Smith recognised, however, that whatever the causes of initial differences, the free movement of goods, technical know-how and factors of production could give an advantage to those who started early, allowing them to maintain or extend their lead.[29]

---

[27] See for example Clerides et al. (1998), Aw et al. (1998), and Bernard and Jensen (1998). Harrison (1996) reports two-way causation.

[28] He offered a number of reasons why some countries lagged behind, including unfavourable cost conditions (which led some countries to forsake manufacturing); a hostile policy environment (which included insecure property rights and misguided trade policy); weak infrastructure (which augmented geographical obstacles to market expansion); and small or scattered populations (which limited the division of labour).

[29] In his *Lectures on Jurispudence* published before *The Wealth of Nations*, Smith noted that "it is easier for a nation, in the same manner as for an individual, to raise itself from a moderate degree of wealth to the highest opulence, than to acquire this moderate degree of wealth" (cited in Vaggi and Groenewegen (2003:113)).

This clearly implies the need to tailor policies to specific national circumstances. David Ricardo, writing some four decades after Smith, was even more aware of the potential for *divergence* (Darity and Davis, 2005). In his world, where capital accumulation, technological change and distributional struggles had begun to assume a much more prominent role in growth dynamics, increased trade could lead countries to very different levels of income depending on whether manufacturing or agriculture was their main source of employment.

Conventional trade models, by contrast, are rooted in a pre-modern agrarian utopia of identical small-scale producers bound by the logic of diminishing returns, where the "best" producers will automatically be selected by free-market forces. In its analytically rigorous guise of a 2 (goods) by 2 (inputs) by 2 (countries) model, this world generalises into a global Pareto-optimal outcome of mutually agreed individual exchanges. In reality, trade takes place among countries at very different levels of development and is shaped by a variety of forces other than factor endowments, including economic structure, firm size, technological learning and political power. This implies that trade takes place in a dynamic and unstable world which is not heading towards some single best outcome and where each country is constantly facing new policy challenges linked to its evolving trading relations with others.

In this world where convergence and divergence pressures are simultaneously at play, the impact of trade on development is much more unpredictable than market fundamentalists assume. In a world where trading advantages are created rather than given, and scale economies and learning are defining features of productive activities, market entry, as a consequence, is slow and expensive, historical accidents have long-run economic consequences, and "market forces do not select a single, predetermined outcome, instead they tend to preserve the established pattern, whatever that pattern may be" (Gomory and Baumol, 2000). Indeed, as Gomory and Baumol insist, given that the modern trading system is so different from the implicit 18th-century historical setting of the free-trade model, the analysis of how trade works needs to start from a very different set of stylised facts. This would also suggest that a "win-win" outcome is just one among a range of possibilities in a more open trading system and that international market forces, in conjunction with varying national capabilities, can produce results that are beneficial for some but detrimental to others.

This section will therefore review some of the less frequently cited empirical studies of the workings of the current trading system which show how (in theory and in practice) the relationships between trade and economic development can generate uneven, uncertain and highly contingent outcomes. It is important to do this in some detail in order to counter the frequently repeated but heavily biased claim that "all the evidence shows" that trade liberalisation is always good for growth and provides the route out of poverty for developing countries.

1. Trading more, earning less

As we have seen, developing countries have certainly been trading a lot more than in the past, including in new areas of manufacturing activity. However, this has been concentrated in just a handful of countries, principally from East Asia. Just how they have managed this is still disputed among development economists, but as Palma (2006) has recently shown, since 1980 regions that have most vigorously pursued neo-liberal policies (Latin America) have extracted less growth from export expansion than those (notably East Asia) that have not.

There is also another less advertised trend, which touches even some of the most successful trading economies in the past 25 years, whereby increased trade has generally failed to translate into commensurate increases in income. In a recent study of 127 developed and developing countries, Dowrick and Golley (2004) found that between 1960 and 1980, increased trade helped productivity to grow in poorer countries at double the rate in richer countries but that this gain was reversed in the period of more open trade between 1980 and 2000, when the marginal impact of trade on productivity growth favoured the richer countries, and indeed turned negative for poorer countries.[30] A similar conclusion is reached by Wacziarg and Welch

---

[30] Dowrick and Golley call for further research to understand these findings. Their own tentative suggestions are that the nature of technology transfer through TNCs has changed in the latter period and that the range of complementary policies that supported successful liberalisation in the earlier period have gone missing in the "one policy fits all" approach of the latter period. Both suggestions are in line with the arguments presented in this and subsequent chapters.

(2003) who, using the previously cited Sachs-Warner methodology, found that the results were period-sensitive, with openness having little impact on growth in the 1990s, and that if anything, more open economies tended to benefit less than relatively closed economies. Developing countries, it seems, have been trading more in a liberalised world but earning less from doing so.

A clear indication of the contingent links between trade liberalisation and development is that increases in the developing countries' share of world manufactured exports during the past two decades have not been matched by a corresponding rise in their share of global value added (Chart 3.4). In a number of cases, shares of global manufacturing income have actually fallen over the past decade or so, while for others it has risen by much less than their share of world exports of manufactures (Table 3.3). Again, this relation appears to have a distinct regional dimension, with the disparity between the two variables being larger for countries in Latin America than in East Asia, but also with differences within East Asia between the first- and second-tier NIEs (UNCTAD, 2002a).

These trends appear to contradict a basic tenet of post-war development thinking, which recommended that developing countries should diversify from primary products to manufactures in order to ensure a more balanced integration into the trading system together with sustained improvements in productivity growth and rising real wages. These were all strongly and positively related in the three decades after 1945 both in the developed countries and in newly industrialising economies such as Korea and Taiwan (Glyn, 2006:92-94). By contrast, in a number of the countries that have pursued more export-oriented policies since the debt crisis of the early 1980s, real wages have been stagnant or falling, as in Argentina, Egypt, Mexico, Morocco and Turkey, and/or currencies have been sharply devalued, as in Chile, Ghana, Malaysia and Pakistan, all of which have seen rising shares of manufactured exports (UNCTAD, 2003a:111).

One of the problems seems to lie with a lopsided reliance on external demand as the basis of sustained growth, a reliance which carries with it the familiar dangers of overproduction and resulting adverse price movements (Heintz, 2003). On its own a small country can rapidly expand its exports in a given market with negligible

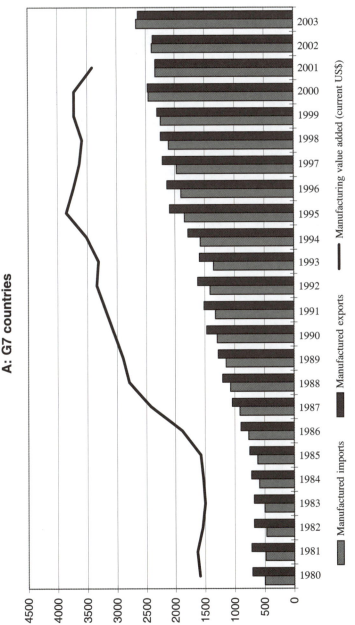

Chart 3.4
Trade in manufactures and value added in manufacturing for two major groups of economies, 1980-2003
(billions of dollars)

A: G7 countries

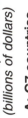

Manufactured imports

Manufactured exports

Manufacturing value added (current US$)

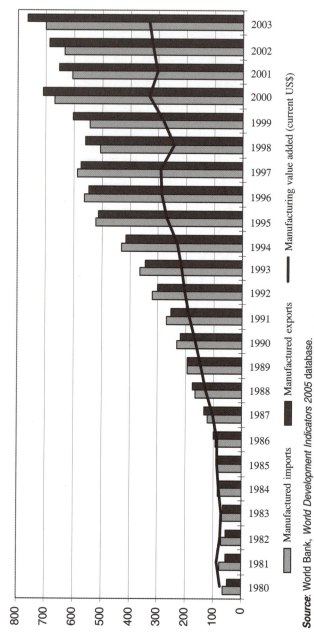

B: D7 countries

Manufactured imports
Manufactured exports
Manufacturing value added (current US$)

Source*:* World Bank, *World Development Indicators 2005* database.
Note*:* The D7 comprises Hong Kong, China; Malaysia; South Korea; Mexico; Singapore; Taiwan, China; and Turkey.
These countries accounted for 60 per cent of developing countries' trade and 40 per cent of their GDP.

Table 3.3

Share of selected regional groups and developing economies in world exports of manufactures and manufacturing value added, 1980, 1997 and 2001

	Share in world exports of manufactures			Share in world manufacturing value added		
	1980	1997	2001	1980	1997	2001
High income	81.4	83.0	79.5	...	78.6	77.6
Low and middle income	15.4	17.3	20.0	16.1	21.5	22.5
Latin America and Caribbean	1.4	3.6	4.1	4.7	6.0	5.3
Argentina	0.1	0.2	0.2	0.8	0.9	0.8
Brazil	0.6	0.7	0.7	2.6	2.4	1.2
Chile	0.0	0.1	0.1	0.2	0.2	0.2
Mexico	0.2	2.1	2.8	1.4	1.4	2.0
South Asia, East Asia and Pacific	0.6[a]	8.3	9.9	5.2	9.7	11.5
NIEs	3.4	9.4	8.8	0.7	2.7	2.7
Hong Kong, China	1.5	4.1	3.8	0.2	0.2	0.2
Korea, Rep.	1.2	2.9	2.8	0.5	2.2	2.2
Singapore	0.7	2.5	2.2	...	0.4	0.4
ASEAN-4	0.4	3.4	3.8	1.1	2.7	2.2
Indonesia	0.0	0.5	0.7	0.4	1.0	0.7
Malaysia	0.2	1.4	1.5	0.2	0.5	0.5
Philippines	0.1	0.5	0.6	0.3	0.3	0.3
Thailand	0.1	1.0	1.0	0.3	0.8	0.7
China	1.1[b]	3.6	4.9	2.7	5.5	7.5
India	0.4	0.6	0.7	1.0	1.1	1.2
Turkey	0.1	0.5	0.5	0.3	0.5	0.4

Source: *World Development Indicators* database 2005.

Note: Calculations in current dollars. Value-added data are based on the definition of manufactures used in industrial statistics, while export data are based on the definition of manufactures used in trade statistics. See Table 5.5, footnotes 1 and 2.

[a] Excluding China

[b] 1984

impact on overall supply and prices – the "importance of being
unimportant" – but once a large number of countries or just a few
large economies (such as India and China) follow the same route there
will be an increased risk of oversupply and declining terms of trade
for the exporters. This increased risk of falling prices, resulting from
a "fallacy of composition", now seems to be facing exporters of some
manufactured goods as a result of widespread efforts to replicate the
successful experience of the Asian NIEs. As was previously the case
with primary commodities, such a risk becomes all the more likely if
there is an asymmetry in the structure of global markets.[31] Where, as
in many advanced countries, there are high barriers to entry and
oligopolistic producers manipulate market dynamics, prices are more
likely to move in line with supply and costs than with fluctuations in
demand. Moreover, price inflexibility is reinforced by labour-market
conditions structured by strong regulations and collective bargaining.[32]
The absence of such conditions – or their erosion under structural
adjustment programmes – in the labour markets of most developing
countries, together with large amounts of surplus labour, implies that
wages there are much more flexible. This flexibility increases the
ability of manufacturing firms to lower wages when prices fall,
enabling them to maintain profit margins and allowing them to compete
on the basis of price in the markets for labour-intensive manufactures.

---

[31] In the case of commodities, the Prebisch-Singer hypothesis assumed that technical
progress in the developed countries led to higher wages and living standards of
those employed but not to lower prices, including those for goods exported to
developing countries; in contrast, in the developing countries increased productivity
tended to result in lower prices for the goods exported to developed countries
rather than to better real wages. Hence, there was a secular tendency for the terms
of trade to move against developing countries and especially for those exporting
primary products. The general pre-war evidence on which Prebisch built his initial
argument is still the subject of dispute but there is little doubting the sharp and
persistent fall in the terms of trade during the inter-war years; see Blattman et al.
(2003).

[32] Certainly, the period of rapid export expansion in the advanced countries in the
three decades after World War II coincided with strong wage growth and the
development of deeper domestic consumer markets (Armstrong et al., 1984).
However, intra-industry trade, strong productivity growth and high rates of capital
formation were not the automatic outcome of market forces in these countries but
were closely interrelated components of a politically fashioned socio-economic
compromise.

Increased capital mobility, which allows large multinationals to exploit these differences in market structure, reinforces this pressure. Consequently, not only is greater price flexibility likely to be found in the markets for developing countries' labour-intensive manufactures in comparison with those exported by industrial countries, but downward pressure on their prices is likely to generate unfavourable movements in their terms of trade. Evidence on the structure of some key markets for developing-country exports, such as clothing and electronic and electrical goods, certainly tends to confirm this danger (UNCTAD, 2002a:121-24).

As a result the markets for many labour-intensive products are beginning to resemble those for primary products on which the developing countries have been seeking to reduce their dependence: that is, they consist increasingly of internationally standardised goods, often tradeable at arm's length, and tending to oversupply in highly competitive markets with declining price trends which, in some cases such as electronic goods, are also more volatile than those for similar goods traded among the developed countries. Indeed, such a process already appears to be having an impact on the terms of trade of those developing countries most dependent on exports of manufactures and leading some observers to revive the idea of "immiserising growth", i.e., increased economic activity resulting in lower standards of living through declining income terms of trade.[33]

Of course, falling prices need not generate welfare losses if they derive from very strong productivity gains and are offset by large enough increases in volume. Whether that happens, however, depends not only on the growth of demand in the advanced countries but also on who is competing against whom and on the type of good being exported. In this respect, the apparent change in the structure of exports by factor intensity, which is suggested by the higher skill content of the goods produced in international production networks, can be seriously misleading as for the most part developing countries' involvement in skill- and technology-intensive products is confined

---

[33] For empirical evidence on this trend, see UNCTAD (1999a, 2002a); Maizels et al. (1998); and Maizels (2000). On immiserising growth see Kaplinsky et al. (2002).

to the labour-intensive parts of vertically integrated production systems.[34] This is most obviously true in the electronics sector where high-tech final products embody a number of low-tech activities involving the assembly of imported parts. But the production of medium-technology automobiles and even low-technology clothing also comprises a range of activities of differing technological sophistication and capital intensity, allowing for the separability and reorganisation of the various components of the value-added chain. In a recent study of 18 developing-country exporters (for which manufactured goods comprised at least 70 per cent of exports) and the 10 largest developed-country importers of developing-country manufactured goods between 1985 and 2001, Blecker and Razmi (2005) find that competition among developing countries does result in a fallacy of composition in low-tech sectors, that this has intensified in recent years, and that there are limited offsetting income gains from expanding sales to Northern markets. In their particular sample of countries this applies to Latin American and North African countries as well as to some in South Asia. For a small group of high-tech exporters in East Asia there was less competition among them and less reliance on industrial-country demand.

2.   *Stuck on competitiveness*

The basic economic challenge for most developing countries, on which most observers would probably agree, is how to combine strong productivity growth with increased employment, rising real wages that ensure higher living standards but do not outpace productivity or worsen the external constraint, and a nominal exchange rate that maintains purchasing power parity. The last section has already suggested that increasing trade, even in dynamic products, is not syn-

---

[34]   For more discussion on international production networks, see Chapter 4. The classification of internationally traded goods by relative factor intensity and other characteristics is generally based, because of data limitations, on the characteristics of those products in developed countries, usually the United States. Applying the same classification to other countries implicitly assumes that the categories are homogeneous with respect to the characteristics in question and that there are no factor intensity reversals among countries. In practice it is the heterogeneity of the standard product categories rather than factor intensity reversals that limits the usefulness of applying such classifications to other countries.

onymous with meeting the development challenge in this sense. Nor, despite its mantra-like status among market fundamentalists, is it synonymous with increased competitiveness. Indeed, the very idea has been described, with justification, as a "dubious ideal" for countries at any level of development (Brittan, 2004). In part, this is because of the danger of the fallacy of composition, but it is also because what is good for any one firm need not be good for the national economy; from a corporate perspective it might not matter whether competitiveness is improved through currency devaluation, tax breaks, wage cuts or productivity growth, but from the perspective of national economic prosperity and social stability it certainly does. Moreover, countries with highly competitive firms in some sectors may still find it necessary to protect others against foreign competition in an effort to build more dynamic industries; and firms that have come to rely on imported inputs and capital goods for their own profitable line of business may resist efforts to build up local suppliers even if such efforts carry the prospects of stronger productivity growth over the long term (Hirschman, 1968).

More generally, of course, the assumption that market prices reflect all underlying cost conditions is doubtful where monopoly conditions are present or where there are significant externalities or incomplete markets. This takes us into the well-mined literature on market failures in developing countries. Focusing on short-term cost conditions, moreover, can all too easily ignore some of the longer-term processes that make for economic "miracles" and particularly the factors behind sustained improvements in productivity (Baumol et al., 1991:1-7).

We have already noted how conventional trade theorists have slipped anchor from their familiar berth in static comparative advantage to be able to sail more freely in a sea of dynamic productivity gains, citing East Asian sailors as their model trade liberalisers.[35] However,

---

[35] Ocampo (1993:122) has complained that the new contributions to trade theory "have had little impact on prevailing orthodoxies regarding trade liberalisation and industrial restructuring in developing countries. In view of the influence that this type of analysis has had on the structural adjustment programmes of the World Bank, this aloofness is both surprising and problematic. The usual recommendation to create neutral trade incentives and to adopt *laissez-faire* industrial policy, in particular, clearly conflicts with the conclusions derived from these new theories".

doing so also severs the simple links between openness and static efficiency gains, with a good deal instead depending on there being a strong and sustained accumulation drive of the kind that underpinned Western European and Japanese growth after World War II, and that was repeated from the early 1960s in the first-tier NIEs and from the mid-1970s in the second-tier NIEs.[36] As a result of their two-decade-long investment drive, and unlike many other developing countries, the East Asian NIEs were already in the early 1980s able to contemplate trade liberalisation from a position of industrial strength; and in all the first-tier NIEs except Hong Kong (China), value added in manufacturing industry continued to rise as fast as, or faster than, the growth of exports and imports throughout the 1980s and 1990s, and in almost all sectors.[37] But while these examples confirm the possibility of a virtuous circle between investment, exports and growth – investing in sectors with significant productivity and market potential, and using export proceeds to finance the imports of capital goods and intermediate inputs required for further productivity increases – the links do not emerge automatically.

We shall return to the role of investment in greater detail in subsequent chapters. What is clear already, however, is that similar linkages between capital accumulation, industrial upgrading and export performance are less easy to find elsewhere in the developing world, including in countries that have undergone a rapid opening up of their economies (Chart 3.5).

Even when such linkages did begin to emerge in the 1990s, they tended to be confined to one or two sectors and a good deal weaker than in East Asia. In a number of countries in Latin America, such as

---

[36] The latter examples also highlight the importance of avoiding boom-bust cycles, such as marked the investment collapse that accompanied the debt crisis of the early 1980s. Not that the Asian NIEs escaped the crisis completely but, given their large tradeable-goods sectors and substantial industrial capacity built up during the 1960s and 1970s, modest currency depreciations and temporary wage restraint enabled them to recover quickly from the shocks of the late 1970s and early 1980s.

[37] Hong Kong (China) is exceptional in that it followed a hands-off policy towards FDI and has been the least successful of the East Asian NIEs in upgrading its manufacturing output and export structures. Its prosperity, however, was underpinned first by its position as a major *entrepôt* centre and then as a major financial centre.

Chart 3.5: Changes in manufacturing value added in relation to changes in exports of manufactures: 1990-2000 compared to 1980-1990

(per cent of GDP)

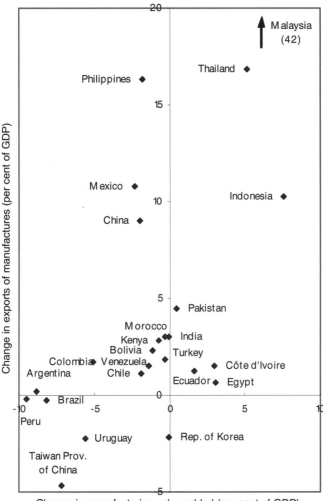

Change in manufacturing value added (per cent of GDP)

Source: UNCTAD, *Trade and Development Report 2003*, Figure 5.2, based on World Bank, *World Development Indicators 2002*.

Argentina, Brazil and Mexico, there were particularly sharp productivity declines in traditional labour-intensive sectors such as textiles and clothing. Productivity growth was better in transport equipment and electrical equipment, and in some cases even exceeded that in the advanced countries. However, in many cases higher productivity was achieved in a context of stagnant or declining levels of employment (Amadeo and Pero, 2000), anticipating a widespread trend of jobless growth. In a few cases, including Mexico, Morocco and the Philippines, exports have risen strongly despite weak investment and productivity growth, thanks largely to their participation in the low-value-added activities of expanding international production networks.[38] But, as we shall see in the next chapter, without spillovers from TNCs to the rest of the economy, and on a significant scale, the transition to a more skill-intensive and sustained pattern of industrial growth is unlikely to proceed through this route. In fact, and this will also be discussed in more detail in the next chapter, the kinds of spillovers that developing countries need and which are often promised, namely technology, intellectual property and skills, are precisely those which the TNC will seek to preserve within the enterprise as these are the sources of its own competitive advantage.

A weakening of the linkage between investment and exports has been particularly noticeable in some middle-income countries, where a combination of (relatively) high wages and low productivity squeezed profits in the face of growing competition. In a number of these countries, particularly in Latin America, weak investment has held back productivity growth and upgrading in the more labour-intensive industries, such as textiles and clothing, and at the same time has arrested the process of diversification to more dynamic areas of manufacturing.[39] In fact, there appears to be a close relationship between the evolution of the structure of exports and the inter-industry

---

[38] It is again worth emphasising, given the unending claims for novelty among enthusiasts for globalisation, that the process of building international production networks dates back to the early 1960s. The first offshore assembly plant for transistors, and subsequently for integrated circuits, was established in Hong Kong in 1961 by Fairchild Semiconductor of the US (Henderson, 1991:50).

[39] Rodrik (2006) identifies similar trends following the collapse of apartheid in South Africa.

pattern of investment in the major Latin American countries, with no significant shift towards technology-intensive industrial categories. Indeed, in almost all cases where a substantial change occurred in the investment pattern, with the exception of the transport sector in some countries, it was towards resource-based or labour-intensive products (UNCTAD, 2002a:115-17). For market fundamentalists this might be interpreted as policy makers getting serious about their comparative advantages, with big efficiency gains expected to follow. But, in an extensive review of the literature on the impact of trade liberalisation on industrial development in Latin America, Dijkstra (2000) concludes that short-term efficiency gains have been achieved at the expense of long-run dynamic efficiency, which he attributes to weak performance in the capital-goods sectors in the major economies. Alice Amsden (2001:260-68) provides further evidence that the sectors commonly associated with successful industrial upgrading have grown particularly slowly in Latin America. Indeed, on her chosen measure of structural change, the economies of Latin America between 1980 and 1994 had some of the lowest rates and lagged far behind East Asia. She attributes this, in part, to a slow growth environment biased towards the destructive rather than the creative forces of market-led structural change, with metalworking industries – a key to sustained industrial growth in most middle-income countries – being particularly weak where neo-liberal policies have driven the reform agenda.

The case of Mexico is particularly telling, given its stellar reputation among market fundamentalists. Since the beginning of liberal reforms in the early 1980s, growth in manufacturing value added has been negligible compared with the surge in exports and imports. Indeed, its share of world manufacturing value added has fallen by a third since then despite a 10-fold increase in its share of world manufactured exports. A principal reason has been weak productivity performance, leading in some cases to a hollowing out of the domestic industrial base in key sectors such as food products, iron and steel, fabricated metal products and industrial chemicals. At a sectoral level most of the increase in exports has been in those industries that are part of international production networks, for example, clothing, non-electrical machinery, and electrical machinery and transport equipment. Even here there has been considerable variation in performance. In clothing, for the period 1980-98, exports grew faster than the average for other manufactures, but domestic value added actually shrunk; a similar pattern is repeated in textiles (albeit with export growth slightly lower). Transport equipment was the fastest-growing category of all exports of manufactures and while the growth in value added was also above average the margin was much smaller than for exports. A similar pattern is repeated in the machinery sectors. In most of these cases, even where productivity growth has been strong, wages have remained stagnant or have fallen. The picture changes little if attention is focussed only on the period since Mexico entered the North American Free Trade Agreement (NAFTA), when exports have become even more closely linked to US-based TNCs, principally in *maquiladoras*, but remain detached from the bulk of domestic economic activity. [40]

Under these circumstances, the rapid exposure of economies to international competition, whether through rapid trade liberalisation or through efforts to attract FDI, may simply lead to the creation of enclaves of manufacturing exports with varying degrees of technological sophistication or even to a reversion to dependence on the extraction and processing of natural resources, even as employment falls in other sectors with a potential for strong productivity growth and greater technological dynamism (UNCTAD, 2003a:106-21).[41] This creates a very real danger of countries getting stuck on a low development road (Pieper, 2000) from which, and while more outward-oriented than in the past, they are unable to generate a rate of growth compatible with rising levels of employment and productivity.

---

[40] World Bank (2003b). On the Mexican experience, see also Hart-Landsberg (2002), and Gallagher and Zarsky (2003). Palma (2004) sees the Mexican example as indicative of the problems arising from an obsession with competitiveness, an obsession that has seen the occasional much-improved player emerge from industries that are constantly being relegated to the lower divisions.

[41] For more on the arrested development of Latin American industry, see Palma (2004). As noted earlier, Chile has something of a distinct profile in the region because of its accelerating economic growth since the debt crisis. However, here too backward and forward linkages in the technologically sophisticated segments of manufacturing have been weakened, raising concerns about its longer-term growth prospects; see Albala-Bertrand (1999).

3.   Constrained growth

The balance of payments – the systematic record of a country's cross-border economic transactions – remains a basic measure of the health of an economy in an interdependent world. Indeed, because it is the point where growth, structural change and integration are most closely intertwined, it has long been recognised as a potentially binding constraint on the development process and a persistent policy challenge for all countries. Prior to 1980, with fixed exchange rates the norm, developing countries routinely tightened their trade regimes when faced with balance-of-payments difficulties, relaxing import controls in periods of surplus. Capital-market liberalisation and flexible exchange rates were expected to offer an escape route from such stopping and going. The standard argument for expecting a smoother ride as market forces take charge of bringing about external balance rests on the unrealistic assumptions behind Say's Law; local resources must always be fully employed and perfectly mobile, prices (including the price of foreign currency) must be perfectly flexible, and, following liberalisation, capital and labour must move effortlessly into those activities judged to be more efficient by global markets. While temporary payments imbalances might still arise, under more open markets these would be underpinned by rational borrowing and lending decisions in the private sector, and should be regarded as benign (the so-called Lawson Doctrine, named after a former UK Finance Minister) and self-correcting.

The underlying idea – that in an interdependent world market forces could be left alone to bring about orderly payment adjustments in the face of persistently unfavourable and highly erratic movements in terms of trade, sharp slowdowns in demand in leading markets, big swings in the principal reserve currencies, and import surges following rapid liberalisation – always required a hefty dose of wishful thinking. In a world of unregulated financial flows, it has proved to be dangerously so, particularly given their volatile nature, as we shall see later in the chapter. In such an untidy world, not only will these flows have a direct bearing on the trade performance of developing countries but their impact will be further complicated by the way in which the performance and policy stance of rich countries impacts on trade prospects in those countries. The relatively slow growth of their markets, continued restrictions on access to them in areas of export interest to developing countries, together with increased global competition, create the obvious danger of increasing developing countries' trade deficits by slowing the growth of their export earnings and generating terms-of-trade losses. Deficits can be further increased by import surges when growth picks up in the developing countries and particularly where policies have not been successful in building competitive industries.

It is thus not surprising, despite all the talk of a new economic order, that the external constraint on growth in the majority of developing countries has remained as tight as ever since the collapse of Bretton Woods. In 51 of 84 developing countries studied by the United Nations Conference on Trade and Development (UNCTAD), the trade balance worsened from the 1980s to the 1990s and in half of them growth rates stagnated or declined (UNCTAD, 1999a:81-84). The majority of countries with worsening trade balances but higher rates of economic growth in the first half of the 1990s – a combination that proved unsustainable – were in Latin America. Deficits largely reflected the failure of exports to keep up with the rapid growth of imports. In the 1970s and 1980s, exports generally rose much faster than imports, although both decelerated sharply in the early 1980s as a result of the global slowdown and the debt crisis. There was a strong recovery of export growth in the 1990s but under the combined pressures of rapid and asymmetric trade liberalisation, the high import content of exports by TNCs and a marked shift in income to groups with a high propensity to import luxury consumer goods, the acceleration of import growth was even greater. In addition, rapid trade liberalisation was generally complicated by mismanaged exchange rates. Instead of maintaining rates that would favour the preservation of international competitiveness and the encouragement of long-term investment, a stable nominal exchange rate was often seen as the way to establish domestic price stability, instead of the other way round, and to attract international capital flows. In most cases the rapid trade liberalisation of the mid-1980s was followed by large inflows of foreign capital, a consequent appreciation of exchange rates, and rising trade deficits.

A more detailed examination of 15 developing countries, five each from Africa, Asia and Latin America, during a 10-year period following liberalisation shows that in the immediate aftermath (two years) imports surged above exports, unless mitigated by a large currency devaluation; more often than not, the problem was exacerbated by currency appreciations. Over the longer period, only in five countries did export growth exceed import growth, but even then deficits did not fall very much, either because the pre-liberalisation deficit was large, the initial surge too strong, or the subsequent growth rate of imports matched that of exports (UNCTAD, 1999a:89-90).

In a slightly larger econometric study of 22 developing countries between 1972 and 1998, Santos-Paulino and Thirlwall (2004) also concluded that liberalisation had had a much larger impact on import than export growth, raising the latter by less than 2 percentage points and the former by over 6 percentage points, with an attendant worsening of the trade balance by over 2 percentage points. This deterioration in the trade balance forced a tightening of macroeconomic policy and a lowering of the longer-term rate of economic growth. China is an exception to this pattern: its economic growth accelerated in the 1990s but a large trade deficit in the 1980s was transformed into a surplus (although the latter has been reduced by a large fall in net incomes from invisibles since the mid-1990s). But even in China, the rising share of FDI in total investment may generate a less healthy picture in the longer run, given the high import content of exports, large profit margins and the likely scale of future remittances abroad. Also in East Asia, although imports grew faster than exports in the 1990s, the difference was much less than elsewhere and the relation between economic growth and the trade deficit is still much the same as in the 1970s.

Thus, overall, the results of most developing countries' efforts to ease the current-account constraint through market-friendly structural reforms and export-led growth have been disappointing. In many countries, the combination of rapid trade liberalisation, opening up the capital account and mismanagement of the exchange rate has produced large trade imbalances without generating rapid and sustainable growth.

D.   Trade liberalisation, adjustment costs and the myth of convergence

The prediction that unrestricted global market forces will, by increasing international trade, benefit poorer countries more than others, rests on hallowed theoretical ground. However, its theoretical elegance is difficult to reconcile with the discussion in the previous section which suggested that the trade performance of developing countries since the early 1980s has at best been uneven, that their gains from trade have weakened, that the pace of structural change in much of the developing world outside of East Asia has slowed, and that there has been a general deterioration in trade balances.

Convergence could of course still occur as a result of a sharp slowdown in growth in richer countries, which has indeed happened, although this is clearly not the message intended (or projected) by most globalisation enthusiasts. In fact, inserting just a little bit of history into the process of global integration by looking for breaks in the time series quickly raises doubts about the convergence scenario, as we saw with the Dowrick and Golley study. They also found that once China and India are removed from their sample of the 22 more globalised developing countries, the remaining countries actually grew more slowly than the less globalised. Matthew Slaughter's (1998) inclusion of a bit more history by examining 10,000 "difference-in-differences" estimates of convergence rates before and after an episode of trade liberalisation also suggests that this failed to trigger convergence; if anything, it did the opposite.[42] At least one comprehensive econometric analysis of the links between trade, tariffs and growth reports a strong positive relation between trade volumes and trade barriers and economic growth in the period 1970-98 (Yanikkaya, 2003), repeating the pre-1914 experience and thus severing again the simple connection from trade policy to economic growth promoted by market fundamentalists. Such findings are

---

[42]   Slaughter examines four liberalisation episodes with a heavy European bias, the formation of the EEC, the formation of EFTA, liberalisation between the EEC and EFTA, and the Kennedy Round of multilateral trade liberalisation, comparing the results on income convergence rates before and after these episodes kicked in, and then comparing these results with changing convergence rates in a randomly selected control group.

consistent with the evidence, noted previously, that exporting is undertaken predominantly by large firms that have expanded in a local market setting, and with sectoral evidence showing that export growth is almost always preceded by a period of successful import substitution (Chenery et al., 1986).

We shall come back to these trends in Chapter 5, but it is still possible we are looking in the wrong place for the big payoff from trade liberalisation. In a speech to the International Labour Organisation (ILO), Michael Moore (2002), then Director-General of the WTO, was convinced that workers of the world should unite around trade liberalisation, arguing that "we do not believe that concerns about adjustment costs and income distribution are meaningful arguments against trade liberalisation. We do believe that with appropriate domestic policies and institutions in place, everyone can gain from trade liberalisation." Exactly what combination of the Stolper-Samuelson theorem (whereby openness raises the returns to the factor used intensively in the rising-price activity), factor price equalisation (whereby free trade equalises factor prices) and the Rybczynski theorem (whereby added supplies of one factor skew production possibilities in favour of the sector using that factor most intensively) Mr Moore deems necessary to guarantee a rosy economic future for all workers in the global economy is not altogether clear. In any case, his beliefs about adjustment costs do not appear to survive closer scrutiny.

Although there have been other factors influencing labour-market conditions during the recent period of trade liberalisation, including those linked to macroeconomic adjustment and labour-market reforms, the possibility that unemployment might increase if tariff and non-tariff barriers are lowered sharply, allowing consumers to switch from non-traded goods to imports, is hardly contentious, going back to Adam Smith.[43] A good deal of evidence from Latin America and Sub-Saharan Africa, where neo-liberal policies have been pursued most intensively, suggests that increases in unemployment and/or increasing wage

---

[43] Buffie (2001). Indeed, even standard trade models which allow for underutilised resources produce indeterminate (or rather multiple) outcomes from trade liberalisation.

inequality have often accompanied rapid trade liberalisation.[44] In one study of changes in the earnings of three different skill groups in 10 Latin American countries in recent years, the wage gap between skilled and unskilled workers increased in nine of them. With few exceptions, the real earnings of unskilled workers fell during the periods covered, with declines of more than 20 per cent in many cases.[45] The difference between the earnings of public employees and workers in larger firms, on the one hand, and skilled workers, on the other, also widened in most countries, although by a smaller margin.[46] Increased wage dispersion in the manufacturing industry has also been reported in a study by the ILO which, for a sample of 30 countries in Africa, Asia and Latin America, compares average real wages in 1975-79 with those in 1987-91.[47] In about two-thirds of the countries real average wages had fallen, and the fall was correlated with a rise in wage dispersion. The economies in which wage dispersion diminished include the first-tier East Asian NIEs, where it was accompanied by large increases in labour productivity.[48]

More important, the observed shift in wage differentials towards skilled labour has not been associated with any significant increase in exports of more skill-intensive products.[49] In some cases the demand

---

[44] For a review of these findings, see Arbache, Dickerson and Green (2004).

[45] UNCTAD (1997:135).

[46] ECLAC (1997:60). Additional evidence is presented in Robbins (1996). Despite the mounting evidence about the impact of trade liberalisation on increased earnings inequality in Latin America, a study by the Inter-American Development Bank (IDB) reports a positive effect of trade liberalisation on personal income distribution. However, no attempt is made to reconcile this finding with all the other evidence to the contrary; see Londoño and Székely (1997).

[47] ILO (1996:Table 5.9 and related text).

[48] The only exception to diminishing wage dispersion in East Asia is Hong Kong (China). A number of explanations have been offered to reconcile increased wage inequality with mainstream trade theory based on comparative advantage. Not surprisingly, technological factors have received particular attention. If trade liberalisation and increased capital mobility accelerate the introduction of best-practice technology in developing countries, and if the use of such technology requires specially trained labour, the increase in demand for skilled labour may lead to a widening of the wage gap. However, a fairly sizeable shift in technology would be required for this to occur, which in turn should be reflected in a sharp increase in imports of capital goods as well as exports of skill-intensive products. But, in general, the greater openness observed in Latin America has not been associated with a significant increase in investment and technology transfer.

[49] UNCTAD (1997:136).

for skilled labour has increased relative to that for unskilled labour without a significant increase in fixed investment to upgrade the industry and expand exports of more technology-intensive products. Industries producing low-technology products have replaced less educated with more educated labour. This upgrading of skills may have been triggered by trade liberalisation, with the industries affected being no longer able to compete with imports. Simply lowering the wages of unskilled labour was not sufficient to restore competitiveness: it required in addition the hiring of more skilled labour (Cragg and Epelbaum, 1996).

The emergence of low-cost producers of labour-intensive manufactures in Asia during this period has no doubt changed the parameters of international trade for other exporters of such products. However, its impact to date has not been uniform. The first-tier East Asian NIEs, where about half of total exports were manufactures in the mid-1980s, responded to this new competition by restructuring and upgrading their labour-intensive exports, and shifting towards more skill-intensive products.[50] This upgrading began before imports were liberalised in the second half of the 1980s. The share of labour-intensive products in the combined exports of Korea and Taiwan fell from over 40 per cent in 1985 to under 15 per cent in 2000, while that of skill- and technology-intensive exports more than doubled, reaching over two-thirds of the total in both countries in 2000. In the Republic of Korea wage differentials narrowed throughout the 1980s, while in Taiwan Province of China the trend of increasing wage inequality was reversed in the latter half of the decade. In both cases, restructuring and upgrading were facilitated by increased supplies of skilled labour brought about by appropriate manpower policies.

Thus, on balance, there is no clear relation (either positive or negative) between trade liberalisation and labour-market performance.

---

[50] Differences in the ability of different countries to respond to increased competition in labour-intensive products are also reflected in movements in the manufacturing sector's terms of trade. During 1979-94 the world price of manufactured exports of developing countries fell relative to that of skill-intensive exports from industrial countries by about 2 per cent per annum. The decline was largest in the least-developed countries (LDCs), followed by the African, Caribbean and Pacific (ACP), Latin American and Mediterranean countries, while it was significantly smaller in East Asia; for the Republic of Korea, the manufacturing terms of trade improved during that period. See UNCTAD (1996:Part Two, Chap. III).

The effect on wages and income distribution differs between countries, depending on the domestic and international conditions prevailing when liberalisation occurred. This – in itself – is an important
result as it suggests that in the real world the distributive predictions
of the standard trade theory are not generally verified. At the same
time, however, the results do not suggest that trade liberalisation always worsens the distribution of income. The distributive outcome
depends on specific factors and circumstances. As these factors vary
considerably from place to place and over time, at the aggregate level
it is difficult to identify a clear relation between trade liberalisation
and inequality.

E.   The liberalisation of international finance

The explosion of international capital flows since the early 1980s
is a prominent feature of the current era of global integration, and
perhaps its defining feature. The global stock of financial assets rose
more than 11-fold between 1980 and the end of 2004, from $12 trillion
to $136 trillion. In 1980 they were roughly equal to global GDP (109
per cent) but by the end of 2004 were more than three times higher (at
334 per cent). This extraordinary growth partly reflects increasing
financial depth throughout the world, including the monetisation of
the formerly centrally planned economies and the rapid development
of countries such as China, but, as we shall see, it also reflects the
influence of asset-price bubbles and rising government indebtedness.
This growth followed the abolition of capital controls by the industrial
countries, which occurred soon after the collapse of the Bretton Woods
system and the shift to flexible exchange rates. The value of daily
foreign-exchange transactions amounted to just $80bn in 1980, but
reached $600bn in 1989 and a staggering $1,900bn in 2004. This 25-
fold increase compares with a 4-5-fold increase in the volume of trade
over the same period. There have also been massive two-way flows
of funds dominated by short-term capital movements in the form of
cross-border bank lending, equities and bonds. The market for
corporate control through cross-border mergers and acquisitions
(M&A) has mushroomed and a good deal of cross-border investment
is in banking, insurance and other financial services. A plethora of

new financial instruments has emerged which promise to mitigate risk, particularly in those emerging markets that greatly excited financial investors after the collapse of the Berlin Wall.

The accelerating gap between the size of the financial and real economies represents a major change from the post-war Bretton Woods regime, which was premised on the assumption that in order to promote economic growth and employment via an open international trading system, international financial flows had to be effectively managed, in particular through the direct control of capital movements. The original design was heavily informed by the basic choice facing macroeconomic policy makers in advanced countries as to which two of the three variables – an independent monetary policy, a fixed exchange rate, or international capital mobility (i.e., capital-account convertibility) – they wanted to influence.[51] With the objective of avoiding a repetition of the failures of capitalism during the inter-war years firmly in mind, the choice was made for a system of fixed exchange rates with flexibility for domestic monetary policy, but with tight controls on international capital movements. Consequently, the original arrangements did not include rules and regulations for capital mobility largely because this was considered incompatible with currency stability and the expansion of trade and employment. But they did allow a good deal of policy space to manage an expanded domestic policy agenda, which included the objectives of faster growth, full employment and stable prices.

As in the case of trade liberalisation, the change in policy orientation reflects deeper arguments over the ways in which market economies are believed to work. One of the major disagreements is whether instability is endemic to the international financial markets, and indeed to the market system in general, or whether it arises from inappropriate institutions and interference with market processes. The neo-liberal position asserts that interfering governments and politicised central banks suppress or distort market signals, and that, left to their own devices, individuals, enterprises and financial institutions will coordinate their various activities in an orderly and predictable way. From this viewpoint, the call for developing and transition economies

---

[51] For a useful history of how this thinking evolved in the context of the emergence of international financial arrangements, see Pauly (1997).

to liberalise their domestic financial markets and their external capital accounts is simply an extension of the argument for free trade in goods. This was expected not only to increase the availability of investment finance from domestic sources but also to provide access to the savings of other countries.[52] Through the search for the most profitable projects, capital mobility would lead to a more efficient use of resources, to increased investment, higher growth rates and the convergence of incomes.[53]

A different view, associated with, but not exclusive to, the Keynesian tradition, is that uncertainty and coordination failures are not due to outside interference but are deeply rooted in the very nature of the system. In contrast to the neo-liberal view, and notwithstanding the evidence of government failures, this tradition regards government intervention as capable of reducing uncertainty and thereby bolstering the animal spirits of investors and stimulating economic growth.[54] From this perspective, not only can directed credit in developing countries play a useful role in correcting domestic financial-market failures, but international arrangements and regulations are also seen as essential for dealing with potential risks and threats to systemic stability.

The collapse of the Bretton Woods system was certainly a pivotal moment in the revival of the neo-liberal vision of the international financial system (Eatwell and Taylor, 2000). Private financial institutions proliferated and began trespassing on each other's territory. Moreover, their measure of economic success was increasingly divorced from the mundane and drawn-out pressures of making productive investment work and increasingly tied to matters of liquidity, speculation and continuously rising asset prices. In addition, as financial interests grew relative to the real economy, their influence

---

[52] For standard accounts see Shaw (1973) and McKinnon (1973).

[53] In recent years, an additional attraction of this approach for the governments of developed market economies has been the suggestion that private capital flows would reduce the need for official financial assistance.

[54] Similar policy conclusions may be reached from both perspectives – for example, that this or that government intervention is harmful or that better regulation of certain financial activities is desirable – but, in the main, the Keynesian tradition would argue the need for various controls on capital movements as a permanent element in the policy tool-box and not just for emergencies; see Felix (2003).

on the political and policy-setting processes also grew and, given their inflation phobia and fixation with being able to move on at a moment's notice, in a strongly neo-liberal direction.

It is certainly the case, even more than with the liberalisation of trade, that freeing finance carries a strident demand for institutional and policy conformity. Despite some disagreement among market fundamentalists about how rapidly financial markets should be liberalised, the basic choice presented to all countries was clear-cut: "either to integrate themselves into the international economy or to become marginalised from it and thus fall farther and farther behind in terms of growth and development" and, not surprisingly, "In order for countries to reap the full benefits of an open and liberal system of capital movements they have to open their capital accounts" (Camdessus, 1997:4). Larry Summers, a former chief economist of the World Bank and erstwhile Keynesian, in an address to the London Stock Exchange in 2001, was even more certain that the reason why some countries were winning in today's global economy was their adherence to an "Anglo-American" model that combined prudent budget policies and open financial markets.[55]

This new agenda was transmitted very swiftly to the rest of the world, thanks in large measure to the transformation of the international financial institutions from guardians of systemic financial stability into proselytisers of financial globalisation. They now became preoccupied with extending the reach of loosely regulated private capital markets, including through domestic structural reforms in debt-ridden developing countries.[56]

---

[55] As cited in Plender (2003:7-8).

[56] As Arestis (2004) notes, the term "financial liberalisation" does not have a standard meaning. He distinguishes between the liberalisation of the capital account described by the removal of regulations on offshore borrowing by financial institutions and non-financial corporations and on capital outflows, and the ending of multiple exchange rates, so that banks and corporations are free to borrow abroad and reserve requirements are kept at a minimum level; the liberalisation of the domestic financial system characterised by the removal of controls on lending and borrowing interest rates, the removal of credit controls and permission to hold foreign currency deposits; and the liberalisation of the stock market in which foreign investors are allowed to buy, earn income from and sell equities without restriction.

At annual gatherings of Finance Ministers in Washington in the 1990s discussion turned to revising the Articles of the IMF to include the promotion of capital-account convertibility. In what with hindsight looks like very unfortunate timing, the then Managing Director of the IMF Michel Camdessus, in his previously cited address in June 1997, left no doubt that surging capital flows to emerging markets not only reflected a more efficient allocation of resources and a stimulus to faster growth worldwide but also provided a powerful incentive for countries to follow more prudent policies and undertake further reforms to improve their domestic investment climate. With equal confidence in that same year the World Bank (1997) had no hesitation in judging Korea, Malaysia and Thailand ready for full liberalisation, with Indonesia, the Philippines, Mexico and Brazil not far behind.

There can be no doubting that the relaxation of controls on international capital mobility led to a considerable increase in the flow of capital to developing countries from the late 1980s (Chart 3.6). In total, net capital flows to developing countries rose by a factor of 20 between 1970 and 1998 (to some $312bn), although in terms of their purchasing power over imports the average annual increase was much less. Moreover, at some 12 per cent a year, the increase in real terms in the 1990s was only slightly more than in the 1970s. Perhaps more significantly, this inflow of capital was characterised by a marked shift in its structure. Private capital flows, freed from controls and attracted by privatisation in many developing countries, rose sharply, from 1 per cent of GDP in the 1980s to 4 per cent in the 1990s, and particularly so after the introduction of the Brady Plan, while official loans and assistance declined, in part reflecting fiscal consolidation in the developed countries.

The greater part (two-thirds or so) of these flows consisted of short-term investments: bank loans, equities and short-dated government securities, inter-bank and other deposits. Portfolio flows accounted for 21 per cent (compared with a mere 2-3 per cent in the 1970s and 1980s), while bank loans and other private credit remained fairly steady at around 25 per cent of the total net inflow. Beginning in the early 1990s, FDI in developing countries also rose sharply, more than doubling between 1995 and 2000, when it reached over $250bn. The factors behind this expansion include the acquisition of privatised assets, especially in Latin America in the early 1990s, the

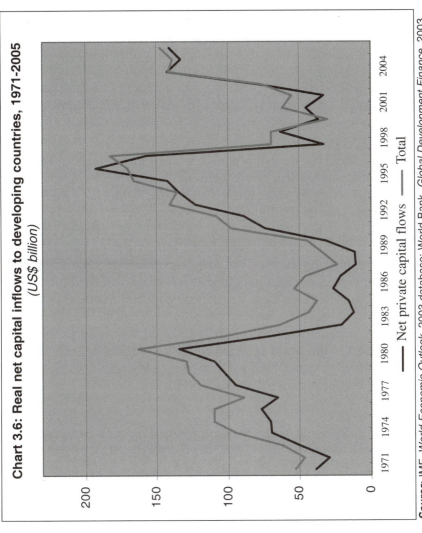

Chart 3.6: Real net capital inflows to developing countries, 1971-2005
(US$ billion)

Net private capital flows ——— Total

Source*: IMF, World Economic Outlook, 2003 database; World Bank, Global Development Finance, 2003.*
Note*: Real flows are nominal flows adjusted for changes in the United States GDP deflator.*

rapid growth of the newly industrialising economies of South-East Asia, and the opening up of the Chinese economy.[57]

This increased mobility of private capital in the 1990s has frequently led to comparisons with the gold standard before 1914. Much of the attention has focused on whether or not markets were more global or more integrated than today, but the more important question is whether increased financial flows, as in the period before 1914, have widened economic divisions in the global economy.[58] The nature of today's financial flows is certainly different from those in the earlier period when they were long-term and principally in the form of bond financing. The greater part of contemporary financial flows reflects international portfolio diversification, hedging and risk-sharing. Much like the earlier period, however, flows today are heavily concentrated on just a few countries. Most of these are advanced industrial countries where gross private capital flows have risen from just 6 per cent of GDP in the late 1960s to over 20 per cent in the second half of the 1990s and over 27 per cent in the opening years of the new millennium. Whether or not Obstfeld and Taylor (2002:57-58) are right to suggest that "The global capital market of the nineteenth century centred on Europe, especially London, extended relatively more credit to LDCs [less developed countries] than does today's global capital market", there can be no disputing that the world's richest country has become its most heavily indebted, absorbing the savings of the rest of the world at an unprecedented $2bn a day, or that the bulk of foreign capital does *not* flow from rich to poor countries – the so-called "Lucas paradox" (Lucas, 1990).

---

[57] According to the calculations of Alfaro et al. (2006:10), based on a sample of 72 countries, between 1970 and 2000, FDI per capita grew at 6.2 per cent a year, average portfolio equity inflows per capita (for a slightly smaller group of countries) at 9.3 per cent, and average inflows of debt per capita (for a larger group of countries) at 3.3 per cent.

[58] As suggested in Chapter 2, before 1914 the international financial markets were concerned with intermediating a "surplus" of domestic savings in Europe to meet the demands for funds for productive and fixed investment in North America, Latin America and other wealthy primary producing countries such as Australia and New Zealand, as well as some smaller newly industrialising economies such as Sweden. This earlier period of globalisation cannot therefore be seen in contemporary terms as integrating a poor South with a rich North. In fact, incomes per head in the capital-receiving countries were often as high as, and sometimes higher than, in the capital-exporting countries.

Concentration is also a feature of flows to developing countries. Thus, the share of low-income countries in net private capital flows to developing countries has been steadily declining since the second half of the 1980s, from 20 per cent (around $6bn) to just 6 per cent in the second half of the 1990s (around $14bn), with an attendant rise in the share of middle-income emerging markets. In recent years more than three-quarters of bond issues have been accounted for by less than 10 borrowers in Latin America and Asia and much of the syndicated bank lending has gone to half-a-dozen countries in Asia. These same countries were also the main recipients of international equity investment.

The greater part of global FDI (some 80 per cent) is also accounted for by flows among the developed countries, much of it linked to mergers and acquisitions rather than fixed investment in new assets. The rising flow to developing countries is also very unevenly distributed: three-quarters of the total in the 1990s went to just 10 emerging-market economies, and China, Brazil and Mexico together took nearly one-half.[59] Indeed, China accounted for about one-third of all FDI in the developing countries in the 1990s and about two-thirds of the total went to East Asia.[60] Other developing regions – Sub-Saharan Africa, South Asia, North Africa and the Middle East – have only marginal shares of the total and, in the case of Sub-Saharan Africa, a falling one.

Although financial flows to developing countries account for a very small proportion of the global flow of private capital, in relation to the size of their economies what they do receive can be very large and thus can have significant consequences for financial and macroeconomic stability. During the 1990s, not only did financial liberalisation give much greater scope to residents in developing countries to purchase financial instruments abroad, but it also deprived governments of a good deal of control over how those funds could be used domestically. For every dollar brought in by non-residents, 24 cents were taken out by residents, compared with 14 cents in the 1980s, and more than 20 cents were put aside for the accumulation of

---

[59] Such a high degree of concentration has changed little since the early 1970s.
[60] The Chinese FDI data, however, are the subject of considerable dispute; see UNCTAD (2005c).

reserves as a safeguard against speculative attacks on the currency and reversals of capital flows. These trends appear to have accelerated in the early years of the new millennium. The latter strategy is particularly costly since reserves are borrowed at much higher interest rates than they can earn in international financial markets. In many cases, inflows have increased the fragility of the banking system as low-cost external financing has been used to acquire local, high-risk and illiquid assets, thus generating a mismatch in currencies and maturities. As will be discussed in greater detail in the next chapter, the extent to which FDI has added to the productive capital stock of the host countries is also not very clear. A large proportion of FDI in the 1990s – between one-half and two-thirds – was due to cross-border M&A, and although this may subsequently lead to additional fixed investment and productivity gains it is essentially a transfer of ownership over existing assets.[61] Although it is widely assumed to be a more stable source of external finance than portfolio flows, the M&A component of FDI is likely to include speculative flows attracted by the prospect of quick capital gains, including in periods of crisis or their aftermath. Thus herd behaviour seems to be ubiquitous among all the various types of capital flow.[62]

The "globalisation" of capital flows is thus somewhat of a misnomer insofar as the developing countries receive only a small proportion of the total and a good deal less than their share of global

---

[61] Usually, acquisitions of 10 per cent or more of voting stocks are treated as FDI; those below are classified as portfolio equity investments. There are many gaps and inconsistencies in the statistics of FDI, which are considerably more problematic than those for international trade. For a good survey of the issues, see Sutcliffe (1998). The figures for FDI are often significantly distorted by "round-tripping". It has been estimated that up to half of China's FDI consists of Chinese capital that has been re-routed through offshore tax havens and Hong Kong (China) in order to benefit from the special privileges given to foreign investors (*Oxford Analytica*, 2003). A similar phenomenon occurred in Eastern Europe, in Hungary for example, in the 1990s. It should also be borne in mind that the OECD statistics on FDI by direction show a large "unallocated" proportion.

[62] A review of the business cycle in 15 developing countries for the period 1970-97 found that FDI was a volatile component of those cycles, and a good deal more so than the official flows that they supplanted (Rand and Tarp, 2002). According to another study of 103 countries for the period 1980-96, portfolio investment was only slightly more volatile than FDI, and among 85 emerging-market economies over the same period the levels of volatility in the two flows were the same; see UNCTAD (2003a:78).

output: their share of global FDI in 2000 was some 16 per cent and of total global capital-market flows less than 7 per cent.[63] Indeed, on balance, the liberalisation of capital movements has had little impact on real resource flows to the developing countries. Taking into account net payments abroad of foreign investment income, including interest payments on outstanding debt, increases in reserve holdings and profit remittances, the picture has been particularly bleak for most developing countries since the Asian financial crisis of 1997, with a cumulative outflow to 2002 in excess of $700bn (UNCTAD, 2003a). This is the backdrop against which we now examine the links between financial liberalisation and economic growth.

F. The siren call of quick fixes: Shocks, cycles and crises in unregulated financial markets

Capital flows were seen as having the leading role in integrating the global economy during the 1990s. The expectation was for faster and more evenly distributed rates of economic growth as these flows would help to finance trade imbalances, to provide more resources for capital formation, particularly in the capital-scarce, poorer countries, and to add depth to local financial markets. Despite the widely shared belief that a more open economic environment would demonstrate the benefits of unrestricted capital mobility and the superiority of markets over government intervention, the period since the collapse of the Bretton Woods system has instead been marked by lower rates of investment in infrastructure and productive capacity and by an increasing incidence of financial crises, in both developed and developing countries, and by their growing virulence in terms of lost output and jobs.

Beyond some rather obvious points of agreement, such as companies being more likely to grow and be more productive when they have access to reasonably priced long-term finance, there is little

---

[63] This compares with their shares of four-fifths of global population, a third of world trade, and over a fifth of global output.

in the way of consensus as to which financial institutions are best for development.[64] As we shall see in later chapters, a good deal of capital accumulation is still financed from retained profits, and there is little evidence to suggest that a more liberal system results in a higher savings ratio or in more of those savings being used to expand productive capacity. Moreover, the fact that private financial institutions tend to be biased against lending to small firms (due to low returns and high risk) is a familiar obstacle to the accumulation process in many poorer countries.

It seems more reasonable to suppose that the impact of financial flows is likely to vary according to the level of a country's development. Again, the cross-country regression literature seems to suggest that a strongly positive impact is only detectable above a certain threshold level of income. This is likely to reflect the simple fact that more sophisticated financial institutions and effective regulations are as much the product as the cause of development. Perhaps more than any other contemporary economist, Joseph Stiglitz has argued the case why policy makers, particularly those in developing countries, should deal cautiously with private capital markets. His work has highlighted the limits of economic rationality in understanding the behaviour of financial-market participants, the role of imperfect information in credit and equity rationing, the dangers of segmentation and the boom-bust nature of short-term capital flows.[65] The upshot is that unregulated capital markets can be a major source of economic volatility, particularly where domestic financial institutions are weak or missing. The underestimation or wilful neglect of these features of capital flows by market fundamentalists has led to an increased risk of financial crises and a major distortionary influence on economic performance and the prospects for growth.

Investment manias, bubbles and crashes are a longstanding feature of capitalist development. Most have been triggered by the relaxation of regulations that were put in place in response to earlier excesses (Kindleberger, 1984). The current era appears to be no

---

[64] Specific financial functions seem to be carried out effectively under different institutional arrangements with similar outcomes. Certainly, the idea of a steady progress towards an optimal Anglo-Saxon model does not meet with strong empirical support.

[65] See Stiglitz (1982, 1985, 1993), and Stiglitz and Weiss (1981).

different in this respect. According to Barry Eichengreen (2002), the period since the collapse of Bretton Woods has seen a sharp increase in the incidence of financial crises, principally in the form of currency crises but also in conjunction with banking crises. On one estimate, during the 1990s the financial system was in crisis for 40 out of 120 months (Plender, 2003:57).

These crises have followed a broadly similar pattern. Financial-market deregulation and capital-account liberalisation are introduced into a system that maintains a stable nominal exchange rate and a tight monetary policy; the resulting interest-rate differential attracts liquid and short-term capital flows which initially reinforce confidence in the stability of the exchange rate; the newly deregulated banking sector expands into new areas of domestic business, and domestic firms borrow abroad to take advantage of lower interest rates, thereby exposing themselves to exchange-rate risks. The new policy configuration eventually begins to put upward pressure on the exchange rate, at the same time as the attempted sterilisation of capital inflows increases the pressure on interest rates alongside a deteriorating fiscal position. These growing imbalances begin to erode confidence and eventually expectations change, triggering a rapid outflow of capital and increasing the probability of a severe crisis as a result of a falling exchange rate, corporate bankruptcies and a growing threat to the solvency of domestic banks.

The precise circumstances in which the vulnerability of individual countries to a reversal of capital inflows arises, and the subsequent impact on economic growth and stability, vary from region to region and among individual countries. The contrast between Latin America and East Asia highlights some of the differences. In Latin America, strategies of import substitution had led to rapid rates of growth in the two decades or so following World War II, and this success was already attracting foreign capital in the late 1960s. Those inflows, largely in the form of syndicated bank loans, accelerated in the mid-1970s in the wake of the first oil shock. However, in most cases, these loans were not used to finance restructuring of the productive sectors and thus failed to increase export capacities on a scale sufficient to meet the mounting burden of debt servicing.[66]

---

[66] The predominance of sovereign debt emerged only after the restructuring of foreign debt in the 1980s; see Diaz-Alejandro (1985).

Consequently, when the United States suddenly switched its monetary policy to a strong anti-inflationary stance at the end of the 1970s, leading to a global recession and a collapse in commodity prices, Latin America sank into a profound payments and debt crisis. This left many countries desperate for external financing, which came at a very heavy price in terms of neo-liberal policy reforms.

The subsequent restructuring of debt at the end of the 1980s under the Brady Plan greatly accelerated this change in policies. Any remaining vestiges of import substitution were abandoned and replaced by a rapid liberalisation of the markets for goods and of the capital account. While the change in policies did bring about a rapid lowering of inflation, the resulting increase in real incomes and wealth, before productive capacity had been rationalised and expanded, fuelled a consumer boom which sucked in a larger volume of imports and led to a growing current-account deficit. In the absence of a new development model to convert export earnings into increased investment in competitive manufacturing industries, such deficits had to be financed by foreign investors attracted by the promise of high returns and low exchange-rate risk.

Recent Latin American experience continues a long history of boom and bust in foreign capital flows and of abrupt changes in development strategy brought about either by internal political pressures or by external events.[67] As such, it stands in contrast to East Asia where development strategies have generally been more stable, gradual and comprehensive, and have included specific policies to reduce their dependence on foreign capital and to incorporate what FDI they did import into a broader framework of domestic investment and technological upgrading. The strategic use of tariff protection and government direction of investment ensured a commensurate growth of export capacities and helped to ensure that ratios of debt service to export earnings never reached the levels that created severe problems in Latin America.

By the mid-1990s, however, as a result of various internal and external factors, including domestic financial liberalisation, foreign bank lending to private-sector borrowers was rising sharply, boosted

---

[67]   See Marichal (1989); Fitzgerald (2002); UNCTAD (2003a).

by low United States interest rates in the early 1990s which stimulated large flows of "hot" money seeking arbitrage profits from international interest-rate differences. Most of the lending was non-syndicated, much was short-term, and a significant proportion was lent to banks and property companies. The accumulation of short-term foreign debt in the Asian economies left them increasingly vulnerable to a turn in foreign sentiment, irrespective of the fact that, unlike Latin America, their basic macroeconomic fundamentals were sound and fiscal policies prudent. Once the shift in market perceptions occurred in mid-1997, the East Asian economies suffered a similar transition from boom to bust in foreign capital flows and hence a major financial crisis. In contrast to Latin America, however, the recovery of the Asian economies from the crisis was relatively fast and complete. It was supported by expansionary macroeconomic policies and by the high degree of regional integration that amplified the effect of the increases in exports that followed the exchange-rate devaluations.[68]

When the Asian financial crisis broke out in 1997, many western commentators were quick to criticise the Asian approach to economic development, blaming it for excessively close relationships between government, banks and business, and for protecting private enterprise from the discipline of market forces. Predictably, the critics also claimed that the model was no longer appropriate in the face of global market forces (World Bank, 2000a). Besides its blatant intellectual hypocrisy, given that these same countries had previously been held up as shining examples of what market-led development could deliver to poorer countries in a globalising world, this claim downplays the role of systemic financial instability in the East Asian crisis.

The global supply of cheap credit had fuelled an investment boom in many of the South-East Asian economies where manufacturing industry was already under increasing competitive pressure from lower-cost producers in other developing countries. The response of the former was a drive to boost productive capacity in an attempt to regain market share, but this only added to an already global excess supply and so exacerbated the fall in prices, especially in

---

[68] For accounts of financial liberalisation in East Asia see Radelet and Sachs (1998), and the various papers in Chang et al. (eds.) (2001).

the IT sector. At the same time banks, which were subject to little or no regulation, moved into new areas of lending, real estate, as in previous crises elsewhere, proving to be one of the most attractive. Banks, manufacturing companies and the property sector thus became extremely vulnerable to a rise in interest rates or a fall in the exchange rate.

The crisis that started in Thailand in May 1997 appears to have been triggered by the expectation of a rise in Japanese interest rates. But once a fragile situation has been created, almost any change in the conjuncture can lead to a sudden reversal of foreign capital and massive downward pressure on the exchange rate. Foreign lenders, seeing the increased exchange-rate risk, started to call in loans as they fell due, and domestic borrowers sought to reduce their exposure by hedging their foreign debts or repaying them. As firms struggled to maintain solvency they simply triggered a downward spiral, typical of a debt deflation, by driving the exchange rate and asset values even lower. The falling exchange rates led to contagion throughout the region as the pattern of relative competitiveness was disrupted.

Although the crisis in South-East Asia had not been caused by budget deficits or a loss of competitiveness due to accelerating domestic inflation, by treating it as a traditional payments crisis the international financial institutions not only failed to halt the fall in the exchange rate and reverse the capital outflows, but actually intensified the debt deflation and pushed the affected economies into a deeper recession. There was certainly some case for a managed reduction in domestic absorption in Thailand, but the actual policies adopted simply increased the degree of financial instability. The essential issue was that, at the new exchange rates, the foreign debt of banks and companies was too large to be serviced by their expected income – and so there was a collapse in their asset prices. Given the high savings rates and strong export capacities in South-East Asia, there should have been few doubts that their debts would be repaid within a reasonable time. Instead, high interest rates and large exchange-rate devaluations led to sharp falls in output and income, rising unemployment and considerable social distress.[69]

---

[69] For accounts of the crisis and its aftermath, see the various papers collected in Chang et al. (eds.) (2001).

Labour-market conditions deteriorated in all countries with the outbreak of the financial crisis. Indeed, it appears that reduced incomes and employment in both organised and informal labour markets were the main conduits for the adverse impact of the crisis on poverty and equality.[70] An expansion of the informal economy and disguised unemployment appeared almost everywhere in Asia, but despite such flexibility and a general decline in participation rates, unemployment rose in all the countries hit by the crisis.[71] Falling wages and growing unemployment combined to produce a sharp increase in poverty throughout the region. In 1998 the number of people living on less than $1 a day was estimated at 65 million in the five East Asian economies hit by the crisis, 10 million of whom were pushed into that condition by the crisis itself. These figures rise to 260 million and 24 million, respectively, if the poverty benchmark is put at $2 a day.[72] Poverty appears to have increased most in Indonesia and the Republic of Korea, where a critical factor was the much larger increase in food prices relative to those of other consumer goods; this was especially the case in Indonesia, where inflation accelerated rapidly.

In Latin America, the impact of financial crises on wages, employment and poverty was similar to earlier crisis episodes. In some cases the adjustment fell most heavily on real wages, which sometimes fell by more than 20 per cent (e.g., in Mexico and Venezuela). The outcome was similar in Turkey. In other Latin American cases, the fall in wages was more moderate, but instead there were sharp increases in the unemployment rate of the order of 6-10 percentage points, as in Argentina during 1995-96 and in Chile during the Southern Cone crisis. The impact on poverty in Latin America was equally severe. Economic growth during the first half of the 1990s had led to a gradual reduction of the high poverty levels inherited from the 1980s, but even so there were still more than 200 million people living below the poverty line before the subsequent crises. One reason for the persistence of such high numbers was that growth in Latin America during the 1990s was generally accompanied by growing income inequality. Taking into account the negative impact of financial crises from the mid-1990s,

---

[70]   Just how badly the poorest sections of society are affected is still unclear.
[71]   Asian Development Bank (2000:51); World Bank (2000a:117-19).
[72]   World Bank (op. cit.:Table 1.2).

the UN Economic Commission for Latin America and the Caribbean (ECLAC) estimated that the decade ended with higher levels of poverty than in the 1980s.[73]

The sharp deterioration in the conditions of labour, particularly among the unskilled, is a major reason why the reduction in poverty levels has so far lagged behind the rate of recovery of output in East Asia. Indeed, empirical studies show that there is a significant asymmetry in the impact of growth and crises on poverty in developing countries: the poverty-alleviating impact of a given rate of growth is significantly weaker than the poverty-augmenting impact of a comparable decline in GDP.[74]

The persistence of widespread poverty and declines in wage income despite the recovery of output provide prima facie evidence that financial cycles result in regressive income distribution. For various reasons related to data problems and conceptual difficulties, however, the standard measures of income distribution are not always able to capture such changes. In the Republic of Korea, for instance, the data show that in the first quarter of 1995 the incomes of the richest 10 per cent of the population were about seven times those of the poorest 10 per cent, while they were more than 10 times higher in the first quarter of 1999.[75] In contrast, Gini coefficients of income distribution appear to have remained unchanged in Indonesia and Thailand, despite substantial increases in the number of people below the poverty line in both countries.[76]

Not everybody has been left to fend for themselves, however. Rising levels of volatility and the fallout from crises have led to a

---

[73] ECLAC (2000:66). The number of households living below the poverty line in Latin America rose from 35 per cent to 41 per cent from 1980 to 1990, rising in all countries except Chile. The ratio had declined during 1990-97, but at 36 per cent it was higher in 1997 than in 1980. During this period the proportion of poor households rose in both Mexico and Venezuela. On the other hand, in 13 Latin American countries for which data for the same period are available, the Gini coefficient rose in nine and declined in four (ECLAC, 2000:Chap. 2, Section 3(c)).
[74] World Bank (2000b:54); and van der Hoeven and Lubker (2006).
[75] Chang et al. (1998).
[76] One explanation is that household surveys of income disregard relative price changes in countries such as Indonesia where the poor faced a significantly higher inflation rate than the rich. Another is that household surveys undertaken in 1998 included questions about household incomes during the preceding year (i.e., 1997) and therefore failed to capture the full impact of the crisis. On these empirical issues, see World Bank (2000a:114-16).

willingness on the part of governments and the international financial institutions to strengthen the "welfare system" for western finance (Plender, 2003), by keeping countries current on their debt payments to private creditors, maintaining capital-account convertibility and preventing default. Thus, the IMF orchestrated bailouts for six emerging markets (Mexico, Thailand, Indonesia, Korea, Russia and Brazil) between 1995 and 1998 totalling over $230bn. From 1995 until the end of 2003 IMF exceptional financing for nine emerging markets (the above six plus Argentina, Turkey and Uruguay) amounted to SDR 174bn, with an average of 637 per cent of quota (IMF, 2005:Table 10). Moreover, placating western financial interests also meant imposing restrictive monetary and fiscal policies on these countries, which not only added to the contractionary pressures but also undercut the productive investment needed to reduce their vulnerability to crises on a more permanent basis (Stiglitz, 2002). Indeed, the danger is that the solution to one crisis simply lays the seeds for another round of boom and bust (Goldstein, 2005).

Thus, even in countries with a record of sound domestic management and sustained growth, financial liberalisation without appropriate institutional arrangements for supervision and regulation can lead to reckless borrowing abroad with disregard of the exchange-rate risk, and so exposing them to the herd-like vagaries of international finance. Although there is plenty of room for improvement in regulatory systems, particularly in the banking and financial sectors of the region, the core of the problem is systemic and therefore needs to be addressed at the global level.

As with the case for rapid trade liberalisation, the arguments for unfettered mobility of capital simply promise too much. But unlike the case for free trade, for which serious attempts, however controversial, have been made to quantify the likely gains, efforts to quantify the benefits of capital-account convertibility are, as one leading international economic specialist has pointed out, virtually non-existent; the case is based on little more than the repeated assertion of an *a priori* argument rather than careful analysis.[77] Domestic investment and national savings rates remain closely correlated across

---

[77]   Bhagwati (1998); Gourinchas and Jeanne (2003).

countries, so that differences in prospective rates of return to investment persist and are not equalised by foreign capital flows. The bulk of international capital flows are motivated more by hedging and risk diversification between the developed countries than by flows of savings from the rich countries into fixed investment in developing countries. The claim that the mobility of capital is an encouragement, to those countries that seek to attract it, to adopt responsible and disciplined macroeconomic policies and thus avoid major policy mistakes, is belied by the prevalence of herd behaviour on the part of international investors and by the evidence of the Asian financial crisis of 1997 when undisciplined capital flows were actually among the factors that undermined macroeconomic stability and contributed to the crisis. Indeed, a widely cited survey has since concluded "it has proven difficult to find robust evidence in support of the proposition that financial integration helps developing countries to improve growth and to reduce macroeconomic volatility" (Prasad et al., 2004:11). Market fundamentalists, however, are reluctant to accept this verdict and continue to insist that financial globalisation is still the only effective way out of poverty for developing countries.[78]

G.   Conclusions

One of the major problems with the political debates and controversies about openness is that too much is claimed for it and against it, both when policy is protectionist and when it is liberalising. Between the extremes of autarky and perfect global competition, the costs and benefits of specific moves in either direction are difficult to quantify, and while the estimates that have been made vary according to the model being used, in general they prove to be quite small. Much larger benefits are sometimes claimed for "dynamic" gains – as opposed to the once-for-all benefits of reallocating existing resources – but the estimates of these are even more sensitive to model specification. Perhaps the more important point for policy makers is that in any case the benefits and the costs are not independent of the

---

[78]   See, for example, Mishkin (2006).

rates of saving and investment, human capital formation and technological innovation.

The variety of developing-country experience with trade liberalisation since the early 1980s certainly suggests that the relationship between trade policy and economic growth is neither simple nor unidirectional. At a minimum, the relationship is likely to depend on a country's initial level of economic development, its institutional strengths and weaknesses, and its position in the international division of labour. What does seem to be more certain is that avoiding large negative shocks is a key ingredient for long-term success. In most successful cases, liberalisation was preceded by a steady process of industrialisation which had advanced on the basis of a wide range of trade and industrial policies specifically designed to encourage the emergence of activities of relatively higher value added per head and the production of high-tech and capital-intensive products. These strategies were outward-oriented, but they did not involve wholesale trade liberalisation. Selective barriers to imports were common and policies deliberately sought to link the development of international trade to investment and technological improvement. The broad strategic objective was to create domestic capacities that would lay the foundations for sustained growth and develop the strengths required to survive the eventual challenges of global competition. Thus, much like the successful stories before 1914, the issue comes back to one of policy space and, more particularly, whether policy makers have the means and flexibility to make trade work in favour of development by harnessing it to broader structural changes associated with a more diversified and integrated domestic economy. The links from financial policy to growth are even more uncertain, but the same basic conclusion stands.

What does seem more certain is that an aggressive mixture of trade and financial liberalisation is not a successful recipe for convergence. Indeed, the evidence presented here suggests that it has consistently failed to create an environment that will support the rising levels of investment that are needed to generate and sustain faster rates of economic growth. In this sense at least, the exaggerated importance given to liberalisation by many governments and international economic institutions is misconceived and likely to be counter-productive. By promising a quick route to overcoming the obstacles to growth and development, it not only risks a backlash from disappointed expectations but also neglects, and more often than not crowds out, a broad range of policies that need to be included in a coherent strategy for development. Trade policy is essentially one policy instrument among several with which countries can pursue their objectives for economic growth and development, and the key question is whether and under what conditions it is effectual.[79] There are signs that the secretariats, if not the member governments, of some of the international economic institutions are aware of this, for example the WTO in its analysis of "coherence" (WTO, 2004) or the World Bank in its exploration of the complex factors behind the weakness of investment in many developing countries (World Bank, 2004). But they have yet to draw the obvious policy conclusion that if the benefits of free trade and international capital movements are contingent on a number of crucial preconditions, there is no logic in giving priority to liberalisation until those conditions are satisfied. Since, on closer examination, those preconditions include the existence of institutions appropriate for a market economy, effective domestic markets and infrastructure, the capacity to pursue sound macroeconomic policies in a market-based environment, and so on, the implication is that opening up to global market forces should follow success, or at least sufficient progress, in meeting these basic challenges of economic development and internal integration. This is why we regard the "export-investment" nexus, which is more sharply focused on strengthening the domestic forces for economic growth, as providing a much better guide as to whether or not policy reforms are bearing fruit. This chapter has argued that on this score, the neo-liberal agenda has failed to deliver for most developing countries, largely because it is fundamentally mistaken about the direction of causation between liberalisation and economic development. Market fundamentalists insist on putting the liberalising cart before the domestic-development horse, a mistake that none of the present advanced market economies made when they were starting to industrialise.

---

[79] As a leading trade theorist, Max Corden, has pointed out: "In relation to GNP, most policies other than macroeconomic ones have small effects … [Hence] the effects of trade policy changes are often overrated" (quoted by Panić, ibid.).

Chapter 4

Transnational Corporations, Foreign Direct Investment and the Uneven Geography of International Production

A. Introduction

THE last chapter cast doubt on the "beautiful" "win-win" logic economists have attached to unregulated international market forces. It suggested that the positive circular and cumulative forces that were expected to be released by opening-up have not emerged in most of the countries that have followed the neo-liberal agenda. In the face of the disappointing benefits of trade liberalisation, the tendency has been to pay closer attention to capital formation. Liberating financial markets and unleashing international capital flows was expected to help establish the right investment climate. Instead there has been the recurrence of boom-bust cycles, financial panics and crashes and a flourishing speculative culture, which hardly describes an environment conducive to long-term productive investment. Evidence that the package of stabilisation, privatisation and liberalisation measures has led to the kind of investment-export nexus that helped to underpin strong growth in East Asia, is difficult to find.

Unwilling to rethink the idea of big gains for all from self-regulating markets, conventional wisdom has looked to bring in new elements in support of its "win-win" logic. Attracting foreign direct investment has increasingly been seen as the preferred option because in addition to providing capital, it also promises to bring, inter alia, up-to-date technology, managerial know-how, corporate governance and ready-made supplier and distribution networks. Here, in a convenient package, were precisely the supply-side linkages missing from earlier reform efforts. This new variant of the investment-export nexus has increasingly been presented as the key to rapid and sustained economic growth and poverty reduction (World Bank, 2003a; Fukasaku et al., 2005).

Again, the debt crisis was a turning point in policy approaches to FDI.[1] In its wake, the architects of structural adjustment were quick to recast the role of TNCs as powerful agents for correcting the distortions associated with industrialisation based on import substitution and to present the prospect of increased FDI as a reward for getting back to "market fundamentals".[2] The pursuit of "responsible" macroeconomic policies combined with an accelerating pace of liberalisation, deregulation and, above all, privatisation were expected to attract FDI to developing countries, thus enhancing their competitiveness and fostering economic growth. Indeed, the claim that FDI would avoid any further increase of debt and was free of the speculative and herd mentalities attached to other capital flows, seemed to confirm it as the development finance of choice (Prasad et al., 2004). As Stiglitz (2002:67) has suggested, getting production right by at-

---

[1]   It is not the case that before the debt crisis developing countries did not want or seek out FDI. However, they were not willing to do so on any terms. Its use was linked to efforts to establish a strong industrial base, a position that could count on a sympathetic hearing from policy makers in developed countries. A little over a decade before the debt crisis hit, Jean-Jacques Servan-Schreiber's *The American Challenge* voiced the fear that European business was being steadily taken over by American TNCs, posing the threat of what he called "cumulative underdevelopment", a fear that clearly resonated in many developing countries, particularly with respect to the exploitation of their natural resources. The resulting policy dialogue between North and South, helped by the oil-price shocks of the 1970s, focused on curbing the power of international big business, with much of the discussion centred on negotiations, at the United Nations, over a New International Economic Order (NIEO). With hindsight, that dialogue appears to have been doomed to failure. Even as the discussions were getting under way, the collapse of the Bretton Woods system, and the move towards floating exchange rates and open capital accounts signalled the unwillingness of the major economic powers to seek multilateral responses to the challenges of increased capital mobility. Indeed, that collapse triggered an accelerating trend towards the deregulation of financial markets that was starkly at odds with the discussions in New York. Just as significantly, Western European corporations were already beginning to penetrate the United States market, to be followed quickly by Japanese firms. In 1975, the stock of inward FDI in the US stood at just $27.7bn compared with over $100bn in Western Europe; by 1985 it had reached $184.6bn, marginally higher than the stock in Western Europe (United Nations, 1988:25). But what changed with the debt crisis was the urgency of filling the financing gap facing many developing countries left by the sudden stop in bank capital and the switch by policy makers from home countries to promoting the interests abroad of their own corporations.

[2]   Opening economies to FDI was one of Williamson's 10 tenets of the Washington Consensus, and it has remained there in his subsequent reappraisals; see Williamson (2000, 2002). From an early date, the World Bank (1991:94-95) insisted that liberalising the rules governing FDI would have to be part of any reform package if the promised gains were to be realised.

tracting FDI has helped to transform the original Washington Consensus (based more narrowly on the idea of "getting prices right") into a truly global ideology of helping poorer countries to trade and invest their way out of poverty.[3]

As with trade liberalisation, the experience of the fast-growing, outward-oriented East Asian NIEs has often been cited as evidence that attracting FDI could act as a catalyst for closing the income gaps between rich and poor countries. In the 1990s, resurgent flows of FDI to Latin America were seen as further confirmation of the potential rewards of comprehensive market reforms. Mexico, particularly after its entry to NAFTA, was held up as a shining example of what a new corporate-friendly development model could deliver in terms of improved economic prospects (Bergsten and Schott, 1997). Indeed, NAFTA has been heavily promoted by market fundamentalists as a blueprint for multilateral investment rules that would help to put more FDI to work in poorer countries (Moran, 2003). In Eastern Europe, policy makers looking for a speedy transition from central planning to free markets saw the hosting of western TNCs as a shortcut to transforming management skills and structures, updating technologies, and indeed as providing evidence that the transition was well under way. In this, they were strongly encouraged by the international financial institutions and, even more so, by the EU, where the promise of future membership was an important catalyst for a comprehensive programme of institutional reform in which the liberalisation of foreign investment was a key element.

Needless to say, the idea that greater freedom for TNCs would salvage the "win-win" logic of market-driven convergence has not met with universal consent. Civil-society groups have been particularly vocal in their opposition to what they see as a corporate takeover of society under the banner of globalisation (Hertz, 2001). But they are not alone. While the Uruguay Round gave a multilateral push to investment negotiations through the inclusion of "trade-related issues" (TRIPS and TRIMs) and the GATS, a more comprehensive in-

---

[3] More recently still, the same policy measures that made up the Washington Consensus have been given a further makeover with the explicit aim of improving the "investment climate" in developing countries and buttressed by tougher governance standards to complement the rigours of global competition (World Bank, 2003a:45-71). But this is more a change in tone than in substance.

vestment agreement was resisted by many developing countries reluctant to cede further control of the development process to large foreign firms (Das, 2003). The acquisition of local businesses at "firesale" prices in the aftermath of financial crises has added to concerns about foreign investors "skimming off the cream" of developing-country firms (Loungani and Razin, 2001). The ILO (2004) has warned about the danger of entering bidding wars to host FDI. On some accounts, the liberalisation of FDI policies has already triggered a "race to the bottom" as the threat of exit (or ostracism) by TNCs compels governments to create more cost-competitive conditions by reducing or abandoning workplace, social and environmental standards (Gray, 1998), and, in the process, threatening fledgling democratic structures in poor countries (Stiglitz, 2002:71-72).

This chapter takes a closer look at the rapid growth of FDI in developing countries, suggesting that both enthusiasts and critics of globalisation are prone to exaggeration. Not only does the bulk of FDI still continue to flow between the rich countries, continuing a pattern established after the Second World War, but flows to developing countries are very heavily concentrated on just a few destinations. Moreover, the impact of FDI, both good and bad, is contingent on a host of domestic economic factors, particularly the rate of total capital formation, the size of local markets and the sophistication of local firms. Indeed, we shall argue that evidence points to FDI as a lagging variable in the growth process, responding to economic success rather than creating it.

B.   The spread of international production

1.   Foreign direct investment and the expanding universe of TNCs

We have seen in Chapter 2 that FDI has been a longstanding feature of the international economy.[4] In the period after 1945 and up to 1980, the increasing volume of FDI occurred predominantly among

---

[4]   As noted earlier, FDI was a prominent feature of globalisation in the late 19th century and only recently did the ratio of the stock of FDI to global output exceed its earlier, pre-1914 peak. For many developing countries, previous peaks in the ratio have still not been surpassed.

advanced countries and was closely connected to their very rapid rates of industrial expansion, particularly in more capital- and technology-intensive sectors, along with rapidly growing and converging levels of income (Hymer, 1960; Rowthorn, 1992). These were predominantly two-way flows, often in the same sector, undertaken by large firms with already well-established export markets. Given these structural determinants of FDI, developing countries offered only marginal attractions to foreign investors. Such investments did continue in primary resource extraction, although technological changes in the consuming countries and rising political tensions in some of the host countries increased the economic risks for foreign investors in these sectors.[5] Expanding local markets also attracted TNCs to sectors requiring medium levels of skill and technology, such as chemicals and transportation, primarily in larger developing countries and particularly where tariff barriers offered assured rent-seeking opportunities.[6]

Since the early 1980s FDI has grown considerably faster than both output and international trade in goods and services (Chart 4.1). During the 1970s, annual global FDI flows averaged $27.5bn. They rose to $50bn in the first half of the 1980s and to $155bn between 1985 and 1990. Following a dip in the early 1990s, they rose dramatically to a peak of $1,400bn in 2000 before declining steadily to $630bn in 2003, since when they have again picked up quite sharply to some $920bn in 2005. The result is that the global stock of FDI has risen more than 20-fold since the early 1980s, reaching the equivalent of close to a quarter of world GDP. In almost all regions, developed and developing, FDI has been rising steadily as a share of gross fixed capital formation (Table 4.1).[7]

---

[5] Such risks only really emerged in the 1970s. Dunning (1984:136) notes that out of 1,369 instances of nationalisation between 1960 and 1976, two-thirds occurred after 1970.

[6] For a useful discussion of the nature and role of such investments, with reference to Brazil, see Evans (1979).

[7] Most of the figures in this chapter come from UNCTAD's *World Investment Report*, which remains the most valuable source of data on FDI and international production trends. However, Vernon's (1999) warning that all such data "must be handled with the utmost care" still stands.

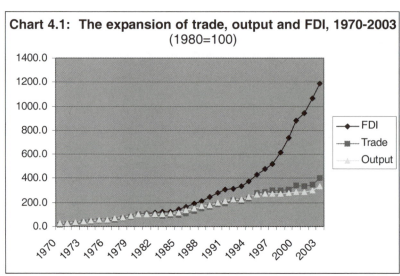

Chart 4.1: The expansion of trade, output and FDI, 1970-2003
(1980=100)

Source: World Bank Online Database and UNCTAD FDI database.
Note: FDI figures which start in 1980 refer to the cumulative stock.

Table 4.1: Share of FDI in gross fixed capital formation			
	1970-79	**1980-89**	**1990-2003**
World	2.2	3.1	8.2
Developed countries	2.1	3.1	7.7
Developing economies	2.8	3.0	9.3
Africa	3.3	2.2	8.6
Latin America and the Caribbean	3.8	3.9	12.9
Mexico	4.0	6.9	13.1
Brazil	4.8	3.2	11.4
Asia and the Pacific	1.9	2.9	8.1
First-tier NIEs*	1.9	1.6	2.7
Second-tier NIEs	5.7	4.5	8.7
China	...	1.6	11.4
India	0.3	0.2	2.1
* Korea and Taiwan, China only			

Source: UNCTAD FDI database.

This acceleration in the growth of FDI has been accompanied by qualitative changes in its composition. There has been a marked shift to services, which now account for close to three-quarters of the total stock of FDI compared with less than 30 per cent in the late 1970s. But even though FDI in manufacturing has grown less than in services, it has still been growing more quickly than global output, generating an expanding network of international production relations. These shifts, in turn, have been associated with important changes in corporate strategy to better manage more dispersed production activities and more extensive and elaborate systems of intra-firm flows of goods and services. This has been variously described as a shift from "simple" to "complex" or from "horizontal" to "vertical" strategies of expansion or, more graphically, the slicing up of the various stages in the corporate value-added chain. What this means essentially is that whereas previously the firm expanded abroad by cloning itself in another location, separate activities are now performed in different locations and valued according to how they contribute to the objectives of the firm as a whole, rather than simply on the basis of their profitability in the host country (Hanson et al., 2002). Moreover, as the universe of TNCs has expanded, inter-firm agreements, networks and alliances of various kinds have emerged alongside FDI to coordinate dispersed activities and deal more effectively with the growing complexity and contestability of international markets.[8]

In the wake of these changes in corporate strategy, policy makers in the developing world, through a mixture of persuasion and pressure, have not only placed much greater emphasis on attracting FDI as a trigger for catch-up growth but have allowed much greater freedom to TNCs to choose how they operate in their countries: of over 2,100 country-level reforms with respect to FDI identified since 1990, almost 95 per cent were liberalising (UNCTAD, 2005c:26); at the same time, however, TNCs have been pushing, with some success, for the greater protection of their assets, including intellectual property, especially vis-à-vis local political and economic actors. The advanced industrial countries, which are the principal headquarters for multinational manufacturing activity and also possess powerful

---

[8]   See Dunning (1997) and World Bank (1997:Chap. 2).

service-sector firms, have pushed hard on both these fronts at the multilateral level (Cornford, 2005). Bilateral and regional treaties and agreements, however, have probably been the more important force behind this "liberalising" trend. In most cases, these moves have been linked to a wider package of measures (including privatisation of state-owned assets) aimed at extending the influence of market forces. Indeed, because affiliates are generally more dependent on imported inputs than domestic firms and rely on close financial relations with their respective parent companies, other affiliates and foreign financial institutions, competition to attract and retain inward FDI has created further pressures to accelerate the liberalisation of trade and finance.[9]

As already indicated in the previous chapter, among the most important changes in the structure of FDI has been the growing weight of mergers and acquisitions (M&A). This shift, particularly in many developing and transition economies, has been partly linked to privatisation. It has also been tied to changes in corporate governance which have made the decision to invest abroad much more subject to the influence of liquidity-driven finance (Grahl, 2001). Whether or not this describes the triumph of an Anglo-Saxon model of corporate governance is a matter on which researchers disagree, but it is certainly the case that the ability of a multinational firm to do one thing with its fixed assets and something quite different in the way it finances them has openened the possibility of a more "footloose" and less stable type of cross-border investment (Hausmann and Fernandez-Arias, 2000:8). In this respect, the simple and popular description of FDI as a non-debt-creating form of finance, locked into specific plant and machinery, is misleading, not only because it carries financing obligations, including in the form of inter-country and intra-company loans, but also because innovations in financial markets have gone a long way to eliminating the idea of a permanent investment in plant and equipment or, at least, the idea that such investments do not involve foreign-exchange and funding risks.

---

[9]   This again underscores the point that the neo-liberal model itself comes as a package. Kobrin (2005) offers a useful but rose-tinted view of FDI liberalisation over the past two decades. Another assessment of the shift in the balance of policy towards attracting FDI suggests it represents a return to a policy environment last seen in the 1950s; see Safarian (1999).

This blurring of the distinction between the various types of capital flow, noted in the previous chapter, also means that FDI is more than ever intertwined with the workings of international financial markets and trade in financial services. Indeed, on some accounts, global financial flows have become the tail wagging the international production dog.[10]

Despite (or perhaps because of) these changes, the geographical distribution of FDI has remained remarkably stable over the past two decades. The 20-fold increase in flows to developing countries since the late 1970s has translated into a small rise in their share of global FDI, albeit one that has been punctuated by pronounced peaks and troughs (Chart 4.2).[11] This is not altogether surprising given the rise of intra-triad (Europe-Japan-USA) flows, the growing weight of M&A, and the shift in FDI towards the service sector, all of which are likely to produce a developed-country bias. Nevertheless, it is the case that export-oriented manufacturing activities linked to FDI have been expanding rapidly in some parts of the developing world and the available (albeit limited) sectoral evidence does show a small shift in the composition of FDI in developing countries towards the manufacturing sector, albeit one that is very heavily coloured by the emergence of China. Perhaps more significantly, the share of manufacturing in the total FDI stock in developing countries rose from 25 per cent to 37 per cent between 1990 and 2003, while the share of developing countries in the global stock of FDI in manufacturing rose from one-fifth to close to one-third.

A possibly related trend, and one increasingly flagged by globalisation enthusiasts, is the rise of developing countries as sources of FDI, leading some observers to talk about a shift in the geography of international production associated with South-South FDI (Aykut and Ratha, 2004). However, this is still a marginal feature of the international production system. Moreover, caution is obviously required

---

[10] For discussions of the growing influence of finance capital on international production and its consequences, see OTA (1993:Chap. 6); Kregel (1996a, 2004); Blackburn (2006).

[11] Taking stock figures, the developing-country share remained at a steady 20 per cent of the world total in the 1980s, rose to around 30 per cent in the 1990s, but has subsequently dropped back to around 25 per cent, which is where it stood in the mid-1970s. It should be noted, however, that the category of developing countries includes some important hosts of FDI which, in the 1990s, effectively became developed industrial economies. These were mainly the first-tier NIEs.

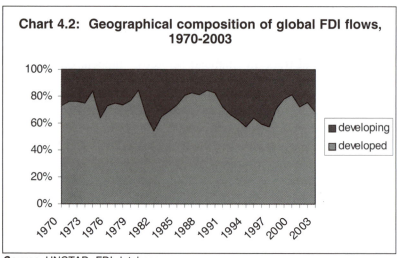

Chart 4.2: Geographical composition of global FDI flows, 1970-2003

Source: UNCTAD, FDI database.

in interpreting these numbers, particularly as some of the countries that are still formally classified as developing have *de facto* graduated to developed-country status; this is the case with the first-tier East Asian NIEs which are already entering the stage of positive deindustrialisation with an allied shift of resources to high-value-added service activities (Rowthorn and Ramaswamy, 1999).[12]

2.   Why firms invest abroad

There is broad agreement that technological developments, greatly reduced transport, communication and coordination costs, and neo-liberal reforms have combined to stimulate the expansion of FDI over the past two decades. However, beyond these familiar pressures there is considerable analytical confusion surrounding the decision of firms to expand their activities abroad. The process certainly differs from other international capital flows where differential rates of return are the principal trigger. Nor does international trade theory provide much of a guide, since its assumptions of identical production functions and competitive markets are far removed from the world

---

[12] To take one striking example, more than half of the FDI in China between the mid-1980s and the late 1990s originated in Hong Kong, a flow that statistically qualifies as South-South but economically is closer to a North-South transaction.

of international big business and because most cross-border flows of investment occur between countries with similar factor endowments.

The creation of TNCs is better understood as an extension of the processes which originally gave rise to national corporations (Hymer, 1960). The fundamental questions are not so much why TNCs exist, but why any kind of multi-plant firm exists, and given that they do, why they tended to be confined within national boundaries for so long and why, when they do move beyond their own borders, they need to *control* assets in other countries. Part of the widely accepted answer to these questions is that national firms become international because they possess specific assets – such as a superior production technology, a distinct product design or superior managerial and marketing skills – and have sufficient economic size to undertake profitable investments abroad despite the higher risk and additional costs that arise from coordinating production activities over large geographical distances and across political borders.

On one prominent account, an "eclectic" approach offers the best way of analysing how corporate and locational advantages might best combine to produce efficient outcomes (Dunning, 1981). Despite its popularity and flexibility, however, this approach has been criticised, with some justification, for offering too general and descriptive a framework which does not go very far in explaining the behaviour of TNCs (Kamaly, 2003a). This is particularly true of its classification of firms into the categories of efficiency-seeking, market-seeking and resource-seeking. Consequently, most conventional accounts of the spread of international production tend to focus on the internalisation process as the key to understanding why firms choose to invest abroad rather than exploit their specific assets through market relations (Markusen, 1995). According to this approach, the decision whether or not to invest abroad reflects the comparative costs of hierarchy and markets in handling more intangible assets.[13] Given the particular mix of factor endowments in the host and home countries, the presence of scale economies in production, and the transac-

---

[13] These points were first established clearly by Stephen Hymer in his doctoral thesis and in subsequent articles collected in Hymer (1979); see also UNCTAD (1996:76-77). The neglect of Hymer's contribution in much of the "new" theory of TNCs reflects the narrowness of a great deal of contemporary economic scholarship.

tion costs arising from trade and setting up production abroad, cost efficiency will dictate whether or not investment abroad emerges as the equilibrium market outcome in industries where firm-specific assets are important. From this perspective, all FDI is efficiency-seeking, which provides a natural complement to the "win-win" logic of trade openness. The development policy implications are straightforward enough; creating an efficient investment climate attractive to TNCs and beneficial to the host country is best achieved by lowering taxes and removing state regulations, including tariff barriers and local-content requirements, and by allowing the parent company the freedom to integrate the affiliate into its worldwide operations as it sees fit.

This argument downplays, if not altogether ignores, the significance of firm size and corporate control in maintaining and expanding profitability, and, crucially, it fails to recognise the potential distortions that can accompany rent-seeking behaviour by large firms (Hymer, 1979:65). Economists, beginning with Adam Smith, who have dug beneath supply and demand curves to explore the realm of production have understood that the same forces that have led to the dynamism of the capitalist system have also led to some firms growing in size to the point where they are powerful enough to shape (distort) market outcomes. These same firms are the ones which also tend to be the first to move into production abroad. Recognising this means abandoning the fiction of price-taking firms in perfectly competitive markets, and contemplating instead an international economic realm structured by hierarchical power relations, inherently imperfect markets and (private) rent-seeking behaviour. Including these features in the argument adds a stronger historical dimension to the FDI story, both by recognising the evolutionary progression of international production and by acknowledging first-mover advantages. Most firms begin by serving a purely local market in some particular region of the national economy. They then expand within the same country by "exporting" from their local base. After a time they establish production facilities elsewhere in the same country until eventually they become an integrated national corporation. Since large firms tend to have more capital at their disposal and to enjoy scale economies, they also tend to have higher levels of productivity, which in turn enables them to enter foreign markets through exporting. Such firms will also be the ones that normally do most of the investing abroad. Here again a sequence is likely: when sufficient sales have been achieved in the new market, it becomes feasible to set up local production facilities on a scale large enough to exploit externalities of one kind or another. Scale economies, however, also bring first-mover advantages and rents that are best protected by seeking to restrict access to markets, technology and finance by potential competitors.[14]

Since a good deal of FDI occurs among the already advanced economies, often consisting of two-way flows in the same industry, a large part of the explanation is tied to the creation and capture of rents arising from technological assets (and related learning externalities) and scale economies. Controlling productive assets abroad reflects the efforts of large firms to fully appropriate or augment the returns on their accumulation of corporate skills and other assets (Rowthorn, 1992).[15] Such intra-industry FDI is either a reflection of competition between firms seeking to access each other's home market for final products by seeking to create regional centres of production and marketing, or an extension of the increasingly fine degree of international specialisation in intermediate products that has been the major impetus for the growth of intra-industry trade (Rayment, 1983). As such, first-mover advantages and strong cumulative dynamics can then make it difficult for newcomers to enter the market for more sophisticated industrial goods. Much the same forces underpin the more rapid growth of FDI in the banking, distribution and other service sectors, where the more limited opportunities for international trade help to explain the explosive nature of these flows since the 1980s, particularly where M&A offer a quick route to market entry.

---

14 The advantages of being first to move into a new market, and often but not always into a new technology, are usually downplayed or ignored in the context of trade liberalisation and especially of opening developing-country markets to TNCs, but they are well understood by enterprises in the developed economies. Thus, the Director of the UK's leading trade association for the environmental technology sector, the Environmental Industries Commission, recently stated that "first-mover advantage in this sector is considerable. But the government must move to boost the market", principally with incentive-boosting regulation and subsidies (*Financial Times,* London, 10 April 2006, p. 3).

15 Since Hymer (1960) this has been the starting point for most theories of the international firm. It should be noted that even with FDI among advanced countries differential unit labour costs can still play a role in the pattern of flows; see Driffield and Love (2005).

Whether or not a particular firm decides to substitute FDI for exports will of course depend on a multitude of factors such as the market structure and technological maturity of the product, as well as the extent of protectionist measures in potential host countries.[16] Macroeconomic factors, including labour costs and currency movements, are likely to play a decisive role in the timing of outward FDI as well as influencing which countries become hosts and the pace at which it occurs. FDI is also likely to follow a different path in extractive and service industries where locational or pull factors have a greater influence than push factors. In all cases, however, bargaining with local firms, workers and governments will have a critical bearing on the size and the direction of FDI, as well as on its impact (Penrose, 1975).

While the cross-border expansion of firms certainly generates closer interdependence among countries, it is likely to do so very unevenly, creating hierarchical relations, spreading the benefits unequally and introducing distortions and tensions in the host economies (Hymer, 1979). The transfer of production abroad is rarely an all-or-nothing affair and certain functions will often continue to be performed in the country of origin. These are likely to be higher-level, strategic functions such as R&D or finance, only the more routine types of production being transferred abroad. Indeed, the capacity of TNCs to slice up the value-added chain may very well translate into an even more rigid hierarchy of activities across countries.[17] Given that TNCs are generally attracted by high rates of economic growth and favourable demand conditions, FDI tends to reinforce – rather than correct – longstanding differences in initial conditions. Countries that are better able to meet the infrastructural and skill requirements of TNCs become, over time, increasingly attractive to FDI and better able to capture its positive benefits, and usually on the back of strong public investment programmes. These same countries have

---

[16]   The important work of Raymond Vernon on the links between the product cycle and outward investment can be seen as complementing Hymer's work, offering one possible explanation of which countries are likely to become the hosts.

[17]   This possibility was suggested by Hymer in the early 1970s. A more complex division of labour in which some of the foreign subsidiaries become almost equal partners with the parent company and a two-way trade in sophisticated products occurs within the firm is also possible, but this tends to be confined almost exclusively to countries at high and similar levels of economic development.

also often used strategic industrial policies to support the emergence and growth of local firms. These developments create bandwagon effects, as markets that become established as desirable locations for leading TNCs attract other investors or producers who are anxious not to miss an opportunity in expanding markets. Thus under some circumstances, and when properly managed, FDI can play an important part in supporting a "big push" to raise the rate of capital formation and deepen industrial linkages (Venables, 1996).[18] There is nothing, however, to suggest that it will happen spontaneously as a result of market forces.

3. The regionalisation of production

As with the trade story in the previous chapter, the dramatic growth in FDI and cross-border production hides a very uneven process that belies much of the popular discussion of global production and TNCs. In the first place, the bulk of FDI takes place among advanced countries with similar factor endowments, where market size and technological infrastructure remain the important determinants.[19] Moreover, large OECD economies, and even some of the smaller ones, are still dominated by firms which produce most of their output within national boundaries. Of the 30 largest TNCs in manufacturing, 23 provide information about the location of their activities (Kozul-Wright and Rowthorn, 1998). Of these, only four employ more than half their labour force outside their country of origin. Most still produce 70 per cent or more of their output at home. In a recent study of the 50 top industrial TNCs between 1980 and 2000, it was shown that they had grown slightly less than world output (De Grauwe and Camerman, 2002). Looking at individual countries, overseas production accounts for less than one-third of the total

---

[18]   However, when not properly managed, and as noted by the Bank for International Settlements (BIS) (1998:32), herd behaviour by TNCs also runs the risk of creating excess capacity in some countries, with the attendant problems of overproduction and adverse balance-of-payments effects.

[19]   It is worth noting that even with flows among advanced countries, exactly who benefits is still a matter of contention among researchers, with at least one recent study finding advantages for the home economy from outward FDI but few or mixed benefits from inward FDI; see van Pottelsberghe de la Potterie and Lichtenberg (2001).

production of manufacturing firms from the United States. In the case of Japan the figure is still well below 10 per cent. Not surprisingly, distinct national characteristics continue to have a strong influence on the strategies of TNCs in key areas such as corporate governance, finance, research and development, and the extent of intra-firm trade (Pauly and Reich, 1997).

Moreover, and again much like international trade, FDI appears to be strongly, and perhaps increasingly, influenced by neighbourhood effects: TNCs still find a disproportionately large number of attractive locations close to home. Within Western Europe, the consolidation of the European Union via the internal market programme has been a steady influence on the growth of intra-regional FDI which, as a result of both M&A and greenfield investment, is leading gradually to the formation of pan-European firms (Dicken, 2003), with an emerging Europe-wide corporate bond market pushing in the same direction (Plender, 2003). This process is quite advanced in North America where the historically close relations between Canada and the United States are being extended under NAFTA, particularly in some key industries, such as automobiles, where regional production structures are quite advanced and beginning to include Latin America (Mortimore, 1998, 2000). In the 1980s, Japan started to invest heavily in some of its neighbouring economies: since 1985 total Japanese FDI in East Asia has quadrupled, much of the investment going into manufacturing (UNCTAD, 1996). As suggested earlier, however, the development gap between Japan and its neighbours is still considerably wider than that within other advanced regions. For this reason, the first-tier NIEs have become an important source of FDI in the regional economy of East Asia, on some estimates already overtaking Japan.

Within these regional blocs direct investment and trade are often complementary, reflecting the development of an internal division of labour within the same firm, whereby plants in different countries of the bloc either collaborate in the creation of a single product or specialise in the production of different finished goods for export to the entire bloc or beyond. Such complementarity is less frequent in the case of trade and investment between regional blocs. Distance, culture and politics continue to create barriers to inter-bloc trade which can often only be overcome by setting up local production facilities.

Since the regional blocs are very large, production facilities within them can be of a sufficiently large and complex scale to undertake most of the activities originally carried out at home by the parent company. Thus, between regional blocs, direct investment and trade are more likely to be alternatives, so that outward investment will often lead to a reduction in exports or inhibit their growth. Manufacturing trade between Europe and North America, for example, is relatively modest in scale. In the early 1990s, manufactured exports from Western Europe to the United States were only 1.2 per cent of European GDP and around 3 per cent of US expenditure on manufactures (Rowthorn, 1999). The United States' exports of manufactures in the opposite direction were only 1.6 per cent of American GDP and around 2 per cent of European expenditures on manufactures. These figures have not changed significantly over the subsequent decade. In the case of Japan the situation is different. The country still exports a great deal to Europe and North America, although importing very few manufactures. It is likely that these exports will be replaced by local production by Japanese affiliates. This has already happened in some areas such as automobiles, but is likely to happen on an increasing scale in the future. Among the factors pushing Japanese firms in this direction in the 1990s were the high exchange rate of the yen and protectionist pressures in the EU and North America (Barrell and Pain, 1999).

Developing countries play little or no part in these two-way intra-industry flows of FDI. When FDI does flow from North to South, lower costs are likely to be a much more prominent part of the decision process, with technological conditions a much less significant part of the story. This, for example, has been the case with the large increase in FDI in China in the 1990s. Moreover, since a reasonably strong and diverse industrial base and a dynamic market are preconditions for attracting and benefiting from this type of FDI, in countries where growth has collapsed or stalled and where there has been premature deindustrialisation, firms are becoming less rather than better equipped to participate in the international production system. Indeed, under these conditions, and with much of the recent FDI reinforcing regional blocs, further divergence rather than convergence appears to be the more likely outcome of increased flows from North to South.

C.   Escaping the simplicities of conventional thinking

Broadening the discussion of the links between openness and economic development to include FDI quickly runs into some of the same methodological problems surrounding trade, but which are further complicated by the limitations of the available statistical data. These arise from the loose definition of what is being measured, as well as from lacunae in collection and coverage.[20] The standard definition of FDI, as a "long-term" relationship involving a "significant degree of influence" on the management of the enterprise, is sufficiently loose to include a heterogeneous group of corporate actors, some with complex integrated production structures in multiple locations, others with little more than a shop-front in a single foreign market.[21] Definitional problems are further aggravated by the fact that FDI is a composite flow including equity flows from abroad, undistributed profits and inter- or intra-company loans. Clearly, some of these do not involve cross-border transactions and their treatment as one-way items in the capital account complicates statistical measurement, as well as the evaluation of their impact (UNCTAD, 1999a:117). The extent to which FDI is simply the "round-tripping" of domestic savings, which for some countries is significant, further complicates the picture. Although the conceptual distinction between M&A and greenfield investment is reasonably straightforward in theory, it is often very difficult to apply to the available statistics (UNCTAD, 2000a:105-06).

Any meaningful discussion of FDI therefore needs to carefully unpack these different components before pronouncing on their likely impact on economic development, but this is rarely done. Greenfield

---

[20] On the general problems surrounding FDI numbers, see Sutcliffe (1998) and Woodward (2001:50-77). On the sensitivity of results about the impact of FDI to country classification, see Bloningen and Wang (2004); on the difficulties of attributing causality in heterogeneous samples, see Nair-Reichert and Weinhold (2001); on the important influence of one or two outliers on the results, see de Mello (1999); and on the danger of hiding important breaks in trend in larger econometric samples, see Kamaly (2003a). Much like the debates on trade policy, very different experiences with FDI, for example among the first-tier East Asian NIEs and between these and the second-tier South-East Asian NIEs, are often lumped together in support of a common policy approach to attracting FDI.

[21] This problem is not resolved simply by calls to standardise the threshold of control, although doing so would make for a more consistent data set.

FDI, for example, which involves a firm constructing a new production facility abroad, financed by capital raised in the firm's home country, clearly makes a positive contribution to capital formation in the host country, creates employment and may crowd-in local investment through backward and forward linkages of various kinds. The acquisition of a controlling interest in an existing domestic firm is likely to have a very different impact, possibly involving little or no new productive capacity[22] and, more than likely, leading to cuts in employment; indeed, M&A are often likely to share more in common with short-term capital flows than greenfield investments. Given that cross-border M&A have accounted for between 30 and 70 per cent of total annual inflows of FDI during the past decade, this is an important distinction to be made when analysing FDI. Indeed, as noted earlier, removing this component of the FDI story already paints a rather different picture of its growth. Moreover, presuming that retained earnings (also classified as FDI) automatically translate into machinery and equipment hides the fact that the available statistics also fail to distinguish among competing types of capital expenditure, including investment in financial assets or speculation in real estate.

These conceptual and methodological pitfalls compromise the frequent use of cross-sectional regression analysis to assess the impact of FDI on development. Such an approach tends to confirm a reasonably robust and positive *association* between FDI and economic growth. However, *causality* is far from being established. Indeed, that relationship appears to be very sensitive to threshold levels and to the influence of extreme observations (Blomstrom et al., 1994; de Mello, 1997; UNCTAD, 2005b; Kosack and Tobin, 2006), and its strength conditional on factors such as trade policy (Balasubramanyam et al., 1996), levels of human capital (Borensztein et al., 1995) and macroeconomic conditions (Akyüz, 1998). These same factors introduce a good deal of country specificity into the relationship between

---

[22] Takeovers are often accompanied by promises by the purchasing company to invest in new equipment and general restructuring, and governments sometimes make this a condition of approving the takeover. The experience of Central European countries in the 1990s, however, was that such promises often fell by the wayside once the deal had gone through, although this was by no means always the case, as the Volkswagen takeover of the old Czech company Skoda illustrates.

FDI and economic growth. Further layers of complexity are added by firm- and industry-level factors.[23]

A growing number of studies find no evidence that FDI is an independent accelerator of economic growth, while others suggest that any positive effect of FDI on growth tends to disappear as greater allowance is made for more country characteristics.[24] Certainly, the idea popular among market fundamentalists, that giving a freer hand to TNCs will lead them to invest much more in poorer countries and to kick-start economic growth, begins to look like an "ephemeral fad" (Lipsey and Sjoholm, 2004). Rather, it seems to us, two "rules of thumb" emerge from the available evidence. The first is that one dollar of FDI, on average, is worth no more and probably less than one dollar of any other kind of investment, although sometimes it is worth much more.[25] The second is that a strong domestic investment drive, a proven growth record and a deep domestic enterprise structure are still the strongest factors attracting TNCs to a particular location, be it to seek markets or realise cost advantages.[26]

These rules help to explain the persistence of FDI among advanced industrial countries as well as the heavy concentration of North-South flows on just a handful of developing countries. Five developing countries accounted for a little under two-thirds of the latter total in the early 1980s and in the early years of the new century, while the 10 largest accounted for close to 80 per cent. The latter figure is little changed from the early 1980s although there has been a shift away from Latin American hosts (three of which accounted for nearly 50 per cent of developing-country inflows in 1980) to East Asia (where just three countries accounted for 43 per cent of the total in 2002).[27] This bias towards East and South-East Asia is very much in line with the account of the pattern of trade in the previous chapter (Chart 4.3).

---

[23] See Nunnenkamp and Spatz (2004); Lall (1995); Aitken et al. (1996).

[24] Carkovic and Levine (2002); Mody (2004); Nunnenkamp and Spatz (2004); Rodrik (1999).

[25] This is a reworking of Rodrik (1999:37) taking account of the different components of FDI identified earlier, the difficulties policy makers face in bargaining with TNCs, but also the potential advantages that these can bring to a host.

[26] See Carkovic and Levine (2002); UNCTAD (2005b). It is revealing that while the bulk of empirical studies reach this conclusion, it is persistently downplayed in the more fundamentalist appraisals of policies needed to attract FDI.

[27] Stock figures show a similar pattern of concentration, although there are some differences in the leading countries.

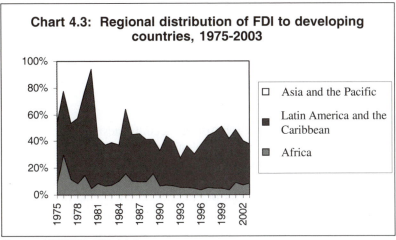

Chart 4.3: Regional distribution of FDI to developing countries, 1975-2003

Legend:
☐ Asia and the Pacific
■ Latin America and the Caribbean
▨ Africa

Source: UNCTAD, FDI database.

Instead of examining carefully the potential unevenness of international production, and how policies might correct it, market fundamentalists have reduced the policy discussion on FDI to the simple proposition that what is good for the TNC is also good for its host country. This is a conclusion inherent in describing FDI as a package of productive assets whose movement is triggered by market failure in the host country, and goes a long way to explaining the hostility to any regulation of international business at the national or international level. The logic was clearly stated by Harry Johnson (1967:61-62) in the 1960s:

> Private direct investment has the great advantage of bringing to the less developed country in one package capital, modern technology, managerial skills, and improvement-mindedness. Direct investment by international corporations through the establishment of affiliates and branch plants has the further advantage of having at its command the technological and managerial innovations of the parent company and its affiliates, so that *automatic progress* is built into its local operations in a relatively inexpensive way...direct private investment, particularly by large international corporations, is a potent generator of political

ill-will and suspicion in the less developed countries. Most
of these reactions are irrational, based on a misunderstanding of the economics of modern industry and especially a
failure to appreciate the economic value of superior technology and the high professional skill required of industrial management.

Following this logic, Johnson reduced the design of appropriate
development strategies to a matter of attracting FDI by abandoning
policies which might hinder the establishment of local affiliates and
distort the way in which they are integrated into the global operations
of the parent company. Much the same policy package of deregulation and liberalisation is commonplace among today's FDI enthusiasts, and 40 years on from Johnson, the dangers of "irrational" nationalist sentiments have become an even more frequently heard warning against those deviating from the faith.

As with the arguments for trade liberalisation, the promise of
"automatic" and "costless" benefits from hosting FDI hinges on a
number of hidden assumptions that essentially prejudge its development impact. The first is that additions to the capital stock from attracting FDI are "bolted down" in new plant and equipment, forcing
firms into long-term commitments and giving policy makers some
degree of reciprocal bargaining power once such investments are in
place. In reality, as we have seen, much FDI takes the form of M&A,
and while from a corporate perspective both are additions to productive assets, this is not so for the economy of the host country. Although long-term considerations may play a role in M&A these can
also be greatly influenced by prospects of quick capital gains, particularly during periods of economic crisis (Krugman, 1998). The
general evidence on the outcome of cross-border M&A suggests that
they add little value at the firm level and have increasingly been driven
by speculative calculations rather than considerations of long-term
productive development. This takeover culture has been described by
a distinguished financial journalist as an exercise in "uncreative destruction" (Plender, 2003).

A second assumption is that the productive assets comprising
FDI readily spill over to the local economy through competition, imitation, labour turnover or vertical linkages. But in a world where

markets fail, scale matters, oligopolistic power is significant, and opaque business practices, such as transfer pricing and creative accounting, are pervasive, keeping control over specific assets is key to a firm's capacity to generate economic rents. In such a world, there are plenty of reasons why a one-sided search for efficiency gains is likely to overestimate the size of positive spillovers from FDI and to underestimate the possible costs, as well as downplaying potential conflicts of interest between TNCs and host governments. On balance, and taking account of the different methodologies employed, there is little evidence of positive spillovers from FDI, particularly in developing countries, and virtually none on a significant scale.[28]

The third assumption is that FDI will crowd-in domestic investment so long as governance is left to competitive markets, with unrestricted entry and exit of firms and minimal state intervention. In fact, no simple pattern of crowding-in or -out by FDI emerges from the data. Regression analysis and country-level studies report both outcomes, although some recent studies point more towards crowding-out due to premature capital-account liberalisation depriving policy makers of the capacity to influence national investment rates.[29]

Given these unrealistic foundations, any tendency to limit the discussion of a healthy investment climate to one which is attractive to foreign firms is unlikely to be a good guide for policy makers. Indeed, as can be seen from Table 4.2, domestic investment and FDI have been moving in different directions over the past quarter-century, in both developed and developing countries. This is further illustrated in Chart 4.4, which shows clearly significant differences among countries in the relationship between changes in FDI and domestic capital formation. In many Latin American countries, FDI as a proportion of GDP, on average, was higher in the 1990s than in the 1980s (by more than 1.7 percentage points), but the share of gross fixed capital formation was lower by 0.6 percentage points. In all the major Latin American countries – Argentina, Brazil, Colombia and Mexico – FDI as a proportion of GDP rose between these two periods

---

[28] See Gorg and Greenaway (2001) for a comprehensive review of the spillover literature. Also Blomström and Kokko (2003); Glass et al. (1999).
[29] See Chapter 5 for further discussion.

Table 4.2: Domestic investment and FDI
(per cent of GDP)

	Gross fixed capital formation			Foreign direct investment		
	1981-1990	1991-2000	2001-2004	1981-1990	1991-2000	2001-2004
World	23.8	22.7	21.4	0.67	1.73	1.91
Industrial countries	22.8	22	20.3	0.75	1.6	1.74
Developing countries	26	25.6	25.5	0.43	2.28	2.57

Source: Akyüz (2006), Table 1.

Chart 4.4: Changes in gross domestic fixed capital formation and FDI in selected developing economies, 1990-2000 and 1980-1990
(per cent of GDP)

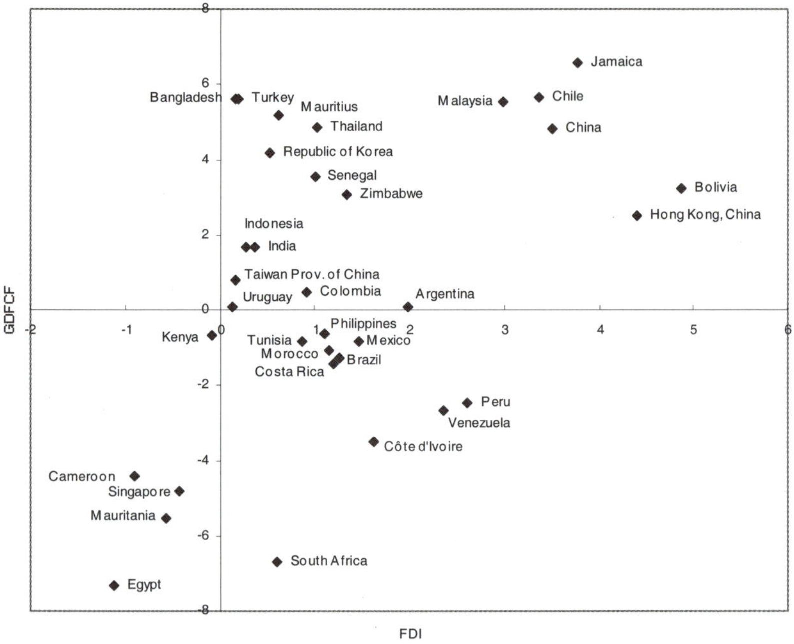

Source: UNCTAD, *World Investment Report* database; World Bank, *World Development Indicators, 2002*; and Thomson Financial Datastream.

Note: GDFCF as a percentage of GDP was calculated using data in current prices, except for Argentina, where constant 1995 prices were used.

while gross domestic fixed capital formation (GDFCF) stagnated or fell.[30] Much the same pattern holds for the major African economies. This suggests that whatever the direct or indirect impact of FDI on domestic capital formation may have been, the conditions that attracted foreign enterprises to these countries were not conducive to a faster rate of total capital formation, and that the two sets of investment decisions can be driven by very different motives.

We shall come back to what drives the investment process in developing countries in later chapters, arguing that its governance requires various institutional arrangements and interventions by the state to generate, distribute and revoke economic rents and to coordinate investments in a way that supports wider development goals. A healthy investment climate, we shall suggest, implies a continuing interaction among, and bargaining between, policy makers and local entrepreneurs. From this viewpoint, it seems sensible to conclude that whether the rents created by TNCs through FDI add to a local accumulation drive is likely to depend on a number of factors, including the specifics of corporate strategy, the levels of industrial, technological and skill development reached by local firms, the presence of a domestic, pro-investment economic policy, and whether or not the local state and private actors have sufficient bargaining strength to face the asymmetric market power enjoyed by most TNCs.

On the evidence in this section, it is plausible to see FDI, just as much as domestic investment, as caught up in a world of cumulative causation. In such a world, even on fairly conventional assumptions, the unpredictable outcome from the growing interaction between FDI, trade and technological change merits a much more measured policy response than is offered by market fundamentalists (Amiti and Wakelin, 2003). The idea that all that matters is how to attract FDI, and that one policy size will suit all circumstances, is particularly inappropriate. On the contrary, carefully weighing the costs and benefits of hosting FDI and designing policies tailored to local conditions and preferences are among the common traits in countries that have successfully used FDI in their development process.

---

[30] Chile and Bolivia were exceptions.

D.   Lessons from success stories

As is clear from Chart 4.4, a high share of FDI in total capital inflows or gross fixed capital formation cannot be taken unambiguously as a benchmark for a healthy investment environment, let alone a guide for policy makers. Moreover, as we have already noted, cross-country regressions do not offer much additional guidance in trying to make sense of the links between FDI and development, at least beyond the basic message that it is a lag variable with cumulative potential. An alternative approach is through individual country case studies. Many of these have focussed on the East Asian NIEs which, in general, have been particularly successful in attracting FDI to compensate for specific deficiencies in their domestic stocks of technological and organisational skills.[31]

In part, their success reflects an early willingness to host manufacturing FDI through fledgling production networks. However, an examination of the diverse group of countries that was involved in these networks from an early date suggests that hosting FDI was not in itself the basis of their subsequent sustainable rates of growth and development.[32] Moreover, in the countries that did benefit from hosting FDI, the inflows usually took off well after they had entered a period of rapid economic growth. This was the case in the second-tier NIEs which enjoyed a decade of relatively strong growth in the 1980s before FDI really took off towards the end of that decade. China has followed the same path, with the FDI boom lagging a decade behind the acceleration in economic growth.

Just as important, however, is the fact that the East Asia region contains a remarkable diversity of experience with FDI. Foreign affiliates accounted for 40-50 per cent of manufacturing sales in Singapore and the second-tier NIEs in the late 1980s, whereas in the Republic of Korea and Hong Kong the figures were 21.5 per cent and 17.3 per cent respectively. No figure is available for Taiwan Prov-

---

[31] For a sample of such studies see Doner (1991), Ernst and O'Connor (1992), Evans (1995), Fields (1995), Hamilton (1991), Jomo et al. (1997), Kim (1997), Lall (1996), Matthews and Cho (2000), and Schein (1996).
[32] Seminal studies from the 1970s include Helleiner (1973), Streeten (1975) and Froebel et al. (1979).

ince of China, but its situation is probably similar to that of Hong Kong.[33] Figures for the share of FDI in gross domestic capital formation also show a similar pattern (see Table 4.1). Foreign direct investment, including that from Japan, did not play such a prominent role in the industrialisation of the two larger economies in the first-tier NIEs, partly because they were very selective and restrictive towards FDI, and partly because Japan had not yet become a major overseas investor. Aggregate figures, such as the share of foreign affiliates in manufacturing sales or the share of FDI in domestic capital formation, do not necessarily measure the full importance of FDI in the industrialisation process. In the Republic of Korea, for example, foreign affiliates accounted for a quarter of all manufactured exports, which is many times greater than their small shares of GDP or gross capital formation. In the key electrical and electronics sector, the share of foreign affiliates was between 65 and 73 per cent.[34] Thus, although development in the Republic of Korea and Taiwan relied mainly on domestic firms, an important role was, and still is, played by FDI in certain sectors of the economy.

Although the share of foreign affiliates in manufacturing sales has been much higher in Taiwan and the Republic of Korea than in Japan, it is higher still in the second-tier NIEs. Broadly speaking, economic development in South-East Asia has been more dependent on FDI (Brooks and Hill, 2004). The second-tier NIEs have been much more willing to allow wholly-owned foreign subsidiaries and have been less restrictive towards FDI. More liberal foreign investment laws were introduced or strengthened in the second half of the 1980s to coincide with concerted moves to accelerate manufacturing exports and with rapid changes in the competitive position of firms in Japan and the first-tier NIEs. Even so, apart from Malaysia, FDI still accounts for a relatively modest share of total investment in the region's latest industrialisers and less than in many Latin American or African countries. In this respect, China, where FDI has accounted for around

---

[33] However, these statistics should be treated with caution since many affiliates are part of joint ventures and may include a large domestic contribution. For example, according to some estimates, in 1986 foreign affiliates employed 11.4 per cent of all manufacturing workers in Taiwan, but when the numbers are weighted by equity holdings the foreign share falls to 6.5 per cent. See Schive and Tu (1991).
[34] See Lee and Ramstetter (1991).

13 per cent of gross capital formation since 1990, albeit on a steady downward trend since peaking at over 17 per cent in 1994, seems to be following a well-established path in the region.

As already noted, there has been a visible regional dimension to the pattern of FDI in East Asia, due to the emergence of Hong Kong, the Republic of Korea, Singapore and Taiwan as foreign investors. In this context, export-promotion policies linked to FDI in the second-tier NIEs have been pursued more vigorously than in the first-tier NIEs, resulting not only in a more rapid shift to manufactures in all these countries from the second half of the 1980s but also in their rapid development of high-technology exports (UNCTAD, 1996). Some observers see this as marking a new trajectory of leapfrogging to higher-technology activities through the use of measures that are more market-friendly than those adopted in the earlier first-tier strategies (Lall, 2004), but this appears to be based on classifying unskilled activities in the same category as the high-skill, high-technology products of which they are only a part.

The more important point that emerges from the available case studies, however, is that policy makers have used an array of instruments to ensure that FDI complemented wider developmental objectives. Certainly, the larger economies of the first tier – following the earlier lead of Japan – adopted a more dirigiste approach to FDI based on an appreciation of its costs and benefits in promoting indigenous enterprise and deepening domestic technological capabilities.[35] Policy makers in both the Republic of Korea and Taiwan consciously chose to tap foreign capital in ways other than FDI, drawing instead on various forms of technology transfer to fill gaps in their productive structure. Managerial and technical assistance from Japanese companies played an important role. Thus, with help from companies such as Kawasaki Shipbuilding and Nippon Steel from Japan, world-class industries were created within the space of a decade in the Republic of Korea.[36] Singapore, which had a much more open policy,

---

[35] See Lall (1996) for details of the Korean experience.

[36] Amsden (1989). If this type of assistance had not been forthcoming, the task of catching-up would almost certainly have been far more difficult and the Republic of Korea would have had to rely entirely on reverse engineering, reading the technical journals and similar – less efficient – ways of acquiring knowledge. To develop major new industries without some form of help from companies in the leading countries is a formidable and sometimes impossible task.

also used a variety of measures to direct FDI into strategic sectors.[37]

There are important questions to be asked about the relative merits of these different approaches, particularly as they relate to sustained improvements in productivity and capturing a larger share of the value added in sectors with FDI. Some of these will be discussed in the next section, but it is worth noting here that policy makers in the second-tier NIEs are searching for more active policies to ensure that FDI delivers its full potential.

Success in the management of FDI is not confined to East Asia. A strong link between FDI and manufacturing exports can also be found in other, frequently cited success stories outside Asia, such as Mauritius and Ireland. Describing their growth as FDI-led, however, again tends to ignore the lagged response of FDI to a prior period of strong growth as well as the heterodox measures that were employed to generate that growth, including the use of strategic trade and industrial policies.[38] In fact, as a share of gross fixed capital formation, FDI was less important in the Mauritius growth story than in many other African countries over the past 30 years, and while the creation of its export processing zone was essential to success in the clothing sector, foreign firms appear to have followed domestic firms in taking advantage of it. Rather, as Subramanian and Roy (2003) have shown, the key to success was the successful management of large economic rents generated by sugar and clothing exports under the Lomé Convention and the Multi-Fibre Agreement. Much the same is true of Ireland, where a "big push", beginning in the early 1970s, reflected a mixture of favourable market conditions, massive amounts of aid from the European Union, and heterodox policies which included pragmatic management of the exchange rate, industrial subsidies and incomes policies, and which together helped to stimulate and sustain almost two decades of economic growth prior to the large-scale entry of FDI in the 1990s (Walsh, 1996).

---

[37] Hong Kong is something of an exception because of its strategic association with China which has allowed it to move into services without first going through a process of industrial upgrading and diversification.

[38] Sachs (1997) is guilty of this in his account of the Irish miracle, as is Moran (2003) on Mauritius.

E. Some warning signals

The widespread tendency to describe the expansion of firms abroad in terms of a simple "win-win" logic is guilty of ignoring the very uneven nature of international production as well as glossing over the details and complexity of specific success stories and in particular the heterodox policies that helped them to manage FDI in the light of local circumstances. Just as significantly, in terms of the design of development policy, market fundamentalists have been far too casual in ignoring the potential downside risks of hosting FDI and the fact that the interests of foreign investors may not always be aligned with those of the host country.

1. A fallacy of composition

The discussion of the previous section notwithstanding, replicating the success of the East Asian NIEs is still often reduced to a matter of accelerating trade and financial liberalisation as a means of attracting export-oriented FDI.[39] Malaysia is frequently held up as the model for others to follow, and certainly both on a per capita basis and relative to GDP, Malaysia has one of the largest stocks of inward FDI in the developing world, much of it in export-oriented sectors focused on Northern markets. There are serious doubts, however, whether it is possible for other countries to attract foreign investment on a similar scale.

There is growing concern, as we saw in the previous chapter, that the entry of a large number of developing countries into the markets for unskilled manufactured exports could have a significant negative impact on their terms of trade. This stems from the intense competition in global markets for low-skilled manufactured goods and appears to be related to the proliferation of international production networks in some of these activities, as well as the emergence of new producers with large amounts of unemployed or underemployed low-skilled labour. But a potential for a fallacy of composition extends also to FDI.

---

[39] See Fukasaku et al. (2005).

Excluding the first-tier NIEs, the flow of FDI into the developing countries averaged $16.5 per capita, or 1.4 per cent of their GDP, in the FDI boom of the early 1990s. For Malaysia the figures were $241.8 and 10 per cent respectively. What would happen if other developing countries were as successful as Malaysia in attracting FDI? Table 4.3 considers two hypothetical cases. In case A, it is assumed that the average developing country receives the same per capita amount of FDI as Malaysia. This would require a 15-fold increase in FDI to developing countries, the total figure reaching approximately $2,000 billion annually. This is 3.5 times the total manufacturing investment of the advanced OECD countries. In case B, the objective is the more modest one of the average developing country seeking to achieve the same share of FDI in GDP as in Malaysia. Even this would require a seven-fold increase in total FDI in developing countries, equal to 1.7 times the manufacturing investment of the North. Even recognising the emergence of new capital exporters such as Taiwan and Korea, the volume of FDI is highly unlikely to develop on such a scale as to make it possible to replicate the Malaysian example more widely. Indeed, looking at the actual flows for 2001-03 in Table 4.3, it is clear how utopian much of the talk on FDI over the past few years has been.

2. *Enclave economies*

The rise in FDI before 1914 was associated with the scramble for the primary inputs needed by the expanding industries of Northern Europe and North America, and was often tied to colonial rule. For the host country, this usually involved an insertion into the international division of labour involving trade relations between the markets of rich countries and their nationals producing abroad in farms or mines. The result was a pattern of development where strong external ties were accompanied by weak internal linkages and, not infrequently, the destruction of fledgling local industries. Foreign firms paid low rents for the right to use land, brought in skilled labour, used imported inputs intensively, hired small amounts of unskilled local labour at subsistence wages, and had minimal impact on the rest of the economy even as they generated large export revenues. Indeed,

Table 4.3: FDI in Malaysia and hypothetical flows to other developing countries
(average annual FDI, 1991-93)

	Total ($ billion)	Per capita ($)	Percentage of 1990 GDP
Malaysia	12.8	241.8	10
Developing countries			
Actual inflow[a]	136.8	16.5	1.4
Hypothetical inflow (i)	2007.8	241.8	20.9
Hypothetical inflow (ii)	957.7	115.3	10
Actual inflow (2001-03)[a]	151.3	30.8	2.7

Source: UNCTAD, *Trade and Development Report 1997*, Table 32 and UNCTAD FDI database.
Note: (i)   assumes FDI inflow per capita to be the same as Malaysia's
       (ii) assumes FDI inflow as percentage of GDP to be the same as Malaysia's
       [a] excluding first-tier NIEs

the gains from trade accrued disproportionately to non-nationals, who repatriated large proportions of their earnings.

Recent work on the links between FDI in natural resources and development prospects suggests that this pattern has persisted (UNCTAD, 2005a&b; Campbell (ed.), 2004). Indeed, under structural adjustment programmes, the distribution of resource rents following privatisation and the deregulation of mining rules has shifted decisively back in favour of large corporations. While the increasing participation of TNCs in oil and mining activities since the mid-1980s has generally expanded production, it has often reduced the share of the rents retained by the host countries, particularly where the role of state-owned enterprises has been considerably reduced (as in much of Latin America and SSA) and fiscal charges for private foreign companies are often very low (Table 4.4). At the same time, the linkages to domestic firms have been limited.

As was shown in the previous chapter, a similar pattern has emerged in some manufacturing industries where TNCs organise the simple, low-skill assembly of imported parts for export. These have certainly been among the most dynamic products in international trade in recent years, but in many cases the growth of manufactured imports and exports has exceeded the increase in domestic value added by a large margin. A recent study of Mexico, for example, estimates that imports for processing constitute as much as one-half to two-thirds of the total sales of affiliates of US TNCs in industries such as computers and transport equipment, while the growth in value added has been negligible (Hanson et al., 2002).

The pattern is different in the second-tier Asian NIEs whose share of global manufacturing value added has risen, albeit lagging behind their growing share of world manufacturing exports. Indeed, while Malaysia and Thailand have reached the level of industrialisation achieved by Taiwan and Korea in the late 1970s, their apparent success in exporting sophisticated products is deceptive. Such exports would normally be associated with a fairly mature industrial economy with a diverse manufacturing base, a robust capital-goods sector, a well-developed local supplier network, large clusters of high-tech-

Table 4.4: Government revenue from international trade and extractive industries, selected countries
(per cent of total current government revenue)

	Import and export duties	Revenue from extractive industries[a]	Year
Algeria	7.3	68.7	2003
Angola	5.9	75.1	2003
Argentina	16.9	7.1	2004
Bolivia	3.5	26.2	2003
Botswana	11	52.7	2002
Chad	17.3	33.8	2004
Chile	5.7	8.2	2003
Côte d'Ivoire	38.6	1.4	2002
Ghana	22.7	3.5	2002
Guinea	19.8	14	2003
Malaysia	5.9	22.7	2004
Mexico	1.7	33.1	2004
Peru	7.3	2.4	2003
Venezuela	3	49.7	2003

Source: UNCTAD, *Trade and Development Report 2005*, Table 3.5.
[a] Government revenue from royalties, income taxes of exporting firms, and profits of state-owned firms transferred to budget.

nology activities, a well-educated and technically proficient workforce, and a significant level of industrial R&D within both the enterprise system and the public sector. Figures on R&D expenditures are particularly striking. On this criterion the second-tier NIEs are still relatively weak, even compared with middle-income developing countries, and a considerable distance behind the first-tier NIEs (UNCTAD, 1996; UNIDO, 2003). Perhaps of more concern for these countries is the absence of medium-technology exports, which were an important stage in the upgrading process in the first-tier NIEs. Indeed, many of the elements of the technological infrastructure needed to allow domestic firms to compete in this middle range of exports are still missing in the second-tier NIEs, and upgrading along the lines already pursued by the first-tier NIEs remains a key policy challenge (UNCTAD, 1996).[40]

Similar concerns are beginning to be voiced in China, where export-oriented FDI surged from the late 1980s, a decade or so into the reform process and linked to a large extent to the transfer of the production of labour-intensive manufactured goods from the first-tier NIEs. While these sectors have certainly produced a very large rise in exports, and also in employment, wages have lagged behind and there is some evidence of domestic investment being crowded out by foreign investors competing with local firms for bank financing. Backward and forward linkages of FDI appear to be quite weak: according to one recent estimate, as much as two-thirds of the value of exports is imported (IIE, 2006) and the high-tech classification of some exports, as we suggested earlier, is a statistical quirk. Indeed, one assessment of the Chinese experience concludes that "In countries with a fraction of the bargaining power of China, which means most developing countries in the world, China's success does not offer great hope for the promise of FDI" (Braunstein and Epstein, 2004:239).

The "footloose" nature of the activities that provide initial starting points for moving up the value-added ladder in manufacturing means that locational advantages are more easily won and lost through small cost changes or the emergence of alternative locations compet-

---

[40] For a discussion of spillovers linked to FDI in the second-tier NIEs, see UNCTAD (1996), Rasiah (1998) and The Brooker Group (2002).

ing to attract TNCs. This is likely to intensify wage and price competition, and almost certainly more so than when the East Asian NIEs
embarked on their more export-oriented development path (Krugman,
1995). Consequently, and as suggested in the previous chapter, the
impact of FDI on a host economy's balance-of-payments position is
likely to vary unpredictably with the share of TNC profits in value
added, the degree of import dependence and the proportion of the
final good sold in domestic markets (Akyüz, 2004). If, as seems likely,
the propensity to import of foreign firms is much higher than that of
domestic firms, and if their export propensities are similar, increased
FDI will add to balance-of-payments pressures (Chudnovsky and
Lopez, 2002). In Brazil, for example, a shift away from net exports
of high-tech goods by foreign firms in the 1990s was accompanied
by a sharp increase in high-tech imports that were not linked to exports. In one survey of foreign firms, an overall export surplus in
1989 had become a deficit by 1997, as their imports rose at more than
double the rate of their exports, and despite a rising share of exports
from domestic firms in high-tech goods (UNCTAD, 2003a:143). A
similar pattern occurred in Argentina in the late 1990s.

These risks are particularly high when trade is based on preferential market access and if countries become too complacent about
their ability to manage diversification to higher-value-added products. Moreover, because much of the technology is embodied in imported parts and components, with limited local value added and related linkages, there is an added threat from external shocks
(UNCTAD, 2002a). This is further compounded when FDI is financed
with loans, including from the parent company, rather than equity.
This pattern of integration, which shares some of the features of commodity enclaves, can hinder the development of domestic supply capabilities, expose countries to the threat of external shocks, and risk
locking them into current trading patterns based on unskilled and semi-
skilled labour-intensive activities.

3.   *Trickling down or racing to the bottom?*

A rising share of profits in national income, together with rising
levels of inequality and unemployment, declining trade-union membership and falling corporate tax revenues have emerged as strong

trends across much of the industrial world during the past two decades of liberalising policy regimes (ILO, 2003). Contrary to the promises of market fundamentalists, however, these trends have been accompanied by a steady decline in the rate of capital accumulation
in the advanced countries (Glyn, 2006). Predictably, policy makers
have responded by insisting that efforts must be intensified to improve competitiveness and attract FDI, and as a result there has been
a steady growth in the range of fiscal and financial incentives offered
to TNCs by national and local authorities (Oman, 2000). In the absence of more expansionary policies, and despite broad agreement
that such incentives are not a major influence on the direction of FDI
(Blomström and Kokko, 2003), the idea that governments must compete to attract FDI has become deeply entrenched in the conventional
policy rhetoric.

For many developing countries, however, this is to substitute
the delusion of a "quick fix" for the much harder task of creating the
institutional, legal and economic environment that will not only attract TNCs but also ensure their commitment to the host country's
long-term development. Creating that environment is tantamount to
development itself, but the shareholders of the TNCs do not consider
that to be a task for their companies. Insofar as TNCs do invest in
countries that lack these background conditions, their investments
are most likely to be confined to very short-term "footloose" activities that can be quickly abandoned as soon as the special incentives
are withdrawn or eroded. Such a situation is not unknown even in the
developed market economies where governments have been tempted
to seek FDI as a solution to specific regional problems of structural
unemployment. But again, in the absence of a broader strategy for
regional regeneration, this is unlikely to be successful: both France
and the UK, for example, have occasionally put their hopes in foreign
investors coming to the rescue of various manufacturers of household appliances ("white goods") in depressed areas and both have
seen the foreign investor disappear at short notice after exhausting
the fiscal and other allowances or seeing them offset by other factors.

Nevertheless, many developing countries have followed the
advice that they must attract FDI and in their efforts to do so have
offered TNCs tax holidays, direct subsidies and exemptions from
import duties, despite a backdrop of ever-tighter fiscal constraints, in

the hope that the gains to foreign firms will eventually trickle down to the local population by crowding-in local investment, creating jobs and raising fiscal revenues. In some cases, such as natural resources, which offer the prospect of a share in large monopolistic profits, the expectation is for a large increase in government revenues even with a lowering of the marginal tax rate. Such a rosy outcome seems unlikely in light of the discussion in the previous section.[41] In fact, countries that have benefited from the presence of TNCs in these sectors, such as Botswana and Chile, appear to have done so as a result of determined bargaining by the state. But attempts to improve cost advantages in the manufacturing sector by liberalising the entry conditions for FDI, by reducing wages and labour standards, or by offering fiscal incentives, run the risk of damaging longer-term growth prospects, particularly if they are introduced without any prior analysis of their costs in relation to the likely benefits from the FDI that they are supposed to attract. As Hanson (2001) has argued, subsidising FDI only makes sense if there is little resulting impact on the factor costs of domestic firms, if the welfare costs of shifting production from domestic to foreign firms are small, and, most importantly, if there are large productivity spillovers. In the three cases examined in his study, two involving automobile producers in Brazil and the other Intel in Costa Rica, the evidence on subsidies points instead to successful rent-seeking by foreign firms.

Incentives have not usually involved direct competition for FDI between developed and developing countries. However, there has been growing concern in the North that the shift towards more liberal FDI regimes worldwide is leading to a general and pervasive lowering of labour standards particularly in the more footloose, cost-sensitive low-skilled industries. Such concerns have been strongly voiced in the context of relocating plants within NAFTA. But FDI is not the

---

[41] An illuminating example is provided by the United States, where inter-state competition to attract out-of-state investment by offering tax breaks and other incentives has proven to be essentially counter-productive. In practice, they have been shown to have little influence on business decisions about where to locate investment and the promised benefits (faster growth, higher tax revenues, etc.) rarely outweigh the cost. They do however divert considerable sums (well over $50bn a year) of tax revenue from spending on infrastructure, education and other public services that, as argued in this chapter, really do have an influence on the decisions of outside investors (Enrich, 2006).

only source of such concern: the subcontracting of unskilled work by TNCs to firms in low-wage countries is seen as adding further downward pressure on the wages and employment of groups of workers in the North (Feenstra and Hanson, 1996), and the debate about the offshoring of services has raised similar concerns and fears. To date, however, the evidence linking FDI to higher levels of unemployment and growing inequality in the advanced developed economies is weak. Although there has been a strong recovery of FDI in developing countries since the late 1980s, it remains small relative to total investment in the North – some 3-4 per cent – and its direct employment effects in the South, if anything, have had a skilled-labour bias (UNCTAD, 1995; Amadeo, 1998). It is true that the threat of exit from advanced-country locations has become more "credible" but, as we have insisted in this chapter, large parts of the developing world – including those where labour and environmental standards are lowest – remain outside the universe of international production because any wage-cost advantages they possess are offset by low productivity and higher levels of risk. Still, as Paul Samuelson (2004) has recently acknowledged, this is less a matter of theoretical dogma and more an empirical issue of weighing the costs and benefits of different types of investment.[42]

F.   Conclusion

At the height of discussions in the 1970s on a New International Economic Order, Charles Kindleberger and Peter Lindert (1978) described the policy debate about controlling international business as one dictated more by irrational instincts than reasonable discussion. Much the same can be said about the more recent discussion about attracting FDI and deregulating international business. In recent years, FDI has been presented as the standard bearer and pre-eminent symbol of globalisation, offering a strong complementary logic to trade

---

[42]   A recent study by Harrison and McMillan (2006) finds that jobs abroad in low-income affiliates are substitutes for US jobs while jobs abroad in high-income affiliates are complementary to US jobs, although the magnitudes in both cases appear to be small.

openness by promising to spread technology and skills more evenly across the global economy. Indeed, since the Asian financial crisis of 1997, attracting FDI through good governance has become the centrepiece of a reworked Washington Consensus promising to deliver a package of assets that will enhance competitiveness and boost economic growth. Difficult questions concerning the possible costs of hosting FDI, not to mention its shortage in relation to the number of eager would-be hosts, have been consistently downplayed or ignored altogether in the excessively enthusiastic and one-sided accounts of the benefits of hosting foreign firms and opening markets.

In this chapter we have argued that a more balanced framework for evaluating FDI needs to weigh carefully the accompanying costs and benefits, and to do so in relation to a range of development goals, many of which are country- and sector-specific. Two broad points are worth emphasising when thinking about such a framework, both of which go against the grain of the market-fundamentalist perspective but which tend to reinforce the conclusion reached in Chapter 3 concerning trade and finance. Firstly, history clearly matters. As elsewhere, past FDI is likely to influence subsequent flows, and the likelihood of their becoming part of a self-sustaining and dynamic investment process, with a strongly positive impact on productivity, depends upon establishing positive complementary interactions with domestic investment, in both the private and public sectors. The failure of capital formation to make a strong recovery since the debt crisis of the 1980s in many developing countries suggests that such cumulative interactions have not taken hold in many of them during the past 20 years. Under such circumstances the tendency of FDI to reinforce enclave-type development appears to be a real danger, with external integration privileged over the internal integration of the local economy.

Secondly, the narrative about attracting FDI through greater openness and downsizing the state is not only open to serious empirical reservations but it also tends to divert attention from the more fundamental determinants of FDI: market size and growth, resource endowments and infrastructure development have been consistently shown to be among the most significant determinants of the distribution of FDI, thus confirming it as a lagging rather than a lead factor in the development process. More than ever, the role of an effective state, able to bargain over rents, still appears to be the key to successfully integrating FDI into a broader development strategy.

FDI is perhaps the most sensitive issue in the polarised and controversial debates about globalisation. Market fundamentalists project the TNC as a totally benign vector of modernisation and development and insist that policy should focus on clearing any and all obstacles in its path, while at the other end of the spectrum anti-globalisers see it as a malevolent and neo-imperial force trampling over local communities and bending governments to its will in its voracious search for profit. The real world, predictably, exists in a messy and confusing position between these extremes and, as we keep insisting, is characterised by a considerable range of different experiences and environmental conditions. There are certainly plenty of examples of rapacious foreign enterprises looting the resources and exploiting the labour of poor countries, often with the cooperation of a corrupt ruling class, but there are also others where FDI has contributed to long-run economic growth and the economic welfare of the local population. For the latter to occur, we have stressed the importance of prior economic and institutional conditions and, above all, the existence of a strong and competent government capable of constructing a coherent strategy for development and of bargaining with TNCs as to where and how they can contribute to national objectives. Where FDI has made an important contribution to development, and the examples stretch from Ireland to Singapore, it has invariably been within the framework of such a strategy and where governments have been able to use a variety of measures to channel FDI into particular sectors or regions. Such success is prima facie a reason to doubt the usefulness of initiatives to lay down multilateral rules for FDI, as proposed by a number of OECD governments and by the International Chamber of Commerce. But another, more fundamental objection to such rules follows from our argument that investment, especially when it is part of a coherent development strategy, represents a population's view or vision about its future and the shape of the society that it would like to inhabit. This is their business, and since the G7 powers have declared their commitment to promoting democratic polities as well as market economies, this is a matter they should respect. We return to this issue in later chapters.

Chapter 5

Globalisation Revisited

A. Introduction

THE deregulation of domestic markets and their opening up to international market forces and TNCs has been driving the economic policy agenda in most developing countries over the past two-and-a-half decades. In this respect, as we have argued earlier, they have been following the lead set by richer countries, although all too often without the checks and balances (and deviations) that have accompanied the process in those countries. The virtues of the invisible hand have acquired an almost mystical status in some quarters and the fervent proselytising of its devotees has helped to create a world with fewer countervailing pressures from governments than at any time since 1945, although, for some, there are still too many (Lal, 2006).

From this perspective, and regardless of historical and economic circumstances, the surest way for poorer countries and communities to achieve lasting economic gains for their citizens is to get rid of the various state-created "distortions" that impede cross-border activity. If they do this, the growth of the world economy should accelerate and draw into the process countries and communities which have hitherto been left behind. The liberalisation of international trade should enable countries to better exploit their comparative advantages. Where this is constrained by a lack of investment, the liberalisation of international capital markets should ensure that investment funds will flow from the capital-abundant North to the capital-scarce developing countries. Attracting FDI will help the latter gain access to new technologies and management practices as well as opening new marketing channels.

Following this line of argument, the success of globalisation tends to be measured in terms of increasing international capital flows, rising trade-to-GDP ratios, and the increased presence of TNCs in national economic activity. It is also clear from the arguments in favour of liberalisation that changes in the spatial distribution of trade and capital flows should begin to accelerate, flattening relations of interdependence among the partner countries and weakening the geographical concentration or clustering of industrial activity. Above all else, growth should pick up sharply in poorer countries and begin to close the income gap which separates them from the richer countries, as well as reducing levels of inequality among their own citizens.

In fact, as described in the previous two chapters, the major channels through which market forces are supposed to invigorate economic life in poorer countries appear to be a good deal less global than often presumed and, far from always being benign, have frequently been shown to be harmful. Moreover, the idea that these forces have generated more stable outcomes is contradicted by the recent record of boom-bust cycles, gyrating asset and currency prices and ever-larger economic shocks that have hit countries at all levels of development. Indeed, the pursuit of a more open economic playing field, far from being a levelling experience for most developing countries, has thrown up new "distortions" and "biases" which are obstructing growth and creating new sources of insecurity. In the face of these developments, calls (whether from political leaders in the richest countries, tenured professors at prestigious Northern universities or business executives surrounded by a battery of corporate lawyers and financial managers) "to keep liberalisation reforms on track", "to go the extra mile" with painful policies or to "forsake narrow national interests for the wider global interest" carry more than a whiff of fundamentalism and a good deal of arrant hypocrisy.[1]

Such calls have often been accompanied by warnings of the dangers of clinging to the norms and practices of a bygone era. Indeed, uncovering such atavistic behaviour is often deemed sufficient to explain why things have not turned out quite as expected. In fact, as we have already suggested, the idea that we are entering uncharted

---

[1]   Quite a few market fundamentalists call to mind the Spanish philosopher George Santayana's definition of fanaticism as doubling one's effort when the original purpose has been forgotten.

economic waters lacks a sensible historical compass. The "universal interdependence of nations" has been ebbing and flowing for centuries, and turning this movement into a new era of global economic development has, as we have argued earlier, ridden roughshod over economic history, both near and distant. Adding a large dose of technological inevitability is also no more convincing in putting an end to the debate as to where things are heading. The shrinkage of time and space due to technological revolutions in transport, communications and information processing has certainly meant that the actions of some countries and citizens reverberate much faster and further than was once the case but, rather than a new departure, this is a very longstanding, progressive development that has also produced some clear winners and losers. It is even more implausible to suggest that we have stumbled into a "borderless world" when there are dozens more new countries than 25 years ago, when three of the most nationally minded developing countries, India, China and Brazil, are emerging as major influences shaping global economic prospects, and when business and governments in the advanced industrial economies are working more closely together than at any other time in the post-war era to define and defend their interests.

In this chapter we shall try to reconnect the features of global interdependence (or external integration) described in previous chapters to those nationally rooted economic forces (or internal integration) that have traditionally helped countries to lift themselves out of poverty, in particular, economic growth, investment and industrialisation. Doing so, we hope, will not just expose some of the more egregious myths that have surrounded the past two-and-a-half decades of market-led development but also provide some pointers to where the search for alternatives might best be focussed.

B.   Catching up, falling behind and growing apart

1.   Globalisation and economic growth

There is no disputing the fact that we have been living through a period in which cross-border economic transactions have been expanding rapidly, albeit, as we have shown in the previous chapters,

very unevenly. Nor should there be any dispute (although one is sometimes hard-pressed to find it acknowledged in much of the globalisation
literature) that this has also been a period of slowing global growth:
the average annual (unweighted) rate of growth of per capita GDP
between 1980 and 2000 was 2 percentage points lower than in the
period 1960-80, and growth in the 1990s was lower than in any decade since the end of the Second World War (Chart 5.1 and Table
5.1).

The gap in real incomes per head between developing countries
and the advanced countries has grown significantly over the past 40
years (Chart 5.2). This dramatic economic divergence is the product
of the higher starting incomes of the latter and their faster rates of
growth (Table 5.2). Although one would be hard-pressed to discover
it in most of the media outpourings on globalisation, in the period
since 1980 the richer countries, on average, have grown more rapidly
than poorer countries.

Table 5.1: Per capita GDP growth in developed and developing countries, 1960s-1990s				
	1960s	1970s	1980s	1990s
Median GDP per capita growth				
Developing countries	2	1.8	-0.5	1.3
Sub-Saharan Africa	1.4	0.6	-1	-0.4
South Asia	1.7	0.7	3.1	3
Middle East and N. Africa	2.4	3.6	-0.2	0.5
L. America and Caribbean	1.8	2.6	-0.7	1.8
Europe and Central Asia	6.2	4.3	1.5	-1.8
East Asia and Pacific	2.1	5.5	1.6	2.9
GDP per capita growth				
High-income countries	4.2	2.6	2.5	1.8
Developing countries	3.6	2.9	0.7	1.8
World	3.4	2.1	1.3	1.3

Source: World Bank (2006), Tables 3.1 and 3.2.
Note: This table refers to a sample of 69 developing countries for which
continuous time series exist.

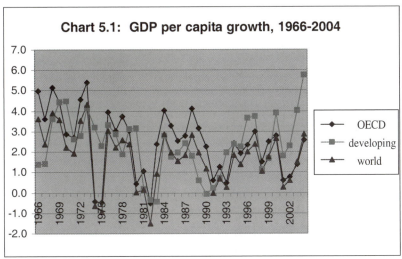

Source: World Bank, World Development Indicators online.

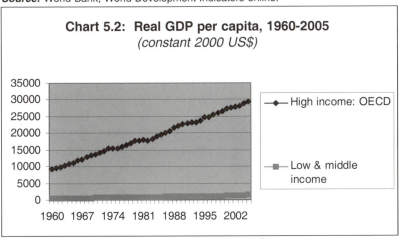

Source: World Bank, World Development Indicators online.

Aggregate figures can, of course, be misleading and there are some important differences within the developing world, with Asia growing much more rapidly than other regions and with catch-up growth a feature of the East Asian experience. Indeed, given that Latin America began this period with the highest per capita income among developing countries, subsequent growth trends have led to convergence across the developing world, even as they have diverged from

Table 5.2: Income levels and growth rates, 1950-2001, selected regions and countries

	GDP per capita (1990 international dollars)				Annual average per capita compound growth rates		
	1950	1973	1980	2001	1950-73	1973-80	1980-2001
Developed	6,298	13,376	15,257	22,825	3.3	1.9	1.9
Eastern Europe	2,111	4,988	5,786	6,027	3.8	2.1	0.2
Former USSR	2,841	6,059	6,426	4,626	3.3	0.8	-1.6
Latin America	2,506	4,504	5,412	5,811	2.6	2.7	0.3
Argentina	4,987	7,973	8,245	8,137	2.1	0.5	-0.1
Brazil	1,672	3,882	5,199	5,570	3.7	4.3	0.3
Mexico	2,365	4,845	6,289	7,089	3.2	3.8	0.6
Peru	2,263	3,952	4,205	3,630	2.5	0.9	-0.7
Asia	918	2,049	2,486	3,998	3.6	2.8	2.3
China	439	839	1,067	3,583	2.9	3.5	5.9
India	619	853	938	1,957	1.4	1.4	3.6
Japan	1,921	11,434	13,428	20,683	8.1	2.3	2.1
Pakistan	643	954	1,161	1,947	1.7	2.8	2.5
Africa	894	1,410	1,536	1,489	2.0	1.2	-0.1
South Africa	2,535	4,175	4,232	4,208	2.2	0.2	0.0
Egypt	718	1,022	1,641	2,992	1.5	7.0	2.9
Ghana	1,122	1,407	1,172	1,311	1.0	-2.6	0.5
Kenya	651	961	1,029	1,016	1.7	1.0	-0.1

Source: Maddison (2001) and UNDESA.

the advanced countries (Chart 5.3). There have also been differences in relative growth performance over time, developing countries outpacing the advanced countries for a number of years in the 1970s and again since the mid-1990s. However, even on a simple extrapolation of recent favourable performance since the start of the millennium, it would still take around 175 years for developing-country incomes to converge on those in the advanced countries.

In both popular and scholarly accounts, the actual and projected tilting of the world's economic axis towards Asia is often seen as

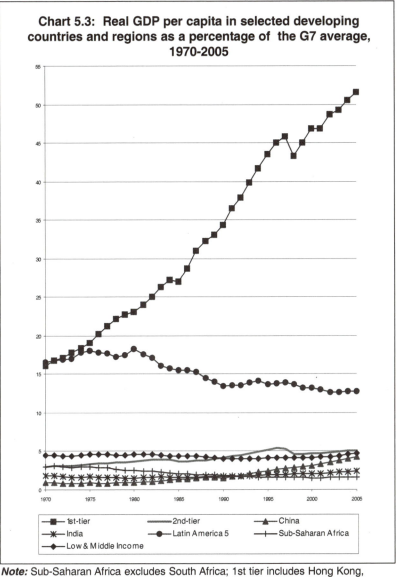

Chart 5.3: Real GDP per capita in selected developing countries and regions as a percentage of the G7 average, 1970-2005

Legend:
- 1st-tier
- 2nd-tier
- China
- India
- Latin America 5
- Sub-Saharan Africa
- Low & Middle Income

Note: Sub-Saharan Africa excludes South Africa; 1st tier includes Hong Kong, China, Korea, Singapore and Taiwan, China; 2nd tier includes Indonesia, Malaysia, the Philippines and Thailand; Latin America 5 includes Argentina, Brazil, Chile, Colombia and Mexico.

Sources: UNCTAD secretariat calculations based on UN statistics and World Bank, World Development Indicators online (for Sub-Saharan Africa and Low & Middle Income regions).

synonymous with globalisation. China and India, but particularly the former, emerged as the new growth hubs in the 1990s, although in both cases the acceleration had started in the 1980s, and perhaps even earlier in the case of China.[2] Both have had a significant impact on the wider regional performance and while neither are yet middle-class countries, they have a large number of citizens who would already qualify as such. Since 1980, growth in South Asia has improved sharply over the preceding two decades, and high growth rates were also maintained in East Asia in the 1990s despite the severe financial crises that hit the region in 1997, although the pace did not match that of the 1970s. However, the idea that these performances can be attributed to their opening up to global market forces is deeply misleading for two main reasons: first, as we have already suggested, there has been a good deal of policy and institutional heresy in how these economies have evolved over the past two decades or so, and, second, many of the structural changes propelling economic catch-up in Asia, including their own shift from rural dependence and rapid urbanisation, are largely independent of globalisation.

Although a significant development, East Asia's rise should not obscure other aspects of the global growth story. After the "lost decade" of the 1980s, Latin American economies enjoyed a brief renaissance in the early 1990s when the intensification of structural reforms enabled them to return to the international capital markets; but after 1997 developments again turned sour and produced another "lost half-decade" (Ocampo, 2002a). Overall, growth in the 1990s was similar to that in the 1960s but well below that in the 1970s. Sub-Saharan Africa, like Latin America, also suffered a "lost decade" of development in the 1980s, but with a weaker (if less erratic) recovery in the 1990s; there was generally little or no inflow of private capital into the region, and no abrupt reversal at the end of the decade, its

---

[2]   China's break with its earlier, highly erratic growth path occurred in the mid-1970s. There are some significant differences between these two awakening giants, notably the much slower pace of urbanisation in India and, with this, a much slower pace of industrialisation and capital accumulation. There is a good deal of dispute among economists as to which of the two development paths is likely to be the more sustainable.

relative poverty thus ironically providing it with some defence against the instability of foreign capital flows.[3]

What is just as telling about recent economic trends as the reawakening of Asia's economic giants is that, relative to their own past, the growth performance of many developing countries has actually deteriorated. Of a total of 124 developing countries, growth in 95 of them (i.e., over three-quarters) was faster in the period 1960-78 than between 1978 and 1998 (Milanovic, 2002a), and only a handful of countries have been able to achieve the growth rates needed to address their economic and social deficits.

Given what we have already said about the determinants of growth, identifying potential growth rates, and the related challenge of setting growth targets, must be seen as a somewhat hit-and-miss business. Assuming that a country's labour force is growing on average at 2-3 per cent per year and that productivity growth needs to match that rate to maintain internal and external balance, then 5-6 per cent would be a minimum annual target for GDP growth. Many, including us, would regard 7-8 per cent as more appropriate if the aim is to make real progress in tackling the massive social deficits that have built up in most developing countries and to start closing the income gaps with the more developed countries.[4] But, regardless of which rate is taken as the benchmark, the vast majority of countries have fallen below it during the current period of globalisation: between 1980 and 2000, of 140 developing countries, only 20 grew at annual rates above 5 per cent, a number that rises to 30 for the period 1990-2000. If a rate of 7 per cent is taken as the benchmark, the number of success stories falls to just 5 and 6 respectively.

Since 1980, countries at the very bottom of the income scale appear to have lost most ground, leading to what some have described as a "twin peaks" global income distribution (Quah, 1996), with a "hollowing out" of the middle-income range of countries (UNDESA,

---

[3]   The recent pick-up in African growth rates is largely a result of an increase in commodity prices linked in no small part to growing demand in China. According to a recent IMF Working Paper, a dozen middle-income and oil-producing African countries have been the principal beneficiaries of a stronger growth performance since 1997; see Tahari et al. (2004).

[4]   This was, for example, the target set by the Blair Commission on Africa in 2005.

2006:8). Milanovic and Yitzhaki (2001) estimate that just 8 per cent of the world's population now fall into the latter category. Polarisation, in large part, can be explained by the fact that the general slowing of global growth over the past two decades has hit poorer countries particularly hard. According to Milanovic (2005:5), the average annual per capita growth rate of the group of least-developed countries (LDCs) was just 0.1 per cent between 1980 and 2002, compared with 1.9 per cent in the "old" OECD economies, and while the former figure hides a very wide dispersion of performance, there were no stellar growth rates of the kind found in East Asia. Moreover, sharp falls in economic growth in this period were much more frequent in these countries than in any other developing-country group.

Most periods of sustained growth have been in East Asia, starting in Japan and followed by a series of such episodes in the 1960s and the 1970s. All established macroeconomic regimes with very fast rates of capital accumulation and avoided sharp slowdowns in economic growth, although the late 1990s proved to be traumatic for some of the previously strong performers.[5] Similarly, the fact that the South Asian economies also avoided the severe shocks of the early 1980s appears to have been an important factor in their subsequent growth acceleration, and the handful of success stories in Africa (most notably Botswana and Mauritius) and in Latin America (Chile) since the early 1980s show a similar pattern.

The global slowdown, however, coincided with a stalling of industrial dynamism in many countries and setbacks to social progress[6], together with a declining frequency of episodes of strong growth and more frequent periods of negative growth. According to Ocampo and Parra (2005), in the 1960s and 1970s about 40 per cent of developing countries had successful growth episodes (with annual average rates of per capita GDP growth greater than 3 per cent over at

---

[5] On the links between the adoption of more liberal policy regimes and financial crises, see UNCTAD (1998) and Chang et al. (eds.) (2001). Avoiding sharp shocks was also a feature of success stories on the European periphery, most notably Ireland.

[6] See UNCTAD (2003a) and UNDESA (2005). The social situation is discussed extensively in Jomo and Baudot (eds.) (2007). Given that there are important social factors that impact on growth performance, setbacks in social progress have almost certainly contributed to vicious growth circles in a number of developing countries.

Table 5.3: Ratio of per capita income to developed countries				
	1950	1973	1980	2001
Eastern Europe	0.34	0.37	0.38	0.26
Former USSR	0.45	0.45	0.42	0.20
Latin America	0.40	0.34	0.35	0.25
Argentina	0.79	0.60	0.54	0.36
Brazil	0.27	0.29	0.34	0.24
Mexico	0.38	0.36	0.41	0.31
Peru	0.36	0.30	0.28	0.16
Asia	0.15	0.15	0.16	0.18
China	0.07	0.06	0.07	0.16
India	0.10	0.06	0.06	0.09
Japan	0.31	0.85	0.88	0.91
Pakistan	0.10	0.07	0.08	0.09
Africa	0.14	0.11	0.10	0.07
South Africa	0.40	0.31	0.28	0.18
Egypt	0.11	0.08	0.11	0.13
Ghana	0.18	0.11	0.08	0.06
Kenya	0.10	0.07	0.07	0.04

Source: Maddison (2001) and UNDESA.

least a five-year period) but this proportion fell to less than 20 per cent through most of the past quarter-century, while in 40 per cent of countries there were negative growth episodes compared with just 15 per cent in the earlier period. Similarly, Hausmann et al. (2004) searched for episodes of rapid acceleration in economic growth that were sustained for at least eight years and found that while there were 23 and 30 such episodes in the 1960s and 1970s respectively, there were only 14 in each decade of the 1980s and 1990s. As we noted in Chapter 3, all this ties into a wider dynamic where developing countries are trading more but earning less from doing so.

Together, these trends have pressed down on the ratio of developing-country incomes to those in the developed world, with countries in East Asia the notable exception (Table 5.3).

The broad picture of the last two decades is thus one of erratic growth around a trend rate that was lower than that before the debt crisis. In some cases, principally in much of SSA, the trend in per capita GDP growth was negative, although there have been a number of strong performers (most notably China and India) whose growth has outpaced earlier performances (Table 5.2).[7] Generally, however, divergence between countries has continued in the period since 1980, at least in the sense that on average per capita incomes in richer countries have tended to grow faster than in poorer countries and the absolute income gap between rich and poor countries, as a result, has grown even wider. This is certainly not what was promised by the proponents of market-driven globalisation.

Market fundamentalists have been encouraged by the pick-up in growth across much of the developing world in the 1990s, as cross-border flows of trade, capital and investment have continued to increase. However, even ignoring the unevenness of this recovery and the crisis that hit some emerging markets at the end of the decade, the evidence of the previous chapters does not point to a simple or unidirectional relationship between trade, capital and FDI flows – let alone the *liberalisation* of trade, finance and FDI – and economic growth. At best, the relationships are ambiguous and even where liberalisation does appear to have had a positive influence on growth, it has invariably been in the context of a broader and more sophisticated package of development policies than that recommended by market fundamentalists. Moreover, as we also suggested earlier, cross-country regressions may not be the best way of helping us to understand the dynamics of growth, not only because they are obviously rooted in the unique characteristics of individual countries (whether described in terms of initial conditions, path dependencies or the effects of cumulative causation), but also because it is the translation of those experiences into a national political discourse that ultimately shapes

---

[7] Some small island economies such as Barbados, Mauritius and Seychelles also enjoyed faster growth after the debt crisis, although their growth takeoff also began earlier. Indeed, outside Asia, perhaps only Chile sustained a significant improvement over its past performance beginning in the mid-1980s, albeit still failing to match Asian rates of growth.

the basic aspirations of the population and determines the legitimacy of politicians and their policies.

Much of the current controversy surrounding development policy revolves around claims that exceptional growth performances are evidence of countries "embracing" globalisation, while growth failures reflect insufficient dedication to reform. We have already suggested reasons why most success stories can hardly be held up as adverts for neo-liberal policy reforms. In fact, what stands out more clearly from the record is that the regions that have been most diligent in applying such reforms, Latin America and Sub-Saharan Africa, have been the slowest-growing and, as the World Bank has acknowledged, are those where growth has consistently failed to meet expectations (World Bank, 2005a:31-32). Even more telling is that in neo-liberal showcase economies such as Argentina, Mexico and the Philippines annual per capita growth rates have not only been less than expected but also below those achieved in the 1960s and 1970s.

There is almost no evidence that the policies of "stabilisation, liberalisation and deregulation" have been able to generate the rates of growth needed by poorer countries to tackle their development deficits. William Easterly, a former senior World Bank economist, is candid about the unhappy experience of adjustment without growth:

> Twelve countries received fifteen or more World Bank and IMF adjustment loans over the fifteen-year period 1980 to 1994: Argentina, Bangladesh, Côte d'Ivoire, Ghana, Jamaica, Kenya, Morocco, Mexico, Pakistan, Philippines, Senegal, and Uganda. The median per capita growth rate for those twelve countries over the period was zero. This is perhaps the most important failing of adjustment: the failure to put in place policies that would promote growth....What is clear is that the hopes for adjustment with growth did not work. There was too little adjustment, too little growth and too little scrutiny of the results of adjustment lending (Easterly, 2001:115).

Updating his assessment, Easterly (2005) confirms that there is no evidence that per capita growth improved with the increased intensity of adjustment lending. This is far from being an isolated assessment.[8] Indeed, some go further. Barro and Lee (2002), for example, taking what they call a "political economy approach" (which suggests that access to IMF programmes is heavily conditioned by political proximity to the major shareholding countries), find that lending has a negative influence on economic growth in the medium to long run, i.e., with a lag of five years. In an extensive empirical review of these programmes, which defines their political dimension more broadly to reflect the interests and actions of local elites, James Vreeland (2003) finds that countries that never entered IMF programmes have had the fastest rates of growth; even when allowance is made for obvious selection bias (whereby countries in serious economic difficulty are the ones attracted to such programmes), the programmes still appear to have had no positive effect on growth performance. When unobserved variables, such as "political will", which have a simultaneous impact on the desire to participate and on economic growth, are introduced, Vreeland also finds that IMF programmes actually had a negative effect on economic growth.

The major issue is thus to explain how changes in policy since the debt crisis have adversely affected economic development. Certainly, most economies applying orthodox adjustment measures have increased their openness to trade and financial flows, have a higher FDI-to-GDP ratio, have sold off state assets, have introduced lower levels of corporate taxation and have achieved greater price stability. However, the idea that this would put an end to stop-go growth cycles associated with excessive levels of indebtedness and periodic balance-of-payments crises, thus facilitating a rapid switch from a distorted inward-looking regime to a more dynamic outward-looking and market-centred one, has proved to be mistaken.

The World Bank now seems willing to acknowledge that growth entails more than the efficient use of resources and that the liberalisation-growth axis is too weak a basis on which to design development strategy; structural transformation, diversification of production, risk-taking by producers, correction of both government and

---

[8]   For critical assessments of the impact of these policies see Killick (1995); Mosley (1999); Przeworski and Vreeland (2000); Rodrik (2003); Evrensel (2005).

market failures, and institutional change all appear to be more important in the longer run (World Bank, 2005a:10). The response has been to construct a wider policy agenda to address social deficits in developing countries and to acknowledge the role of institutions in shaping development outcomes. This belated acknowledgement of past failures is based on what has been apparently left out of the agenda (omissions) while implicitly assuming that there is nothing really wrong with its original core components. This begs the question, which too many erstwhile supporters of the Washington Consensus continue to evade, of what damage might have been, and continues to be, done by economic policies with serious design faults.

Two aspects of "policy hysteresis" can be identified in the context of the highly uneven growth performance just described. The first is the way in which neo-liberal policies to eliminate inflation and regain fiscal discipline have left some countries more vulnerable to shocks and less capable of managing them when they occur. In particular, the combination of tight macroeconomic policies, rapid trade liberalisation and capital-account opening has led in some cases to gyrations in the real exchange rate and persistently high real interest rates, which have shortened investors' horizons and impaired the restructuring of industry needed to improve productivity and competitiveness. As a result, there has been a failure to ease the external constraints on growth, resulting in persistently high levels of indebtedness and increased non-resident claims on the current account in the form of profit and dividend remittances to foreign investors. The expectation was that getting prices right would bring about an automatic adjustment to payments (and fiscal) imbalances, without too great a sacrifice in terms of growth. In fact, for those countries that became "seriously" (a debt-to-gross national income (GNI) ratio above 50 per cent) or "heavily" (a debt-to-GNI ratio over 100 per cent) indebted following the rise in interest rates in 1979 and 1980, few have been able subsequently to eliminate their debts. Changes in the composition of the budget and the external accounts, resulting from the build-up of internal and external debt and a concomitant rise in interest payments and profit remittances abroad, also mean that traditional deflationary policies have to be more severe to bring about the required corrections in fiscal and external balance, again damaging the potential for economic growth.

Secondly, inconsistencies between macroeconomic, trade, FDI and financial policies have also undermined the process of structural change. Efforts to upgrade technologically to match more advanced economies have been damaged while at the same time weak productivity performance in more labour-intensive sectors has led to increased competition from lower-wage producers.

Evidence of the resulting damage to growth can be found across much of Africa, where the sharp deterioration in the external economy in the late 1970s and early 1980s shattered the profitability of private firms, led to a collapse of state revenues and added to the debt that had begun to accumulate in the late 1970s. A vicious downward spiral followed in many countries: with little prospect of raising export earnings to maintain import levels, macroeconomic policies were tightened further, which in turn tightened the constraints on investment, diversification and growth. This was the genesis of Africa's debt overhang, the bulk of which was accumulated after 1982 when economic policy came under the close supervision of the international financial institutions (IFIs) (UNCTAD, 2004). As we shall see in Section C below, declining capital formation (both public and private), often to below replacement levels, and regressive structural changes held back recovery.[9] By leading to lower investment in critical areas such as transport, health and education, the debt overhang compromised some of the most essential conditions for sustainable economic growth, development and poverty reduction. Declining flows of official development assistance (ODA) in the 1990s only compounded the problem.

Africa's experience, however, is not unique. Indeed, international banks were particularly aggressive in pushing loans to the Latin American economies during the 1970s as part of their efforts to recycle petro-dollars. The subsequent "big bang" introduction of ad-

---

[9] Real GDP per capita in SSA peaked in the early 1970s, while the terms of trade only turned sharply down in 1977. The initial spurt of industrial growth in many African countries following independence was already stalling in the mid-1970s, dropping from an annual average in SSA of over 8 per cent between 1965 and 1973, to just 4 per cent between 1973 and 1980. As a result, by the late 1970s only a handful of African countries had reached a level of manufacturing activity that would allow domestic firms to break out of the vicious circle of small markets and low productivity, to strengthen the links between investment and exports, and thereby improve their prospects of entry into foreign markets.

justment programmes, particularly in Argentina, Mexico and Peru, in response to the sudden ending of these flows in the early 1980s failed, as noted earlier, to trigger the corporate restructuring, technological deepening and structural change needed to raise productivity and diversify production. Following the implementation of the Brady Plan, monetary conditions in Latin America remained much too stringent to provide a sound basis for macroeconomic stability and encourage growth based on capital accumulation, and restrictive fiscal policy (adopted in response to the rising burden of debt servicing) served to depress domestic activity (UNCTAD, 2003a:133-36).

As discussed in Chapter 3, in many cases the decline of employment that accompanied the initial shocks of the early 1980s accelerated sharply following the implementation of adjustment programmes and increased competition from imports. However, the destructive potential of these policy measures was not confined to the 1980s. A similar outcome followed the impact of adjustment programmes in a number of East Asian economies in the wake of the financial crises of the 1990s, and again the bias towards job destruction was slow to be reversed when recovery eventually set in. Perhaps even more telling, as the ILO has documented at some length, is that employment growth remained subdued in the 1990s even as growth picked up (ILO, 2003): estimated employment elasticities indicate that for every 1 percentage point of additional GDP growth, global employment grew by only 0.30 percentage points between 1999 and 2003, a drop from 0.38 percentage points between 1995 and 1999. Again, the familiar regional pattern is visible beneath the aggregate figures, with economic expansion in East Asia sufficient to generate growth of both employment and productivity and to reduce the high incidence of poverty in the region. Even so, as the Asian Development Bank (2006) has noted more recently, this virtuous circle may be faltering; in the period since the Asian financial crisis, 15 out of 18 Asian developing countries have had rising unemployment, with an estimated 29 per cent of the labour force underemployed.

The flipside of weak labour-market performance has been the growing size of the informal economy, estimated in 1999-2000 to account for over 40 per cent of output and close to half the size of the formal labour force in Africa and Latin America, rising to 60 per cent or more in individual cases (Schneider, 2002). These figures alone testify to the deep failure of adjustment programmes. Moreover, in a world of cumulative and interdependent developments, the expansion of the informal sector is likely to throw up further barriers to sustained growth by holding back the emergence or expansion of large domestic firms, both private and public, that have traditionally been the driving forces behind rapid accumulation, thereby limiting the opportunities to exploit scale economies, further stunting the process of employment creation and in all likelihood lowering labour standards (Galli and Kucera, 2004). It also leads to mounting fiscal pressures on the state, which are only exacerbated by growing urban problems, as the share of the population living in cities rises at a rapid pace.

There appears to be little in this record to suggest that the neo-liberal policy programme has established what Stiglitz (2005) has called a "moral growth path", i.e., one that is sustainable, that increases living standards not just today but for future generations as well, and that leads to a more tolerant, open society. This conclusion, it seems to us, is often obscured amid the political and intellectual recrimination that has emerged from the literature examining whether or not globalisation has added to or reduced global poverty.

2.   Global inequality and poverty

Where an individual stands in the global income order remains largely a matter of the passport he or she holds: the commonly cited figure is that 70 per cent of global inequality is explained by differences in countries' mean incomes, the rest being due to variations *within* countries (Milanovic, 2006). It is probably the case, however, that the latter remains the more powerful influence on everyday political and social life. Still, in an interdependent world, how these two components of income distribution interact is a question policy makers must address in one way or another, and perhaps more urgently than in the past. Martin Wolf (2006), for one, has begun to wonder whether rising levels of inequality in what he dubs the "new gilded age" will damage political, and with it economic, stability at both national and international levels.

Efforts to measure inequality at the global level are of recent vintage, and massive lacunae in the data, which persist despite considerable efforts to improve on their collection and collation, only add to the difficulties in addressing what has long been one of the most challenging analytical issues in economic and political theory. Efforts to fill the gaps in the data are still very much assumption-driven, and the results appear to be very sensitive to what is actually being measured and how, to country selection and weighting, to the time periods covered, to the exchange rate used to make local data internationally comparable, and so on. Most researchers would accept that for comparative purposes, purchasing power parity (PPP) is the appropriate income measure (Sutcliffe, 2003), although this is not without its methodological difficulties (Pogge and Reddy, 2002; Dowrick and Akmal, 2003).[10] Certainly, the sharply rising trend in global inequality since 1980 which arises from using market exchange rates gives way to a much fuzzier picture on the basis of PPP rates, with weaker trends in both a positive and negative direction (Svedberg, 2004).

Using income gaps and ratios, the previous section suggested a very uneven pattern in income distribution among countries, with divergence probably a stronger trend than convergence. However, income gaps and ratios are not the only way of measuring international inequality. The Gini coefficient is a more integral measure that aims to account for all members of a chosen set.[11] On this measure a number of studies have reported a reduction in international inequality since 1980. As Sutcliffe (2007) has noted, however, there is little agreement on how significant this is and, more importantly, it is a result that hinges on the performance of a single outlier: removing China from the country sample transforms the resulting trend to one of rising international inequality, and one that has been increasing even

---

[10] The difficulties centre on the relative prices of non-tradeables such as many services and foodstuffs.
[11] The Gini coefficient derives from the Lorenz curve which shows the cumulative share of the income received by the cumulative shares of the population, starting from the poorest income-receiving units. The coefficient measures the area between this curve and the diagonal of perfect equality, and varies from 0 (maximum equality) to 1 (maximum inequality) or from 0 to 100 when expressed in percentages. Milanovic's review of the literature notes that there is little disagreement on the degree of international inequality, with most studies finding a Gini coefficient in the range of 63 to 68, a figure that is higher than the coefficient in highly unequal countries such as Brazil or South Africa (Milanovic, 2006:140-42).

more sharply than before 1980. The Theil decomposition of international inequality gives a similar result (UNDESA, 2006:14). Given its size, China's performance is obviously central to the analysis of global trends. From a comparative perspective, however, what happens in a single country (however large) should not be used to obscure what is in fact a highly variegated picture (Berry and Serieux, 2004).

Perhaps because of such problems, critics and supporters of globalisation have shifted their attention to the issue of poverty. There is of course nothing new in putting poverty at the centre of policy and political debates or linking it to globalisation (Stedman Jones, 2004). Moreover, poverty is probably easier to measure, or at least easier to grasp – the meaning of living on less than a dollar a day is almost certainly more comprehensible for a wider audience than the Gini coefficient or the Theil index. However, the poverty debate is especially complicated because it acts as a lightning rod for a whole range of contentious issues that divide supporters and critics of market-led globalisation.

The resulting polarisation of positions has shed little light on income distribution and its links to economic growth. Nevertheless, there are some emerging points of agreement. There is, for example, almost no disputing that the really big divergence in global incomes occurred in the 19th century and the first half of the 20th, that this was largely driven by countries growing apart, and that these differences still dominate within-country differences. In terms of the recent period, there is also no dispute that absolute income gaps between the North and South have been widening for most of the postwar period and continued to widen during the past two decades: the gap in per capita (PPP) income between the rich (OECD) and poor (low- and middle-income) countries more than doubled between 1985 and 2004 from $12,000 to over $27,000; and the gap between the poor and the poorest (those countries classified by the United Nations as least developed) also more than doubled, from $1,150 to $3,300, over the same period. There is also no disputing that the number of people living in absolute poverty, i.e., on less than a dollar a day, declined during the 1990s by around 140 million but that this was not a global trend, rather the net outcome of diverging regional trends, with a dramatic improvement in China offsetting increases in Central

Asia, Latin America and Africa (United Nations, 2005:50-55). Finally, there is also more or less (but not complete) agreement that a sufficiently rapid growth rate in poorer countries can have a large and fairly rapid impact on poverty figures, without necessarily having any immediate impact on global inequality.[12]

Disagreements remain on how to combine country-level comparisons of per capita incomes with income inequality within countries, in order to attain a real measure of global inequality, and how to determine its direction and pace of change over the past two decades. Such exercises should, as Milanovic (2006) rightly insists, be concerned with the position of households in the global income pyramid but this poses huge data problems. Efforts to redistribute the global population into income groups have been a popular way of moving beyond country comparisons to a global picture, albeit with plenty of hidden assumptions and creative estimates. Such exercises, using the Gini measure of concentration, tend to report an improving average picture over the past two decades but with a striking worsening at the extremes, as measured by the ratio of the top 1 or 5 per cent to their counterparts at the bottom (Sutcliffe, 2007). There remains, however, plenty of scope for serious methodological disagreements. One of the few studies actually based on household data has reported rising global inequality since the late 1980s, largely due to rising inequality within China and India, although the fact that most of the deterioration occurs between 1988 and 1993 suggests that the collapse of communism might also be implicated (Milanovic, 2006). Inevitably, the reliability of this exercise has also been questioned by some researchers.

What is perhaps particularly telling is that on most assessments, inequality within countries, both developed and developing, has been on a worsening trend over the past two decades.[13] Here again the pattern has been set in the advanced countries, with those that have adopted a more overtly neo-liberal policy regime (such as the United

---

[12] The drop in the numbers living in poverty seems to be linked to a shift of population from the rural to the urban sector, but the link is not uniform. Differences in this respect between China and India go some way to explaining why the former has been more successful in reducing its poverty numbers.
[13] See Firebaugh (2003) and Atkinson (2001).

States and the United Kingdom) showing the largest increases in income inequality.[14] In a study commissioned by UNU/WIDER (Cornia (ed.), 2003), for a sample of 73 developed, developing and transition economies, there was a surge of inequality in 53 of them in the 1980s and 1990s. Among developing countries, inequality rose sharply in the 1990s. In many cases, typically in much of Latin America, the large increases in the 1980s were not reversed during the recovery of the early 1990s and the financial crises at the end of the decade worsened the situation further.

This trend is certainly consistent with our earlier discussion of the impact of the rapid liberalisation of trade, finance and FDI, of which financial openness is likely to have had the largest effect. The liberalisation of finance, particularly in middle-income developing countries, has led to a massive explosion in public and private debt, and with it the emergence of a new class of "rentiers" whose incomes depend on capital gains and interest payments (Dumenil and Levy, 2004). Large segments of the industrial and commercial classes have been borrowing and lending, and buying and selling existing assets, as a source of income rather than investing in commercial or industrial ventures or construction as they had previously done under conditions of "repressed finance". As a result, in many developing countries the richest 20 per cent of the population, which tends to capture a larger proportion of total income than the same quintile in the developed countries, has tended to increase its share of total income since the early 1980s at the expense of the middle class as well as those at the bottom of the scale. In more than half the developing countries, the richest 20 per cent now receive more than one-half of national income (UNCTAD, 1997). On one recent estimate, the middle 20 per cent of the income distribution in Brazil capture less than 10 per cent of total income, and earn just $4.50 per day (Birdsall, 2005). Similar developments in many other countries have reversed the pattern of relative gains made before 1980.

---

[14]   On the extent of rising inequality in the United States since the early 1980s, see Piketty and Saez (2003), and for a comparison with other developed countries see Glyn (2006).

But perhaps the most characteristic feature of a neo-liberal world has been the rise of super-elites – loosely defined as the top 1 per cent of each country's population – closely connected with each other but increasingly distanced, economically, politically and culturally, from their fellow citizens.[15] These connections are made in an international "paper economy" where a shared preference for liquidity and familiarity with a variety of short-term financial instruments have spurred the growth of financial activities "that generate high private rewards disproportionate to their social productivity" (Tobin, 1984). The widening gap in ownership of financial assets is now estimated to exceed that in incomes (Davies et al., 2006).

All things considered, there is something rather odd about the debate on global inequality. Income gaps have been widening among most countries and there has been growing inequality within most countries, yet there is still a good deal of dispute about the overall global trend during the past two decades. Perhaps, as we suggested in Chapter 3, the problem is that most researchers are looking for simple links between globalisation and inequality which are simply not there. Much depends on domestic circumstances, with initial conditions, policy priorities and other factors having a major bearing on the outcome.

Beyond the numerical controversy, it is perhaps possible to detect an emerging consensus that existing levels of inequality are unacceptable, particularly in developing countries, that these can be politically destabilising and that advanced countries will find it increasingly difficult to protect themselves from the shocks and instability that are likely to be created by an increasing sense of injustice. There is also a greater willingness to acknowledge that inequality may be an obstacle to growth. According to some analysts, the hollowing out of the middle class (both wage-earning and professional) threatens economic instability by depriving society of a more robust savings base and limiting investment. In a recent report on Latin America, the World Bank (2006) has revived the language of Gunnar Myrdal, explicitly acknowledging that the region may be caught in a

---

[15] Svedberg (2004:23-24) also sees signs of an emerging global elite which may have a distorting influence on policy in developing countries.

vicious circle of persistent poverty impeding higher growth, thereby reproducing still higher rates of poverty.

This seems to us to be a sensible conclusion, and with relevance that extends well beyond Latin America. Our own reaction to this debate is that efforts to achieve a systematic reduction in poverty will require a policy framework that is not only able to generate much higher growth rates than those achieved in the past two decades but will also include more explicit distributional goals at both the domestic and international levels. Such a framework will also require, as we shall discuss more fully in Chapters 6 and 7, the creation of a popular and democratic consensus for change. Unfortunately, with the neo-liberal compass continuing to set the general economic direction, some of the most crucial links between distribution, growth and poverty alleviation continue to be left out of the development debate and the design of policy (UNCTAD, 2002b). In particular, and despite all its talk of improving the investment climate, the neo-liberal approach has surprisingly little to say about the process of capital accumulation.

C.   Change in the policy climate: Investment trends since the debt crisis

For many market fundamentalists, the disappointing record since 1980 can be explained by temporary adjustment difficulties in moving to a more open economic environment. If this is so, allowing the rich to get richer should still eventually bring large gains, given that they have a much higher propensity to save and invest than other sections of society and that they tend to be more supportive of greater openness, which, it is also assumed, will raise incomes generally as a result of efficiency gains.

Even accepting that some increase in inequality is probably unavoidable in the process of raising domestic savings and providing incentives to invest, any resulting distribution of incomes and wealth must be seen to be legitimate and socially acceptable. What is acceptable will vary from society to society, but a crucial factor is whether the prevailing distribution is seen to benefit society as a whole through what Keynes (1919:16) identified as "some continuous improvement

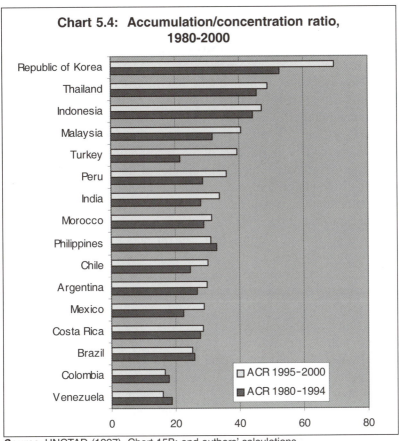

Chart 5.4: Accumulation/concentration ratio, 1980-2000

Source: UNCTAD (1997), Chart 15B; and authors' calculations.
Note: The ratio of the share of private investment in GDP to the share of the richest quintile of the population in total income. As income-distribution data are only available for individual years at varying intervals, the data for the two periods refer to different individual years, or to the average of a subset of years within each of the two periods.

in the daily conditions of life of the mass of population" and espe-cially its poorest members. Making this assessment means, as Keynes recognised, taking a much closer look at how the richest strata earn their income than is common among market fundamentalists. This is because investment in market-based economies depends not simply on the availability and efficient use of savings, but also on the spend-ing habits of the rich. This, of course, picks up a very classical theme, where each functional income category defines a particular socio-economic class, from which it follows that capital accumulation is financed to a large degree out of profits rather than household savings. The profit-investment nexus is discussed in more detail in the next chapter.

However, there is little doubt that the extent to which the rich save and invest their incomes in productive assets varies considerably among countries and plays a key role in relative economic performance. Chart 5.4, which presents the ratio of the share of private investment in GDP to the share of the richest quintile in total income, offers an (admittedly imperfect) indicator of the extent to which the rich, in different developing countries, spend their incomes on investment rather than personal consumption, or of what Keynes called their "animal spirits". Productive investment on a sufficient scale acts like a tax on profits, restricting their use for personal consumption. It thereby provides both a social and an economic justification for concentrating a large proportion of national income in the hands of a small minority.[16] As has been repeatedly emphasised in previous chapters, examining these links is key to understanding the successful development strategies adopted in East Asia, which deployed selective import controls, taxed luxury consumption, targeted credits and fiscal subsidies, fostered close relations between government, business and finance, and strategically managed foreign investment in an effort to boost savings, profits and fixed investment.

Given the steady rise in the minimum scale of investment needed to launch and maintain an industrialisation drive, there can be little doubt that the very fast pace of capital accumulation that characterised Japanese development in the 1950s and 1960s, the Korean experience in the 1960s and 1970s and the Chinese take-off in the 1980s and 1990s – as well as some ephemeral success stories such as Brazil in the 1960s and 1970s – will need to become a much more central feature of the development landscape, with an attendant flourishing of "animal spirits" among entrepreneurial elites. Since the debt crisis of the 1980s, the balance in all regions has shifted towards private

---

[16] As such, this is consistent with one of the conditions required to satisfy the "difference principle" of John Rawls' theory of justice. The other condition is that social and economic inequalities should be "attached to offices and positions open to all" (Rawls, 2001).

Chart 5.5: Public and private domestic investment and FDI in selected groups of developing countries, 1981-99
(per cent of GDP)

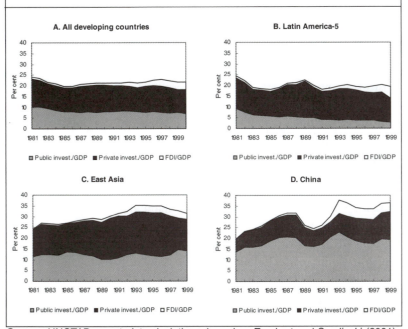

Source: UNCTAD secretariat calculations, based on Everhart and Sumlinski (2001); UNCTAD, *World Investment Report, 2002*; and World Bank, *World Development Indicators, 2002*.
Note: Latin America-5 comprises Argentina, Brazil, Chile, Colombia and Mexico. East Asia comprises Indonesia, Malaysia, the Philippines, the Republic of Korea and Thailand. Percentage shares are weighted averages of the values for these countries. Private investment is defined as total gross domestic investment (from national accounts) less consolidated public investment and FDI inflows.

investment, including by foreign corporations (Chart 5.5). However, the pre-crisis peak was not surpassed in the developing countries as a whole until 1996, albeit somewhat earlier in East Asia, later in Latin America and not at all in Sub-Saharan Africa. Moreover, the influence on the aggregate trend of China, where the share of private investment rose from under 4 per cent of GDP in 1980 to 17 per cent in 2000, again distorts the overall picture for developing countries. In contrast, the declining share of public investment after the debt crisis has been persistent in most developing regions, from an average of over 10 per cent in the early 1980s to 7 per cent by 2000.

While a central assumption of structural adjustment programmes is the greater efficiency of private investment, with significant improvements in the investment climate therefore expected from downsizing the public sector, evidence in support of this crowding-in hypothesis is hardly conclusive.[17] A simple exercise of within-country correlations between public and private investment found an almost even split between episodes of crowding-in and crowding-out in 63 developing countries for the period 1970 to 2000. Public investment in communications and transport, however, did appear to consistently stimulate private investment.[18] Repeating the exercise for the period 1985-2000 shows little change, four countries (Papua New Guinea, Thailand, Tunisia and Uruguay) shifting from crowding-in to crowding-out and two (Chile and Brazil) moving in the opposite direction. Many of the countries that maintained a high rate of investment after the debt crisis also had stable or rising shares of public investment in total income together with a crowding-in of private investment. This was the case in Chile, China, Korea, Malaysia and Mauritius, all success stories of the past 20 years or more. In contrast, the sharply declining trend in public investment across much of Latin America since the debt crisis appears to be associated with deindustrialisation (see next section), and in the countries of Sub-Saharan Africa the same trend is closely tied to the weak performance of agriculture and the slow pace of diversification.

Outside East Asia, trends since the debt crisis belie the claim that the policy changes of the past two decades have been good for capital formation. In many countries, the investment pause of the 1980s continued in the 1990s, or was followed, at best, by weak recoveries. These have failed to reach earlier peaks (Chart 5.6) and, by and large, have failed to cross the thresholds needed for strong and sustainable growth (UNCTAD, 2003a; ECLAC, 2000).

---

[17]   The difficulty of interpreting trends is typified by a recent study of Latin America during the period 1983-93, which at the same time found a positive association between public investment and economic growth, evidence that public investment crowds out private investment, due to inefficient state-owned enterprises and public trust funds substituting for private investment, and a significantly negative impact of defence expenditures on private investment (Ramirez and Nazmi, 2003).

[18]   Everhart and Sumlinski (2001:Tables 2.2 and 2.3) and World Bank (2003a:104).

The previous chapter suggested that the advocates of neo-liberal reforms have often oversold the contribution of FDI to development, with insufficient attention paid to its costs and an exaggeration of its benefits. In this respect, the tendency to associate a healthy investment climate with measures to attract more FDI is particularly misleading, with significant differences at the country and regional levels between trends in gross domestic fixed capital formation and FDI (see Chart 4.4). As noted in the last chapter, not only is FDI a heterogeneous mix of cross-border flows with potentially very different spillovers, but it can take place at the expense of domestic capital formation if it displaces domestic producers or pre-empts their investment opportunities. One study of 32 developing countries between 1970 and 1996 found the strongest evidence of crowding-out in Latin America, whereas in Asia crowding-in was stronger, and in Africa the effect was neutral (Agosin and Mayer, 2000). In a more comprehensive study of 98 developing countries between 1980 and 1999, a significant relation between FDI and domestic investment was detected in 52 countries, with 29 experiencing net crowding-out and 23

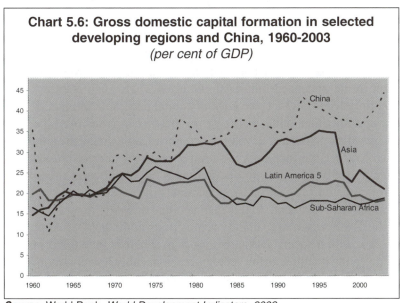

Chart 5.6: Gross domestic capital formation in selected developing regions and China, 1960-2003
(per cent of GDP)

Source: World Bank, *World Development Indicators, 2002.*
Note: Latin America 5 comprises Argentina, Brazil, Chile, Colombia and Mexico; Sub-Saharan Africa excludes South Africa.

crowding-in, with Latin American countries again proving most vulnerable to crowding-out (Nagesh and Pradhan, 2002). A study by Ghosh (2004) finds a stronger tendency for crowding-out by FDI in the period 1990-97 compared with earlier years, a change that may reflect the growing share of FDI being devoted to M&A (Mody and Murshid, 2002).

Comparing the crowding-in and -out effects for both public and foreign direct investment is revealing. A crowding-in of domestic private investment is most likely in Asia, particularly in Korea, Thailand and Bangladesh, but less so in China and Malaysia, where the FDI coefficient is neutral. Conversely, both public and foreign investments appear to crowd out private domestic investment in a large number of Latin American countries. On this evidence, the number of countries where a structural adjustment programme might have given a strong impulse to the investment process, through a combination of increased FDI and lower public investment, appears to be quite small.

It was suggested in Chapter 3 that the kinds of linkage established between industrial and financial capital are likely to have a bearing on the composition of investment and that these have almost certainly changed significantly under neo-liberal policy reforms. Such reforms have usually been defended on the grounds that they help unleash the "animal spirits" of entrepreneurs that had been restrained by the dirigiste leash of post-war statist regimes. This was the argument in the advanced industrial countries where such reforms were first introduced. In fact, the pace of capital accumulation has slowed down, sometimes quite markedly, in these economies over the past two decades.[19] In many developing countries, adjustment programmes have led to large increases in nominal and real interest rates which have not only added to production costs but also biased the investment climate in favour of financial assets over restructuring through productive investment. In this manner, the Latin American FDI boom in the 1990s was dominated by acquisitions in the public and private sectors, with a strong service-sector bias, whereas greenfield investments in the manufacturing sector were noticeably less common. The impact of higher financing costs also tended to be greater for firms in

---

[19]   The growth of the US capital stock did pick up strongly from 1992, although even at its peak in 2000 it did not reach the peaks of the 1960s or 1970s.

the export sector which face strong competition on world markets, whereas the non-tradeable sectors, usually operating in oligopolistic markets, could more easily raise prices to compensate for the higher cost of capital. At the same time it was difficult to offset the impact on exports with devaluation, for fear of triggering capital flight and an inflationary spiral. Indeed, in many cases appreciating exchange rates further weakened the investment-export nexus.

A common feature of weak investment regimes in the 1980s was a sharp rise in the share of residential construction in total investment, reflecting a diminished expectation of profits in more productive activities, particularly in tradeable goods, during and immediately after the debt crisis. In Latin America, only in Chile and Costa Rica, where there were strong investment recoveries in the second half of the 1980s, did the share of residential construction remain relatively low throughout the decade. In countries where the recovery of investment was delayed until the 1990s, there was often a large increase in residential construction. Across Latin America, with the exception of Chile, Costa Rica and Bolivia, residential construction was the strongest component of investment in the 1990s. This was particularly pronounced in Argentina, where it rose steadily to 45 per cent of gross fixed capital formation by 1997-98. The trend, although not absent, was less apparent in those countries, mainly in East Asia, where investment remained resilient after the debt crisis.[20] In these cases, however, the fact that construction was no more pronounced, and usually less so in the 1990s, than the other components of investment, suggests that over-investment was a more general response to mounting competitive pressures in a more liberal policy environment characterised by excessive capital inflows (UNCTAD, 2000c).

In contrast to acquisitions or residential housing, investment in machinery and equipment is generally recognised as central to a vibrant investment regime and a key source of sustained productivity growth, particularly in the initial stages of development (de Long and Summers, 1991). Indeed, the combination of a rising share of such

---

[20] This was the case, for example, in both Korea and Thailand, where residential construction peaked (in the early 1990s) at close to 25 per cent of gross fixed capital formation. The declining incremental capital output ratio in East Asia in the first half of the 1990s (World Bank, 2000a) is probably explained by this trend.

investment, together with expanding non-residential construction, particularly in physical infrastructure (much of which is likely to be in the public sector), would seem to be the defining features of a strong development-oriented investment performance. Certainly in many developing countries with a declining share of total investment in the 1980s, the share of investment in machinery and equipment was also declining, and while productivity improved during the punc-tuated recoveries in the 1990s, mainly because of large cuts in em-ployment, a strong and sustained recovery of investment failed to materialise.

These trends in capital formation over the past two decades re-flect the complexity of the decision to commit investible resources to future wealth creation. However, they give little support to the notion that a standard package of austerity, liberalisation and deregulation measures has been any more successful in reviving investment in developing countries than it has in more advanced countries (Glyn, 2006).

D.   Deindustrialisation and enclave development

Capital accumulation can help raise per capita incomes by al-lowing a fuller use of underutilised labour and natural resources with-out altering underlying efficiency. Longer-term economic success, however, depends on sustained improvements in productivity; on some assessments, economic miracles hinge on little else (Baumol et al., 1991). Here again, the consensus of opinion seems to give a key role to capital accumulation, particularly through its close links to techno-logical change and the evolving structure of economic activity.

The broad sweep of historical evidence certainly suggests a close relationship between a rising share of industrial employment, rapid growth rates of industrial output and productivity, vibrant market de-mand and a diversified trading profile. This is almost certainly what triggered the major 19th-century divergence, and these same forces, when working in tandem, are what carry a country to an income level consistent with a state of economic maturity.[21] We have already in-

---

[21]   See UNCTAD (2003a), Rowthorn and Wells (1987), Imbs and Wacziarg (2000).

sisted on the existence of a diversity of successful industrialisation paths, reflecting differences in natural-resource endowments, country size and geographical location, all of which are independent of policy action. Structural change is also the product of policy and institutional reform. Indeed, managing such change is what distinguishes success stories in the 19th century and in the period since 1945 (Adelman, 2000). Perhaps the main point that needs to be stressed is that successful industrial development opens up a world of cumulative and interdependent causation between growth in productivity, growth in employment and growth in output. Moreover, this pattern of development has traditionally had a strong spatial dimension linked to the growth of the urban economy, where supply- and demand-side externalities add to the growth dynamic. We shall return to this in greater detail in the next chapter.

In the past two decades or so, the East and South-East Asian NIEs have continued to industrialise at a rapid pace and to upgrade to higher skill and technology sectors, with some first-tier NIEs already close to industrial maturity or entering a phase of "positive deindustrialisation" where the service sector begins to absorb a sharply increasing share of the labour force (Rowthorn and Ramaswamy, 1999). As was noted in earlier chapters, the second-tier Asian NIEs have also been moving along this path, albeit less surely and with a less diversified industrial profile. In part, this appears to reflect a longer period of dependence on natural resources in the early stages of development and a greater reliance on FDI for their industrialisation (Jomo et al., 1997). Their progress contrasts sharply with many Latin American and Sub-Saharan African countries that appear to be undergoing "premature" deindustrialisation, in terms of declining shares of industry in total employment and output, at a level of income well below that associated with maturity and before passing through the more complex stages of diversification. Much of this has been policy-induced. Albert Hirschman (1987:163-66) observed this to be the case in Chile and Argentina in the early 1980s, where deindustrialisation resulted from a cocktail of misguided neo-liberal policies, including a shock reduction in tariff protection and a radical monetary experiment aimed at rapidly squeezing inflation out of the system. The resulting overvaluation of the currency and high domestic interest rates squeezed profits, particularly in traditional consumer-goods indus-

Table 5.4: Manufacturing output as a share of GDP, by region, 1960-2000
(per cent)

Region	1960	1970	1980	1990	2000
Sub-Saharan Africa	15.3	17.8	17.4	14.9	14.9
West Asia and North Africa	10.9	12.2	10.1	15.6	14.2
Latin America	28.1	26.8	28.2	25.0	17.8
Southern Cone	32.2	29.8	31.7	27.7	17.3
South Asia	13.8	14.5	17.4	18.0	15.7
East Asia (excl. China)	14.6	20.6	25.4	26.8	27.0
First-tier NIEs	16.3	24.2	29.6	28.4	26.2
China	23.7	30.1	40.6	33.0	34.5
Developing countries	21.5	22.3	24.7	24.4	22.7
Developed countries	28.9	28.3	24.5	22.1	18.9

Sources: UNCTAD secretariat calculations, based on data for manufacturing output and GDP at current prices from World Bank (2003a) and UNCTAD (2003a); and Government Statistical System of the Republic of China, online.
Note: Sub-Saharan Africa includes Benin, Botswana, Burkina Faso, Cameroon, Central African Republic, Chad, Congo, Côte d'Ivoire, Democratic Republic of the Congo, Gabon, Ghana, Kenya, Lesotho, Malawi, Mauritania, Mauritius, Niger, Nigeria, Rwanda, Senegal, South Africa, Togo, Zambia and Zimbabwe; West Asia and North Africa includes Algeria, Egypt, Morocco, Oman, Saudi Arabia, Tunisia and Turkey; Latin America includes the Southern Cone countries and Colombia, Costa Rica, Dominican Republic, Ecuador, El Salvador, Guatemala, Honduras, Jamaica, Mexico, Nicaragua, Panama, Paraguay and Peru; Southern Cone here includes Argentina, Brazil, Chile and Uruguay; South Asia includes Bangladesh, India, Pakistan and Sri Lanka; East Asia includes Hong Kong (China), Indonesia, Malaysia, the Philippines, the Republic of Korea, Singapore, Taiwan Province of China and Thailand.

tries and among smaller enterprises, even as borrowing abroad became attractive for larger resource-based firms.

The pattern seems to have become more widespread in the 1990s following the adoption of the Brady Plan, which led to policy-making in much of Latin America being narrowly focused on reducing the debt burden and satisfying the demands of the international financial markets (Table 5.4). Emphasis continued to be placed on price stability, through exchange-rate stabilisation and tight control of the

	Manufacturing value added as a share of GDP[1]				Exports of manufactures as a share of merchandise exports[2]		
	1970-79	1980-89	1990-99	2000-03	1980-89	1990-99	2000-04
Argentina	34.9	29.4	18.5	17.9	24.6	32.1	30.3
Bolivia	13.1	13.3	16.1	13.1	2.8	18.6	18.1
Brazil	27.6	31.1	22.1	20.6	50.4	54.2	53.4
Chile	15.7	15.0	17.4	18.0	11.0	13.6	15.1
Ecuador[3]	17.8	19.3	14.0	6.7	2.0	6.9	9.1
Mexico[4]	16.4	19.9	18.8	17.4	52.0	77.8	82.7
Peru	14.3	15.0	15.6	14.6	15.3	16.1	17.0
Uruguay	24.7	26.7	21.0	17.3	45.9	46.0	41.5
Venezuela[5]	18.1	20.0	17.2	12.0	12.6	12.5	11.2
Indonesia	9.4	15.2	23.7	25.1	13.0	47.5	54.8
Malaysia	17.3	21.0	27.0	31.2	33.1	73.3	78.2
Philippines	25.7	25.0	23.3	22.9	28.2	71.4	91.1
Rep. of Korea	18.2	24.1	24.4	24.4	91.8	90.1	90.9
Taiwan, China	33.5	36.8	29.6	26.0	90.8	93.6	94.0
Thailand	19.2	22.8	24.8	29.0	43.1	71.1	75.3
Côte d'Ivoire	12.8	13.5	19.0	18.2	12.1	14.9	19.7
Egypt[6]	15.5	14.9	17.0	18.8	21.2	37.0	29.0
Kenya	10.4	10.4	9.4	11.4	13.2	26.7	22.5
Morocco	16.7	17.9	17.6	17.0	40.5	56.5	65.8
China	..	..	..	..	61.8	83.5	90.1
India	14.0	14.8	15.0	14.6	61.4	74.2	75.7
Turkey	16.5	20.2	21.2	20.0	56.0	73.9	83.8

Sources: UNCTAD secretariat calculations, based on the UNCTAD Handbook of Statistics 2005, Table 4.1; the United Nations Statistics Department; and WTO estimates.

[1] Manufacturing corresponds to ISIC Rev.3 code D.
[2] SITC Revision 2. Manufactures comprise SITC sections 5 to 8 excluding 68 (non-ferrous metals).
[3] Ecuador, 1970-79: Manufacturing excludes petroleum refining.
[4] Mexico, 1988-2003: Basic petroleum manufacturing is included in mining and quarrying.
[5] Venezuela, 1970-97: Manufacturing includes petroleum refining.
[6] Egypt, 1996: Manufacturing includes non-petroleum mining activities.

money supply, but with privatisation, attracting FDI and opening the capital account assuming a more prominent role. This policy mix succeeded in attracting foreign capital, thus fending off balance-of-payments crises, even as rising domestic asset prices added to incomes and consumer demand. The result was an appreciation of the real exchange rate (due to price stickiness, nominal appreciation or both) and persistently high interest rates; both were higher and more volatile in Latin America in the 1990s than in the past or in relation to competitors (UNCTAD, 2003a:134-35). At the same time, restrictive fiscal policies accompanied rising debt-servicing obligations as governments refinanced and issued new debt to meet the increased demands of interest payments on government expenditure. This was hardly an economic environment conducive to the expansion of domestic industry. Nor, as we have insisted in previous chapters, does a more outward-oriented strategy (whether defined in terms of exports or attracting FDI) automatically establish a more dynamic growth path. Indeed, the combination of a declining share of manufacturing value added and a rising share of manufactured exports has been a common pattern in many countries (Table 5.5).

In some cases in Latin America, and as was already apparent in the Southern Cone crisis of the late 1970s, there has been a reversion to primary exports or resource-based industries, often with a strong FDI presence; in other cases, a generally weaker industrial performance has been consistent with the emergence of pockets of industrial excellence including some in medium- and higher-skill activities, such as chemicals and transportation, which have been able to build on earlier episodes of industrialisation based on import substitution. Particularly in countries neighbouring the United States, restructuring has occurred through an expanding *maquiladora* sector, where the strong growth of exports was highly import-intensive and dependent on low wage costs. But all too often, surging imports have been accompanied by a hollowing out of dynamic middle-ranking industries, such as metalworking, which have traditionally been pivotal in building strong backward and forward linkages across a range of sectors. In general, this deindustrialisation trend in Latin America has taken place in the presence of a marked slowdown in economic growth and a weak productivity performance.[22]

Sub-Saharan Africa has exhibited some of the same tendencies, albeit starting from a much lower base. The share of manufacturing output in GDP dropped sharply in SSA between 1980 and 1990 before stalling at a level below that in 1960 (UNCTAD, 2003a). Moreover, between 1980 and 2000 per capita manufacturing output fell in SSA. In 1980, there were seven countries in SSA with a level of per capita manufacturing output comparable to, and often higher than, Thailand, but by 2002 all of them except Mauritius had been overtaken. Various studies have traced this development to the sharp slowdown of output growth under adjustment programmes. Stein (1992) provided an early assessment along these lines, while later studies by UNCTAD (1998) and by Noorbakhsh and Paloni (1999) found signs of a deteriorating industrial performance in SSA countries undergoing structural adjustment, beginning in the mid-1980s but becoming more apparent in the early 1990s when investment, productivity and technology indicators all pointed to a sharp deterioration. A more recent study of African "deindustrialisation" by Thirlwall (2004) confirms this finding for the period 1980-96, with a cumulative decline in industrial productivity of 50 per cent. This study also reports that those African countries that managed to maintain some industrial dynamism tended to have a more rapid rate of total output growth as well as a stronger balance of payments. Moreover, these and other studies show that differences in productivity and export performance in the industrial sector explain much of the variance in growth rates within Africa in the period following the debt crisis.[23]

---

[22]   The empirical evidence suggests that successful development is characterised by eventual deindustrialisation and a move towards concentration on fewer sectors, with empirical studies finding that both tendencies occur at a level of per capita income of around $9,000; see Rowthorn and Wells (1987) and Imbs and Wacziarg (2000). Deindustrialisation as such is a "natural" product of success in the advanced industrial economies in a context of strong productivity growth in manufacturing, full employment and rapid output growth.

[23]   See Pieper (2000) and Thirlwall (2004).

In many developing countries, and regardless of their income levels, the combined impact of slow growth, deindustrialisation and informalisation has resulted in growing urban poverty, and what one observer has described as an "urban climacteric" whereby urbanisation has been "radically decoupled" from industrialisation, and even from development:

> ...in Sub-Saharan Africa, Latin America, the Middle East and parts of Asia, urbanisation without growth is more obviously the legacy of a global political conjuncture – the debt crisis of the late 1970s and the subsequent IMF restructuring of Third World economies in the 1980s – than an iron law of advancing technology. Third World urbanisation, moreover, continued its breakneck pace (3.8 per cent from 1960-93) through the locust years of the 1980s and early 1990s in spite of falling real wages, soaring prices and skyrocketing urban unemployment (Davis, 2004:9).

But just as troubling, in predominantly agricultural economies (such as those in much of SSA) where neo-liberal policies were promoted as the way to rebalance decades of distortionary policies against the rural sector – bringing farmgate prices into line with market prices, by reducing the fiscal burden on agriculture and, thereby, stimulating a more diversified rural economy – in practice they have proved particularly insensitive to the production, environmental and market conditions associated with specific crops (Karshenas, 2001). Moreover, given its dependence on appropriate public investment, both tailored to the rural economy (such as transportation) and more generally (such as communications infrastructure), private investment in agriculture has been further damaged by the rolling back of the public sector. In fact the growth of agricultural output in SSA has actually been slower than that of manufacturing industry over the past two decades. This is not altogether surprising given that raising agricultural productivity is perhaps even more sensitive to investment, including in transport and other areas of public-sector infrastructure, and building closer links with the food-processing industry and other parts of the fledgling industrial sector. Such inter-sectoral linkages are unlikely to emerge under conditions of deindustrialisation and tight macroeconomic policies; indeed, without the stimulus from a dynamic urban economy, there is unlikely to be any steady advance in agricultural productivity.

In countries that have failed to establish a strong pattern of internal economic integration, the combination of geographical, historical and structural legacies tends to attract FDI only to enclaves of export-oriented primary production, using a good deal of imported technology and with limited linkages to the rest of the economy. This pattern of insertion into the global economy is of long standing in commodity-exporting economies and, as we saw in the previous chapter, persistent. But we also suggested that a similar process describes manufacturing activity in the context of international production networks and in all developing regions. The dynamics of these networks were discussed in Chapter 4 in terms of both growing competition among countries leading to a fallacy of composition and countries getting stuck with technologically weak and import-dependent activities. These factors can inhibit the development of domestic supply capabilities and increase the risk of the host country getting locked into a position in the international division of labour that is dependent on low-wage labour.

Various writers have identified the rise of enclave production in developing countries with a "race to the bottom" in which excessive competition results in the under-pricing of existing (economic, social, political and environmental) assets in a scramble for quick returns. Certainly, there have been clear signs of this tendency in Africa in recent years (UNCTAD, 2005a) and its pernicious effects on investment and growth are well known. However, in the absence of comprehensive input-output tables, the wider significance of enclave production can only be indirectly gauged by the extent to which a country's GDP (a measure of the value of output generated within national boundaries) is higher than its GNP (a measure of the income actually earned by national citizens), by a high ratio of export earnings to domestic value added, and by the presence of a large informal economy (Todaro, 1983:357). Enclave economies also tend to exhibit periodic profit surges, often well in excess of FDI inflows. On all these measures, there are plenty of signs that enclave development has become an endemic feature of the neo-liberal development experience.[24] The example of Mexico, often presented as a neo-liberal success, is particularly telling. Mexico enjoyed large inflows of FDI (in the 1990s it was the third largest recipient after China and Hong Kong), relatively unrestricted access to developed-country markets (thanks largely to its membership of NAFTA) which helped to raise the share of non-oil exports in total GDP, and improved governance (as symbolised by its becoming a member of the OECD). Despite all this, the external engines of growth appear to have been largely disconnected from the domestic economy.

E.   Conclusions

In the opening chapter we quoted Tony Blair's homily on market-led economic success and the irrelevance of debating whether or not globalisation was moving in the right direction. In fact, as is clear from his, and other like-minded, remarks, attributing such success hinges on the performance of just one (very big) economy, China. Leaving aside the point that western commentators never refer to this as a (Communist) Party-led success story, on the evidence of this and the previous chapters we believe that the need for discussing alternatives is more important than ever, particularly in many developing countries, where a quarter-century of neo-liberal policy reform has failed to deliver in terms of growth performance, employment creation (particularly in the formal industrial sector), capital formation and poverty reduction. Before picking up this thread in the following chapters, we conclude here by reflecting on why, contrary to the insistence of market fundamentalists, international market forces over the past two decades appear to have contributed to such a highly uneven pattern of development, including the persistence and, it appears, the intensification of inequalities among and within countries.

It is important to stress again that competitive markets do not arise in nature through some form of asocial parthenogenesis or as

---

[24]   For a recent discussion of the persistence of enclavism in the African context, see UNCTAD (2005b).

the default position of social organisation. Markets are above all social constructs and, as Adam Smith recognised, can never be disembodied from the political, social and legal structures from which they arise. This means that markets are always managed, most fundamentally by the values and social constraints of the society in which they operate and which are reflected in the structure of incentives which bestow approval on certain types of activity and behaviour and discourage others. This is a much larger point than simply claiming that markets are invariably imperfect, which they are, because of overpowerful economic actors, asymmetric and imperfect information, and so on. Insofar as price signals emerge from an institutional framework that incorporates a prior set of social values and preferences, it follows that there will be no single, ideal market structure that will generate optimal outcomes for all the population groups participating in the international economy. The varieties of capitalism, for example, both in its evolution over time and at any given period in time, are rooted in the variegated institutional expressions of such different preferences and values. The revival of interest among economists in the institutional foundations of market structures is a positive development, but this will be counter-productive if all it leads to is the promotion of a single institutional structure for all in place of a single economic policy for all. The rejection of one model for all has to be the starting point for any serious discussion of the failed policies of the last two-and-a-half decades, not simply to take account of different local and initial conditions but also to respect different social preferences.

A second point is that market forces are not pre-programmed to generate stable equilibria, let alone social harmony, but rather tend to be caught up in processes of cumulative causation which can certainly give rise to rising (and widely shared) incomes but can just as easily confine communities and countries to a low-growth path where the scramble to augment private returns comes at the expense of larger social returns and where rent-seeking takes on more destructive forms. A major difficulty with relying solely on market forces to achieve development is that, in a world of dynamic scale economies, those who are first in the field have an advantage over those who lag behind at the starting post. First-mover advantages can be squandered, but they are certainly an advantage and, if successfully exploited, can be increased and passed on to the next generation of entrepreneurs, companies and individuals; but this is a process that also contributes to raising the threshold investment requirements for newcomers. Catching up is therefore a problem of creating and/or acquiring ownership of capital stocks, which is not an easy task for those who lag behind or start from scratch.

As we have argued already, the principal vectors of globalisation – liberalised trade and capital markets and the spread of internationalised production – have not generally worked in the direction of a significant redistribution of the global stocks of productive capital. International trade and foreign capital movements remain largely dominated by transactions among the already-rich countries. FDI rarely flows to the poorest countries where economic growth and accumulation have failed to take off or remain weak and uncertain. By definition, FDI means that ownership of the capital assets remains in foreign hands and so the initial returns will accrue to them. The key test of FDI as a contributing force for sustainable development and a reduction in income inequalities is therefore whether it has a positive, catalytic effect on domestic investment. The evidence on this, as we have seen, is very mixed, and where liberalisation policies have been most energetically pursued, the effect is often negative. Moreover, we have also shown that although FDI can incorporate a developing country into internationally integrated production chains, it often confines it to those functions requiring unskilled labour, often the assembly of imported components. In principle, this is not necessarily a bad place to start, but if the backward linkages to the domestic economy are weak or non-existent, and the evidence suggests this is usually the case, FDI will not contribute to a reduction of inter-country inequalities and is likely to exacerbate income differences within the host country. The finding that despite a rising share of world exports of manufactures, the developing countries' share of global value added (i.e., gross factor incomes) in manufacturing has been falling points to FDI as widening rather than narrowing the income gap between the rich and the poor. In other words, the economic benefits of a more dispersed and specialised international division of labour have tended to accrue disproportionately to the foreign owners of capital.

Finally, markets can be a major source of failures and shocks. That markets fail should no longer be taken as a deviant line of thinking: the record of under-regulated financial markets speaks for itself. Shocks can be transmitted by cross-border flows of technology and trade but also by premature liberalisation. The severity of any post-liberalisation shock will depend on how far domestic output, employment and relative prices have to change in response to the new competitive pressures from abroad, and that in turn will partly depend on the degree of outward orientation achieved prior to the shock. But in the end, just how far freer trade and market forces can be allowed to determine the levels and structures of production and consumption is a political question of whether governments are able and willing to intervene in order to handle adjustment costs and distribution issues. This helps to explain why, historically, more liberal trade policies in the present developed countries invariably followed rather than preceded development. In general, the historical record provides little evidence that trade policy in itself has any significant independent effect on the pace of economic growth and development. The basic lessons we draw from the Asian model of development is that the mobilisation of domestic fixed investment is the basis of successful industrialisation and that integration with the global economy needs to be approached gradually, strategically, and in line with local conditions and preferences.

If, as we have argued, the world economy is permeated by processes of circular and cumulative causation, it would in fact be surprising to expect a reduction of income inequalities, within and between countries, to come about as a result of market liberalisation *unless* it also leads to a marked acceleration in the rate of capital investment, in both physical and human assets, in the poorer countries. In a market economy, income accrues to those who possess and have secure title to such assets and the distribution of endowments helps to explain the distribution of incomes.[25] Reducing inequality is

---

[25] Human capital should be interpreted broadly to include not only the possession of skills and a good education but also all the other factors, including good health, that enable individuals to function effectively in society. Privileged positions, in violation of the Rawlsian principle of justice, should also be regarded as capital assets for those lucky enough to enjoy them.

thus in large measure a problem of increasing the capital endowments of the poorest countries and individuals. A key issue therefore is whether a more equal distribution of capital stocks is likely to emerge spontaneously as a result of market forces or whether it will require some form of intervention to get the process of accumulation under way in a sustained and productive manner. Market fundamentalists put their faith in spontaneity. The evidence suggests that this is misplaced.

Chapter 6

Towards an Alternative Framework for Development Strategies

A.   Introduction

THE economic record since the debt crisis of the early 1980s, as discussed in the previous chapter, is hardly a ringing endorsement of the neo-liberal agenda, and raises serious doubts about the "weight of evidence" so often cited by its supporters when faced with criticisms as to its damaging consequences for many poorer countries and communities. Such doubts have already forced some of those supporters to take more seriously the need to include social goals in development programmes, to place a greater emphasis on the role of institutions, and to give closer attention to the sequencing of reforms. Indeed, having "discovered" poverty in the course of the 1970s (under Robert McNamara) and then rejected it after the debt crisis (in favour of structural adjustment), the World Bank has now returned to "working for a world free of poverty". Nevertheless, the core policies for economic adjustment have survived largely unscathed.[1]

The adoption of those reforms in many developing countries followed a period in which unprecedented growth across the developing world, albeit subject to cycles of stop-go development and periodic balance-of-payments crises, had stalled, and policy makers were struggling to deal with the consequences of a series of sharp external shocks. From the late 1970s, restrictive macroeconomic policies in the advanced industrial countries provided the catalyst for turning

---

[1] For a critical self-assessment of the Bank's policies in the 1990s, see World Bank (2005a&b).

what might otherwise have been routine external payment crises and "slowdowns" across the developing world into "meltdowns" and an international debt crisis, particularly after international lending shuddered to a virtual halt following Mexico's decision to default in August 1982.[2] The crisis certainly exposed structural weaknesses in economies that had failed to find the right balance between domestic resource mobilisation, export orientation and foreign capital inflows. But the decisive factor in defining a new reform agenda in developing economies was the pressure for policy change brought to bear on them by the international development community, pressure that reflected a mixture of self-interest and ideological conviction that the developed countries had themselves now discovered the best route from economic stagnation to sustainable economic development.[3] More often than not, that new policy course was imposed on developing countries as a condition of extending various forms of economic assistance or of being admitted to certain international institutions, such as the OECD or the WTO or, in the case of the transition economies of Central Europe, the European Union. Albert Hirschman's (1987:184) description of the change in tone and tactics towards Latin America in the early 1980s captures the shift in approach:

> This is not the first time that the United States or multinational institutions, strongly influenced by the United States, have convinced themselves that they possess the key to progress and development for all those wayward, hence backward, foreign countries. In the fifties, the World Bank attempted to condition its lending on countries' establishing some form of overall economic planning. In the sixties, the Alliance for Progress strongly encouraged Latin

---

[2] See Ben-David and Papell (1995) for an initial attempt at dating "slowdowns" and "meltdowns" in the developing world. Arguably the first signs of an international debt crisis were seen in Poland a year earlier. For a useful discussion of the debt crisis and the role of the IMF, see IMF (2001). On the causes of the Mexican default and its aftermath, set against a broader historical background, see Marichal (1989).

[3] A number of heterodox responses to these weaknesses emerged in the late 1970s and early 1980s; see Hirschman (1987) for an assessment.

American countries to institute land and fiscal reforms – the latter then meaning stiffer taxes for the rich. But never have Latin Americans been lectured and admonished as insistently as in the eighties, this time along very different lines – on the virtues of free markets, privatisation, and foreign private investment, and on the perils of state guidance and intervention, as well as excessive taxation, not to mention planning. Moreover such lectures now claim a captured audience of top Latin American economic policy-makers, who must frequently make trips to Washington to renegotiate and reschedule the heavy debt burdens that most of their countries have accumulated during the seventies.

As Stiglitz (1998:21-22) has noted, the fact that a set of bold policy recommendations – "stabilise, liberalise and privatise" – could be distilled from a very sophisticated analytical framework, which, at the same time, appeared relatively easy to administer in practice and promised quick results, certainly helped to convert a new generation of international economic advisers and their local policy acolytes. The agenda often found domestic constituencies that either shared the same underlying ideology or were looking to use external pressures as a convenient cloak for furthering their own reform programmes (Vreeland, 2003). As Hirschman suggests, the seeds of a neo-liberal backlash had been sown by earlier policy advice. In the case of Latin America, for example, various domestic business groups were already pressing for the liberalisation of trade and finance in the 1970s, their arguments only becoming more persuasive following the debt crisis of the early 1980s, and more widely implemented at the end of the decade in the wake of the Brady Plan.[4] Moreover, the more

---

[4] Named after US Treasury Secretary Nicholas F. Brady, the Brady Plan, launched in March 1989, aimed for an orderly process of (market-friendly) debt reduction, through creditor banks agreeing voluntarily to reduce the value of their claims in return for guarantees on the remaining portion of the debt. To encourage the banks to accept debt reduction rather than hold out for the original amounts, the IMF and the World Bank were urged to guarantee new bonds issued by debtor countries in exchange for existing debt or to make loans to allow countries to buy back debt on the secondary market.

local elites shifted the locus of their economic interests from productive investment to financial assets (both domestic and foreign), and the more Finance Ministries became the focus for protecting those interests through "responsible" measures to keep inflation in check, reduce the risk of default and ensure the free flow of capital, the more such policies became "locally owned" and defended (Fitzgerald, 2002).

Nevertheless, as suggested in Chapter 1, the broad thrust of these policies tends to reflect the experience, interests and current concerns of the developed countries as much as the problems of poverty eradication, structural stagnation and lagging development. There are two major elements in this extrapolation of developed countries' policy perspectives to the less developed: one is the historical narrative which policy makers in the former believe provides a good description of how they reached their present position of economic superiority; the second concerns the restrictive assumptions, usually hidden or only implicit, in the economic theories on which they base their policy prescriptions for getting economic development under way. Following a review of why these elements do not provide an adequate basis for contemporary policy-making in the developing world, this chapter suggests an alternative framework around a number of interrelated concepts drawn from political economy, in particular those of cumulative and interdependent development, the profit-investment-export nexus, the developmental state and democratic gradualism.

B.   Myths, biases and simple assumptions

The appeal to history to underpin the presuppositions of current thinking about political institutions and economic policies in a globalising world has invariably involved some variation on what has been called the "Whig view of history" (Butterfield, 1931). This is the tendency, deliberate or unconscious, to document a steady and linear progression from an inferior past towards a superior present. While this may have a useful political role to play in providing narratives to support a sense of national identity and purpose in fledgling states or in times of crisis, as a vision of economic development it runs the very real risk of degenerating into what the philosopher Henri

Bergson once called "the illusions of retrospective determinism". Certainly, such illusions permeate much of the current debates on globalisation. An immediate consequence of this view of history is that by diminishing the variance of past experience it leaves out or glosses over awkward facts and, in doing so, suggests that the consequences of each intermediate step were anticipated, thereby claiming an excessive degree of rationality and foresight for the policies that accompanied the process of change. In this perspective, progress tends to be depicted as a polarised struggle, between modernisers and traditionalists, internationalists and nationalists, free-traders and protectionists, Keynesians and Monetarists, etc. This in turn casts the policy-making process in an overly simple light, diminishing the range of possible options that might be used to meet a particular goal, downplaying the trade-offs which characterise a healthy policy-making process in more open societies and excluding a learning dimension through which policy makers can improve on their decisions and actions.

A second damaging consequence of this use of history is to create a false sense of inevitable futures, not only for the countries whose histories are being described but also for those who wish, or are urged, to emulate them. Western politicians and policy makers see their values and institutions as universally applicable to all those seeking economic development and modernity, and so the key to the western past and present is also presented as the key to everyone else's future. The dangers of designing policies around externally conceived historical narratives are compounded for developing countries by the fact that changes to the storyline are likely to be made in response to the needs and challenges of the developed countries. Looking back from the 1960s, developments over the previous century could be viewed as being dominated by the spread of democracy, the rise of organised labour, the reduction of inequality and, in sum, the taming of the worst excesses of unbridled capitalism, culminating, after World War II, in the welfare state. As suggested earlier by Hirschman, something of this history marked early development policy advice and technical assistance programmes. Where Soviet influence was stronger, a different kind of narrative prevailed in which the ineluctable rise of the international proletariat, state ownership and central planning pointed the way to a more rational post-capitalist future.[5]

From the 1980s, however, western views of their economic history, especially in the United States and Britain, returned to a more traditional, and largely uncontested, late-19th-century narrative. This sees the industrial revolution and the path to modernity as a largely spontaneous movement by innovative entrepreneurs supported by private finance and subject to minimal interference by government. Low taxes, free trade and a general attitude of *laissez-faire* were the incontestable keys to success. In this perspective, the mixed economy, planning, progressive taxation and the welfare state were all seen as deviations from or obstacles to a "normal" path to economic success.[6] The advice for reforming moribund western economies in the 1980s and 1990s was therefore to "roll back the state", cut taxes, maintain strict monetary discipline, increase the flexibility of labour markets by removing generous state benefits for the poor and the unemployed, and generally to set the business sector free by reducing government interference in the workings of the market by liberalising international trade and finance as far and as quickly as possible.

It was out of these preoccupations with the state of the western economies (in the wake of rising labour militancy, the collapse of the Bretton Woods exchange-rate system and the oil shocks of the 1970s) that the basic package of current policy advice to developing countries, and to the Central European economies emerging from central

---

[5]   East-West ideological competition was a principal reason why intellectuals from the periphery played a prominent role in the rise of development economics in the decades following 1945 and were able to project a different set of historical experiences into wider economic policy debates. For a useful history of these developments, see Arndt (1987). The United Nations played an important role as an incubator and disseminator of a more pluralistic development policy agenda. Ironically, given the obsession of market fundamentalism with the virtues of unrestrained competition, such pluralism has been replaced since the collapse of communism by market triumphalism and ideological conformity in much of the current policy debates.

[6]   As suggested in Chapter 2, this narrative only really began to take shape in the emerging policy battles after World War I. An inspirational text for such histories among today's globalisation enthusiasts is Hayek (1944). For a contemporary critique of Hayek's extreme liberalism see Durbin (1945).

planning and Soviet domination after 1989, was formulated.[7] As Adelman (2000:50) summarises it, the resulting reform agenda rested on the contention that "the process of government-sponsored accelerated development had given rise to incorrect relative factor prices that did not reflect fundamental relative economic scarcities". In practice this meant transforming a series of specific concerns about the structure of price incentives in poorer countries into a blueprint for bringing their economic and political structures and their social norms and values into line with the requirements of unrestricted global market forces.[8] Such thinking gained technocratic respectability in the guise of the "Washington Consensus" on development policy. Although this was originally conceived in response to the macroeconomic imbalances that had emerged in Latin America during the 1970s, the call to stabilise, liberalise and privatise soon crystallised into a policy paradigm for guiding the expanding development mandates of the Bretton Woods institutions.[9]

---

[7] Most advanced economies had ended their use of multilateral finance in support of adjustment by the late 1970s. This in turn had major consequences for the workings of the international monetary system, particularly in redefining the role of the IMF and triggering an ideological and programmatic convergence with the World Bank; see Ahluwalia (1999:2-5) and Pauly (1997), who usefully locates this transformation in a longer history of international financial management.

[8] There had been a growing body of research inside the Bretton Woods institutions since the late 1960s which focused on the market-distorting impact of imprudent policy interventions in the areas of agriculture, trade and finance, research that was associated with the work of Schultz, Little, Scitovsky and Scott and McKinnon and Shaw respectively; for a useful history see Toye (1993). With particular reference to trade openness, Anne Krueger has described the agenda of "getting prices right" as a struggle among economists to reclaim the truth about markets from the narrow interest-group politics of bureaucrats and politicians (Krueger, 1997) and more generally to promote the view that government failures are always a greater obstacle to development than market failures (Krueger, 1990). It should be noted, however, that concern about imbalances in the economic structure of developing countries was not the preserve of neo-liberal economists at the end of the 1960s. At much the same time, the ILO was drawing attention to the employment biases of more capital-intensive industrialisation strategies.

[9] Despite this Latin American inflection, one of the earliest Washington Consensus texts was the World Bank's 1981 report on Africa, often referred to as the Berg Report after its senior author. Nevertheless, there were precedents, beginning with the debates on inflation in the 1950s, in the Southern Cone economic experiments of the 1970s, notably in Chile under General Pinochet, and in the IMF's dealings with Jamaica in the late 1970s.

Implicit in the programme was the idea that beneath the apparatus of the centrally planned economy or obscured by the interventionist policies of industrialisation based on import substitution, a fully fledged market economy was lying dormant awaiting the reviving forces of competition and free trade. As noted in the opening chapter, John Williamson, who originally coined the term, has subsequently described (and defended) the Washington Consensus as seeking to end an era of "global apartheid" during which the "right" pattern of prices and incentives for developing countries had been buried beneath a pile of ill-judged attempts to outsmart the market and rapidly build modern industrial economies (Williamson, 2002).[10]

All too often, however, such calls for clearing away the intellectual debris left by a half-century of nationalistic, statist and collectivist ideologies are accompanied by mythical accounts of global economic integration before 1914 (World Bank, 2002b:23-31). A number of the myths were exposed in Chapter 2. One of the principal pieces of current advice to developing countries, supposedly drawing on the globalisation experience before 1914, is that trade liberalisation is a powerful catalyst for economic growth and therefore they should open up their economies to international competition as quickly as possible. In fact, in the first wave of countries that set out to catch up with Britain's industrial revolution in the 19th century, few if any of them considered free trade as a serious policy option.[11] Generally this emerged only in the later stages of industrialisation when confidence in the ability of domestic industries to withstand, or preferably dominate, the pressures of international competition had been established. The strategies adopted by these countries in their attempts to meet the challenge of Britain's industrial power varied according to national conditions and perceptions, but none could be described as "rolling

---

[10] While Williamson's aim was to distil the most widely accepted policy principles, his own view was cautious about liberalising financial flows. However, as we have already pointed out, in a world where capital flows were fast becoming the principal force shaping global interdependence, technocrats were only one of the interested parties seeking to influence policy. In any case, a mechanical separation of the trade and financial spheres, as we have seen earlier, was difficult to maintain in practice for many countries as trade liberalisation opened up current-account deficits and TNCs became more prominent in their economies.

[11] Even for Britain, "all the figures suggest that... it was the success of British industries that caused exports to grow, not the success of British overseas trade that made industries grow" (Ogilvie, 2000:123).

back the state": all used a large variety of instruments to promote industrialisation (including general and targeted subsidies, tariffs, incentives, monopoly grants, quantitative restrictions, licensing, tax privileges and state-owned enterprises); most were closely engaged in building markets (through infrastructure development and government procurement); most also substituted for missing domestic factors (including through immigration of unskilled labour, investing in education, importing technology and ideas, and promoting financial intermediaries). Our own reading of these experiences is that the rapid expansion of trade before 1914 was less the product of trade policies narrowly defined and more a matter of creating a growth dynamic where investment, structural change, technological upgrading and exporting could become mutually and cumulatively reinforcing. As we noted in Chapter 3, and with due allowance for the specificities of time and place, a similar conclusion can be drawn from the recent experience of the East and South-East Asian NIEs.

The mainstream body of advice from western governments and international financial institutions to developing countries as to how they should set about improving their economic performance is coloured not only by historical myths about western economic progress but also by the exaggerated technocratic claims of much modern economics, which, for the most part, is rooted in the same (Victorian) mindset of progress through steady improvement, book-keeping accuracy and self-reliance (Heilbroner, 1980:130-61).

The idea that the market economy possessed certain general properties similar to those of the natural world, and that economics should therefore be regarded as a "science" on a par with the natural sciences, was of course part of the classical tradition. Adam Smith, strongly influenced by the views of Bacon and Newton, certainly saw parallels between the natural order and a well-organised civil society. More explicitly, Jean-Baptiste Say regarded the task of economics as elucidating the actual laws determining the creation, distribution and consumption of wealth and these were to be seen as essentially independent of social and political organisation (Fontaine, 1996). Thomas Malthus tied these same laws of economic life even more deterministically to biological reproduction. Karl Marx famously suggested he had discovered the laws of evolution of human society to match those discovered by Darwin for the natural world. But as Stedman

Jones (2004) has argued, this "classical" vision, far from being an intellectual precursor of *laissez-faire* individualism centred around the idea of a self-regulating market, is better understood as an attempt to forge a political discourse which could protect emerging commercial and industrial interests from the lingering resistance of a feudal, military and aristocratic past while fending off (or in Marx's case amplifying) new social threats of the kind that had already materialised in America and France.[12]

It took the marginalist revolution of the late 19th century to move the idea of a self-regulating market onto a new plane. It was Edgeworth, Jevons, Walras, Marshall and others who set about reducing social relations to a profit-and-loss calculus which could be captured in precise mathematical formulae. Theirs was a world of rational human beings whose calculated matching of ends and scarce means brought about stable and satisfactory outcomes for all through the maximisation or minimisation of strategic economic quantities, without resort to conflict or the need for government intervention. Growth was taken for granted and recurrent classical anxieties about technological unemployment, food shortages and economic crisis simply disappeared from their discourse. This "new economy" of the 19th century was a world of abundance and opportunity in which disorderly behaviour was kept firmly in check by the intertwined logic of profit (and utility) maximisation and diminishing returns. The idea of a competitive equilibrium, where each and every interest was satisfied to the fullest extent, became the central organising principle around which the workings of an autonomous economic sphere could be constructed (Milgate, 1987).[13]

---

[12] Indeed, as any passing familiarity with the four authors just mentioned would confirm, the classical view included a prominent place for conflict, struggle and crisis. There is also a parallel here in seeing Adam Smith as part of the 18th-century struggle against authoritarian and mercantilist rule, rather than as a precursor of 19th-century economic liberalism (and thence as a founding father of globalisation); Winch (1978) offers a clear interpretation of why the former is the more apt description.

[13] Albert Hirschman (1995:136) referred to this tendency amongst conventional economists to describe the social and economic world by means of a sober and transparent system of equations as "physics envy". This approach has contributed to the widespread view, especially among economists, that economics is the most "scientific" of the social sciences, an assessment that is based on its capacity to deduce testable propositions from a theory of general equilibrium in which rational individuals maximise utility and efficiency. The standing of economics as the only social science with Nobel status has only strengthened this perception.

It would be foolish to deny that the intellectual endeavour generated by this programme has made progress over the years: powerful concepts have been developed and empirical analysis, supported since 1945 by increasingly sophisticated statistical methods and abundant sources of data, has led to more rigorous testing of hypotheses. However, a fundamental problem with this framework when applied to development issues is, as John Hicks (1973) acknowledged in his Nobel lecture, that it is pre-programmed to find optimal outcomes among dispersed market participants, rather than seeking to understand why some nations are rich and others poor. Indeed, in a world where property rights are taken for granted, information is costless, and the main drivers of economic growth, capital, labour, technology, knowledge, etc., appear exogenously, *dei ex machina*, the idea of *continuous* and *cumulative* development is all but ruled out of the analysis.[14] As another Nobel laureate has put it:

> Neo-classical theory is simply an inappropriate tool to analyse and prescribe policies that will induce development. It is concerned with the operation of markets, not with how markets develop. How can one prescribe policies when one doesn't understand how economies develop? The very methods employed by neo-classical economists have dictated the subject matter and militated against such a development. That theory in the pristine form that gave it mathematical precision and elegance modelled a frictionless and static world. When applied to economic history and development it focused on technological development and more recently human capital investment, but ignored the incentive structure embodied in institutions that determined the extent of societal investment in those factors. In the analysis of economic performance through

---

[14] For a remarkably prescient and still relevant discussion of the issue of statics versus dynamics in economic analysis, see Harrod (1948:1-34). This is not, of course, to deny the efforts by more conventional economists to include time in their analysis, but rather to note that, by and large, it remains a mathematical parameter subordinate to the maximisation principle, an approach that has long worried economists such as Arrow, Hicks and Hahn. Hicks once remarked that while he could put time in his models he could not get his models into time.

time it contained two erroneous assumptions: one that institutions do not matter and two that time does not matter
(North, 1994:359).

Having reduced economic man to his simplest motivations, extracted institutions and expunged history, conventional economics not
surprisingly finds little time for the specificity of time and place.
Markets and the behaviour they inspire are as universal as they are
predictable. The only deviant actor in an otherwise immaculate market landscape is the state, whose visible hold on the reins of political
power brings with it an unpredictable and unwelcome element of blus-
ter and irrationality. Consequently, while politics as the art of government was treated as an exogenous variable as far as neo-classical
economics was concerned, for things to work properly, government
had to be firmly subordinated to the "natural" laws of economy, at
most occupying a "night-watchman" role responsible for delivering
the basic public goods needed to guarantee the market rules of the
game. We have already suggested in Chapter 2 just how far this view
deviates from the historical record of the 19th century. More generally, Polanyi (1944) has described how the emergence of national
markets was not a gradual or spontaneous emancipation of the economic sphere from government control, but rather the outcome of a
conscious and often violent intervention on the part of government
which imposed market organisation on society for a mixture of economic and non-economic ends.

Today's market fundamentalists, nevertheless, boldly carry their
brand of "revolutionary anarchism" (Hobsbawm, 1994:40) onto the
global stage, where they present a putative world economy as a self-
regulating market system unrestrained by "artificial" political boundaries, where undistorted price signals can be safely left to guide the
flow of goods, factors and technology to their most productive uses.
In such an economy all producers have access to the same technologies; there are no economies of scale; everybody is a price taker;
resources are fully employed; and adjustment costs are minimal or
non-existent. In this world, markets generate all the information necessary for rational decision-making and provide sufficient incentives
and penalties to ensure that individuals make the right choices to
maximise their welfare. Every player is an optimiser, untainted by

his or her past, with complete knowledge of current market circumstances and with fully rational expectations about what the future will bring.

Economists have long insisted that only through the severity of their abstractions can a clearer understanding of our complex reality be reached.[15] In practice, such fundamental real-world economic phenomena as large price-setting firms, increasing returns to scale and technological learning have proved difficult to introduce, at least without undermining the original abstract structure on which the "win-win" logic depends. A vast body of literature documenting when and how markets fail as one or another of the original assumptions is relaxed has, of course, been an important influence in expanding the domain of economic policy (Meade, 1975). But perhaps more importantly, in a world where initial conditions, historical processes and social institutions shape a country's growth experience, there can be no legitimacy in reverting to an idealised state as some higher authority against which to judge reality. Paul David (2000) has noted, rightly in our view, that restricting policy space on the basis of a set of propositions that were originally derived from a purely static and deterministic model is hardly convincing and, given its abstraction from history, highly misleading:

> The static framework of welfare analysis within which too many economists are still being taught to do their thinking tends to suppress the natural disposition to conceptualise the whole flow of current economic life as contingent upon the results of antecedent choices. Seen in truly historical perspective, a great deal of human ingenuity, especially the sort that is said to be "mothered by necessity", is devoted to trying to cope with "mistakes" that are threatening to become "serious" in their economic consequences; to assuring, somehow, that their more pernicious effects will be moderated, if not abated altogether. This is done *ex*

---

[15] Krugman (1994) provides a sterling defence of model-building with particular reference to development economics, a defence that is rebutted by Taylor (1994). On the attractions and limitations of building and testing mechanistic models among economists, see the excellent confessions of a one-time macro-modeller Paul Ormerod (1994).

post, by contriving technological "fixes" and "patches", by commandeering temporary task forces to handle emergencies that established organisational structures are discovered to be handling badly, by sustained efforts at "reforming" (not reinventing) long-standing institutions, and, yes, by concerted educational campaigns to un-train people who have acquired dysfunctional habits of one sort or another.

The process of abstraction and simplification, an intrinsic characteristic of any theory, does not mean that policy recommendations will not be highly sensitive to different assumptions and different social contexts.[16] It should be obvious to most observers that an economy, however organised, is part of a wider system of political and social organisation. This was certainly understood by Adam Smith and was also part and parcel of classical political economy which was concerned with the distribution of gains and losses accompanying technological progress and an increasingly fine division of labour, including its extension across national boundaries. Even before Marx made it a guiding principle in his analysis of capitalism, there was a general interest in how these tendencies eased or exacerbated class tensions. The need to place economic behaviour in a broad societal context was also well understood by the German historical school in the mid-19th century. Later, Vilfredo Pareto saw the economy as a part of a larger social structure and he tried to elucidate the dynamics of the system as a whole in which the competition and tension between conservative and radical forces played an important role. In the 20th century, institutional economists from Veblen to Galbraith have insisted that both the consumer and the private corporation are motivated by much more than calculations of profit and loss, that size

---

[16] Encouraged by the successes of, especially, microeconomics, and with more than a touch of hubris, a number of mainstream economists have applied their concepts and techniques to a wide range of social issues such as education, crime and punishment, family relations and discrimination (Lazear, 2000), but these are essentially narrow excursions into non-economic areas and do not amount to an analysis of the socio-economic system as a whole (Fine, 2000). The idea that following the method of natural science means abstracting from the complexity of society and constructing simple models of independent economic behaviour is itself a simplistic interpretation of how the natural sciences have progressed (Rose, 1997).

matters in shaping economic outcomes and that specific cultural practices and organisational characteristics give a distinct shape to national business systems. Keynes, Schumpeter and Polanyi, in their different ways, described how a self-regulating market society could eventually give rise to deeply disruptive strains, economic crises and social collapse.

From this heterodox perspective, institutions, the formal and informal codes of conduct, the social values and "moral sentiments" that govern and shape the system as a whole, all have a major influence on economic behaviour that is not simply instrumental. At the same time, economic developments, including the profit motive, the accumulation process and technical change, will in turn influence social and political behaviour and institutions. Social reality is thus inherently complex: not only is the economy itself constructed through interdependent relations both within and between nations but social and economic phenomena are interrelated and the economy is driven (and constrained) by more than economic variables. It follows that the transition from, say, a centrally planned to a market-based economy, or from an agrarian to an industrial economy, or, indeed, from a closed to an export-oriented economy, is not simply a matter of economics but of societal (Stiglitz, 1998) and probably also of cultural (Kay, 2004) transformation. The economic realm itself describes a world of persistent disequilibria, irregular fluctuations, cumulative developments and unforeseen shocks, as much as incremental moves towards or away from a state of stable equilibrium. It is a world where institutional diversity and history matter.

Many academic economists are aware of all this but their "health warning" is frequently ignored, not always innocently, by politicians and their advisers when they are promoting a favoured programme. Say's view about the independence of economic analysis from political and other factors supposedly exogenous to the economic system is the preferred vision, reflected in the position of many economists who consider that their task, qua economists, is simply to present a range of (positive) technical possibilities for dealing with particular problems while the politician's task is to make the (normative) value judgements as to which particular course of action is to be followed (Robbins, 1932). The difficulty with this dichotomy is three-fold. First it assumes that there is no bias in the economists' analysis of the feasible set of options, either from the analyst's own political preferences or from the analysis being bound to a particular economic and social structure. On both counts we share the scepticism of Gunnar Myrdal that such objectivity can be taken for granted. Indeed, the basic language of conventional economics shapes how it sees the world and in ways that are often strongly supportive of individual group interests, particularly, as might be expected, those of the most fortunate, articulate and politically influential in the larger community (Galbraith, 2004). Second, the distinction between economic and non-economic factors can only make sense as a useful abstraction when most of the latter can be taken for granted or as belonging to a stable background to the workings of the economy. This may be a reasonable starting point for the analysis of developed economies where the appropriate institutional structures are in place, where markets work more or less effectively and, in cases where they do not, there is a long history of managing the consequences. But it is certainly not reasonable in countries with very different economic and social structures, where markets are weak or missing, where political and social attitudes may not be so strongly attached to market-determined behaviour, and where market forces can transmit external shocks that are not only very sharp but can also be long-lasting. Thirdly, the dichotomy ignores the tendency of politicians to be biased in favour of their own national interests and for economists and others in the public service (including those in international institutions) to shape their advice to support the wishes, not always explicit, of their political masters. Such bias is nearly always in an opportunistic direction. The ruling ideas of an age, as the saying goes, usually reflect the interests of the most powerful.

Inevitably, standard economic theory is constantly running into behaviour that seems to contradict the basic model. The first reaction of generations of economists has tended to be similar, namely, to cast doubts on reality rather than the model. The early neo-classicists, including Marshall and Pigou, for example, were concerned that the labouring classes were failing to save enough to enable them to survive periods of unemployment and to provide for their old age. This was regarded as "irrational behaviour" and due to a lack of foresight or self-control (Peart, 2000). Education was seen as the cure and, once obtained, there would be no further need for government intervention. The lingering influence of such thinking can still be found in much of the human-capital literature. During the inter-war years, conventional economists were preoccupied with politicians interfering with the "natural" workings of the gold standard and obstructing a "return to normality"; restraining their irrational behaviour and correcting for their lack of foresight required budgets to be balanced and central bankers to be given more independence (Eichengreen and Temin, 1997). Again, we can hear a strong echo of this in today's development policy debates.[17] Whenever the reforms demanded by donor governments and international institutions fail to be implemented or to generate the expected results, the explanation is usually given in terms of personal failings on the part of the target population or their government: they are short-sighted, against progress, corrupt, lacking in discipline, tenacity and commitment, etc. Adding "good governance" to today's package of policy advice again appears to save conventional economic thinking from addressing any problems with its own logic.[18] Thus the possibility that initial conditions, national context, institutional capacities and the incentive structure for reform may be radically different from those prevailing in the developed countries, and such differences matter for the design of policies, has only slowly been gaining ground over the last decade and, so far, without seriously questioning the limits of the underlying economic analysis.

1.   Corruption and rent-seeking

The problem of corruption among ruling elites and its effects on economic development typifies the ad hoc response of conventional analysts to the policy challenges in poorer countries. This question has only come to the fore in the last 10 years or so and, again, largely as a result of the governments of the developed economies discovering (or rediscovering) the problem at home. A few economists had raised the issue in the 1950s (for example, Mende, 1955) and Myrdal

---

[17] Polanyi (op. cit.:232-33) refers to the programme of subordinating social stability and organisation to the needs of the international monetary system as the "Geneva programme", given its association with the League of Nations during the 1920s. The parallels with the Washington Consensus are obvious; see also Mazower (1998:106-17).

[18] See for example Burki and Edwards (1996) and Krueger (2004).

highlighted it in his major study of Asian development (Myrdal, 1968, especially Volume II, Chap. 2), arguing that corruption was one of the causes of the "soft state" and a major drag on development. But western governments remained largely silent on the subject. It was only in the aftermath of the Watergate scandal in the United States, in the early 1970s, and the subsequent focus on the overseas behaviour of US corporations that corruption moved up the agenda of the developed countries. The passing of the US Foreign Corrupt Practices Act in 1977 led to a more active stance against corruption and that intensified when the collapse of the Soviet Union removed many of the political and strategic considerations that had previously softened the assault on corrupt behaviour. Even so, the principal motive was not so much concern at the impact on development as seeking a "level playing field" for US corporations (UNECE, 2001:50-51). Such opportunistic thinking saw the World Bank effortlessly recast the "East Asian Miracle" economies from paragons of market-friendly virtue (World Bank, 1993) to pariahs of "crony capitalism" when the region suffered a severe economic crisis in the late 1990s (World Bank, 2000a) – a crisis that, predictably, in the Bank's view required the rapid dismantling of state controls if the region was to benefit from the emerging opportunities of globalisation.

Something of the same opportunistic thinking can be seen in the debates on aid, where an alleged negative association with economic growth is claimed to justify aid scepticism and fatigue, even though, at least in part, it can be explained by the geo-political calculations that have consistently distorted aid flows. On this basis, and despite a plethora of studies showing that development aid under many circumstances is good for growth (UNCTAD, 2006b), eliminating corruption through good governance is seen as a *precondition* of receiving aid by much of the international economic policy community, and with a focus that is almost exclusively concerned with the size of the public sector and the alleged distortions of state policy.[19]

---

[19] Thus the IMF could also effortlessly switch from denying that "Dutch Disease" was a problem with aid flows, as in its 2003 *World Economic Outlook*, to seeing it as a major reason for scepticism about the proposal to double aid to Africa, as it did at the time of the G8 Summit at Gleneagles in 2005. On the complex links between aid and growth, see Hanson and Tarp (2000); Roodman (2003); and Clemens et al. (2004).

This opportunistic bias has inevitably had an impact on the wider analytical framework for examining the difficult issue of government-business relations and handling the role of rents and rent-seeking in relation to the development process. In a purely static framework rents signal a move away from competitive market efficiency due to some kind of restriction on entry or exit that prevents the emergence of market-clearing prices. Often on the grounds of adding an institutional dimension to economic analysis, rent-seeking has been turned into a form of deviant state behaviour taking economies further away from their most efficient allocation of resources and imposing huge welfare losses, particularly when the rents derive from illiberal trade policies. For economists who have long understood the institutional nuances of modern capitalism, rents associated with entrepreneurial innovation have always played a dynamic role in a capitalist economy. Schumpeter famously linked these to the process of "creative destruction", but this focuses too narrowly on technical innovation. Rents arising in a range of other activities, such as organisation, human-capital development, design improvements, etc., can all be linked to economic progress. Indeed, Taylor and Ocampo (1998:1531) have argued, when the assumptions of perfect competition fail to hold and in the absence of uniform enterprise responses and fully utilised resources, rents can accelerate capital accumulation, raise productivity and contribute to a more dynamic economic climate. Scholars of the East Asian experience have also insisted that the management of rents helped to boost capital formation and to direct it towards more dynamic sectors.[20] A similar lesson emerges from other successful development experiences such as Botswana and Mauritius in Africa.[21] In fact, outside a world described as being at or around a competitive equilibrium, the creation, distribution and use of rents is a normal feature of the development process although one which can yield very different outcomes depending on how these are managed (Khan and Jomo (eds.), 2000).

---

[20] Interestingly, the Congressional Budget Office (1997:43) of the Congress of the United States seems to recognise this point in its discussion of the Korean experience.

[21] See the studies in Rodrik (2003).

2.   Liberalisation and opportunism

Opportunistic bias also colours the urgent calls by the developed countries and international organisations for developing countries to liberalise their international trade and remove all barriers to foreign investment as a condition of and a spur to development. Indeed, on some recent assessments developing countries should do so whether or not there is reciprocal action by rich countries (World Bank, 2004). As was shown earlier, the relationship between liberalisation and the take-off into sustained growth is actually very weak and, historically, free trade has generally been adopted only after industrial development was well under way. As such, it is a policy for the strong and the successful. This is certainly true of the trade agenda that has evolved since the 1980s in response to corporate pressure in the most advanced economies. The difference between pure logic and actual practice is manifest in a mixture of aggressive unilateralism, ad hoc protectionism and strategic multilateralism, including the addition of so-called "trade-related" issues.

Critics of trade liberalisation are often characterised as simpletons who fail to understand the wealth-augmenting effects of the division of labour[22], let alone the more sophisticated mechanics of computable equilibrium models, and whose apparent ignorance is denying spectacular income gains to the world's poorest communities.[23] Most critics do in fact understand the theory of comparative advantage: given its assumptions, the logic is unassailable. The problem is with its assumptions. When they fail to hold, unregulated market forces can just as readily trigger processes of "circular causation with cumulative effects" whereby countries with higher levels of productivity

---

[22] See, for example, the review of four books on globalisation by Henri Astier (2005:6-7).

[23] See, for example, Cline (2005) and Bhagwati (2005) for claims that critics of the Doha Round are so motivated. The claim that trade liberalisation is against the vested interests of the powerful is rooted, as we suggested earlier, in a very different historical era but is still deeply embedded in the economists' DNA. Even a sceptically minded economist such as Paul Krugman (1987:131) believes that not only is comparative advantage "an idea that conflicts directly with stubborn popular prejudices and powerful interests" but even its imperfections stand in a favourable light compared with those in the political world.

and incomes gain further while those at lower levels fall further behind (Myrdal, 1970:275).

In a world dominated by manufactured goods, large firms and fast-moving technological change, market forces are a source of unavoidable conflicts in international trade (Gomory and Baumol, 2000).[24] In this world of "retainable industries", both economic and political power have a bearing on the outcome; thus "whatever dispassionate economic analysis may indicate about the identity of the industries that are appropriate candidates for encouragement and assistance, the government's selection will in actuality be influenced heavily by political pressures" (ibid.:65).[25] Certainly, in those high-tech and skill-intensive activities, including services, where western companies anticipate future growth and expect to establish a dominant market position, they are not only eager for their governments' support through R&D budgets and fiscal breaks, but they also pressure them to seek the removal of trade barriers in developing-country markets so that they can consolidate their advantage. In the current Doha Round of WTO trade negotiations, the EU and the USA have been aggressively demanding large cuts in developing countries' industrial tariffs and the opening up of their nascent service sectors to foreign companies, in return for which the former are offering small reductions in their agricultural subsidies, subsidies that have long been regarded as derogating from WTO principles. In contrast, comparable demands to support the infant industries of the developing countries are immediately dismissed as trade-distorting while every effort is made to delay the opening of developed-country markets to the products of the many labour-intensive activities where developing countries have, or could be expected to create, comparative advantages. By denying that the interplay of economic and political interests is an integral part of the trading system, conventional thinking ends up by

---

[24] New trade theories do acknowledge that market failures (scale economies and imperfect competition), history and accident can dictate trade patterns, although at the policy level the nuances between new and old are often difficult to detect. Recall Ocampo's complaint (quoted in Chapter 3, footnote 35) about the orthodox free-traders' disregard of these new trade theories.

[25] A retainable industry is one characterised by high start-up costs which give a significant advantage to established producers in maintaining their position.

providing a thin cover for powerful vested interests, particularly those from the more advanced economies (Helleiner, 2000).[26]

The more sophisticated trade economists understand this very well and do not call for trade to be liberalised as rapidly as possible. In this, they are echoing the sentiments of the founding fathers from Adam Smith through Ricardo to John Stuart Mill, all of whom adopted a pragmatic approach to translating theory into practice (Panić, 1988:132-37). Even Alfred Marshall, towards the end of his life, came to recognise that foreign trade grows out of industrial strength, and to acknowledge the case for appropriate policy responses to strengthen industrial development in line with a country's own obligations and resources (Panić, ibid.:136). Unfortunately, these more sophisticated views are not the ones with any great influence on multilateral trade negotiations.

Factor mobility is another source of opportunism and deceit. According to the logic of conventional economics, labour and capital mobility should produce considerable gains for source and host countries in equal if not greater measure than does trade (Krugman and Obstfeld, 1997:159). However, in a recent report on globalisation prepared for the European Commission by the Centre for Economic Policy Research (CEPR) (2002), whose central message was that the "true benefits" of international liberalisation "strongly outweigh the costs", it was the "possible negative effects" of labour migration from South to North that were emphasised.[27] Similarly, while constrained labour mobility in the developed countries is used to justify their own exceptions to free trade in order to protect "sensitive" industries and vulnerable regions, no such consideration is extended to policy makers in the developing world looking to better manage their integration into the global economy. As noted in Chapter 3, proponents of rapid

---

[26] The idea that only "protectionists" pander to a narrow political constituency while "free-traders" seek to promote a broader cosmopolitan viewpoint was dismissed by Lionel Robbins in his discussion of British classical economists, noting of the latter that "there is little evidence that they often went beyond the test of national advantage as a criterion of policy, still less that they were prepared to contemplate the dissolution of national bonds. If you examine the ground on which they recommend free trade, you will find that it is always in terms of a more productive use of *national* resources...." (cited in Panić (1988:132)).

[27] On the hypocrisy of this position, see Rodrik (2003).

trade liberalisation have often been reticent financial-market liberalisers, usually on the grounds that there is more to capital mobility than meets the eye. Krugman and Obstfeld (op. cit.) put this down to "political difficulties" in hosting foreign capital. But the idea of capital as a given endowment, comparable to land or labour, is vital to the "win-win" logic on which calls for trade liberalisation are premised. Of course, this is an idea that has long been subject to a simple but decisive challenge to its meaning and measurability, with devastating consequences for the analytical integrity of the production function and the attendant theory of income distribution (Harcourt, 1972). This is because capital is not an homogeneous factor, cannot be aggregated, and is itself produced. On these grounds, John Hicks (1973:3) thought it "better not to live in the world of production functions and elasticities of substitution between factors globally defined". This advice has not been heeded by conventional trade theorists or their policy disciples in western capitals. The latter's drive for "deeper integration" is, in effect, an attempt to impose the policies, laws and institutions of the advanced countries on their weaker partners in various trade and cooperation agreements.[28] Consequently, Western trade officials and corporate interests who press for rapid liberalisation continue to use the "win-win" language of the simple Heckscher-Ohlin model, knowing very well that the major gains from trade arise not so much from improvements in static, allocative efficiency but from increased economies of scale and dynamic gains from increased specialisation, where those who are first to enter a particular market not only stand to gain most but are well placed to maintain their economic and technological dominance.

Another important assumption of mainstream economic theory, and one which is central to the case for rapid liberalisation, is that changes in the economic system are usually small and continuous, thus generating little disruption and allowing the gains to far out-

---

[28] This attempt by the strong to impose their system on the weak has uncomfortable echoes of Stalin's boast that "whoever occupies a territory also imposes on it his own social system. Everyone imposes his own system as far as his army can reach. It cannot be otherwise" (Djilas, 1962:93).

weigh any possible costs.[29] Indeed, estimates of the gains from trade generated by computable general equilibrium models depend on rapid supply responses and minimal adjustment costs (Akyüz, 2005). In a dynamic world economy, however, changes in technology or organisation can cause spectacular discontinuities in production possibilities, profit opportunities and relative productivity levels. This, for example, is what appears to have happened as a result of Britain's industrial revolution which caused a major disruption in the 18th-century pattern of trade. Suddenly "competition among industries was no longer merely a matter of tiny cost differences... The new machines and factories produced cotton textiles, small wares, and soon other manufactures, which could be profitably sold at prices a quantum leap below those of most existing proto-industries" (Ogilvie, 2000:119). The result was a considerable shock not only to the economic system of continental Europe but also to the social and political arrangements in which it was embedded; and because adjustment had to overcome social barriers and traditional institutional privileges the process in many countries took most of the succeeding 19th century to work itself through (Ogilvie, 2000:121). Those countries that adopted some form of infant-industry protection did so not in order to insulate themselves indefinitely from the challenge of British manufacturing but to give their domestic firms and entrepreneurs time to adjust, to adopt and adapt the new technologies without undermining social peace, and to prepare to participate effectively in an open trading regime.

Given the wide productivity gap between themselves and the G7 economies, it is hardly surprising that developing countries would share similar fears to those countries that followed the British revolution in manufacturing, namely, that their entire social and economic

---

[29] Joseph Schumpeter was explicit about this when he defined economic growth as "changes in economic data which occur continuously in the sense that increment or decrement per unit of time can be currently absorbed by the system without perceptible disturbance" (Schumpeter, 1935) but at the same time marrying this to a discontinuous process of "creative destruction". Alfred Marshall famously adopted the motto *natura non facit saltum* for his *Principles of Economics* but although generally desirable it was perhaps more of a hopeful assumption than an iron law. It is curious that neither Adam Smith, perhaps understandably, writing at its start, nor Marshall, writing at the time of its maturity, saw the industrial revolution as a major shock to the economic system.

systems could be destabilised by premature exposure to the forces of global competition. Indeed, as discussed in previous chapters, premature liberalisation has had a significant negative impact on wages and employment and has damaged the long-term growth prospects of many developing economies both by exposing producers to heightened shocks, increasing uncertainty and shortening investment horizons and by shifting the pattern of production away from more dynamic sectors into enclaves of varying technological sophistication, i.e., premature liberalisation has led to premature deindustrialisation.

3. The contingency of liberalisation

This brief overview of the selective appeals to history and the simplifying assumptions that underpin western policy makers' approach to development suggests that the confidence with which it is propagated is deeply misplaced. Far from providing a universally applicable model for the rest of the world, the history of western economic development shows that contingency was more important than ineluctable laws. Within a broadly common framework of more or less market-oriented economies and evolving democratic institutions, not only are there marked differences in the political and economic structures between North America and Western Europe, but the variations within the latter are also significant and persistent. Such variation, as we have seen, is just as true of the successful newly industrialising economies of East Asia, beginning with Japan.

Clearly, all these advanced capitalist countries share a core set of institutions and values without which they could not qualify for the description of market economy (or democracy). Private property rights are generally regarded as an essential component, as is their skewed distribution. Profit-making firms with effective corporate governance structures are another. So too are market-based incentives both to encourage risk-taking – what Kaldor (1972) called the creative role of markets – and to coordinate the wishes of consumers with the ambitions of producers. But none of these stand alone: they require complementary legal and financial bodies, shared values and agreed modes of behaviour, and an array of formal and informal rules of interaction. Moreover, because these institutions are largely forged within a national economic and political territory, they are intimately and distinctly shaped by the strategic actions of the state. The potential scope for variation is apparent in the specific mechanisms of ownership and control that govern corporate behaviour, the links, both formal and informal, between industrial firms and banks, as well as other types of financial institution, and in the rules and regulations that states implement to reach and maintain a balance between private profits and social consensus (Rosenberg and Birdzell, 1986:31-32).

The contingency of the western experience is further highlighted by historians, such as Mark Mazower (2005), who remind us that it was only in the 19th century that Western European economies moved decisively ahead of Asia, China's GDP probably being greater than Europe's until the mid-19th century.[30] John Hobson has argued cogently that the rise of Europe as a global power was greatly assisted by the successful assimilation of eastern ideas, inventions and institutions (Hobson, 2004). Moreover, while democratic institutions can be a powerful and positive force for innovation and economic progress, the roots of liberal and democratic ideas can also be found in Asia and Africa, not only in Europe (Sen, 2005).

Thus, far from offering a universal blueprint for economic and political development, the considerable achievements of Western Europe and North America point to their capacity for experimentation, eclecticism and pragmatism, to their ability to shape external influences to their particular domestic situations, and to their tolerance of different preferences regarding the trade-offs between efficiency and equity and between faster economic growth and social stability. The tendency of the last two decades for western policy makers to present a single scenario of successful development is thus sharply at variance with their own histories.

---

[30] According to Maddison (2000:263), China accounted for close to one-third of world GDP in 1820 compared with a little under a quarter for Western Europe, although the figure for all of Europe, including Eastern Europe and Russia, was similar to that for China. By 1870 the shares are 17.2 per cent, 33.6 per cent and 45.3 per cent, respectively. On a per capita basis, however, Western Europe overtakes China at a much earlier date. Historians such as Pomerantz (2000) have argued that the "great divergence" between Europe and Asia occurred only after 1800, but more recent work, based on empirical data for wages and prices in the two continents, suggests that it was well under way before 1800 (Broadberry and Gupta, 2006).

An alternative framework for development policies, and for western and international assistance in support of them, therefore needs to recognise the considerable differences in social and political systems between countries and in the present or initial conditions in which they are attempting to develop. Policy makers must have a clear understanding of the social and political context in which economic reforms and policies are expected to bring benefit; analytically, they must accept that one model will not fit all and, at whatever cost to the construction of elegant models, the need to allow fully for socio-political reality must place a premium on political economy.

C.   Cumulative and interdependent factors of development

Economic development is a process where history and politics intertwine to govern the evolution of income and the distribution of wealth. The complexity of the linkages and positive feedback mechanisms means that path dependence and institutional readiness are central in determining outcomes that are a good deal more unpredictable than presumed by market fundamentalists.[31] There is widespread agreement among economists that a rapid and sustained rise in productivity is a *sine qua non* for sustained rises in living standards, including for the poorest communities. But despite the periodic appearance of "new" growth models (and a plethora of attendant empirical studies), there is surprisingly little agreement about what really counts for particular countries seeking to raise productivity and close the gap between themselves and those that have already achieved high levels of income.[32] We have suggested in the last section that this has a lot to do with the limits of conventional economic thinking, and, in particular, the assumptions underlying general equilibrium analysis.

---

[31] This has been recognised by Gary Becker, one of the stars of Chicago economics: "Multiple steady states mean that history and luck are critical determinants of a country's growth experience…Many attempts to explain why some countries and continents have had the best economic performance during the past several centuries give too little attention to accidents and good fortunes" (Becker et al., 1990:14).

[32] Kenny and Williams (2001) provide a good overview of the literature; they note that well over 100 variables have been subjected to millions of regressions with what at best can be described as "disappointing results".

It is worth recalling at the outset the warning of Charles Kindleberger that anyone who claims to have found the key to the secret of economic growth "is likely to be a fool or a charlatan or both" (Herrick and Kindleberger, 1983:xvi). Nevertheless, there is plenty that we do know about the "characteristics" of long-term growth, at least in the Kaldorian sense of "stylised facts" or "empirical regularities" which, however, are historically contingent and change over time with the transformation of the economic system.[33] We know that it is a process of continuous change in which each new step is greatly influenced by those preceding it and that together these steps describe a progressive transformation in the structure of economic activity, including a change in production methods, mainly in the direction of more advanced techniques and larger productive units, along with a diminished weight for raw materials and an increased one for intermediate inputs, including those with a high knowledge content. We know that new final products are constantly being developed, with related shifts in consumption patterns; that the output of domestic industry is likely to contain a growing tradeable component; and there will be a redistribution of labour between different industries and occupations and of population from rural to urban locations. We know that various coordination failures can lead to the process breaking down. We also know that this is not a process which describes a movement towards equilibrium; rather, as Toner (1999:21) notes: "...successive rounds of increasing returns, real price reductions, demand and output expansion, investment and increasing returns, act not to equilibrate supply and demand but to perpetuate disequilibria. Growth, says Albert Hirschman, should be viewed as a chain of disequilibria...that nightmare of equilibrium economics, the endlessly spinning cobweb, is the kind of mechanism we must assiduously look for as an invaluable aid in the development process." Finally, we also know that growth can be contagious particularly among neighbouring economies, but that the process also tends to be very uneven both within and across countries. Thus geography continues to matter in all kinds of ways that are important, but not neces-

---

[33] See Toner (1999:120-21); Adelman (2000:65) talks about pulling together "very general common strands evident from both the nineteenth century continental European development and the post-WWII development of developing countries".

sarily definitive, in determining the pace and direction of the growth process. [34]

In surveying the experience of today's advanced economies, including the latest graduates in East Asia, it is difficult to avoid the conclusion that a broad industrial base is critical to establishing and sustaining a robust process of economic growth. At a fundamental, conceptual level, industrialisation can play a pivotal role in promoting the circular and cumulative processes of development which break definitively with the straightjacket of equilibrium economics. A number of empirical regularities are associated with industrialisation and more particularly with its manufacturing component which is especially important: its contribution to growth has been found to be greater than its share in total output, i.e., it tends to be an engine of growth; faster growth in manufacturing output generates faster growth in manufacturing productivity; and faster growth in manufacturing is linked to faster growth of output and productivity in other sectors of the economy.[35] Industrial development and accompanying changes in the pattern of employment also appear to be closely associated with reaching a high threshold level of income and a sustainable pattern of insertion into the international economy. There is an additional reason why industrialisation should be given a prominent place in the design of development strategies. It is closely associated with the expansion of productive capacity, the creation of new capital equipment and the progressive substitution of capital for labour, i.e., with the process of capital accumulation.

Putting these elements together in a coherent development strategy is no simple matter. Gregory Mankiw, a former head of the Council of Economic Advisors to the US President, has suggested that "basic theory, shrewd observation and commonsense" remain the most reliable guides for promoting economic growth (Mankiw, 1995:308-09). Such advice leaves plenty of room to discuss local heresies, but in this spirit, an examination of the linkages and feedback mechanisms

---

[34] These characteristics are taken from Kuznets' 1971 Nobel lecture and from Svennilson (1954), which is an unjustly neglected study of the growth process.

[35] These regularities are associated with the empirical studies of Verdoorn and Kaldor (Scott, 1991:Chap. 12).

between investment, structural change and trade seems a sensible starting point for a general discussion of development strategy.[36]

The profit-investment-export nexus

Harry Johnson long ago described economic development as "a
generalised process of capital accumulation" and this still has much
to commend it. As discussed in the previous chapter, fixed investment simultaneously generates income and expands productive capacity. It is also closely attached to other elements in the growth
process, such as technological progress, skills acquisition and institutional deepening.[37] Moreover, due to the sensitivity of the investment
decision to the level and stability of economic activity, investment
plays an important bridging role between the cyclical and longer-term
features of economic development. A given rate of accumulation can
of course generate different rates of output growth depending on its
nature and composition as well as the efficiency with which production capacity is utilised. All this means that policies will have a significant bearing on the outcome.[38] This was certainly understood by
the founding fathers of development economics:

> ... any theory of development must start with a consider-
> ation of the forces that determine investment in underde-

---

[36] There are, of course, dissenting voices; see Easterly (2002).
[37] Thus, most astute observers of the role of technological innovation in the growth
process recognise an unavoidable degree of interaction with investment (Baumol
et al., 1991:164).
[38] This is perhaps one of the main reasons why econometric studies have failed to
establish a one-to-one relation between the rate of investment and economic
growth. Still, it is the case that of the many variables fed into growth equations,
investment emerges as one of the few with a robust and independent impact on
economic growth, particularly for rapidly growing middle-income economies
(Bosworth and Collins, 2004; Ros, 2000; IMF, 1997:80-81; Levine, 1992). A
recent study by Bond et al. (2004) of some 98 countries for the period 1960-98
found that a higher share of investment in GDP predicts a higher level of output
per worker in the steady state and that an increase in the share of investment
predicts a higher growth rate of output per worker, both in the short run and the
steady state, with the long-run effects on growth rates quantitatively substantial
and statistically significant. This study also stresses the importance of heterogeneity
across countries reflecting differences in economic policies and institutions.

veloped countries, especially when it is realised that savings are by no means the only limiting factor, and may be low because investments are low rather than vice versa....Current writings on development are almost devoid of attempts at building up a theoretical framework to answer this question. One finds in them valuable hints on how investment should proceed, and on investment criteria useful for policy makers, but little systematic discussion of the forces that govern the process of capital accumulation (Hirschman, 1958:35).[39]

As suggested in the previous chapter, that discussion needs to focus more closely on the links between accumulation and the functional distribution of income, i.e., what we have called the profit-investment nexus. Profits not only provide an incentive for investment but are also an important source of financing it. Ideally, these should be mutually reinforcing; indeed, cumulative and interdependent links between profits and investment are central to any healthy growth regime in any market-based economy. However, the link from profits to investment is neither spontaneous nor direct, not least because the firm is comprised of owners and managers with potentially different objectives and strategies to realise them, and because most investment involves debt and equity financing in addition to retained profits (Bhaskar and Glyn, 1992).[40] The link can be broken by competing claims on profits, including by labour, or through alternative ways of spending those profits, whether on consumer goods or financial assets.[41] Thus while accumulation is necessary to the survival

---

[39] This conclusion applies, we believe, to much of the recent discussion, initiated by the World Bank, on how to improve the "investment climate" in developing countries.

[40] Conventional theory has long struggled to fashion a convincing theory of investment on the back of its own assumptions of perpetual market clearing, rational expectations, efficient markets, small owner-managed firms, etc. In particular, the investment decision, whether following Tobin's Q or Jorgenson's user cost model, is an essentially riskless and reversible decision, involving no sunk costs, site specificity, inter-temporal profit trade-offs or debt burdens.

[41] All this was lost sight of after the debt crisis when the focus shifted from growth as a policy objective to the removal of price distortions as the surest way to improve allocative efficiency, a shift that was linked directly to the mobilisation of domestic savings through the deregulation and liberalisation of the financial sector and the attraction of FDI (World Bank, 1991).

and expansion of the firm, it is also a source of risks and tensions. Dealing with these makes investment an institutionally and histori-cally grounded process (Crotty, 1990).

As discussed earlier, a good deal of evidence shows that after the initial stages of industrialisation, when agricultural and commer-cial incomes provide the main source of investment finance, capital accumulation is financed primarily by the retention of corporate profits, often in a symbiotic relation with long-term bank loans. A recent study of 30 developing countries in the late 1980s and early 1990s finds a strong relationship between a high savings rate, a large share of manu-facturing output in GDP and a high profit share in manufacturing in the successful East Asian NIEs (Ros, 2000:79-83). This contrasts with other regions, such as Latin America, where savings rates are lower than expected, given the share of profits in national income, and where a fall in the savings rate has been associated with stagnant or falling shares of manufacturing industry in GDP. This profit-investment nexus provides an important criterion for assessing policies in search of faster growth.[42]

On the argument made in this chapter, emphasising investment, both private and public, is also important because it allows for a more encompassing analysis that highlights the interdependent nature of socio-economic relations and also raises questions about their legiti-macy. Keynes (1919:16-17) saw the repressed consumption habits of the "new rich" as key to the legitimacy of the 19th-century system: "If the rich had spent their new wealth on their enjoyments, the world would long ago have found such a regime intolerable. But like bees they (the rich) saved and accumulated, not least to the advantage of the whole community." As we noted in Chapter 5, investment acts like a social tax restricting the use of profits for the personal con-sumption of the capitalists, thus making for less personal inequality but also bestowing legitimacy on the broader pattern of distribution.[43]

---

[42] For more on the profit-investment nexus, see UNCTAD (1995, 1997); Singh (1999); Ros (2000); and Amsden (2001).

[43] At more advanced levels of development a wage-led growth dynamic is feasible. Indeed, in many accounts the transition to such a new social contract was precisely what gave the richer countries their strong growth impulse after the Second World War (Armstrong et al., 1984:123-211).

Just how this legitimacy problem is handled opens the way for variations in the organisation of a capitalist economy. In many developing countries, where the basic policy challenge is to increase the rate of investment significantly, it cannot be taken for granted that markets will generate sufficient levels of profit to fuel accumulation or that elites will behave in the manner described by Keynes. The coexistence of a high share of profits in value added with a very unequal distribution of personal incomes, for example, suggests a low propensity to save and invest by the rich. The rich in developing countries do not always save and invest a large proportion of their incomes, but spend them on goods and services that, by developing-country standards, fall into the category of luxury consumption. Alternatively they often choose to siphon profits into financial assets at home or abroad. They also tend to consume goods with a relatively high import content, which, besides emphasising consumption over savings, also has the effect of tightening the balance-of-payments constraint on accumulation and growth. Just as significantly for the argument of this chapter, in most of the countries that have succeeded in generating sizeable resources for investment, market forces have not been left alone to dictate either the pace or the sectoral pattern of accumulation.

In an interdependent world, however, it is wrong to regard the profit-investment nexus as a sufficient condition for sustained economic growth. There must also be markets available to absorb the potential expansion in output that this implies. To paraphrase Young (1928), the profit-investment nexus is constrained by the size of the market just as the size of the market is constrained by the profit-investment nexus. Indeed, a set of feedback mechanisms between the supply and demand sides of the economy must figure prominently in any consistent growth story. Some of these mechanisms will involve recurring structural linkages between the urban and rural sectors, others are likely to involve government policy. However, there is a potential for breakdown if output runs ahead of markets.

In this respect, exporting is likely to play a major role in the process of industrialisation and economic growth, although that relationship can be envisaged in a number of ways. In more heterodox approaches, the advantages come from market size, whether through the gains from a more intricate division of labour, technological upgrading or by achieving minimum efficient scales of production. In these latter respects, exporting manufactures brings dynamic advantages through a virtuous circle of higher demand, greater investment and more rapid productivity growth. But for many developing countries, exporting is simply a matter of expediency, because in the absence of a domestic capital-goods sector, financing the imports necessary for faster growth is likely to meet a balance-of-payments constraint. In this case, the shift in the structure of economic activity towards the production and export of manufactured goods requires a "vent for surplus" to ensure that structural changes are not impeded by macroeconomic imbalances. Whatever the underlying rationale, however, successful exporting is itself contingent on a favourable investment dynamic. As incomes increase, rising labour costs and the entry of lower-cost producers can rapidly erode the competitiveness of labour-intensive manufactures, and new investments are needed to maintain productivity growth and to upgrade to higher-value-added activities. Indeed, as was argued in Chapter 3, to the extent that "making openness work for development" is contingent on capital accumulation, the export-investment nexus provides a second criterion for assessing development policies.[44]

It is clear that the varied policy challenges facing most developing countries stem from these overlapping relationships connecting growth, structural change and integration; in our view, the profit-investment-export nexus provides a useful way of framing those challenges. The effort required to raise investment and exports in the initial stages of industrialisation increases considerably as the production process becomes more dependent on scale economies and knowledge-intensive activities: the technological and organisational capabilities required to compete internationally become more exacting, more difficult to master and more costly to acquire, and the investment climate becomes more uncertain.

---

[44] Rodrik (1999); and for further elaboration see UNCTAD (1996, 2003a).

D. Developmental states

The last section suggested that development policy is about triggering and sustaining a cumulative growth process around a profit-investment-export nexus to generate more productive jobs, rising incomes and better social conditions. From this perspective, one of the least helpful ideas promulgated by policy makers and their advisers in the western market economies since the early 1980s is that the state is an obstacle to economic progress and should be "rolled back". After the collapse of communism in Eastern Europe in 1989 the constantly repeated slogan was to "get the state out of the economy", and suggestions that industrial policy, for example, might have a useful role to play in restructuring and influencing the future path of economic growth were usually caricatured as an attempt to restore central planning. Despite romantic, conservative notions of a return to the "night-watchman state" that would be confined to the tasks of defence, education, law and order, and the protection of property rights, the weight and role of the state in the rich market economies remains large, in the region of 40 per cent of GDP or more, and has changed only marginally in the last 20 years or so.[45]

The anti-state rhetoric, however, employs language that implies the state is somehow external or foreign to the market economy and that it "intervenes" or "meddles" in matters that should be none of its business. This is largely ideology and ignores the fact that the state has always been an important actor *in* the market economy and indeed an integral part of it. Historically, the state has always been an instigator of innovation in successful economies: it was institutional development by the state that laid the basis for the "efficient set of markets that make possible the growth of exchange and commerce" (North, 1990:130). Neo-liberal rhetoric, however, has helped to obscure the real problem for transition and developing countries, which is not so much to roll back the state as far as possible but to transform

---

[45] There is, needless to say, a vast but thoroughly inconclusive body of econometric literature attempting to discover a relationship (positive or negative) between the size of the state (whether measured from the expenditure or revenue side) and economic growth; see Agell et al. (1997).

it in order for it to perform efficiently the functions required of it in a market-based democracy.

In the years following World War II, the major achievement of the western democracies was to temper the violence of the competitive individualism of the 19th century and to avoid a repetition of the failures of capitalism in the inter-war years of the 20th in such a way that full employment and economic growth, driven mainly by market forces, could be combined with objectives for equity and social justice. Governments set out to improve the efficiency of the market system by correcting for market failure, especially in non-competitive markets, and to accelerate growth by promoting collaboration among enterprises and governments in the areas of long-term investment, research and development, education and training, and so on. Doing so involved a new set of policy instruments, which ranged from nationalisation, indicative planning and incomes policies at one extreme to fiscal reform, active labour-market policies and measured trade liberalisation on the other. Such policies, in combination with "Keynesian" demand management, laid the basis of what was known at the time as the "mixed economy" and, in retrospect, is now often referred to as a "golden age".[46]

None of this should be taken to imply that states are invincible or unable to fail, which is clearly not the case. Rather it is to recognise that when we compare the European countries, let alone North America and Japan, we find that the market economy can operate efficiently within a wide spectrum of different political and social arrangements. Moreover, when the market economies are compared over time, we see a considerable evolution in their various political and social arrangements, suggesting on the one hand that what works in one period may fail in another and, on the other, that successful economies are those that have or develop the capacity to adapt their institutions and behavioural conventions to changing circumstances and evolving political and social preferences. To repeat, this means that beyond a few core elements there is no single homogeneous model of state-market relations. Each country must experiment and find the configuration of institutions and conventions that will work best in its

---

[46] For a detailed and still useful survey of these developments see Shonfield (1965).

national conditions and meet the expectations of its population. What will work, however, and whether the system will prove adaptable to changing circumstances, will depend on the interaction between cultural, political and economic factors.[47]

We have to admit that our knowledge of such interaction is at best rudimentary and is often insufficient for precise recommendations. The unprecedented rates of economic growth during the "golden post-war years" in Western Europe suggest that capitalism is most productive when it is embedded in a political and social system where its more destructive characteristics are subject to effective constraints. But the positive role of the state in managing capital accumulation and structural change along with a rapid pace of output growth in poorer countries has been generally downplayed by market fundamentalists. Such a role was certainly present in catch-up economies after 1945, notably in Japan, but also in some smaller economies on the European periphery such as Finland and Austria, and more recently Ireland. Not only did these economies have a strong encompassing vision of development which was not entrusted entirely to the care of market forces, but a defining feature of their success was the design of effective mechanisms to encourage and discipline private investors by raising profits above those generated by competitive market forces alone and directing them to areas where the economic and social returns might be particularly high.

In all these cases, policies to ensure that profits would be used to increase productive capacity and employment and encourage technological progress included credit rationing, subsidised credit, fiscal concessions, targeted industrial policies and active labour-market measures (Vartianen, 1995). Governments enjoyed a substantial degree of autonomy, particularly with respect to the local business class and international capital, as well as the requisite degree of capacity and credibility to act in the wider public interest. Moreover, this combination of autonomy, capacity and credibility was essential to adapting policy to changing circumstances as these economies climbed up the development ladder.

---

[47] This is very close to North's (1990) notion of "adaptive efficiency" and is discussed in the next chapter.

The previous section suggested that most developing countries are also faced with the task of designing appropriate incentives and disciplines to raise the rate of investment and direct it to the most productive activities. The potential advantages of "economic backwardness" (Gerschenkron, 1962) have usually implied a more prominent role for the state in providing the institutional and financial resources to turn that potential into sustained and rapid rates of industrialisation. The record in this respect, however, has often fallen well short of expectation, in part because there has been a narrow focus on scale effects rather than on the linkages and feedback mechanisms discussed earlier.

From his study of socio-economic change in Asia, Gunnar Myrdal (1968:Chap.18) had already concluded in the 1960s that a dividing line between developed and underdeveloped countries was the presence in the latter, to varying degrees, of "soft states", that is, states with "low levels of social discipline" that were vulnerable to capture by narrow interest groups and unable to address the various bottlenecks and hurdles blocking the path to faster rates of catch-up growth. Myrdal did not provide a blueprint for a "hard" state, although fighting corruption and land reform were uppermost on his agenda for creating harder states in Asia.[48] Irma Adelman (2000:71-76) has provided a clearer notion of the elements that make up a hard state. These include a substantial degree of autonomy, capacity and credibility to set policies in the national interest; leadership commitment to economic development; good economic policies; and a necessary degree of economic autonomy with respect to the international environment.

Somewhat ironically, given Myrdal's own pessimistic assessment, the states that evolved in East Asia during the 1960s and 1970s exhibited these kinds of qualities.[49] They created a predictable economic environment involving reasonably secure property rights, a predominant role for market competition and a broadly pro-business stance. They also invested heavily in human capital to bring the labour

---

[48] Myrdal seems to have had in mind the states of North-West Europe in the late 19th century, which had achieved high levels of integrity in politics and administration along with effective intervention to raise productivity.

[49] They certainly acquired some of the characteristics of the late-industrialising Scandinavian countries; see Chang and Kozul-Wright (1994).

force closer to international standards. But beyond this the state also saw its central task as increasing the supply of investible resources and socialising long-term investment risks. State-sponsored accumulation involved variously the transfer of land and other assets, control and manipulation of the financial system, a pro-investment macroeconomic policy, as well as direct public investment in some lines of activity. This did not mean setting policy according to the dictates of the business community: instead, there was a considerable amount of state supervision to "govern the market" in accordance with a politically defined notion of national development (Wade, 1990).

These "developmental states" (Johnson, 1982) did not simply measure success in terms of raising investment to fuel economic growth, but also in terms of guiding investment into activities that could sustain a high-wage future for their citizens. This meant a co-ordinated effort to shift resources from traditional sectors by raising agricultural productivity and channelling the resulting surplus to emerging industrial activities (Grabowski, 2003). It also meant deliberately reducing risks and augmenting profits in industries deemed important for future growth (Wade, 1995:120). Like their 19th-century precursors, this meant making full use of innovations induced by the creative impulses of markets, even as some domestic producers were being protected against excessive competition, particularly from international markets. This did not so much involve the state in inventing a new set of policy instruments as in adapting a familiar set of macroeconomic, industrial, educational, financial and trade measures to a set of goals that were themselves evolving with each new stage in the development process (UNCTAD, 1997:177-79).

A key feature of such successful policy regimes was the state's growing ability to manage rents in support of infant industries and to foster a more strategic pattern of integration into the global economy. This included ways to discipline the recipients of those rents through the setting of performance criteria and by managing the decline of exceptional rents as firms became more competitive on world markets (Akyüz et al., 1999:15-18). Doing so often meant the state devising institutional arrangements to better coordinate its relations with the business sector (World Bank, 1993) and also with organised labour (UNCTAD, 1997). This institutional learning helped policy makers to be highly selective in providing support, not so much in terms of

"picking winners" but rather in pursuing competitive advantages based
on a longer-term vision of developing activities of ever-increasing
technological sophistication, capital and knowledge intensity (Weiss
and Hobson, 1995:148-56). In other words, in their vision of the future, policy makers did not accept an historically determined set of
comparative advantages but instead decided what they wanted them
to be in the future.

Significantly, these states had previously been accused of clinging to conservative practices and of lacking the competence to organise
their economic development. Moreover, their evolution into harder
states did not follow a single path. Rather, the organisational resources
and potential political leverage reflected distinct historical and cultural roots. Korea's interventionist policies under the Park dictator-
ship (1961-79) relied heavily on close consultation between (compromised) business leaders and government, with a notable role played
by very large diversified corporations and a state-controlled financial
sector. In contrast, the state-business relationship in Taiwan, particularly in its formative years, was more distant and fragmented, in large
part due to strained relations between the transplanted political structures (bureaucracy and military) and the indigenous business elite;
large state-owned corporations in some key sectors coexisted with
smaller firms elsewhere, and with room for the evolution of a good
deal of strategic planning in between. The pattern of business-gov-
ernment relations in the more commodity-dependent and ethnically
mixed South-East Asian NIEs was different again.[50] In all these cases,
however, it was only through persistent efforts to reform recruitment,
promotion, compensation and training that their bureaucracies were
improved. Much the same can be said of other related institutions
that helped to create and strengthen the profit-investment nexus, such
as industry associations, semi-public trading agencies and various
public research institutes (Evans, 1999; Cheng et al., 1998).

All this was ignored or played down in the 1980s when the advice from developed countries and international financial institutions
focused on defining private property rights and giving full rein to
market forces, via liberalisation and privatisation, and diminishing

---

[50] On these differences see Haggard (2004); Jomo et al. (1997).

the role of the state. This emphasis was supported by the cynical assumption of neo-liberal public choice theory that politicians and civil servants are motivated only by their self-interest, which they try to maximise in just the same way as private enterprises focus on profit.[51] This is little more than prejudice, but when constantly repeated it can help to undermine confidence in democratic politics and honest administration. There is plenty of evidence of a strong public ethos governing the behaviour of bureaucrats and politicians, despite the inevitable exceptions to the rule, but this has to be nurtured by appropriate institutional structures. Moreover, the history of West European countries provides many examples of corrupt and inefficient bureaucracies being successfully reformed, Britain and France in the 19th century being prominent examples (Wraith and Simpkins, 1963) and the United States in the early 20th another (Glaeser and Goldin (eds.), 2006). The danger perhaps is not so much that political leaders and civil-service elites pursue their private interests but that they lose touch with civil society and grassroots institutions and conclude, like many other professional elites, that only they know what is best in the public interest. But this is a risk that can be better handled with the help of an active civil society and appropriate institutions than by minimising the functions of the state and neglecting the need for an effective public service.[52]

This is not to deny that for many developing and transition economies the issue is how to reform a dysfunctional, underdeveloped and, sometimes, corrupt administration. Rather, as Mkandawire (2001) has argued in the case of Africa, it is to recognise that many such problems have emerged (or been reinforced) in the context of adjustment programmes which are aimed at creating an enabling environment for the private sector but which instead often lead to "soft authoritarian states". As he notes: "Wanton liberalisation of markets without careful consultation with business classes, privatisation that provides

---

[51] For critical reviews of the public choice approach, see Self (1993) and Orchard and Streeten (1997).

[52] Persistent denigration of the state and public servants by neo-liberal ideologues and naïve conservatives has achieved little by way of reducing the size of the state in the more developed market economies, but by undermining the morale of civil servants and, often, by holding back their salaries relative to those in the private sector, it can undermine the efficiency of the bureaucracy.

no special privilege to local capitalists, cessation of directed credit or development finance, high interest rates, all these underscore the distancing of the state from local capitalist interests and the pre-eminent position of IFIs' interests and perceptions in policy-making" (ibid.:309). Restoring an effective role to the state will require a break with these programmes and much less intervention by the international financial institutions. Honest, impartial and competent administrative, judicial and law-enforcement systems are crucial not only for upholding the rule of law, protecting property rights and ensuring personal security but also for building an atmosphere of trust in public institutions without which any state may prove highly fragile. Reforming these institutions and weeding out criminal and corrupt elements is perhaps the one area where carefully prepared "shock therapy" may be highly effective. Again, East Asia provides some lessons in this respect. Large salary increases for the civil service, the judiciary and the police, combined with rigorous selection procedures for new entrants, should be considered an urgent priority, and support to cope with the budgetary implications should be regarded as an appropriate candidate for international financial assistance.[53]

The need for highly qualified and dedicated bureaucracies in the developing countries is not simply based on the need for effective implementation of the usual demands on the state. As we have shown earlier, in all countries where economic development has been successful, whether Britain in the 18th century, North-West Europe and the United States in the 19th, or East Asia in the 20th, the early stages of growth have always been assisted in varying degrees by the active intervention of the state. The developmental state is essentially a version of the mixed economy, namely, one where policy makers leave market forces to determine as far as possible the prices and quantities supplied of most goods and services but where they consider certain key objectives will not automatically be generated by markets or that

---

[53] Following the so-called "rose revolution" in the Republic of Georgia in November 2003, 15,000 police officers were dismissed and salaries were raised 10-fold for the new force, a popular move with a population that had previously regarded the police as enemies of the people; salaries were also raised considerably for tax inspectors and anti-corruption officials, a move that should lead to higher tax revenues; and the budget, supported with significant funds from the UN Development Programme (UNDP), was raised four-fold in order to pay civil servants a decent salary.

they will not be achieved fast enough or in a manner desired by government policy. Among these objectives are the institutions that shape the incentives that determine whether markets behave efficiently and lead to socially acceptable outcomes. As we have suggested throughout this chapter, for most developing countries the focus is likely to be on stimulating, directing and coordinating the process of capital accumulation.[54]

The developmental state, we have argued, requires the creation of civil-service capacities and agencies capable of drawing up coherent development programmes and implementing specific policies, such as the development of infant industries, for example, so that they serve the broader national interest and are not captured by private, corporate interests. The burden on national bureaucracies, however, is now much heavier than it was for earlier developers because an increasing number of microeconomic policies have become subject to international negotiation, while at the same time the international coordination of macroeconomic policies has weakened. This shift in the balance of micro- and macro- in international policy coordination reflects the rise of neo-liberalism and the liberalisation of international capital markets since the early 1980s. For market fundamentalists, the mixed economy, as an expression of incomplete trust in market forces, is anathema, while the free movement of capital is held to make macro-policy coordination unnecessary or unfeasible. Developing countries, however, find themselves in a relatively weak position in such negotiations as they are conducted for the most part in the IMF, the World Bank and the WTO, where the developed countries have the financial leverage and organisational abilities to defend their own interests and determine the overall agenda. The understaffing, in terms of numbers and expertise, of developing-country delegations to the WTO, for example, is cynically exploited by the EU and the USA through manipulation of the agenda, by holding several meet-

---

[54] We have not discussed the contribution of the new institutional development economics associated with the work of Acemoglu et al. (2001). However, while their empirical work is ingenious, we do not think its particular brand of geographical determinism provides a convincing account of colonial development, let alone the challenges facing developing countries today. For a critique of that approach, see Rodrik (2004c).

ings or working groups simultaneously, drafting proposals in closed meetings, and generally using informal consultations among small groups to push forward much of the serious work of interest to the rich countries. Although, formally, all the members of the WTO are equal, unlike in the IMF and the World Bank where voting is weighted by contributions, a large number of the developing countries are effectively marginalised in the WTO.[55] To defend their interests effectively in such forums, the developing countries need a significant strengthening of their civil-service capacities for policy analysis and negotiations. This will require, inter alia, policies to attract able graduates to stay at home instead of rushing off to better-paid jobs in the developed world or in international institutions, and greater cooperation in regional bodies that are still very weak in the developing world compared, for example, with the European Union.

E.   Democracy and economic development

It was mentioned earlier that, despite its many shortcomings in practice, the principles and processes of representative democracy are now generally accepted by most members of the United Nations as providing the basis for legitimate government. Democracy, however, is considerably more than a set of formal institutions that can be put quickly into place as a result of elections and a new constitution. It is rather a broad political culture that requires time to evolve in such a way that it responds to the particular needs and preferences of the population that chooses it, and it cannot be imposed by force, diplomatic pressure or according to an outsider's timetable.[56]   It is

---

[55]   For a detailed account of the workings of the WTO, see Jawara and Kwa (2003) and Das (2003).

[56]   The evolution of democratic institutions in today's advanced western economies is measured in decades if not centuries. Certainly, the use of foreign armies to bring liberty and a new constitution to a country is more likely to unite progressive and conservative elements of the population in opposition to the foreign invader, as suggested by the rejection of the revolutionary armies of France bearing liberty to its European neighbours. In addition, ethnic, religious or linguistic divisions may be exacerbated and thereby weaken the prospects for more democratic institutions and for economic development. The reader is unlikely to need reminding of more recent examples of the limits of armed force in spreading democracy.

also a large political mansion with many rooms in it, as the diverse arrangements of Western Europe and North America demonstrate. Nascent democracies must therefore be free to choose the institutional forms and processes that suit them best: sometimes they may succeed in copying western models but success is by no means guaranteed (North, 1994). In any case, democratic tradition and process is not unique to the west and new institutions may be less fragile if they are encouraged to take root in established national traditions.

This is not the place to enter a discussion about the ethical criteria for judging different forms of government.[57] Here our interest is in whether democratic processes are more or less supportive of economic development than alternative political arrangements. A prominent feature of the current globalisation era has been the close identification of free markets and democratic principles. Market fundamentalists tend to focus on a positive link between participatory democracy and economic freedom through the acquisition, protection and use of property rights. This seems to be premised on the view that once a minimum set of institutional prerequisites are in place, the market economy will acquire a life of its own which should not be subject to political pressures. In fact, the association owes more to the dramatic collapse of the Soviet Union than to any "natural" symbiosis between the two. Indeed, the rise of democratic principles, his-

---

[57] It seems clear to us that concern for human rights and the equitable treatment of all citizens, male and female, are part and parcel of any search for a just, or more just, society, and this in turn is part of a still wider search for international peace and security. The thesis of the "democratic peace", that liberal democracies never go to war with one another, is, of course, a familiar and appealing one. A consensus is often claimed for Kant's proposition on the grounds that democracies are notably successful at managing and settling disputes and institutionalising their agreements and obligations. This is an attractive model, not least because violent conflict, actual or threatened, whether intra- or inter-state, is still a major obstacle to economic development in many parts of the world, and institutional reforms, at both national and regional levels, are a priority if a stable environment for development is to be created. Assessing whether or not democracies go to war depends in part on what subset of characteristics qualifies a country to be called a democracy: in Western Europe, the current shape of democracy has evolved over a very long period, the right to vote, for example, being extended to women in many countries only from the 1940s, and in some only in the 1970s. Democracy was considered at the time to have triumphed in Europe in 1918, but its roots were shallow and, with calamitous consequences, it failed to compete with authoritarian forms of political order in providing solutions to social and economic problems (Mazower, 1998).

torically, has more often than not been driven by a desire to tame the unpredictability and brutality of unregulated market forces. By insisting that economic policy choices be narrowly restricted and, as far as possible, be treated as purely technical issues, there is a real danger that today's market fundamentalists will succeed, at least in the short run, in their attempts to remove more and more aspects of market behaviour and economic performance from democratic scrutiny and accountability. But diminishing the domain over which democratic choices can be exercised increases the risk of a backlash that will damage both political and economic development in the longer run. The incantation of political elites that "there is no alternative" to liberal economic reforms has already begun to fuel resentment and discontent in Europe (West and East) and in Latin America.[58] What is patronisingly dismissed as economic nationalism by market fundamentalists usually reflects their disdain for any national preferences that are not revealed by the market and their unwillingness to support effective policies to ease the adjustment costs of economic change, especially those that fall on the least-advantaged.

An alternative argument sometimes heard is that human rights, social policies and democracy are political luxuries that can only be afforded at later stages of economic development. There is no doubt that economic advance, at least in the shorter run, has been achieved under some authoritarian regimes, or that democracies have sometimes failed spectacularly in the face of economic crisis. However, when presented as some kind of ineluctable principle of development, we believe this view also to be deeply mistaken.

Effective mechanisms of participation and voice, as well as respect for and defence of human rights, can actually have a very positive impact on the daily economic lives of individuals, especially those of the poor in developing countries, who are often remote, in more than just the geographical sense, from representative institutions in the capital cities: the peasant with undefined or unprotected property rights, subject to grasping landlords; the slum dweller subject to arbi-

---

[58] The latest opinion surveys undertaken in Latin America by Latinobarómetro, a Chilean organisation, suggest support for democracy is lower in a dozen countries today than in 1996, although it is still generally seen as the least-worst option. See "Democracy's ten-year rut", *The Economist,* 27 October 2005.

trary arrest from an undisciplined police force and brutality from criminal gangs; the precarious position of women and children in many societies. The elementary, positive freedom to survive is greatly increased in the presence of democratic institutions. Amartya Sen has shown that famines have often occurred in the presence of plentiful supplies of food because vulnerable groups (landless agricultural workers, for example) lack appropriate entitlements or ownership rights. In contrast, and despite many natural catastrophes, there has not been a single case of famine in India since independence (Sen, 1981; Drèze and Sen, 1981). The key factor is the ability of the affected population to give "voice" to its predicament and to maintain pressure on governments to respond rapidly and effectively to social distress. Such a situation contrasts sharply with that in many states of Sub-Saharan Africa and some of those in Latin America. In countries with democratic government and an array of democratic freedoms, disasters, man-made or natural, are difficult to keep secret (as happened with the great Chinese famine of 1958-61).

Still, the question is whether or not this same logic extends to everyday matters of development policy; to put it in its simplest terms, can a poor democratic state be expected to raise its growth rates from 3 or 4 per cent per annum to 7 or 8 per cent on a sustainable basis? There are certainly plenty of naysayers and the broad body of cross-country evidence remains confusing, partly for familar methodological reasons discussed in earlier chapters, on the strength of the link between democracy and economic growth (Przeworski and Limongi, 1993; Brunetti, 1997). There is also evidence pointing to different types of growth paths, with more authoritarian regimes relying on resource mobilisation and exhibiting a greater degree of volatility, while growth in more democratic regimes relies on raising productivity and innovation, and tends to exhibit greater stability (Przeworski et al., 2000). Others have suggested that the more decisive test lies in the comparative strength of political regimes in managing economic transitions, suggesting positive results for democracies (Rodrik and Wacziarg, 2004). There is also plenty of evidence to suggest that, from a purely economic standpoint, democracies perform better than authoritarian regimes in producing more stable rates of economic growth, in handling negative shocks from whatever source, and in producing better distributional outcomes (Rodrik, 2000). Restricting

the policy options available to developing countries thus increases
the risks of undermining the prospects of both economic and democratic development.

This is not, of course, a matter that is likely to be resolved by
econometric studies. The sensible position is probably to accept that
political and economic progress are never tied together in any straightforward or functional way (Hirschman, 1994:229). That position still
leaves plenty of room (and enough empirical evidence) to support the
argument that democracy, involving not just periodic elections but
the broader qualities of the participatory open society, can have and
has had a significant, positive effect on economic growth.[59] The fact
that the link is not automatic implies a need for more careful attention
to the possible channels through which positive synergies can be
realised and the possible gaps that might have to be filled. Some have
linked democratisation to less corruption and more efficient bureaucracies which in turn are associated with higher investment ratios,
suggesting improvements in the bureaucracy might be as important
as political stability (Mauro, 1995; Wei, 2001). Dani Rodrik (1998)
has found a close correlation between the openness of an economy
and the size of its government, a relationship that he suggests reflects
an explicit *quid pro quo* for labour agreeing to trade liberalisation,
which in turn suggests a greater sensitivity of democratic governments towards those who bear the costs of generally advantageous
policies and whose cooperation is needed for their success. Others
have found a strong link between democracy, investment in human
capital and growth (Tavares and Wacziarg, 2001). Similarly, the introduction of democracy has been associated with reductions in inequality of incomes and, despite some fears to the contrary, this does
not appear to have negative effects on economic performance, either
because higher wages for workers may reflect more efficient labour

---

[59] States that hold free elections but ignore these other dimensions of the democratic
process, including respect for the rule of law and respect for individual rights,
have been labelled "illiberal democracies" (Zakaria, 1997). In many cases this
may reflect the problems of "transition" mentioned earlier. Disenchantment with
half-way democracies as a block on development was a focus of the UNDP's
Human Development Report in 2002. More generally, on the positive links between
development and democracy, see Leblanc (1997); Nelson and Singh (1998); Isham,
Kaufmann and Pritchett (1997); Siegle, Weinstein and Halperin (2004).

markets or because it encourages the emergence of a middle class and a thickening of market relations or because it produces a more stable investment climate (Rodrik, 1999). A related approach associates social divergence with a weakening of the interaction between individuals that is needed to boost innovation and accelerate the diffusion of ideas which in turn raise productivity (Grafton, Knowles and Owen, 2001).

The more general point, it seems to us, is that because dynamic market societies progress through both creative and destructive forces, they are bound to trigger tensions and conflicts. Such conflicts can emerge from technical progress, investment cycles, opening up to foreign competition and TNCs, shifts in the structure and location of economic activity, etc. These can be dealt with either by suppressing the underlying forces that give rise to them, and at the same time foregoing the benefits of such dynamism, or by learning to manage the conflicts through bargaining, arguing and negotiating. Albert Hirschman (1994:242-48) has suggested, and we agree with him, that there is a greater likelihood of learning to better manage the "steady diet of conflicts" generated by market forces under a democratic than an authoritarian regime.

Economic development is a continuing process of transformation in which economic, political and social factors are closely interrelated. As such, it requires popular assent and that, in turn, needs institutions for consultation, discussion and participation; changes in the economic system require innovations in the framework of institutions that incorporate the incentives that can either stimulate development or retard it; and the ruling elites must be willing to respond to popular pressure and accommodate change. The capacity of the state to provide a coherent vision of the future and to manage the conflicts that change brings, including disciplining the behaviour of elites when they undermine the broader national interest, is perhaps the greatest challenge it faces in poorer countries. If a large part of the ruling class of politicians, officials and businessmen are unwilling to give up or modify some of the benefits and social position they enjoy from the status quo, then very little can be achieved until the structure of power has been changed either through evolution or revolution, preferably of the "velvet" rather than the violent sort.

Outside pressure, under some circumstances, can play a constructive role in deepening the participation process and building consent. In different ways that was probably the case in Japan, South
Korea and Taiwan.[60] But we have already argued that outside pressure and advice for economic and institutional reforms is frequently
influenced by mythical narratives of the outsiders' own histories and
by the misleading, universalist assumptions of mainstream economic
policies. An additional problem is that international technocrats, business advisers and others tend to see the problems of development in
relatively narrow, apolitical terms. Economists who overlook the wider
political and social issues are unlikely, in our view, to provide useful
advice and, by extension, economic development is unlikely to be
achieved with economic instruments alone. If, as seems likely, productivity and growth are, in part, explained by politics, policy and
institutions (Hibbs, 2001), then the elegant simplicities of the neo-
classical and endogenous theories of economic growth are unlikely
to be the source of many valid, general policy recommendations for
countries seeking economic development.

The proposition that democratic processes and institutions are
more generally vital for promoting development was central to the
political thinking of Karl Popper, who argued in 1945 that democratic
societies were much better at solving their problems and achieving
their aims than authoritarian regimes (Popper, 1966, 5th edition). This
is because problem-solving involves experimentation, processes of
trial and error, tolerance and encouragement of open criticism, and a
willingness, or at least incentives, for governments to change direction as a result of that criticism. Writing at the same time as Popper,
Karl Polanyi (1944) recognised that extending "freedom in a complex society" also meant challenging the anti-democratic tendencies
of the market to remove economic life from the influence of political
voice and from collective and cooperative action. More recently, Joseph Stiglitz has taken up this theme, arguing for the importance of
democratic process for economic development: inter alia, strengthening the mechanisms of "voice" helps to reduce the risks of disrup-

---

[60] We suspect that the outlook inspired by the Marshall Plan had a decisive impact
in these cases; see Chapter 7.

tion by disappointed groups, and institutions for participation and consultation make it easier to create the necessary consensus for reform (in Chang, 2001, especially Chapters 7 and 8). This line of thought, as with Sen's argument for the importance of participation in public decision-making, government by discussion and public reasoning (Sen, 2005), is closely connected to the ideas of political theorists of deliberative democracy.[61]

All these approaches challenge the view that the political process can be reduced to another form of market behaviour where self-interested competition is governed by bargaining and rational choice. In the Popper-Sen-Stiglitz framework, democratic political engagement can be an end in itself, encouraging citizens to think beyond their own immediate interests towards larger public interests, an educating process that strengthens civic virtues and supports the evolution of shared values and norms of behaviour that a long list of writers, including Adam Smith in his *Theory of Moral Sentiments,* have identified as essential for an effective economy and a stable polity. Nevertheless, while accepting that political institutions and processes cannot simply be reduced to their instrumental effectiveness in raising GDP, it is still important, especially for the poor, to be confident that democratic processes are effective in promoting economic development.

None of this can be captured in the market-fundamentalist dogma of minimal government, which lacks any recognition of the state's economic role in preserving and fostering social cohesion, instead replacing this with a set of universalistic policy recommendations ostensibly derived from the "win-win" logic of economic theory (Gray, 1998:203). Instead of prescribing specific institutional arrangements and policy options for a developing, transition or post-conflict economy – those are for each individual country to discover – it is perhaps more useful to highlight the tasks that the government of a market-based democracy can be expected to perform and for which it must establish, through trial and error, and in tune with the political and social culture of the country, the most appropriate set of institu-

---

[61] For a useful collection of papers on the concept of deliberative democracy, see Bohman and Relig (1997).

tions for carrying them out. We will return to this theme in the next chapter. Here we wish simply to reiterate that it is a strategic error to relegate political institutions to the category of "second-generation reforms": instituting effective democratic processes is more urgent than creating stock markets or liberalising the capital account of the balance of payments. Apart from the obvious key requirements of democracy – that the legitimacy of government is derived from popular consent and is periodically tested in competitive political elections in which all adults are free to vote or stand as candidates, that voting is secret, and that the basic freedoms of speech, press, assembly and organisation are open to all – our argument for democratic gradualism, as well as the works cited above, stress the importance of participation, consultation and negotiation as a means of deploying local knowledge and local interests as a check on governments (and their foreign advisers) acting in an authoritarian manner between elections.

By encouraging and strengthening these local or micro-foundations of democracy, governments can be helped to design more effective strategies for reform and to build a broad coalition for societal change. This is no small matter given that one of the most important determinants of policy success is whether a government is able to create and maintain credibility in its programme. This is a difficult task and requires not just economic understanding but political skills of a high order, but the process is made easier if there is a genuine interaction between policy makers and effective local organisations. The credibility of a government's programme is also enhanced if it can set out a coherent and convincing multi-year programme of reforms and objectives. Coherence here means setting out the basic strategy, the interrelationships between social and economic factors, and a credible sequence of actions that will increase the probability of success. If economic agents expect a reversal of policy they will act accordingly and undermine it before it even gets under way.

Since we have stressed that promoting economic development is still an advance into *terra incognita*, governments will need to experiment and therefore there are bound to be setbacks and mistakes. In order to handle these without seriously damaging expectations and losing popular support for change, we suggest in the next chapter a framework along the lines of the post-war Marshall Plan, a framework that will be stronger the more it takes into account local knowledge and interests. Since some of these interests will inevitably be hurt by changes in the structure of the economy, and because of *ex ante* uncertainty about the likely distribution of the benefits and costs of change – the costs often arriving ahead of the benefits – such "Marshall Plans" will need to make explicit provision for distributional policies. This will include safety nets for those directly affected by increased imports or market liberalisation: taking care of the wounded, in other words. But more general policies are also needed to focus specifically on poverty reduction and more equal income distribution in order to underpin the institutions of participatory democracy and, in turn, sustain popular support for programmes of change. The dangerous consequences of sections of the population being left behind in the development process include threats not only to the process itself but also to security within and beyond national borders. It is marginalised communities that constitute those "pools of disaffection" that provide at least a passive cover for terrorist groups, the leaders of which normally come from the ranks of the middle class rather than those of the poor. Although explicit distributive policies, including at the international level, may frighten the corporate sector in the rich countries, the G7 countries would be wise to support them.

Thus, we are arguing that creating and strengthening effective democratic institutions and introducing mechanisms for handling distribution issues should be among the top priorities for institutional reform, not relegated to some "second stage" when growth is under way and they can be more easily "afforded".[62] Underlying these re-

---

[62] The concept of "second-stage" reforms is not very helpful in that it suggests a series of finite steps which should be followed in sequence *and* that we know what it should be. The general idea of a credible sequence of reforms is understandable in the sense that proceeding with A before B can increase the probability of success for both, whereas the opposite sequence may raise expectations that both may fail. But apart from recommending that the trade account should be liberalised before the capital account, economists have little general advice to give about correct sequencing. This will have to be determined largely on pragmatic grounds and on the basis of local knowledge. The "second-stage" concept is to a large extent a belated recognition of matters that should have been in the "first stage" but were overlooked by those advocating shock therapy in Eastern Europe in the 1990s.

marks on the importance of democratic processes is the recognition that although a competitive framework is essential in a world of scarcity, cooperation is also crucial for the success of market economies, and that cooperation is nurtured by political arrangements that allow and encourage participation by the citizens at large. It is within such arrangements that the population can help to change the formal and informal rules that govern their economic behaviour and gradually move them in a direction more favourable to sustained growth, although there is no guarantee that they will succeed. If, as suggested by North (1994), culture is a key ingredient of path dependence, then the probability of altering direction is much higher if changes in rules and conventions emerge from and have the support of grassroots democratic bodies than if they are imposed by elites or authoritarian governments; from this perspective, it is "adaptive" rather than "allocative" efficiency which is the key to long-run growth (North, 1994:367). Although we are not sure how to create adaptive efficiency or what institutional arrangements are most likely to nurture it, democratic practices do appear to be particularly suited to supporting the learning and experimental processes that characterise dynamic societies.

F.   Conclusions

In this chapter we have insisted on development as a process of societal change, that the market economy is only one dimension of a highly complex interaction of political, social and economic factors, and that there is no universally applicable set of institutions and values or lessons from the experience of the west for developing countries to follow. The pretence that the secret of development is known to western policy makers and international bureaucrats is at best a "fatal conceit", to borrow Hayek's description of the claims of socialist economics, and at worst a form of intellectual imperialism. The importance of institutions and politics means that only the local population can decide what it wants and what it must do to achieve its aims. This does not mean holding a closed or insular perspective, far from it; only that without a deep knowledge of local conditions, outside policy advice is more likely to be a hindrance rather than a help. A similar consideration applies to the importance of local and tacit knowledge for the adoption of innovations and making them work. Valuable technical and financial assistance is available abroad, but it needs to be designed to support a development agenda determined principally by the developing countries themselves, not vice versa.

Our understanding of the causes of economic growth and of the ways in which it interacts with social and political variables is still very limited. There is widepsread agreement, however, that capital accumulation plays a crucial role in the process and in this chapter we have used the profit-investment-export nexus to examine some of the linkages and feedback mechanisms that, from this starting point, can help define development strategies, albeit contingent on social and political factors and on the nature of a country's institutional structure which embodies many of the incentives and other variables that influence the propensity to invest.

We have argued that this general uncertainty about the sources of progress points to the necessity for careful experimentation with institutions and policies in order to discover what will be effective in a particular national context where history, culture and initial economic conditions all have an important influence on the possibilities for growth and development. Given the premium on flexibility and "adaptive efficiency", and given also the absence of universal laws of economic growth, restricting the policy space available to developing countries is more than likely to be counter-productive. It is unacceptable for the IFIs and developed countries to rule out certain policy instruments, such as various supports to infant industries, capital controls, start-up subsidies, and a wide range of other types of government intervention that have proved very effective in the past but which are now declared to be inconsistent with the neo-liberal view of the world.

We have argued that neo-liberalism, far from providing a universal set of prescriptions for economic growth and development, is contaminated with historical myths about the economic development of the industrial market economies, with implausible theoretical assumptions, and with opportunistic bias; moreover, the empirical evidence is that it fails to deliver what it promises.

We have also stressed that if the requirements of democratic process are ignored, the risks are increased of a popular backlash against reforms if they promise too much too soon and expectations are disappointed, or if technocratic elites, whether home-grown or from abroad, press ahead regardless of local customs and preferences. The issue was clearly understood more than 100 years ago by the British Conservative Prime Minister, Benjamin Disraeli, in a speech on the 1867 Reform Bill (extending the male franchise): "In a progressive country change is constant; and the great question is, not whether you should resist change which is inevitable, but whether that change should be carried out in deference to the manners, the customs, the laws, and traditions of a people, or whether it should be carried out in deference to abstract principles, and arbitrary and general doctrines" (Kebbel, 1882, Vol. II:487). Thus, Disraeli, the 19th-century Conservative, and Stiglitz, the 21st-century social democrat, come together on the importance of democratic process and the limitations of technical expertise when fundamental issues of economic development and social change are at stake. In comparison, "shock therapists" and market fundamentalists belong more to the Leninist tradition in wanting to introduce systemic change with a minimum of delay, with little or no discussion of alternative transition paths, and, if not totally indifferent to the social costs, by downplaying or assuming them away.

In all democratic societies gradualism tends to be the rule, one of the major democratic arts being to negotiate compromises and solutions to the conflicts of interest to which change invariably gives rise (Kozul-Wright and Rayment, 1997). In terms of market and democratic forces combining for progressive economic change, it should be emphasised that this requires the presence of institutions that can help fashion a broader and longer view of the national interest than one limited to those with privileges and position in the status quo. This is far from being the case in many developing countries. Indeed, we have suggested that one of the most damaging consequences of 25 years of ill-conceived adjustment programmes is to have made this institutional hiatus even wider. Even when a majority of a population is convinced that it could benefit from the new order, there may still be resistance to change if there is *ex ante* uncertainty about the actual distribution of the costs and benefits, i.e., if *individuals* are unsure whether they will benefit personally (Fernandez and Rodrik, 1991) and there is insufficient confidence in the institutions that are available to manage the potential conflicts.[63] In such a situation the majority could vote against its own perceived interest. The task of political leadership in creating and sustaining support for a development programme is therefore crucially important for the prospects of success. This requires considerable political skills, but some frameworks for policy are likely to be more effective than others. In our judgement there is much that can be learned from the Economic Recovery Programme or Marshall Plan for Western Europe in the late 1940s when considering alternatives to the failed policies of market fundamentalism. We turn to this experience in the next chapter.

---

[63] The problem was set out clearly in the early 16th century by Machiavelli when he explained why there is "nothing more difficult to take in hand, more perilous to conduct, or more uncertain in its success than to take the lead in the introduction of a new order of things" (Machiavelli, 1961, Penguin edition:51). He gave two reasons: one, the resistance of those benefiting from the status quo and, two, the lukewarm support of those who should benefit from the "new order" but are uncertain about the outcome, "never trusting new things unless they have tested them by experience" (loc. cit.).

Chapter 7

Resisting Market Fundamentalism

A.   Introduction

OVER 30 years ago Gunnar Myrdal concluded his book, *The Challenge of World Poverty,* by reminding his readers that "development should be seen as a movement upward of a whole system of interdependent conditions, of which economic growth, assuming that it could be properly defined and measured, is only one of several categories of causally interrelated conditions". Myrdal was convinced that through a judicious mix of prices, policies and international cooperation, the forces of justice, equality and productivity could be united to establish just such an upward movement in developing countries, thereby eliminating global poverty. We share his conviction and like Myrdal, we have argued that searching out alternatives to the neoliberal idolisation of market forces means putting institutions, values and politics back onto the development agenda.

In 1970, Myrdal predicted that if neo-liberal abstractions were allowed to dictate policy options in poorer countries, the whole development process would eventually come to a "grinding lame walk and, finally, general retrogression" (Myrdal, ibid.). The past 25 years have certainly witnessed retrogression of the type that Myrdal feared, principally at the regional level in Latin America and Sub-Saharan Africa, as well as in parts of the former communist bloc. General retrogression, however, has been avoided, thanks, in no small part, to strong and sustained growth in East Asia and, more recently, in parts of South Asia. Although Myrdal underestimated the potential for economic growth in these regions, their success has in no small measure been due to their adopting many of the policies and institutional reforms that he associated with a "virtuous circle" of cumulative and interdependent development.

We argued in the last chapter that one way to distil clearer lessons from these experiences is to focus on the profit-investment-export nexus. This was not offered as an alternative development "paradigm" but rather as a heuristic framework for discovering development policy options that focus on the main factors of economic growth while at the same time being sensitive to historical legacies, institutional structures and democratic practices. The importance of raising investment and exports is fully recognised, of course, by those who support the rapid liberalisation of international trade and capital markets. And few would disagree that profits play a central role in the dynamics of capitalist development. The crucial disagreement is over whether the mutually reinforcing links between trade, investment and economic growth can be brought about by rapid opening up to market forces, establishing an investment climate attractive to private foreign capital, and removing the direction of the economy from democratic accountability. This, as we noted in the opening chapter, was the prescription for faster growth and convergence offered to the international community in the early 1980s by US President Ronald Reagan and its evolution into a development "consensus" has been accompanied by the persistent refrain that "there is no alternative" to getting prices right and accepting the sovereignty of nomadic capital.

Such confidence has been shaken in recent years by the sub-standard growth performance of many countries pursuing the neo-liberal agenda, by the virulence of financial crises, including in economies previously deemed to be proof of the benefits of globalisation, by persistent and widening income gaps and social inequities, and by the failure of a booming trading system to deliver stable jobs and rising wages. The discussion in the previous chapters has suggested that these problems lie as much with what has been included (policy commissions) in the neo-liberal agenda as with what has been left out (governance omissions).

Simply put, the one-size-fits-all prescription of leaving things to the free play of market forces has been, and continues to be, bad economics for developing countries. In part, this is because by continuing to measure policy programmes against the utopian yardstick of perfectly competitive markets, the instinctive reaction of its proponents is to deny policy makers the requisite space to correct market failures, to better manage boom-bust cycles and to deal effectively with exogenous shocks. Also, by ignoring the uneven power relations in the global economy, it (inadvertently or not) promotes the interests of the advanced economies which effectively insist that developing countries must integrate into the world economy on their terms. But principally it is because the drive to policy conformity under the cloak of market-driven globalisation fails, or is unwilling, to acknowledge the considerable differences among countries in their initial economic conditions and their national preferences, as well as denying a role for institutional "rootedness" in effective policy design and implementation (Berger and Dore, 1996).

Such "rootedness" implies that successful institutional reforms are unlikely to result from large shocks or to "travel well", and that policies to stimulate growth must be designed around a clear understanding of local capabilities, constraints and opportunities – and that in turn requires sufficient space for experimentation in order to discover what will actually work in a specific context. Such "rootedness" also implies that institutional deepening, both of a formal and informal nature, is path-dependent. In all these respects, the nation state has a pivotal role in articulating and building an economic future. That role, of course, will change over time, and because growth and development essentially involve a societal, not just an economic, transformation, a nation's perception of where it wants to go should be treated with respect.[1]

For some observers, the uncontested rise of global markets and firms has unleashed an anarchic maelstrom that precludes alternatives centred on national economic institutions (Gray, 1998). For others, shifting geo-political structures along with the tightening of policy rules and regulations through regional and multilateral fora greatly frustrate that search, if not curtailing it altogether (Gallagher (ed.), 2005). Some see the growing detachment of local elites from their domestic economic and political environment and their lowering of expectations about national development projects as firmly closing the door on local development options (Sklair, 2001). All highlight

---

[1] In this spirit, Johann von Thünen (1783-1850), the agricultural economist and founder of marginal analysis, once argued that savings reflect a society's capacity to imagine a future for itself and its confidence to create it.

some important truths, but their denial of the possibility of national development strategies seems to us too pessimistic. Indeed, in the absence of strong state actors from the developing world, the alternative approach of trying to create overarching mechanisms of global governance seems to us to be as utopian as the agenda of market fundamentalists.

The challenge facing policy makers in most developing countries is how to define, expand and, where necessary, reclaim the policy space they need for more development-oriented economic strategies, in a manner consistent with an increasingly open and integrated world economy and without falling into the trap of substituting a myth of unfettered national sovereignty for the myths of market fundamentalism. In the next two sections, we take a closer look at the idea of policy space and then begin the task of thinking about alternatives by reflecting on the policies adopted in Western Europe in the years following the end of World War II, policies that managed to strike an acceptable balance between national sovereignty and international responsibilities. We then look at some of the "nuts and bolts" policy issues that emerge from putting the profit-investment-export nexus at the centre of development strategy. Finally, we consider some of the changes to the international framework, including at the regional level, which might better encourage an environment of experimentation, diversity and democratic gradualism in support of development.

B.   Democratic gradualism and policy space

Following the collapse of communism in Eastern and Central Europe in the early 1990s, there was heated debate about the appropriate pace at which these economies should move towards decentralised market systems. Apart from general agreement on the need to move quickly in order to prevent accelerating inflation in several countries, and although admitting that many institutional changes would take a long time to implement, "shock therapists" were generally in favour of rapid price and trade liberalisation, the speedy removal of controls on foreign capital flows, the pegging of exchange rates to a hard currency, and the privatisation of state-owned enterprises as quickly as possible in order for a new private sector to emerge and be able to respond to the new environment.[2] Underlying this approach was considerable optimism about the ability of these economies to respond to the new environment of competition and the change in relative prices, but there was also an expectation that with the fall of the Berlin Wall the international economic environment would become a good deal more supportive in terms of the size and quality of capital flows, both official and private, and of improved access to western markets. Those in favour of a more gradual transition were much less optimistic about the speed of response, pointing to the problems of missing institutions and the effective loss of a large proportion of the countries' political and organisational capital as a result of the revolutions of 1989 (UNECE, 1990). Suggestions that something along the lines of the 1947 Marshall Plan might be an effective way of handling these problems were swiftly rejected by western governments and the IFIs, which, in their belief that rapid liberalisation was the answer, seriously underestimated the costs and the time required for transforming centrally planned into market economies and, in the process, failed to anticipate the collapse of output that followed the upheaval in institutional frameworks.[3]

This was not a new debate, however. The term "shock therapy" had already come into use in the 1980s in the context of structural adjustment programmes in the developing world, where a similar package of reforms, quickly adopted, was seen as the most effective means not only of correcting past policy mistakes but also of pre-empting those interest groups who might otherwise block the reform process (World Bank, 1991). But the roots go back even further. In the 1950s, the IMF had advocated a form of shock therapy for Latin

---

[2]   "Shock therapy" was also influenced by fears that if the new economy were not quickly established the old *nomenklatura* would try to "turn the clock back". Instead, it was all too ready to move with the times and many of its members enriched themselves quickly by obtaining state assets at "fire-sale" prices.

[3]   A considerable body of literature arose over the question of whether shock therapy or a more gradual approach supported by a new Marshall Plan was the best way to effect the transition from a centrally planned to a market economy. For a small sample see UNECE (1990); Kostrzewa, Nunnenkamp and Schmieding (1990); Kaser (1990); Hare (1990); Kregel, Matzner and Grabher (1992); Köves (1992); Dabrowski (1996); Wei (1997); and Davis and Foreman-Peck (2001).

American countries, where rates of growth were decelerating and prices rising, a therapy that included credit constraints, public-expenditure cuts, devaluation, deregulation and a rapid liberalisation of foreign trade (Felix, 1961). Then, as now, the optimists judged that adjustment would be more or less spontaneous as long as "prices were right" and private enterprise given free rein.[4] As we have tried to show in previous chapters, this policy orientation failed to produce the kind of economic environment in which investors and firms would be encouraged to support the expansion and improvement of productive capacity, but it did succeed in unleashing the often "destructive" forces of global competition.

Differences between shock therapists and gradualists have often been exaggerated in the heat of polemical debate. This has not been very helpful because it falsely implies just two paths of adjustment and was often pitched in terms of "historic" choices. In fact, what was required in developing and transition economies alike was a combination of sufficient time to fill the "institutional hiatus" and policy space to undertake effective adjustments in the light of the specificities of each country's circumstances. A second generation of neo-liberal strategists has gone some way to acknowledging this and has called for more careful thinking about establishing the right "sequence" of reforms. As we noted in Chapter 3, this was principally focussed on finding a more constructive way of handling capital inflows. However, as Fanelli and Frenkel (1993) have pointed out, this approach still ties policy design to an abstract notion of a fully liberalised economy rather than situating concrete reforms in a specific historical and institutional context. Moreover, much of the literature on sequencing still denies the possibility that the reforms themselves might generate persistent forces for decline or stagnation.

---

[4]   In contrast, structuralists and institutionalists, such as Raúl Prebisch and Gunnar Myrdal, thought that institutional and coordination failures would block or weaken the mechanism for the efficient allocation of resources and distort the broader process of development. Moreover, for adjustment to be productive, a supportive international environment would be needed to provide the time and the resources required to allow countries to avoid defensive measures that might damage not only their own longer-term prospects but also those of their neighbours.

Rodrik (2004a:6-7) has argued that with no guide to setting priorities or mixing policies in a second-best world, "sequencing" offers few pointers to judging the costs of neo-liberal reform or discovering what works under local conditions.[5] What we have called democratic gradualism is essentially a political mechanism for introducing a range of economic and social outcomes beyond a narrowly conceived business interest and handling a wide variety of adjustment costs that accompany real-world reforms and policy changes in pursuit of those outcomes. Among the important elements in the process we note the following: firstly, those who see profitable opportunities in reforms will want them implemented as quickly as possible, and will usually want to "leave things to the market", i.e., to leave themselves with a free hand; secondly, those likely to bear the burden of reform will try to extend the adjustment period for as long as possible or to socialise the costs in order to minimise the impact on their capital (physical, human or communal) assets; and thirdly, there ensues a bargaining process, usually under the auspices of the government, to reconcile these two positions. The results are not always economically or socially optimal and there is the danger that organised interests will bias the outcome. But these problems can be dealt with, in part, by ensuring that there is transparency in the policy-making process, that the targets for adjustment are credible, and that sanctions are available if those targets are not met. If credibility is achieved in this way, then the signals for reallocating resources will be clear and the process of adjustment will begin to operate as soon as the policy is announced. This, as we saw in the previous chapter, is how gradualism can be effective, not simply in dealing with specific problems of adjustment but more generally in managing the creative and destructive forces of a market economy.

With hindsight, the successes and failures of the transition process tend to bear out this conclusion. The countries of Central

---

[5] Conventional economists have known, at least since Jacob Viner's work on customs unions, that in the absence of full and immediate liberalisation, the consequences of partial liberalisation are impossible to predict. Consequently, the kinds of positive spin put on the partial-liberalisation packages (whether bilateral, regional or multilateral) found in the real world should always be treated with a healthy degree of scepticism.

Europe where the transition to a functioning market economy was most rapid were those where initial conditions were most favourable, where political and economic reforms had started well before the collapse of central planning and where different interest groups were given some voice over possible outcomes.[6] Similarly, success stories in the developing world – South Korea and Taiwan in the 1970s, Mauritius in the 1980s, India and China in the 1990s – were in countries that had gradually introduced reforms and had institutionalised voice, albeit in different ways. Nor were they significantly subject to detailed pressure from the international financial institutions in terms of the trade-offs they were allowed to make in organising and managing their reforms.

We have already argued that attempts to transplant existing institutions from one environment to another are unlikely to be successful if they strangle the processes of trial and error, of institutional and policy experimentation, that have characterised all previous examples of successful development. It is also inconsistent, many would say hypocritical, for the developed countries to promote, on the one hand, the principles and institutions of democracy in developing countries and then, on the other, to seize every opportunity to force them to adopt the institutional arrangements that have evolved in response to the conditions and preferences of the countries and populations of North America and Western Europe. Again, this is not to deny that successful market economies tend to share a basic core of institutions, capacities and objectives, but only to insist there is no unique mapping from these to specific arrangements in individual countries. Thus, for example, there is general agreement that market

---

[6]   There was always considerable uncertainty about the precise nature and intensity of the alleged shocks and the reality of shock therapy was often much less than the rhetoric suggested. Governments would claim they had made their currencies convertible, an important element of the shock programme, while retaining an array of controls on access to foreign currency. Romania, for example, announced current-account convertibility in November 1991 but did not abolish import controls. Poland was widely regarded as having introduced shock therapy in 1991 but in fact the policies, including the target for disinflation, were markedly softened soon after their introduction. To some extent East European policy makers were echoing the rhetoric of shock therapy coming from western advisers while being forced by events to be gradual (or more pragmatic) in many important areas.

economies usually function best under a system of private property rights, although various forms of social or mutual ownership have also been shown to work, as most recently in China (Nolan, 2004). Yet even in the advanced economies, property rights are never absolute or unlimited: they are, for example, subject to inheritance and zoning laws, the uses to which they are put may be regulated, and private interests may be overridden by the public interest (to make way for public roads, for example). The key principle is not that property rights should be completely unfettered (although some extreme conservative groups hold this view) but that the restrictions should be transparent, predictable (although not immutable) and subject to the rule of law and constitutional restraints. In a democracy these restraints reflect the legitimate preferences of the population, and for an international institution or a developed country to insist that they be altered to reflect another set of preferences is a gross interference in the democratic process. It is up to each country to decide how to define, protect and qualify property rights and to judge how far these arrangements support other objectives such as promoting entrepreneurship and fixed investment.

Similarly, it should be a matter for democratic choice in each country to decide where the boundaries are drawn between the state, private and social sectors. By extension, it should also be a matter of democratic choice to decide the extent of foreign ownership of domestic assets and how foreign investment should be distributed sectorally and regionally. This last point follows from two related observations: one, that economic growth is a vector, that is, it has not only quantity but also direction; and two, that the composition of investment in a country reflects a view of the future structure of its economy and, hence, of the future shape of its society. Opening a developing economy to unrestricted foreign investment in the belief that this will boost development is not, as we have seen earlier, based on strong empirical foundations. But in addition it risks effectively transferring important decisions about the future to foreigners who will not necessarily share the interests and preferences of the local population. Although developing countries want to "catch up" with the levels of income and welfare prevailing in the developed world, it is still legitimate for them to ask whether they want to be like the United States or Sweden or Japan, or something quite different.

We have already emphasised that none of the most developed economies reached their present levels of prosperity by practising the type of free-market capitalism that they now urge upon poorer countries. Historically, the evolution of today's successful economies has above all been marked by what has earlier been described as "adaptive efficiency", the capacity to develop institutions that provide a stable framework for economic activity but at the same time are flexible enough to provide the maximum leeway for policy choices at any given time and in any given situation in response to specific challenges. The emphasis on flexibility and the need to experiment reflect the realities of operating in an uncertain world where our knowledge of the best ways to promote economic growth and development is limited, and what we do know suggests that success is characterised by diversity, contingent on national political and social cultures, on historically determined path dependencies, and on the behaviour of the ruling elites. Experimentation, together with rules and conventions to ensure that failed experiments are dropped rather than retained to avoid embarrassment, is thus crucial for raising the probability of success.

In the particular case of state institutions, this notion of adaptive efficiency implies that policy makers must have the requisite amount of space to articulate priorities, choose their preferred policy instruments and implement what they see as the most appropriate policy "mix". Some time ago, Jan Tinbergen established that for the mix to work at a macroeconomic level there had to be at least as many instruments as there are goals. If a programme includes more goals than instruments, at least one goal will not be met; whereas if it contains more instruments than goals, there will be more than one way of achieving the combination of goals. Arguably, and as is certainly the case with most development strategies, where a variety of microeconomic, macroeconomic and structural goals are being pursued simultaneously, maximising the number of instruments would seem to be the sensible option. However, simply reducing the issue of policy space to the number of instruments and goals is not a sufficient guide to the complexities involved. Not only are different instruments likely to have different degrees of effectiveness in meeting a particular goal, but because goals are *interdependent*, a particular instrument can potentially influence many goals at the same time, and not always in the expected or desired direction.[7] Moreover, the distinction between goals and instruments is neither entirely unambiguous nor obvious. What is a target for one set of policy makers (or in one set of circumstances) may well be an instrument for another (or in another set of circumstances).

All this means that policy makers are continuously forced into thinking about trade-offs in a particular programme. Typically, policy goals are rarely of the "either or" type (growth or price stability, open or closed, state or private ownership, fixed or flexible exchange rates, etc.), but of various in-between shades. This would already suggest that learning to mix objectives and instruments is an unavoidable component of policy-making, and experimentation becomes all the more important given that there are different ways of achieving faster growth, macroeconomic stability, openness and a more equitable distribution of income (World Bank, 2005a:13).

Some means must still be in place for setting priorities and judging the extent to which they can be met. Consequently the room available to policy makers depends, as we noted in the previous chapter, on their autonomy from the array of interest groups that are looking for support from the state, as well as the strength of political leadership on economic-development issues. At the same time, deciding on the appropriate mix will also involve judgements about the likely magnitude of the adjustments arising from a particular programme. Accordingly, before such a programme is finalised, there must be preparatory discussion and quantitative work examining the likely effectiveness of various instruments to establish whether the extent of the adjustment needed is politically feasible. In any event the combination of leadership, experimentation and judgement is certain to make for an open-ended policy-making process.

---

[7]   To give just one microeconomic example: in parts of East Africa the subsidisation of school meals by the World Food Programme not only helped to improve the nutrition of schoolchildren, a primary objective, but also led to an increased enrolment of girls, another major development target, parents being only too willing to have their daughters fed by someone else and thereby leaving more of the family food supplies for working sons.

In contrast, the certainty (and the arrogance) of the neo-liberal agenda stems from its lop-sided focus on instruments, or more precisely its preconceived conviction that some instruments are almost desirable ends in themselves (trade liberalisation, privatisation, attracting FDI, a balanced budget, etc.) while others (tariffs, higher taxes, nationalisation, printing money, etc.) are intrinsically bad. That is not only because the preferred instruments, such as trade liberalisation, are seen as synonymous with the incentive structure of an idealised market economy, but also because it is assumed that there is an automatic and linear relationship from efficiency gains to other desirable outcomes, such as a faster rate of economic growth. In such a framework there is no place for debate and experimentation in the policy-making process. On the contrary, such experimentation is deemed a potential threat to economic efficiency, and deferring to technocratic authority on which instruments matter is seen as a way of curtailing the unruly ambitions of political actors and guaranteeing economic stability.[8]

Restoring a broader set of development ends which privilege the real economy will almost certainly require adding more instruments to the policy tool-box than is allowed to the developing countries by the Washington Consensus. However, recasting policy space in this way must still recognise the contingent and uncertain effects of particular policy instruments, as well as the potential trade-offs and adjustment costs of choosing one set of policies rather than another. Moreover, as we suggested in the last chapter, at any particular time, there is an unwritten social contract about the rules that make an economy work and which set the boundaries to the state's economic role. The process whereby that consensus is forged, priorities set and attitudes shaped is just as important a part of defining policy space as technocratic competence.

Given the importance of experimentation in finding what works for a particular developing country, governments must also have sufficient autonomy not just from domestic vested interests but also from

---

[8]   This was a central argument in the "Treasury View" used by policy makers to justify the status quo in inter-war Britain, and repeated in more recent times by public choice and rational expectations theorists in the reaction against the policy activism of Keynesianism.

international pressures on their economic agenda-setting (Adelman, 2000:73). *Ceteris paribus*, the more open an economy is, the greater its dependence on events outside the immediate control of domestic economic actors and policy makers. However, whether (and how much) policy space is foregone in the process of opening up is not a straightforward issue. Political independence is obviously a factor; this is clearly the case if policy decisions are decided on and imposed from outside. A country's size will also matter, as will the depth of its economic structure: a small country which is dependent on just one commodity for a large part of its output and exports is likely to enjoy, *de facto*, less policy space than a very large, diversified industrial economy. Another factor is economic strength. The nature and effects of liberalisation in East Asia during the 1980s (from a position of economic health) were different from those in Latin America (from a position of economic stagnation). The institutional framework within which markets are embedded also introduces degrees of insulation from external influences. To take an obvious example, lowering tariff barriers may not have much of an impact on local markets if informal firm ties, government procurement and consumer loyalties maintain existing patterns of demand or if policy makers can find new ways of supporting local firms; arguably, the strong positive correlation between increased openness and the size of the public sector should provide plenty of scope for thinking about such support.

Indeed, because, as we insisted in the last chapter, institutional diversity is good for economic growth, and because the resulting institutional boundaries introduce discontinuities and transaction costs (Rodrik, 2002), international markets are likely to remain more fragmented than national markets. Moreover, in practice, the economic authority of international markets is circumscribed by the political authority of states (including how much economic sovereignty they are willing to concede) and by their willingness to cooperate with one another, for example, in setting the rules governing capital mobility. This allows for a good deal of policy space even where legal barriers to cross-border flows are low or absent.

Of course not all global market forces carry the same impact, and arguably the rise of cross-border financial activities has been a more potent force in curtailing policy space through its emphasis on monetary and fiscal discipline and the defeat of inflation as an overriding policy objective and because of the apparent ease and speed with which financial assets can be moved if policies do not conform. While the financial sector has naturally been in the lead demanding financial liberalisation, it is important to recognise that the rise of finance as a political force, domestically and internationally, has been closely linked to larger changes in political forces and choices in richer countries that were pushing for a downgrading of economic growth, full employment and income distribution as independent policy objectives (Glyn, 2006). In the case of developed countries there is still considerable diversity in the degree to which finance is a dominant force and it would be wrong to underestimate the capacity for re-establishing effective surveillance and regulation of finance given its propensity for corruption, instability and crisis. In developing countries, where financial markets and institutions are much thinner, the pressure for policy conformity following financial liberalisation is arguably much greater. But even here, the links between financial and industrial interests are far from identical (and are often in conflict) and, as post-crisis Malaysia and Argentina, in their different ways, have demonstrated, the room for manoeuvre is far from being closed.

Almost certainly, reinstating real-economy policy objectives implies, as Colin Bradford (2005) has noted, reducing the autonomy of financial markets to the point where macroeconomic policy instruments can be deployed to support a development mandate dedicated to rapid output growth, structural change and exporting. Arguably there is still plenty of scope for this. The broad body of evidence continues to suggest, for example, that the negative impact of inflation on economic performance is only really detectable above a fairly high threshold figure, usually around 40 per cent per annum, with no clear association below that figure. Similarly, while strongly overvalued exchange rates have damaging effects on long-term growth, the impact of moderately overvalued or undervalued currencies is less easy to determine, and is certainly less important than the stability of the currency. Greater regulation of financial markets cannot be undertaken in isolation: it also requires giving more attention to aspects of development strategy, such as industrial, technology and labour-market policies. Indeed, such policy coherence will influence perceptions of country risk and the ways in which financial markets impact on economic prospects (Mosley, 2006). This is not simply a matter of adding more instruments, but also of changing institutional behaviour and regulatory norms in the banking system, labour markets, corporate governance, etc. As Stiglitz (1999:22) has argued, the case for moving beyond the Washington Consensus by broadening goals and adding policy instruments requires accepting an untidy notion of policy space, where the political process has a much more important say in national economic choices.

What is also clear, however, is that if the effects of trade and foreign investment on economic growth and development are contingent on political leadership and consensus-building, on the state of national institutions and local economic conditions, the case for the rapid liberalisation of trade and capital accounts as a necessary precondition for sustained growth collapses. But instead of drawing the conclusion that developing countries should be given more room to experiment with both policies and institutions in order to discover what actually works in their particular environments, the developed countries have institutionalised the neo-liberal stance against an active development role for the state by restricting the scope for policy intervention and institutional innovation. The two principal institutions for promoting this agenda are the IMF, which has extended the conditions on which it makes funds available to developing countries far beyond its original requirements for fiscal, monetary and exchange-rate policies[9], and the WTO, where the developed countries have forced through an enlarged agenda to include rules in such areas as investment, competition policy, government procurement and trade facilitation.[10] In addition, bilateral trade agreements between developing countries and the EU and the United States respectively often contain even more stringent demands than those made by the WTO.

---

[9] One result of this enlargement of conditionality is that compliance with IMF-supported programmes in the 1990s was much lower than in the 1970s and 1980s, an outcome that reduces the catalytic effect of such programmes in raising inflows of private finance (Toye and Toye, 2004:281).

[10] These are known as the "Singapore issues". They were introduced by the developed countries at the 1996 Ministerial Conference, held in Singapore, the highest decision-making body of the WTO which meets at least once every two years. The Uruguay Round had earlier extended the remit of the WTO, at the insistence of the developed countries, to cover services and intellectual property rights. One effect of the latter has been to raise the price of essential medicines to developing countries.

Although there has been some slight softening of the neo-liberal stance on certain issues – following the 1997 financial crisis, the IMF, for example, is less insistent on rapid liberalisation of the capital account – the emphasis on "second-stage" reforms reveals another bias in the direction of institutional arrangements, essentially towards a stylised "Anglo-Saxon" model. This is the origin of the good-governance debate mentioned earlier. There are no more grounds, however, for assuming that institutions can follow a common trajectory than there are for policies. This simply exchanges one Procrustean bed for another. Rodrik (2002) has suggested that governments face a constant trilemma in choosing two priorities from among national sovereignty, deeper economic integration and democracy. If, as he suggests, and we would concur, the nation state remains the locus of democratic and developmental politics, then it is necessary for policy makers to settle for a less muscular version of globalisation and a much more strategic approach to integration with the global economy. This again simply underscores the fundamental point that there are institutional and political limits to how far integration can and should go and that governments should be free to reassess and rethink their actions in this regard without prejudice or opprobrium.[11]

The real issue that emerges from this debate is not a matter of choosing between extreme options but of judging correctly the time required for a particular policy or strategy to be successful and being able to select among a suitable range of objectives and to experiment with policies and channels of implementation. Even when large, rapid changes are desirable in principle, in practice the feasible rate of change in any country depends largely on the nature and strength of its economic and political institutions, on its social cohesiveness, on the ability of its political leaders to maintain that cohesion during a period

---

[11] In any legal system, there are grounds for a retrial if process is breached or new evidence comes to light. What is particularly difficult to comprehend in the current multilateral trading regime is that, despite professing its adherence to the rule of law, this avenue is denied participants. Bhagwati (2005:7) has recently pointed out that virtually all trade rounds have involved renegotiating issues dealt with previously. However, this is an essentially ad hoc process.

of radical and often painful adjustment, and on the resources available to help manage those adjustments. Political leaders can influence the pace of reform, although not always by as much as many of them like to imagine, if they can establish credibility in their programmes and create and sustain a popular consensus for change behind a positive vision of the society at which they are aiming. They will also need to make candid estimates of the likely short-run costs involved, not promising a "blooming landscape" in a very short time[12], and prepare measures to ensure they do not fall disproportionately on the most vulnerable sections of the population.

C.   Regaining policy space: Lessons from the Marshall Plan

Faced with complex and apparently intractable problems or with the consequences of major disasters, politicians, particularly those in Western Europe, have increasingly called for a "Marshall Plan" as part of the response. The UN's Economic Commission for Europe (UNECE) seems to have started the fashion in early 1990 when it argued the need for a programme on the scale of the Marshall Plan to assist the countries of Eastern Europe in their transition from centrally planned to market economies (UNECE, 1990). This was taken up by German Chancellor Helmut Kohl and his Foreign Minister, Hans-Dietrich Genscher, who called for a Marshall Plan for Russia in 1992. In 1997 the then European Commission President, Jacques Santer, described the programme and costs of EU enlargement as "a veritable Marshall Plan" for Eastern Europe. In April 1999 British Prime Minister Tony Blair called for a "Marshall Plan" for the Balkans[13] and in October 2001 the Italian Prime Minister, Silvio

---

[12] This was Chancellor Helmut Kohl's promise to the population of the former German Democratic Republic in 1990.

[13] Blair's proposal for a Balkans Marshall Plan seems to have alarmed his own officials – "We have never used that phrase" was the lofty comment from a Foreign and Commonwealth Office spokesman. In February 2002, at the World Economic Forum in New York, a somewhat bitter Zoran Djindjic, the reformist Prime Minister of post-Milosevic Serbia, was warning Afghanistan not to count on western promises of aid to support post-war reconstruction and reform.

Berlusconi, proposed one for solving the economic problems of the Palestinians on the West Bank[14]. None of this rhetoric came to very much, partly because finance ministers in the rich countries in the 1990s were grappling with fiscal deficits, many of them trying to meet the Maastricht criteria for entry into the European Monetary Union, and the last thing they wanted to hear were proposals for large increases in aid budgets. Moreover, the resurgence of neo-liberal ideas from the early 1980s meant the developed world was more in favour of free markets and foreign private investment than official aid or planning as the remedy for the problems of transition and under-development.

The terrorist attacks in the United States on 11 September 2001, however, led to rather more urgent calls, at least in Europe, for action on the scale of the Marshall Plan to deal with the problems of under-development. Within a few weeks, Mr Blair was citing the North-South divide between rich and poor as a fundamental factor in the growth of terrorism and in December 2001 British Chancellor of the Exchequer Gordon Brown proposed a "New Marshall Plan" which would double the aid provided by the rich countries to the poor ones. Both Blair and Brown stressed the security objectives of such an initiative. Three years later, on 17 December 2004, Brown, speaking in New York, continued to stress the tensions between the rich and the poor and argued that if the west failed to open its markets to developing countries, forgive debt and provide more generous aid, there was a real risk of "permanent guerrilla war fought not by conventional armies or nation states but by cliques and factions". Having implicitly condemned the idea that the "war against terror" can be won by the military, he declared: "We need to make an offer as bold as the offer that was made in the Marshall Plan of the 1940s." The links between terrorism and under-development, including grinding pov-

---

14   The appeal of the Marshall Plan has not been confined to statesmen with their eyes on global issues: in June 2002, the Mayor of Toulouse declared "*un plan Marshall*" was needed to deal with the aftermath of the explosion at the AZF fertiliser factory in his city; and, soon after, Richard Rogers, the architect, was proposing a "a sort of regeneration Marshall Plan for public building in the UK – a massive infusion of planning, design and engineering skills". One suspects that the "Marshall Plan" has become a somewhat empty metaphor for any major or exceptional effort judged to be necessary to deal with particularly difficult situations.

erty and mass unemployment among young males with few or no prospects, are invoked more often by politicians in Europe than in the United States although US Secretary of State Colin Powell, during his post-tsunami visit to Indonesia in early 2005, stressed the need for cooperation to dry up "the pools of dissatisfaction" that led to terrorism. Prime Minister Blair and Chancellor Brown again called for a "Marshall Plan approach" in the run-up to the G8 summit in Scotland in 2005. It is never clear, however, whether those proposing "new Marshall Plans" see them as anything much more than a goodwill financial gesture to countries in need, and indeed there are many critics who dismiss such ideas on the ground that such large sums cannot be absorbed efficiently by the receiving countries and that they are likely to fall into the hands of corrupt politicians and government officials.[15] The Marshall Plan, however, was much more than just a financial package and it is far from clear that those attached to neo-liberalism and the idea of the irresistibility of market forces will be keen to embrace its other features.

The Marshall Plan of 1947 was certainly generous, providing Western Europe with some $12.4 billion over a four-year period, most of it in the form of grants rather than loans. The programme amounted to just over 1 per cent of the US's GDP and over 2 per cent of the recipients'. The Marshall Plan did much more, however, than supply Europe with lots of dollars; it also introduced a framework of organising principles intended to ensure that the aid was used effectively and to encourage policy makers to forge a new kind of "social contract" that would be radically different from the deflationary and divisive actions of the inter-war period (Mazower, 1998:299). These aspects of the Marshall Plan are almost entirely absent from current suggestions for a "new" version, but it is precisely here that useful lessons can be drawn for development policy.

It is also relevant, in light of the experience with adjustment programmes, to recall that the Marshall Plan was actually a belated recognition of the fact that policy makers in the United States, especially in the US Treasury, had been far too optimistic about the time it

---

[15] For a cross-section of opinion on the current state of the aid debate see IDS (2005). On two sharply differing views on the aid and planning debate, see Easterly (2006) and Sen (2006).

would take to return to "normality" after the cessation of hostilities. By this was meant a return to a system of multilateral free trade and payments, in accordance with the rules of the new Bretton Woods institutions which were to provide the basic architecture of the post-war economic system. The attempt to put these new arrangements into place rapidly, an early example of "shock therapy", had foundered in a series of European dollar crises and particularly the sterling convertibility fiasco of 1947. Large amounts of relief assistance had been pouring into Europe before 1947 and members of the United States Congress were complaining about their taxpayers' dollars disappearing down a European "rat-hole", a story with a familiar ring today.

When the United States Secretary of State George Marshall made his famous speech at Harvard in June 1947, the economic and political outlook for Europe was far from encouraging. The post-war recovery in output appeared to have stalled and there were fears of rising social unrest and of communist parties winning elections in several countries. Marshall was explicit that the economic dimension of security was uppermost in his mind[16]: "Our policy is directed against hunger, poverty, desperation and chaos ... so as to permit the emergence of political and social conditions in which free institutions can exist." Marshall would thus have agreed with Chancellor Gordon Brown in seeing poverty, not a hatred of freedom, as an incubator of terrorism. It is also notable that Marshall saw free institutions emerging from "economic health", not the other way round. When critics object to proposals for "new" Marshall Plans for certain countries on the grounds that they are not democracies or do not possess market economies, they forget that Marshall Aid was not so demanding: Italy and West Germany adopted democratic institutions only in 1948 and 1949, and in Italy many of their provisions were ignored as part of the strategy to keep the communists out of power. Although most of the institutions of a market economy did not have to be built from scratch, the various European economies had been highly regulated and subject to direct controls for the best part of a decade, and with large sections of the population still suffering considerable privations, quick

---

[16]   The text of Secretary Marshall's speech, from which this and the following quotations are taken, is published in OECD (1978:227-29).

fixes and shock therapy for a return to "normal" market conditions were considered neither economically feasible nor politically acceptable. Once again there is a sharp contrast between the policies rich countries adopted for themselves and those they consider appropriate for others. It is true that the Marshall Plan was ultimately directed at keeping the Soviet Union out of Western Europe and communist parties out of West European governments, and the US administration may not have been too particular about the democratic credentials of some of the recipients of aid. But it would anyway have been unwise to have set stringent democratic preconditions for receiving economic assistance. If the lack of assistance were to have made the economic situation worse, the outlook for developing democratic institutions would also have been likely to deteriorate.

With this background in mind, there are at least seven major virtues of the Marshall Plan which provide useful lessons for rebalancing the policy environment facing developing countries today. *First*, it set a time frame for the post-war adjustment process that was more realistic than that envisaged by the US Treasury or by an IMF programme. Instead of thinking in terms of 18 months, the time scale was changed to four to five years. *Second*, Marshall made it clear that there was to be an end to the piecemeal assistance which had suffered from a lack of coordination and had less impact than expected in stimulating economic recovery. A key requirement, therefore, was that each state recipient of aid had to produce a four-year outline plan for recovery, setting out targets for the main economic variables and providing an account of how the government intended to achieve its objectives. *Third*, Marshall insisted that these plans, together with estimates of the need for assistance, had to be drawn up by the West Europeans themselves: "It would be neither fitting nor efficacious for [the United States] to undertake to draw up unilaterally a program designed to place Europe on its feet economically. This is the business of Europeans ... The role of this country should consist of friendly aid in the drafting of a European program and of later support of such a program ..." Marshall thus acknowledged national sensibilities, admitted that the recipient countries were better informed about the facts of their situation than outsiders, and generally showed a deference towards European traditions and preferences that has been conspicuously absent in the subsequent attitudes of the rich countries and international institutions towards the rest of the world.

A *fourth* feature of the Marshall Plan was that aid was released in tranches that depended on the countries' intermediate targets being met. The removal of the recovery programme from the Bretton Woods framework did not therefore imply an escape from conditionality, but the Marshall Plan conditions were different, more flexible and were to be met over a longer period than allowed by IMF rules. Conditionality was important not simply to ensure that the aid was being used effectively but also to gain, and sustain, the support of the American taxpayer.[17]

Fifth, the Marshall Plan acknowledged that the damage to European productive capacities and the great disparity in economic strength between the United States and Europe meant that rapid liberalisation of trade and payments would quickly lead to European payments crises. It was accepted that Europe would gradually dismantle a wide range of direct and indirect controls on its trade according to an agreed timetable within the framework of the European Payments Union between 1950 and 1958. This gradual liberalisation of trade provided European producers with protection against American competition and gave them time and encouragement for the reconstruction of enterprises capable of producing competitive substitutes for dollar imports. At the same time, the US agreed to a more rapid improvement in access to its own market for European exports, a policy of asymmetric liberalisation that stands in marked contrast to the present approach of the EU and the United States which insists on a rapid opening of developing countries' markets and on restricting the range of policy options available for their development. Another, largely forgotten aspect of American restraint towards the relative economic weakness of Europe in 1947 was a moratorium on foreign investment in Germany until monetary equilibrium had been more or less achieved (Kindleberger, 1989). The prospect of US capitalists buying up Mercedes, Siemens and other major companies at derisory

---

[17] This in turn was needed in order to strengthen the hand of the State Department and the Marshall Planners in overcoming the opposition of Senator Taft and his Republican supporters in Congress who were against not only the Marshall Plan but also the United Nations and anything else that smacked of multilateralism.

prices did not appear to the State Department as a useful contribution to winning the "hearts and minds" of a defeated population and a future ally.[18]

Sixth, effective leadership requires generosity. Marshall Aid consisted largely of grants and the small proportion of loans contained a large element of grant: they were usually for 35 years at 2.5 per cent interest with repayments starting in 1953. It is worth emphasising this structure of financial help at a time when "aid" and "assistance" are used loosely to cover everything from gifts to loans at market (or above-market) rates of interest. The wisdom of adding to the debts of already heavily indebted economies is highly questionable, the more so when they are grappling with economic restructuring and institution-building, which is typically the case for countries trying to accelerate their development or to recover from the chaos that normally follows the end of violent conflict. A generous supply of grants, monitored within and conditional on a coherent economic programme on the lines of the Marshall Plan, can be more effective than loans in lifting countries out of a "stagnation trap" where heavy debt-servicing obligations hold back the domestic and foreign investment that could improve the longer-run performance of the economy, including its capacity to service debt. Another advantage of grants is that they are not usually subject to the long and complex negotiations, legal and financial, associated with loans. This is important because one of the lessons of the Marshall Plan is that prompt assistance at the start of a promised programme can help to sustain positive expectations, which most likely will have been raised by politicians, and instigate a momentum for change that will stand a chance of becoming self-reinforcing. Aid is usually provided with a close eye on the interests of the donor, to strengthen a bilateral alliance, secure supplies of raw materials, boost exports and so forth. That is to be expected, but a lot depends on whether donors see their interests narrowly or broadly, short-term or long-term, and whether larger public interests prevail

---

[18] For economists involved in the Marshall Plan, such as Charles Kindleberger, this was a sensible policy based on the theory of second best, namely, that when markets fail to work, or do not exist, they should not be used. Instead, the priority should be to create or rebuild the institutional framework that will ensure they do work efficiently. Even in one of the most advanced economies of the day, that was expected to take some time.

over narrower corporate ones. There are public-goods aspects to aid if it succeeds in raising the prospects for growth and development and thereby reducing threats to regional and global security, easing the pressures for migration, and so on. Grants may therefore generate a higher rate of return in terms of the donors' larger interests than loans.[19] Marshall Aid grants were arriving in Europe in well under a year from General Marshall's speech in June 1947, a painful contrast with the assistance efforts of the G7 over the last few decades which have been dominated by loans and characterised by large discrepancies between pledges and deliveries, long delays in disbursement, and weak coordination among a large number of donors with often competing interests.

Finally, the *seventh* virtue of the Marshall Plan that we consider relevant to current problems was its insistence that there should be a degree of united and cooperative effort among the Europeans themselves, and that the plans of the 16 recipient countries and the allocation of aid should be coordinated in a regional body.[20] This requirement partly reflected US foreign-policy objectives for a more integrated Europe, but it provided a structure for cooperation in areas where there are significant externalities, economies of scale and other trans-boundary issues. The peer review of national programmes provided national policy makers with a regional perspective for their own policies and encouraged a culture of regular contact and cooperation among national bureaucracies which today is taken for granted in Europe.

Regional bodies are now frequently opposed by the G7 countries, which tend to prefer global institutions where they can assert more control over decisions.[21] That of course is one reason in favour of them from the standpoint of countries in a region, an advantage that many members of the EU often stress. But for most countries, most of the time, many of their pressing everyday problems involve their neighbours. Regional cooperation to lower trade barriers and other obstacles to doing business within the region can provide larger

---

[19]   Economists will no doubt raise the "free rider" problem but that should be irrelevant to these broader, strategic interests of the G7 countries.

[20]   This was the Organisation for European Economic Cooperation, founded in April 1948, and which was later converted into the OECD.

[21]   Concerns about regional trade agreements are discussed in the next section.

markets for small, low-income countries and make it easier for them, if it suits their development strategies, to attract FDI.[22] For small, fragmented economies infant-industry policies may be more effective in a regional than a small national market. Regional cooperation can also make it easier to deal with black markets, organised crime and other activities which have the power to undermine democratic and market institutions. The very fact of increased efforts at such cooperation is itself a sign of increasing stability and security in a region and that can be an important influence on economic activity in general and fixed investment in particular.

One of the important aspects of post-war regional cooperation in Europe, in institutions such as the OECD, the UNECE and the EU, is that it encouraged a focus on "nuts and bolts" cooperation in resolving possibly mundane but nevertheless important practical problems, such as trade facilitation, harmonising standards for various traded products, trans-boundary air and water pollution, and so on, where all the parties can see that they will gain from agreed rules or norms and therefore have an incentive to cooperate.[23] The practical consequence, however, is the gradual evolution of a form of regional or international governance as countries seek ways to reconcile their pursuit of national objectives with international constraints, an activity based on local knowledge that can also contribute to developing the autonomous learning capabilities that we identified earlier as crucial for promoting both development and democracy. This suggests that the necessity and benefits of collective action, on the one hand, and the evident desire of peoples to preserve as far as possible their autonomy to decide national policy, on the other, can be balanced in many areas without the need for overarching global bodies.

---

[22] As we have suggested in the case of Mexico, the regional option should not be seen as a panacea.

[23] The UNECE, for example, with the most comprehensive membership of the European region, brought together countries that were bitterly divided over political and social values, and yet they succeeded in reaching agreement on a range of practical issues. "The UNECE's experience shows that cooperation can move ahead by accepting certain differences in preferences and values. This does not imply accepting murderous behaviour and violations of human rights, but it does imply recognition that there are differences and preferences that may not be reconcilable and should therefore be accepted and recognised by others" (Berthelot and Rayment, 2004:130).

What we are suggesting is that the *processes* of the Marshall Plan can help to provide a coherent framework for coordinating national economic-development plans with international assistance. Without an articulate account of a government's macroeconomic objectives and their relation to detailed programmes for infrastructure investment, education, health, housing, etc., it is difficult to see how limited supplies of foreign assistance, financial and technical, can be really effective. Official assistance is essentially a form of intervention to ease shortages, bottlenecks and other constraints on growth and structural change, but it is difficult to target aid to where it will be most effective without some idea of priorities and the potential marginal effect of removing one bottleneck, say, before another. Similarly, the impact of assistance will be reduced if complementarities are overlooked: the value of funds for treating the victims of HIV/ AIDS and other major diseases, for example, will be diminished if the planning and funding of health support services is neglected or underestimated.

Despite the demonstrated success of the Marshall Plan framework in Europe in the 1940s, "aid" has developed over the years into a mixture of assistance for an assortment of specific projects and ad hoc responses to unexpected shocks with little apparent coherence, either in the countries that receive it or in its global distribution. Donor conferences are more like bazaars, driven more by what donors want to promote than by the desire to support specific multi-year, national programmes. It is difficult to see how aid can ever be really effective without an articulation of macroeconomic objectives and detailed programmes for infrastructure investment etc., and without a coherent account of priorities – what should be done in what order – and a sense of the necessary complementarities among different investments and projects.

National development programmes along the lines of the Marshall Plan would also make it easier to provide general, non-project assistance to government budgets or the balance of payments, as was done for a number of European countries under Marshall Aid. Development (even more than reconstruction) programmes essentially deal with deep-rooted structural problems and both fiscal and current-account deficits are usually unavoidable if constructive, long-run adjustment is to be achieved. The need to provide financial assistance to deal with long-term imbalances is usually seen by the international financial institutions as evidence of a weak commitment to reform and as encouraging a slackening of discipline by postponing necessary adjustment. This was not the view of the Marshall Planners, who regarded such assistance as an investment in structural change and as providing governments with the breathing space required to bring difficult and often painful policies to success. When such policies threatened to cause social upheaval on a scale that might upset the adjustment process, as was the case in post-war Italy at one point, Marshall Aid was available to support the government budget in order to cushion the social costs.

Another major attraction of a Marshall Plan framework is that it can serve an important political function. A multi-year programme of economic and social objectives, setting out their interrelationships, the means to achieve them and their contingency on outside assistance, effectively sets out the government's vision of the structure of society at which it is aiming. That is highly political, and so the proposed programme provides a basis for the democratic discussion and the negotiation between competing views that should take place. This is not an easy task, as the history of French indicative planning shows (Cohen, 1977), but obtaining popular support for such a programme can be a major stimulus for change. This will not always result in what the international financial institutions regard as the "best" policies, but the advantage of democratic processes, as we suggested in the previous chapter, is that they generate pressures to correct mistakes: they may reach the "best" policy more slowly than if driven by autocratic outsiders, but politically the slow route may be superior. A "new Marshall Plan" could thus be a way to provide a concrete operational basis for such ideas as "ownership" and "partnership", which otherwise risk degenerating into empty slogans. Moreover, a coherent national programme with popular support, indicating where outside assistance could be most effective, *ipso facto* becomes a powerful argument for persuading potential donors to respond to national priorities rather than following their own preferences from a basket of seemingly unrelated projects. The emphasis on *national* programmes is deliberate because the problem with recent suggestions for a new Marshall Plan for Africa, for example, is that they seem to imply that the continent is homogeneous, which is very far from being the case. The approach in Europe in the late 1940s was to treat each country as a specific case but to bring them together in a regional framework of cooperation that would support both national objectives and regional coherence.

D.   Strengthening the profit-investment-export nexus

We have insisted throughout this book that the task of moving from strategic development goals to specific policy measures can only be done through experimenting, arguing and bargaining at the national level where "local heresies" will be decisive (Rodrik, 2003:13), an approach that, despite the differences in the nature and the magnitude of the challenges facing Western European reconstruction, was very much followed by the Marshall Planners. We have also insisted that in a non-linear, non-equilibrium and multi-dimensional economic world, institutions and policies cannot be taken as given or static but must evolve over time as development proceeds. By implication the functions and activities of the state will also change as industrialisation proceeds and institutional development deepens.

In trying to move the discussion of development strategies forward, it seems to us useful to draw from our comparative analysis of the trends in capital formation, export performance, industrialisation and growth a more disaggregated classification of where developing countries stand in relation to one another after a quarter of a century in which the pendulum has swung strongly towards international firms and market forces:

- *Mature industrialisers*: This group includes the first-tier NIEs, notably the Republic of Korea and Taiwan Province of China, which achieved industrial maturity through rapid and sustained accumulation of capital, growth in industrial employment, productivity and output, as well as manufactured exports. In the 1990s these economies enjoyed a share of industrial output in GDP above the levels of advanced countries, exports had shifted to more capital- and technology-intensive goods, and industrial growth was starting to slow down as resources shifted towards the service sector.

- *Rapid industrialisers*: A number of countries had a rising share of manufactures in total output, employment and exports, based on strong investment in resource-based and labour-intensive activities, and were beginning to upgrade to middle-range technology products. This group includes the second-tier Asian NIEs, but also isolated success stories from other regions, as well as the waking giants of China and India.

- *Enclave industrialisers*: Some countries moved away from dependence on commodity exports by linking to international production chains, often by attracting large amounts of FDI and with a heavy reliance on imported inputs and machinery. Export growth was often very rapid, as in the Philippines, Mexico and to some extent Morocco. However, overall performance in terms of investment, value added and productivity growth was often quite weak.

- *Premature deindustrialisers*: This group includes most countries in Latin America, which had achieved a certain degree of industrialisation but were unable to sustain a dynamic process of structural change through rapid accumulation and growth. In a context of rapid liberalisation, declining shares of manufacturing employment and output and a downgrading to less-technology-intensive activities were common trends.

- *Commodity-dependent exporters*: Many poorer economies, particularly in SSA, remain heavily dependent on one or two commodity exports. In the face of relatively stagnant markets, volatile prices and declining terms of trade, investment weakened, diversification stalled and productivity was stagnant. In some cases enclaves of faster export growth emerged in the extractive sectors, usually tied to FDI, but with weak linkages to the rest of the economy. However, some of the wealthier developing countries, notably Chile, did achieve a faster pace of investment and growth based on their natural-resource endowments.

This is not of course intended as a definitive typology, but in designing policies for development, it is essential for the considerable differences in national conditions to be explicitly recognised in an organised way.

1.   Policy-making in a diverse world

It is a truism that in countries where the working population is predominantly employed in agriculture, growth in GDP per capita requires either rapid growth in productivity in that sector or very rapid growth elsewhere in the economy. Moreover, in the early stages of their industrialisation, and even where they rely on external markets for their growth, a basic objective will be to create a net surplus in the agricultural sector that can be used to support nascent manufacturing. Given that many commodity-dependent economies face a combination of low levels of income, very low rates of investment and high population growth, low household savings are likely to be a binding constraint. In many cases the small size of farms makes for additional problems in generating an investible surplus: in the case of SSA, for example, food output has actually been stagnant since 1980. Dealing with the challenge of domestic resource mobilisation in such economies presents specific policy challenges. Sachs et al. (2004) have identified soil fertility, access to seeds, limited water availability, lack of appropriate crop technologies and weak and gender-biased property rights as some of the main constraints on raising rural productivity.

There are no quick or general solutions, but an effective set of incentives must be in place to give farmers a predictable financial surplus and encourage them to invest some of it to raise productivity and diversify output. Exchange-rate and pricing policies can be used to reduce income instability and influence the relative profitability of different activities. Extension services need to focus on specific supply-side problems, improving the technical knowledge of farmers, making it easier for them to obtain better inputs as well as credit, and encouraging diversification and the improvement of marketing skills. Such specific measures to strengthen productivity and extend markets can be greatly enhanced by basic infrastructure investment (Temple, 2003:162-66).

Achieving higher rates of capital formation will require public-sector investment, and it seems likely that ODA and "soft" multilateral loans will remain a crucial source of financing in the medium term. Just how big a push is needed will vary from country to country, but managing it will require that increased aid goes hand-in-hand with appropriate institutional reforms that will give greater freedom to policy makers to discover the policy mix best suited to specific local conditions. The institutional hiatus facing poorer agricultural economies can seem daunting, although comparison with far more advanced economies often leads to an exaggeration of the scale of the challenge (Sachs et al., 2004). The initial degree of institutional capacity needed to start raising the rate of capital formation, for example, is probably not that great. However, predictability is a principal condition if investors are to commit resources to an uncertain future and while more secure property rights are part of the story, the premature abolition of state institutions, such as marketing boards and development banks, has been unhelpful in many cases. Measures to fill this gap will require restoring some of these functions to state institutions, strengthening others, as well as more generally restoring a degree of professional integrity and respectability to public offices, both of which have been lost under adjustment programmes (Van Arkadie, 1995). Financing the public sector remains a major issue in many poorer countries. The combination of dwindling tariff revenues and dependence on aid is not sustainable and widening the fiscal base as growth picks up will be a priority. This will also require local government reforms to ensure taxes are collected fairly and efficiently and that they are well spent in support of local development.[24]

For countries that have large mineral and fuel resources the policy challenges are likely to be somewhat different. Most extractive industries have a limited local market and are driven to maximise export revenues. This can generate significant profits and valuable foreign-exchange earnings which, if properly managed, can ease a number of potential constraints on faster growth. Nevertheless, doing so has proved to be a far from simple task. The problem of "Dutch disease", whereby an expanding mineral sector triggers a real currency

---

[24] In some cases, the highly charged issue of land reforms will be a necessary component of progressive reform. That, however, can never be sufficient in itself to introduce a process of progressive structural reform in agriculture. For a discussion of why it worked in East Asia after 1950, see UNCTAD (1997:121-22).

appreciation and a fall in output and employment in other tradeable sectors, can introduce serious macroeconomic imbalances and increase the volatility of the economy. However, the broad body of evidence suggests that this is manageable providing policy makers have the requisite policy space (IMF, 2003). More damaging to long-term prospects is when this kind of expansion generates a pattern of lopsided internal integration through the creation of enclave economies. The structure of international commodity markets means that when policy makers invite TNCs to develop this sector they will face very large international firms armed with asymmetric information and financial, technological and market strengths, including the threat of capital flight, all of which make for unequal bargaining. Moreover, unpredictable rents associated with price volatility can seriously distort the wider incentive structure, adding a speculative dimension to investment planning in both the private and public sectors. Neither state nor foreign ownership, by themselves, offer a solution. The challenge is how to best manage resource rents with long-term development goals in mind. In recent years, as discussed earlier, the pendulum has swung much too far towards trying to attract FDI to these sectors, with insufficient attention given to strengthening the bargaining position of host governments to obtain better returns from their natural-resource base and stimulate the upgrading and diversification of national output. Focusing the profit-investment-export nexus more sharply on long-term development will require changes in existing fiscal and legislative arrangements in order to increase revenues and ensure that a greater proportion of value added remains in the host economy. Just as important, policy makers will have to enhance their tool-kits: input-output tables, cost-benefit analysis, linkages, leading sectors and development blocs are just some of the concepts that can be usefully revisited in developing a more balanced framework.

Reforms in the primary sector which succeed in raising productivity, improving the fiscal base and generating additional export revenues will almost certainly be accompanied by a significant shedding of labour as farm size and the technological intensity of production increase. The challenge of absorbing surplus labour from the agricultural sector will have to be met, in part, by a significant rise in public investment in the expanding urban economy. However, its sustainability will depend on private investment increasing capacity in low-skilled manufacturing activities and related services. If this does not happen, countries face the risk of being stuck on a low-growth path with burgeoning problems of urban unemployment and insecurity.

Historically, the successful development of such manufacturing activities has been characterised by reinforcing linkages between increasing specialisation, market expansion, investment and growing firm size. China is currently building these linkages, albeit with an uncharacteristically high export bias for an economy of its size. However, the urban expansion already under way across much of the developing world, and which is expected to accelerate over the coming decades (UN-HABITAT, 2003), has, under the impact of structural adjustment, coincided with reduced state capacities, lower rates of public investment and a lack of diversification which, in some cases, has triggered a process of premature deindustrialisation. One glaring consequence, as discussed in Chapter 5, has been an expanding informal economy. This presents an unprecedented challenge to policy makers in many poorer, commodity-dependent countries looking for ways to start (or restart) catch-up rates of growth.[25] But the same combination also poses a major challenge to countries that are stuck with an increasingly outdated industrial base which is vulnerable to new competitors. Indeed, the institutional challenge may be even greater in these countries, not only because entrenched interests may be harder to dislodge, but also because the range of complementary activities needed to upgrade to more dynamic industries will require an even higher level of investment in the transition period.

Raising investment can face multiple constraints in such countries and committed leadership by the state in search of new advantages will be all the more important. As mentioned earlier, rapid industrialisation is likely to imply an increasing dependence on imports of capital and intermediate goods, which in turn will require a rapid growth of export earnings and a steady expansion of export capacities. The evidence quoted earlier suggests that opening up will

---

[25] The HIV/AIDS crisis, particularly in SSA, adds another dimension to that challenge.

not automatically lead to export-led growth: indeed, the broad tendency is for domestic firms already successful in their home markets to become successful exporters – and in this respect size matters: large firms tend to invest more, have easier access to financial markets, and achieve higher productivity.

While simple imitation is ruled out by country specifics, a number of broad policy lessons can be drawn from successful industrialisers. First, a broader pro-growth macroeconomic stance is essential. This requires adopting a full range of macroeconomic instruments both to stimulate investment and to counteract any damaging effect on capital formation from economic shocks and volatility (Ocampo, 2005). Certainly, as Bradford (2005) rightly notes, prioritising growth and introducing more instruments to the policy mix opens the way to heterodox strategies. This will involve different combinations of fiscal, monetary and exchange-rate policies including capital controls calibrated to specific conditions to allow countries to meet their objectives for employment, price stability and external balance. Other instruments, including debt restructuring, wage and price controls, and labour-market policies, might also be needed to help maintain growth at the desired rate. Secondly, the state will need to raise enterprise profits to levels above those that would have emerged from a purely free market. This means using fiscal instruments such as tax breaks and accelerated depreciation allowances to directly boost profits, and to allow firms to set up various reserve funds against risk which can be used to defer paying taxes on profits. The effects of such policies will be amplified if they encourage commercial banks to make loans more easily available for investment. A number of other measures can also be used to increase rents: for example, selective import protection, controls over interest rates and the allocation of credit, managed competition involving government encouragement of specific mergers and restrictions on entry into certain sectors, the screening of imported technology, and the promotion of cartels for particular purposes such as product standards or export promotion. Such measures will set the tone for a different kind of competition policy which, rather than promoting competition for its own sake, fosters industrial depth and economic development. Competition that leads to price wars or sharp falls in profit or declining wages is unlikely to stimulate investment on the appropriate scale or

of the right kind. In some instances the right strategy may be to restrict competition, at other times to promote it vigorously. In most
cases, policy makers will again have to discover for themselves the
appropriate blend of competition and cooperation to achieve faster
rates of long-term growth (Singh, 2002).

While most of the fiscal and other instruments can be applied
deliberately to specific industries at specific times, investment should
be especially promoted in industries with the greatest potential for
upgrading skills, reaping economies of scale and raising productivity
growth, thereby increasing the rates of return on investment. Total
investment can also be boosted by favouring sectors with important
forward and backward linkages to the rest of the economy. Such
policies can lay the basis for a dynamic manufacturing sector which,
in turn, can greatly ease the balance-of-payments constraint on the
import of capital goods.

Adopting this more strategic approach does not mean favouring
universal protection, as is sometimes suggested; rather, it prescribes
liberalisation, protection and subsidies in various combinations, depending on a country's resource endowments, macroeconomic circumstances and level of industrialisation. Such an approach, a staple
feature of the rise of today's advanced countries throughout the 19th
and 20th centuries, is not synonymous with public ownership or picking winners, although these are not precluded *per se* from the strategy; rather, it is part of the process of discovery and coordination
whereby firms and governments learn about the underlying costs and
profit opportunities associated with new activities and technologies,
evaluate the possible externalities associated with particular projects,
and push towards a more diversified and higher-value-added economy.

Dani Rodrik (2004b:25-28) has discussed a possible package of
six industrial policies which are most likely to make a difference.
These include subsidising the early stages of developing new products or the adaptation of imported technologies with a view to
maximising high learning spillovers; developing mechanisms to increase the supply of higher risk finance with longer time horizons
than those of commercial banks; addressing coordination failures;
public spending on R&D; subsidising general technical training; and
engaging the skills and financial resources of nationals abroad. The
challenge here is not simply one of resurrecting "old style" industrial

policy for the diversification and upgrading of domestic output, but of redeploying existing measures which have tended to favour exports and foreign firms.

There are a number of factors which appear to be important for the success of such policies and whose absence helps to explain the failure of past efforts in developing countries. First, the rents created by these measures should be provided only to productive activities that support the broader national economic strategy. Second, subsidies and rents should be made available only as a condition of enhanced performance, especially of exports and of technological upgrading. Third, large, diversified business enterprises, together with close, interlocking ownership relationships with banks, enable firms to resist short-term demands to distribute profits to shareholders and instead invest for the longer term. This form of business organisation can be particularly effective in countries with relatively weak endowments of capital, entrepreneurship and skills, and it can help the government in its coordination efforts by facilitating the exchange of information and reducing the risks of investment. Fourth, the effectual implementation of such an industrial strategy depends on the creation of an appropriate structure of public and private institutions and, not least, on the development of a strong and competent bureaucracy. Finally, industrial policy needs to be linked to labour-market policy at an early stage to ensure that structural change proceeds as smoothly and as fairly as possible. The record of active labour-market policies is mixed but there is an array of measures that combine transfer payments with work programmes and training that can be used to improve the effectiveness of labour markets (Auer et al., 2005). One possible arrangement to support the investment-profit nexus is profit-related pay, which can help to promote stable levels of employment, thereby improving the distribution of incomes, as well as raising levels of saving by workers and of investment by enterprises.[26] Again

---

[26] Bonuses in East Asia tended to be paid as periodic lump sums and, in general, the marginal propensity to consume out of what is regarded as transitory income is significantly lower than for regular income. The system also helps to introduce a degree of labour-market flexibility which does not depend on firing people in response to a downturn or other external shocks: instead of unemployment leading to a loss of skills, the greater stability of employment preserves skills and the bonus system helps to encourage learning by doing.

the objective is to think locally and beyond the conventional policy framework, given that there is no one policy for all occasions.

As noted earlier, a strategy to boost profits by creating rents and encouraging the retention of corporate profits runs the risk of increasing the consumption of luxury goods and the acquisition of foreign financial assets rather than boosting fixed investment. Managing the potential conflicts surrounding rent creation will have to pay close attention to the structure and efficiency of fiscal regimes. In many developing countries, including many middle-income countries in Latin America, for example, tax revenues are below the level that might be expected given their per capita income. Efforts to curtail tax evasion will need to be stepped up, progressive components (on personal incomes or property taxes) increased and regressive aspects reduced. The ad hoc fiscal impositions that have accumulated haphazardly in response to persistent fiscal crises will need to be rationalised, particularly those that deter productive investment. Measures to curb luxury consumption may also have a useful role to play in the early stages of industrialisation: these may include import controls of varying severity, differential rates of value-added or sales taxes, credit controls, and government propaganda to encourage the rich to exercise self-restraint when much of the rest of the population is enduring much lower standards of living. A complementary approach is to encourage the domestic production of luxury goods such as motor cars and consumer durables which are known to have strong backward linkages to the rest of the economy. After an initial period of serving a limited domestic market to acquire experience, exports can be encouraged to grow faster than output by combining the incentives mentioned already with measures to reduce domestic consumption.[27] This contrasts with the more usual experience where TNCs establish local plants behind import barriers either to produce for the local market, which will tend to lower domestic savings without necessarily creating the basis for eventual exports, or to assemble imported components for export, which generally involves a very high level of imports, low domestic value added and weak backward linkages.

---

[27] This was the approach adopted in the Republic of Korea to develop the automobile industry. See Amsden (1989) and, for a comparison with the Mexican experience in this sector, Mortimore (1998).

The sectors where policies can make a difference are broadly circumscribed by a country's initial labour and resource endowments. Even so, these do not dictate a country's industrial future; even in the early stages, developing the sectors that use these inputs intensively and raising their relative value added requires a rapid rate of fixed investment. Also from an early stage, fiscal and other incentives will have a role to play in encouraging the growth of more sophisticated industries. Additional measures will also be needed to encourage the creation and expansion of technological capacities, such as local research and development facilities, the expansion of educational institutions and a wide range of vocational training.

Boosting profits, raising domestic investment and curbing luxury consumption are demanding goals that will often require the use of new or revived policy instruments. Some of the constraints negotiated in the WTO, however, no longer allow such an expansion of policy space, and the relentless pressure to further cut developing-country tariffs is certainly unhelpful. Nevertheless, scope for innovation in these areas still exists and many of the policies needed fall outside the current rules: these include, for example, some "disguised" subsidies to industry (through infrastructure investment, cheap food, subsidised housing, incomes policies, etc.) as well as "targeted" subsidies (such as tax rebates, support for R&D or temporary monopoly privileges).[28] Any efforts to enlarge policy space will also need to address weak domestic institutional capacity, including the education system. New policy initiatives are possible with respect to science and technology, regional problems and export facilitation, all of which, so far, remain untouched by the new trading rules. Moreover, developing-country policy makers need to pursue closer interaction between government and the private sector, already a prominent part of the policy environment in advanced industrial countries. This implies paying closer attention to start-up financing, improving the transfer of intellectual property from public agencies to private firms, more effective use of procurement contracts, the provision of financial and infrastructural support for export promotion, and so on. As Akyüz (2005) has rightly insisted, however, because the sequencing process

---

[28]   This distinction is suggested by Adelman (2000:76).

differs from country to country and is non-linear, all developing countries should also be allowed to retain the option of using tariffs, on a selective basis, as and when needed to encourage diversification and upgrading. Whether or not this requires a renegotiation of trading rules, it will certainly need a sharpening of the political skills of policy makers and trade negotiators in support of more development-sensitive trade agendas.

We are therefore proposing a development strategy where the central focus is on the creation of local enterprises with a high propensity to invest as a necessary prelude to closer integration with the global economy, and on encouraging the development of a business class that will eventually be able to maintain the dynamic of industrial change and technological upgrading on its own. Although the "shock" exposure of an economy to the forces of global competition has not proved to be an effective way to encourage the creation of a competitive local manufacturing base, this does not mean that the role of FDI and TNCs in the development process should be ignored or rejected. It does mean, however, that the starting point for policy should be an evaluation of the likely net gains from hosting FDI rather than simply attracting it, and, because the interests of TNC shareholders do not necessarily coincide with national development objectives, bargaining should be at the centre of any appropriate policy regime. Evaluating the net gains will be country- and sector-specific, with policies towards FDI needing to be tailored accordingly and in full knowledge that there will be trade-offs and a potential for conflicts of interest between TNCs and host governments. It is therefore important that the governments of host countries adopt a strategic approach to FDI, preserving a range of policies to ensure that it supports the objectives of domestic development.

As suggested in earlier chapters, this implies moving away from a narrow view of FDI as an efficiency-raising response to local market failure and, instead, asking how the costs and benefits of FDI can best be managed to complement the broader objective of strengthening profit-investment linkages in such a way that internal integration is deepened. This requires policy makers to ask different questions from those concerned simply with attracting FDI. Is FDI likely to raise the production costs and lower the profitability of domestic firms? What is the likely extent of positive spillovers and linkages from FDI, and are domestic firms likely to benefit from them? What is the likely scale of increased import dependence and future profit repatriation? What are the potential problems of nurturing new domestic firms in sectors where TNCs have gained an early dominance?

There are no easy answers to these questions and no hard and fast rules for striking the right balance between nurturing domestic enterprises and attracting foreign ones. What is clear is that policies have to be adapted to individual circumstances. Sometimes they may need to include restrictions on entry to certain sectors, prior approval for joint ventures, domestic-content agreements, and so on. At other times it may be advisable to have an open-door policy with few restrictions, and sometimes it may be desirable to provide incentives to attract FDI to preferred sectors. A key point for policy makers to keep in mind is that technological spillovers and other potential benefits from FDI are unlikely to occur without the presence of strong local firms able to take advantage of them. This goes against the more conventional strategies which continue to give a leading role in the development process to FDI and TNCs, and against the policy stance of most developed countries which deplores any restriction on the free movement of foreign investment. Nevertheless, countries which have adopted policies to guide FDI within a national development strategy do not appear to have had much difficulty in attracting it – coherent national policies and good prospects for growth seem to be the key attractions for TNCs while at the same time increasing the bargaining power of the host country.

Direct credit allocation at preferential rates, as noted earlier, played an important role in animating the profit-investment-export nexus in the Asian NIEs in the 1960s, 1970s and 1980s. All the evidence confirms that firms grow faster, and are more productive, when long-term finance is available. Moreover, while the impact of financial development is likely to differ depending on a country's level of economic and industrial development, banks remain a key element in the institutional framework. With the demand for investment in the development process, the premature dismantling of development banks has proved unhelpful.[29] We have seen in previous chapters that in a

---

global economy where dynamic scale economies and prolonged learning processes are the rule rather than the exception, market-based
allocation of financial resources on the basis of existing comparative
advantages may simply prevent a developing country from moving
into new industries and progressing towards higher-value-added activities. Intervention to ensure that such an evolution is not frustrated
by a lack of finance is a key element of a more sophisticated approach
to infant-industry protection. Market failures are widespread in finance, especially in developing countries, and the boom-and-bust
cycles of international capital flows are highly detrimental to national
development efforts. There is now a growing acceptance that financial liberalisation is a very risky policy and should only be embarked
upon with the greatest caution. As the experience of many countries
in Asia and in Western Europe has shown, a failure to liberalise finance is not necessarily an obstacle to rapid rates of economic growth
– indeed the contrary seems more likely, especially in developing
countries.

Reclaiming policy space from the stranglehold of finance is a
basic challenge in many middle-income developing countries where
high and volatile interest rates and overvalued exchange rates have
damaged investment prospects, particularly in the traded-goods
sectors. An independent central bank is no panacea and, if anything,
is likely to impart an unhelpful deflationary bias to macroeconomic
policy. Certainly, a key element in any development strategy designed
to enable a country to benefit from gradual integration into the global
trading system is successful management of the exchange rate. The
objective is to sustain a rate that will support competitiveness over
the longer term and to retain enough policy autonomy to make orderly
adjustments in the face of external shocks (Helleiner (ed.), 2003).
The major obstacle to achieving such stability and autonomy, however,
is the instability of private financial flows motivated by the prospect
of arbitrage and speculative gains.[30] The greater part of these are
unrelated to international flows of goods and services and fixed

---

[30] The distinction between "short-term" and "long-term" capital has been largely
eroded by the development of derivatives and other financial instruments. As
pointed out earlier, FDI can also be unstable, subject to surges and sudden stops.
The crucial aspect from the point of view of vulnerability to instability is liquidity
rather than the maturity of liabilities.

investment; as noted earlier, they have acquired a life of their own and are primarily driven by the prospect of short-term gains. They make little contribution to a better allocation of resources or the diffusion of technology; instead they undermine stability and growth by creating general uncertainty, increasing real-exchange-rate fluctuations, sometimes impeding fixed investment, and increasing the risk of financial crises. No exchange-rate regime – floating, flexible, currency board, dollarisation or nominal peg – can deliver stable and competitive exchange rates in the face of large and volatile capital flows. Nor will development strategies be able to combine steady growth with financial stability in the presence of such capital movements.

The damage can be prevented, or at least limited, only if there is effective regulation and control over such destabilising capital flows. A key objective is to prevent a large build-up of foreign liabilities that can be quickly reversed. Controls on capital flows therefore need to become a legitimate feature of the policy maker's tool-kit. The techniques are well known and range from market-based measures – intervention in the foreign-exchange market, more flexible exchange-rate bands, non-interest-bearing reserve requirements on foreign liabilities, or taxes to reduce the international arbitrage margin – to direct controls on, say, banks' net external positions, borrowing abroad by non-banks, or on foreign equity participation in domestic firms. A number of developing countries have used such measures to manage capital flows: the key to success is a flexible and pragmatic approach that will support stable exchange rates without deterring trade-related capital flows and FDI.[31] Indeed, a coherent and transparent approach to managing short-term capital flows should help to improve the environment for both trade and FDI.

2. *Regional options*

To be effective, many of the measures required for a more strategic intervention in the international economy must be tailored

---

[31] Chile, Malaysia and, in Central Europe, Slovenia are among the countries that have successfully deployed controls on short-term capital flows without endangering their longer-term growth prospects.

to and embedded in their specific local setting. However, they may also find a complementary setting at the regional level. There is a considerable body of economics literature, mostly in the branch of international trade, which views the regionalisation trend with alarm and sees it as the result of trade-diverting agreements which threaten to undermine the global trading system.[32] Regional trade agreements may have played some role in boosting regional trade at the expense of multilateral transactions, but it is far from clear that this is inevitably the case[33]; indeed, there are a number of more fundamental forces making for regionalisation that tend to be ignored by mainstream trade theory. As mentioned earlier, intra-regional trade in Europe, North America and, increasingly, in East Asia is largely dominated by intra-industry exchanges of intermediate manufactures and capital goods, and these reflect a very high degree of specialisation in the various stages of the manufacturing production process. Intra-industry trade tends to be most intense among industrialised (or industrialising) countries at similar levels of development and is driven by dynamic economies of scale and specialisation and by the search for long production runs. These processes tend to generate economies of agglomeration and to trigger cumulative processes that reinforce the degree of concentration over time. Once such processes are under way there will be pressure from producers within the region to lower or remove the various barriers to intra-regional trade, including bureaucratic red tape, conflicting legal restrictions and administrative procedures, etc., as well as demands for better transport and communications infrastructure. These various demands are likely to be accompanied by the creation of institutions for closer regional cooperation, as has happened for example in Europe.[34] At first, such cooperation will tend to focus on technical issues (trade barriers, standards and the like) but as regional production systems become ever more integrated, so the regional policy framework is likely to expand. This can be seen in Europe's evolving financial arrangements,

---

[32] See, for example, the papers in Frankel (ed.) (1998).
[33] The development of an East Asian regional economy, for example, has been described as "open regionalism"; see Kirkpatrick (1994:191-202).
[34] Intra-industry trade in Western Europe was already important in the 1950s, but the drive to keep reducing transaction costs by removing administrative and other obstacles often came from the enterprise sector. This was the case with the 1992 Single Market programme.

beginning with reconstruction aid and balance-of-payments support under the Marshall Plan, extending to financial support to poorer regions and the financing of regional public goods (particularly infrastructure) channelled through the European Investment Bank, and culminating in regional exchange-rate arrangements and ultimately monetary union under a common central bank.[35]

In the case of East Asia, a close association between the pattern of industrialisation and its regional location has been linked with the upgrading of economic activity from resource-based and labour-intensive industries to more and more sophisticated manufactures by the lead economies, which in turn has opened up opportunities for the less developed countries in the region to enter the regional division of labour by engaging in less demanding activities. To stay ahead, the countries which developed first have been forced to move up the trade hierarchy and export more sophisticated products where they now have a comparative advantage, with FDI providing one possible route for recycling comparative advantage. This idea of a regional division of labour, combining an industrial and locational hierarchy, has been described as the "flying geese" development paradigm. However, as we insisted earlier, government policy has been central to the regional impact of FDI, and when drawing wider lessons from this experience, it should not be forgotten that much of the international spillovers within East Asia have been ultimately generated because of the success of the industrial policy of the first-tier NIEs, rather than through a purely market-generated process.

As described in earlier chapters, three major regional blocs have already formed and are likely to consolidate still further, with large firms organising a complex international division of labour within them. Trade between these blocs is already quite limited, and may continue to atrophy as direct investment becomes the principal route to penetrating markets in other regions. This is likely to mean more investment by European and Japanese firms in North America, and more North American investment in Europe. It is less clear what will happen in Japan, since European and North American firms seem to have great difficulty in penetrating Japanese markets through either

---

[35]   See the papers in Ocampo (ed.) (2006) by Charles Wyplosz and Stephany Griffith-Jones, Alfred Steinherr and Ana Teresa Fuzzo de Lima on the European financial experience.

exports or investment; both trade and investment intensity ratios of North America and Europe in East Asia are still low. Predicting future trends is, of course, hazardous, particularly given the still uncertain role of China. However, regional economic ties are likely to become closer under the combined impact of successful industrialisation and increased trade and investment flows. Large-scale exports of labour-intensive products from the poorer countries of East Asia to Europe and North America are likely to continue to increase. There is also likely to be some increase in exports of more sophisticated technology goods, but these face serious economic and political constraints. To penetrate the markets of Europe and North America, the larger East Asian firms will probably rely increasingly on direct investment and this will limit the volume of sophisticated exports. The result will be a consolidation of existing regional structures, with a more closely knit regional bloc developing in the east to take its place alongside those of Europe and North America.

Whether and how similar regional dynamics will emerge elsewhere in the developing world, such as in Latin America and Southern Africa, will depend to a large extent on how quickly leading economies, such as Brazil and South Africa, can establish robust and sustained rates of growth. Political will on the part of governments to coordinate policies in some areas and give up certain options in others is certainly a prerequisite for building regional integration. There are signs, after a series of false starts and disappointments, that such integration is again gaining converts in parts of the developing world. Proposals to forge greater consistency with respect to trade and investment policies are back on the agenda in both Africa and Latin America. Indeed, renewed discussions on South-South cooperation seem likely to flourish initially at the regional level in the hope that enlarged markets can attract FDI from neighbouring countries in the way that has emerged in East Asia. In addition, there has been renewed emphasis on regional infrastructure projects. The UN Report on the Millennium Development Goals (MDGs) (2005) recognised the importance of channelling ODA into regional programmes in order to meet development goals; aid for such programmes could also be increased through more innovative forms of financing (UNDESA, 2005). One important area where regional policy initiatives could make an important contribution is in curtailing "races to the bottom" as a result of wasteful bidding by countries hoping to attract TNCs, particularly, but not exclusively, in the extractive sectors. Indeed, efforts by developing countries to harmonise their codes and policies towards contract enforcement, tax and other incentives, etc. would increase their bargaining strength vis-à-vis the TNCs, thereby improving their chances of following their own preferred growth path consistent with their priorities.

This sketch of the underlying forces for regionalisation suggests that much of the alarmism about regional arrangements and regional blocs is misplaced. Most of the actions taken to enhance regional cooperation need not be associated with discrimination against out-siders. But the crucial point is that dynamic economies of scale and specialisation lead to cumulative advantages in concentrating eco-nomic activities in particular locations. Mainstream economic theory tends to ignore these processes and so its adherents interpret regionalisation as an obstruction to the realisation of a truly global economy. It is significant that rapid economic growth in East Asia has been accompanied by a marked increase in mutual economic in-terdependence among the countries of the region via intra-regional trade and investment. But while such interdependence can amplify the forces for growth, it can also increase the threat of contagion to external shocks, as was experienced during the 1997 financial crisis. Designing more formal regional financial arrangements to ensure fu-ture stability is thus likely to be a necessary complement to any search for alternative development strategies (Ocampo, 2002b).

E.   Reforming the global architecture

Suggestions for a more measured pace of integration of devel-oping countries into the global economy are often portrayed as a sign of reluctance to implement the necessary reforms required to com-pete in global markets. This is a caricature based on a gross simplifi-cation of the problems faced by most developing countries. The is-sue for them is not whether they want to integrate with the global system, but how to proceed, under what conditions and at what pace.

Over the past 25 years developing countries have made consid-erable efforts to integrate more closely with the rest of the world through trade and capital-account liberalisation, and for the most part have done so on the terms laid down by the leading economic powers. However, the promises of liberalisation – that it would stimulate faster growth and reduce poverty, and that per capita incomes would start to catch up with those in the developed economies – have been realised in only a few countries and, in almost all cases, they have done so on the basis of a gradual integration with the global economy rather than the neo-liberal agenda. The most recent wave of attempts at closer integration have been frustrated by the fact that the international system itself has been developing in a way that has not in general been supportive of rapid growth and development. The international economic system that emerged after 1945 was, inevitably, a compromise. It was nevertheless an agreement struck among countries with shared histories and similar levels of economic development and based on a common view of what needed to be avoided, namely the incoherence and turmoil of the 1930s, and with a broad tolerance of different national policy choices so long as they avoided damaging the economies of other members of the system. Its subsequent evolution, to include countries at very different levels of development, was more ad hoc. The resources were never made available to tackle effectively the deep-seated structural problems facing most of these countries. However, multilateral arrangements were premised on the assumption of putting growth and employment first (a premise that travelled well from North to South) and it was accepted that the difficulties facing most developing countries seeking to integrate with the international economy could best be managed by allowing some derogation from the rules that essentially had been agreed by, and in the interests of, the richest countries.

For most developing countries, the international trade and finance system that has evolved since the debt crisis has not only failed to provide sufficient long-term financial and technological resources to enable them to achieve rapid and sustained rates of growth but also broken with the working principles of the post-war system. Indeed, under present arrangements and policies, developing countries almost invariably find themselves obliged to adjust to international imbalances through domestic retrenchment. The IMF, since the mid-1970s, has abandoned the objective of ensuring stable exchange rates in an orderly international financial system and, instead, international financial flows have been allowed to return to levels similar to those that caused instability in the inter-war period, generating exchange-rate instability and misalignments and leading to sudden disruptions in the pattern of international competitiveness. In contrast to its early history, the IMF now lends exclusively to developing countries, substantially blurring the distinction between the short-term liquidity requirements of a stable financial system and the long-term financing requirements for the development of lower-income countries. The World Bank has also given up its emphasis on longer-term infrastructure projects and now concentrates on "structural adjustment" lending and poverty reduction. The governance of international trade has moved towards a single-tier system of rights and obligations, in which developing countries have generally the same level of obligations as the developed countries. The recognition that full employment should be a key measure of the success of an increasingly free trade system has been weakened. Trade liberalisation has been given priority over economic growth and full employment, thereby rekindling mercantilist agendas, not least in the developed countries.

Implementation of the commitments undertaken by most developing countries during the Uruguay Round, together with continued restrictions on market access in some of the major industrial countries, have generated payments imbalances that cannot be financed on a sustained and reliable basis by private international capital flows. As we noted earlier, these have proved to be highly concentrated on just a few countries, pro-cyclical and very volatile. Moreover, despite sustained international pressure to increase them, official financial flows declined throughout the 1990s and there has been only a hesitant recovery since the start of the new millennium. The outcome of the Monterrey Financing for Development conference in 2002 highlights this inconsistency: the additional pledges made there fell far short of the amounts needed to close the resource gap which, according to estimates made by UNCTAD, the Zedillo Panel and the World Bank, requires a doubling in the flow of official aid. Since then, more recent commitments have promised to raise ODA flows to $120 billion a year by 2010. While there is no doubting the change of political heart behind these promises, the real numbers are still highly contentious, with one charity talking of too little real aid and too much "phantom aid" (ActionAid, 2005). Perhaps more importantly, it remains very uncertain whether the institutional and policy changes required to support a major push for development will be forthcoming (UNCTAD, 2006b).

Ideally, the international community should be looking for more extensive reforms of the international financial system so that it can support a more balanced integration of developing countries into the international trading system, an integration that will allow them not only to trade more but also to earn more from doing so, and will ensure that any adjustments are made through expansion rather than contraction. In other words, the interest of developing countries in the stability of the international financial system is whether it will allow them to combine increased participation in international trade with the full exploitation of their development potential.

On some assessments this can only be achieved by completely closing down current arrangements; for others it means a radical overhaul of existing institutions, including the introduction of new rules and institutions to regulate more effectively the array of global public "goods and bads" that have emerged as a result of closer economic interdependence.[36] The Asian financial crisis and subsequent aftershocks elsewhere in the developing world gave a strong impulse to calls for major reform, such as those from the Meltzer Commission, established by the US Congress in 1998. The former chief economist of the IMF, Kenneth Rogoff (1999:28), for one, has acknowledged that there is a case for major institutional change in order to deal with persistent shocks and the risk of further crises.

Our intention here is not to add to such blueprints. However, it is the case that, to date, proposals to reform the international financial system have placed undue emphasis on what should be done at the national level and, even here, the approach has not been even-handed.[37] In the financial sphere, efforts have concentrated on disciplining debtors, setting guidelines and standards for major areas of domestic policy, principally in debtor countries, and providing incentives and sanctions for their implementation. Debtor countries have been urged to better manage risk by adopting stricter financial standards and

---

[36] The specific proposals for reform of existing institutions and for the creation of new ones are numerous. See Nayyar (ed.) (2002).

[37] See UNCTAD (2001b:Part Two), particularly Chapter III for a survey of the issues.

regulations, to hold larger international reserves, establish contingent credit lines, and make contractual arrangements with private creditors so as to involve them in crisis resolution. The international financial system has continued to be organised around the principle of *laissez-faire, laissez-passer*, and developing countries are advised or cajoled to adhere to the objective of open capital accounts and convertibility. All this has extended the global reach of financial markets without a corresponding strengthening of global institutions or recognition of the need for them to coordinate the trading and financial systems in a coherent way.

As things stand, there is a general recognition that current arrangements fall far short of providing developing countries with sufficient resources. IMF quotas have lagged considerably behind the growth of global output and trade: according to one estimate, they stood at just 6 per cent of world imports in 2000 compared with 58 per cent in 1944 and 15 per cent in 1970 (Buira, 2003:9). Moreover, the bulk of IMF lending is now given to crisis management in emerging markets. Perhaps more telling is that net transfers from the International Bank for Reconstruction and Development (IBRD) have been negative in almost every year since 1990, both for low-income and middle-income countries, leaving concessional International Development Association (IDA) credits as the only real source of development finance (Akyüz, 2006).

It is not just the shortage of financial resources, since the collapse of the Bretton Woods system, that has biased adjustments in a deflationary direction. A key assumption behind the founding Bretton Woods Conference of 1944 was that the leading countries would be willing to forego or attenuate the pursuit of their own immediate interests in favour of a larger concern for systemic stability.[38] On this basis, Harry Dexter White, who with Keynes was one of the two principal architects of the Bretton Woods system, insisted that:

> To use international monetary arrangements as a cloak for
> the enforcement of unpopular policies, whose merits or
> demerits rest not on international monetary considerations

---

[38] The potential of unfettered capital flows to disrupt international trade and undermine financial stability was clearly recognised by both Keynes and White.

as such but on the whole economic programme and philosophy of the country concerned, would poison the atmosphere of international financial stability (cited in Felix, 1996:64).

It was taken for granted by Keynes and White that controls on international capital movements would be needed in order to maintain an open international trading and monetary system, even if this meant limiting the options open to the financial-market institutions in their own countries. The conditionalities – understood broadly as the "means by which one offers support and attempts to influence the policies of another in order to secure compliance with a programme of measures" (Buira, 2003:3) – attached to multilateral financial flows were limited. There were, of course, regular assessments of development policies and prospects of individual recipient countries, but this was primarily to ensure project implementation and the creditworthiness of borrowers, and not with a view to specifying detailed policy conditionality. That only changed in the early 1980s with the expanding development mandates of the IFIs. As multilateral flows concentrated more and more on adjustment lending, conditionalities were crafted with the explicit aim of shifting policy-making in borrowing countries towards more market-friendly development strategies (Ahluwalia, 1999:3-5).[39] In contrast to White's wise advice, surveillance was intensified to ensure the correct policy line was being followed in borrowing countries (now exclusively from the developing world), in the process failing to protect weaker and smaller economies against the adverse effects of changes in monetary and financial policies in the major industrial countries.

There is now a groundswell of opinion, from a former head of the IMF, Horst Kohler, to the Blair Commission on Africa, that conditionalities need to be dramatically pruned.[40] But even if this is done, the general thrust of reform continues to work against establishing a dynamic profit-investment-export nexus in most

---

[39]   As was noted earlier, the combination of adequate resources and tolerant leadership in the interest of lifting all boats together was very much the spirit behind the Marshall Plan.

[40]   On ways to revise conditionality, see Kapur and Webb (2000) and Buira (2003).

developing countries. In particular, the volatility of exchange rates, high real interest rates and the proliferation of arbitrage and unproductive rent-seeking opportunities in a world of deregulated financial markets have generated sub-standard capital formation and stunted industrial restructuring. In these circumstances, the premature liberalisation of capital accounts has not only been highly damaging to economic performance but threatens to lock many countries into a longer-term path of slow and erratic growth. It is now widely recognised that financial liberalisation was pushed much too hard in the 1990s but, to date, this has failed to lead to concrete measures of reform.

The logic of rejecting the one-size-fits-all model must be for these institutions to adopt a much more open and balanced discussion of policy options. The consequences of this were spelt out by the German Development Minister to the IMF-World Bank Development Committee in Washington in October 2004:

> Development institutions, in particular the [World] Bank and the [International Monetary] Fund, should actively advise on a range of policy alternatives and thus create "policy space" for the countries. Here, it is not so much a question of "policy advice" in the classic sense. Rather, the role of the IFIs is to identify trade-offs, show possible alternative policy options, make experience from other countries accessible and contribute to the establishment of national analytical capabilities. A further streamlining of conditionality and focusing of performance criteria on output indicators would also contribute to ownership.

Managing nominal exchange rates in order to reduce fluctuations in the real rate, combined with controls on short-term capital flows, is a rational choice for developing countries and should be accepted as such by the international financial institutions and the developed countries. Avoiding pro-cyclical macroeconomic policies, particularly when shocks are triggered through the capital account, is also essential to building a stable growth environment in developing countries. This will almost certainly require an increase in the size of multilateral financial resources to match the growth of international economic transactions and the greater vulnerability that accompanies increased interdependence.

Given the scale and unpredictability of capital flows, however, even a well-managed economy may succumb to a sustained and major attack on its currency, and a liquidity problem can then be rapidly transformed into an international debt crisis. The growing literature on managing such crises accepts the premise that international finance is under-regulated and that avoiding the downward spiral of a debt deflation, which is a likely outcome if the standard remedy of higher interest rates and tighter fiscal policy is adopted, requires new responses (Eichengreen, 2002).

The multilateral arrangements designed at Bretton Woods did not include a global regime for capital movements, given that capital mobility was assumed to be limited by the wider workings of the international system. However, no such regime has emerged even after the breakdown of these arrangements, and despite the growing importance of private capital flows. Various codes and standards have been established through institutions such as the IMF and the Bank for International Settlements (BIS), with respect not just to the financial sector but also to macroeconomic policy, data collection and dissemination, auditing and accounting, etc. But while their application should be generally beneficial, particularly over the longer term, they will not necessarily contribute to financial stability and in many cases they will involve substantial costs (UNCTAD, 2001b:79-107).

Rethinking the role of financial regulation might usefully begin with hedge funds, which are a recognised source of systemic vulnerability and which have already come close on a number of occasions to triggering financial meltdown.[41]

---

[41] Hedge funds emerged in response to the exchange-rate and interest-rate volatility that followed the collapse of Bretton Woods. They handle an estimated $1-1.5 trillion of funds, equivalent to the eighth-largest country in the world. In 1998, the hedge fund Long-Term Capital Management, with assets of $125bn (financed by just $4.1bn of its own capital) and holding 50,000 derivatives contracts (notionally involving more than $1 trillion), came close to collapse, triggering a $3.6bn bailout organised through the New York Federal Reserve.

This argument recognises, first, that large bailouts organised by the international financial institutions have been neither successful nor equitable and, second, that although domestic financial institutions and regulation need to be greatly strengthened this cannot be done quickly.[42] It also recognises that the burden of adjustment should be shared more equitably between borrowers and private-sector creditors, who tend to move in and out of individual countries in a herd and thereby increase the risks of transforming a liquidity squeeze into a solvency crisis and then a major recession.

Whether or not sufficient funds are likely to be made available to the IMF to act independently in response to a crisis, there remains a moral-hazard problem with such bailouts that could perpetuate instability. A sensible response would be to combine an injection of liquidity with a debt standstill and a programme for restructuring the debt (UNCTAD, 2001b). This proposal, inspired by Chapters 9 and 11 of the United States Bankruptcy Code, would stop an escalation of the crisis in its tracks. It would involve a temporary standstill on debt servicing and the IMF "lending into arrears", and so provide breathing space while debts are restructured. It is thus a proposal for preventing financial crises from being more serious than they need be and, by ensuring that private-sector creditors share the costs of adjustment, it may even reduce the probability of such crises occurring in the first place.

In the case of international trade, the fashioning of a standardised set of rules ought to act as a bulwark against arbitrary action by the powerful and provide effective surveillance to prevent the adoption of beggar-my-neighbour measures. This, however, has not been the case. In part the problem has arisen, as Helleiner (2000) has argued, from restricting the design and monitoring of international trade rules

---

[42] IMF rescue packages have sometimes exceeded several times the accepted quota limits (an annual limit of 100 per cent of a member's quota and a cumulative limit of 300 per cent), and in some instances were put together with funds from development banks and bilateral contributions from major industrial countries. IMF rescue packages for six emerging markets (Mexico, Thailand, Indonesia, Korea, Russia and Brazil) between 1995 and 1998 reached $231bn, of which 44 per cent came from bilateral donors, 38 per cent from the IMF, and the rest from development banks. From 1995 until the end of 2003 IMF exceptional financing for nine emerging markets (the above six plus Argentina, Turkey and Uruguay) amounted to SDR 174bn, averaging 637 per cent of quota. See also Akyüz (2006).

to liberalisation (or deregulation), thereby ignoring a broad swathe of issues from unfavourable movements in the terms of trade through restrictive business practices to technology transfer, where re-regulation should be a legitimate provision in international arrangements. In part the problem has arisen from a widening hiatus between the increasing demands of a "single undertaking," whereby countries are required to agree to and implement an entire set of rules, and diminished capacities on the part of the state in developing countries, a combination that makes it increasingly difficult for them to take advantage of their rights, defend their interests and even meet their obligations.

In terms of the arguments of this chapter, the international trading system has also become systemically biased against the establishment of a dynamic profit-investment-export nexus in developing countries. The strong bias in the Uruguay Round towards gains for the rich developed countries should have been a signal to the international community that things were moving in a lop-sided manner, i.e., the rules of the game were a source of divergence, not the much-promised convergence. Two specific areas are in urgent need of correction. The first is that, despite the reduction of trade barriers in the Uruguay Round, the developed countries still heavily protect their domestic markets for a wide range of products in which developing countries have or could quickly acquire a clear advantage – agricultural products, processed foods, textiles and clothing, and a range of labour-intensive manufactures. The willingness of the developed countries to liberalise their markets for such products, to eliminate peak tariffs, end their abuse of anti-dumping actions, and abolish trade-distorting subsidies to their agricultural producers is thus the real test of the credibility of *their* commitment to a more open global trading system. At the same time, the global trade rules continue to allow plenty of room for advanced countries to nurture new industries through government support for science and technology, venture capital for high-tech start-ups, public-private partnerships, etc. Making sure that the rules are equally flexible in areas where developing countries want to support their own "new" industries should be part of a more balanced system.

The second area where the trading system is increasingly biased against the developing countries is in the extension of global rules to matters that go far beyond the traditional domain of international trade policy. Thus, the Uruguay Round removed or restricted the developing countries' ability to subsidise their local industries or to introduce investment-promotion measures, such as local-content rules or limiting imported inputs to a given percentage of exports (the Agreement on Trade-Related Investment Measures (TRIMs)); and the Agreement on Trade-Related Aspects of Intellectual Property Rights (TRIPS), which obliges developing countries to protect intellectual property rights with the same rigour as the developed countries, hinders both the absorption of modern technologies by developing-country firms and their technological development. Proposals to extend WTO rules to areas such as investment, competition policy, government procurement and environmental standards should be rejected. The effect of such extensions of the rule-based system, which essentially favour western corporate interests, is to greatly reduce the policy options available to developing countries to promote their trade and development. Indeed, some of the measures employed successfully by the NIEs of East Asia, and by the developed economies themselves at various times since World War II, are now being denied to developing countries.[43]

Despite the narrowing of developing countries' policy space, however, there are still various financial, fiscal and macroeconomic measures that can be but are not always fully used to direct investment, promote exports and allow some degree of infant-industry protection.[44] In this respect, the failure of elites in developing countries to establish effective state institutions and to forge a consensus around an alternative vision of economic progress to that offered by market fundamentalism is arguably the single biggest obstacle to building the requisite policy space needed to achieve faster growth and structural diversification. We have already suggested some reasons why market-driven globalisation has contributed to this failure.

Nevertheless, the narrowing of the policy choices allowed to developing countries due to international rules, norms and pressures is particularly disturbing because it implies that the options that are

---

[43] See Chang (2002) for an excellent account of the array of trade and other policies employed by today's advanced countries to promote their own industries and economic growth.

[44] See UNCTAD (1996:156-57); Amsden (2000).

permitted are known to be sufficient for promoting growth and development. This, however, is very far from being the case. Although there is increasing agreement as to the crucial importance of the factors emphasised above, the precise ways and circumstances in which they interact effectively in one country but not in another are very far from being well known or understood.[45] Developing countries therefore need more room to experiment, not less, in order to discover what will work in their own specific circumstances. If nothing is done to address the systemic biases in the trading rules, and if greater flexibility is not allowed to developing countries in their pursuit of effective development strategies, the legitimacy of the entire multilateral rules-based system that has been painstakingly developed over more than 50 years will itself be undermined.

---

[45] It is salutary to be reminded that "all the thousands of pages of controversy about the causes of the Industrial Revolution have still not come up with one clear identifiable factor that Britain had and every other European (or Asian, or African) economy lacked" (Ogilvie, 2000:118).

Chapter 8

The Conditions for a Sustainable Global Order

SINCE the collapse of the Berlin Wall there has been a veritable boom in articles and books, not to mention newspaper and TV commentary, on the subject of globalisation. Most extol its virtues and see it leading towards a new world of greater prosperity more equally shared. Explaining how it works to the benefit of all was the *leitmotif* of early pundits; demonstrating the boundless potential of the latest technological breakthrough, unravelling the mysteries of comparative advantage (to a befuddled public), revealing the intricate workings of international financial markets (to a more eager public), extolling the virtues of the new global corporation, welcoming the end of business cycles (as well as history), all were wrapped in the language of globalisation. Recently, as some of the trends outlined in this book have become more and more difficult to shrug off, a more cautious note has been sounded, with the debate turning on why globalisation is worth defending, the error of falling back on the models of a bygone age, and the dangerous allure of outdated political habits. But across most of this commentary, globalisation is seen as taking us ineluctably towards a world without borders, whose promised gains will only be fully realised if markets and technology are left alone to drive the process, allowing a full transformation not just of the economy but also of all the social, cultural and political structures that surround them. The only "rational" course, we are repeatedly told, is to adjust to this emerging world or be crushed by it. Just how difficult that adjustment could be provokes differences of opinion, sometimes quite sharp, but the constant refrain is that there is "no alternative", no "turning back the clock".

This is a particularly odd choice of metaphor, not least because for many of those using it, the preferred economic model not only allows for roll-back, but sees it as a rather effortless, if not altogether painless, process! Across whole areas of economic life, turning the clock back is precisely what globalisation has been about: reversing high levels of trade-union membership and labour-market legislation that favoured workers, reversing the steady decline of profits in value added and the shift towards a more equal distribution of income, reversing state ownership of industry, correcting the commodity-price hikes and budget deficits of the 1970s, reversing the rise in corporate-tax rates, reversing a policy emphasis on economic growth as the best route to facilitate adjustments, and so on.

What actually seems to us to have been distinct about the last quarter-century is that there has been a concerted political drive, initiated by ruling elites in the advanced industrial economies, to recast the boundaries of state, corporate and market power around the idea of an autonomous and self-adjusting economic realm. From this viewpoint, globalisation is essentially a policy-driven process that emerged from conflicts in the developed countries in the 1970s and which has been driven to a large extent by their corporate sectors. This is not to deny that it has the potential to deliver wider benefits, but a special feature of arguments for globalisation since the early 1980s is the demand that in one way or another political and social arrangements should bend to the demands of the market economy. Indeed, if globalisation is an unavoidable and irresistible force, as the fundamentalists insist, then there is no room for negotiation or mutual adjustment: a society must adapt or become marginalised. This goes against the principle established in most nation states, and especially in the western democracies in the decades following World War II, that activity in the private corporate sector is subject to constraints established within the broader framework of political and social institutions of which the economy is a part. Persistent attacks over the last 25 years or so on state intervention in the economy, usually on the ground that it is always inefficient or counter-productive, combined with repeated assertions that the nation state is redundant, amount to an attempt to reverse this direction of legitimacy, to insist that political and social arrangements and preferences must be justified according to whether they meet the requirements of corporate interests rather than the reverse.

It would be wrong, however, to take the "rolling back" ideology at face value (although this is usually the language adopted by market fundamentalists). What has been happening is better described as a general "softening" of state power. This does not just mean that the state agrees to let markets and corporations look after themselves, relinquishing various policy instruments and foreclosing on its regulatory authority, although this has certainly happened, but also that it adopts the yardstick of private profit and the values and practices of the business and financial community to recalibrate and reshape both the activities of the public sector and a broad swathe of social and political life. Moreover, it involves not only shifting authority over many economic matters from politically accountable actors to the marketplace, but also deferring judgement on a wide range of public issues to a new body of actors such as "independent" central banks, regional bureaucratic authorities, quasi- and non-governmental organisations, international financial institutions and, not least, management consultants. Indeed these new (or at least newly emboldened) actors have been particularly aggressive in de-linking the public domain from the national political sphere, and reinterpreting much of the public domain and the provision of public goods as an essentially technocratic exercise, best served by harnessing the efficiency-promoting properties of international market forces and private enterprise. These ideas, of a global market destiny, economic convergence and technocratic responsibility, have been combined in a powerful political ideology that denies any real choices for policy makers over the direction of economic activity. Reflecting on the particular way in which this ideology has transformed French society during the course of the past two decades, Alain Supiot (2006) has described the current problems which those reforms have encountered (manifest most visibly in violent urban protests) in terms which carry much wider resonance:

> A number (of reforms) have been imposed from on high and don't answer to the real living and working conditions of those they affect; other, undeniably necessary ones were

not undertaken at all because they would have disturbed powerful vested interests. In reality the French "délitement" or "unbedding" reveals something much more serious than a mere delay in the glorious march towards an economy without barriers: it reveals the chasms into which the march is dragging us. The subjection of the public sphere to the laws of the market is having a deleterious effect on the old nation states and this has taken a particularly virulent form in France: institutions are giving way from within, social justice is being abandoned and there is a loss of direction on the international stage.

In an interview he gave in 1991, one of the doyens of liberal philosophical thinking, Isaiah Berlin, expressed his hope that a "world which is a reasonably peaceful coat of many colours, each portion of which develops its own distinct cultural identity and is tolerant of others, is not a Utopian dream" (Gardels, 1991). In a somewhat similar vein, we have argued in this book that a more prosperous and peaceful world has to be comprised of interdependent economies with distinct institutional identities and with sufficient policy space to be able to design effective development strategies to meet the rising expectations of their citizens and to handle the myriad conflicts and unpredictable twists and turns that inevitably accompany economic development. In this perspective, as John Ralston Saul (2005) has recently argued, echoing Adam Smith, the very idea of a self-regulating global marketplace is not only a utopian dream, but a dangerous one, precisely because it rules out of court the institutional basis on which distinct economic identities can flourish. Contrary to the insistence of the globalists that one market view (whether it be vulgar Marxist or neo-liberal) must prevail in all circumstances, the search by citizens across the world for security, dignity, inclusion and prosperity continues to rest on the institutional foundations of the nation state and on some notion of positive or "civic" nationalism which is grounded in local experiences and choices.[1]

However, after more than two decades of neo-liberals peddling their dangerous utopia, the question is whether the kind of international trade and financial system required to support such a world can be said to exist at all at present when currency and financial markets are dominated by speculative transactions and regular outbreaks of herd behaviour, and when there is virtually no coordination at all between the macroeconomic policies of the most developed industrialised countries. Most of the financial crises in the developing countries have resulted from various shocks and policy changes that originated in the major reserve-currency countries, but at present there is no assurance that international liquidity will be supplied on a sufficient scale to enable the developing countries to make measured adjustments to such shocks rather than worsen an economic contraction. Nor is there a system of multilateral surveillance that can insist on greater coherence in the monetary and exchange-rate policies of the richest countries. Similarly, an international trading system that generates greater volumes of trade but without commensurate increases in incomes and employment, and which bends too easily to the interests of the strongest economic powers, leaves the weaker countries and communities increasingly anxious about their future economic prospects. As their resources are increasingly stretched at home, poor

---

[1]   Saul's notion of nationalism is closely linked to Berlin's plea for tolerance: "You could say that all nationalism is about belonging, about place and about imagining the other. It can take a positive civic form, one in which belonging brings the obligation to reach out and to imagine the other in an inclusive, multiple way. It can also take a negative form, above all ethnic, dedicated to belonging as an expression of privilege and exclusion. The positive form of nationalism is tied to self-confidence and openness and to a concept of the public good. Negative nationalism is dependent on fear and anger and a desperate conviction that one nation's rights exist by comparison with those of another nation, as if in a competition that produces winners and losers." A recent attempt by the UNCTAD secretariat to introduce the concept of "open nationalism" as a way of describing the kind of strategic integration policies needed by developing countries to benefit from closer ties with the global economy was immediately met with accusations of negative nationalism by the representatives of richer countries. At the same time, they were insisting that the real issue was whether or not developing countries were adopting the right (market-friendly) policies to allow them to compete amongst each other and against the advanced industrial economies for the spoils (opportunities) of a globalising world.

countries see fewer and fewer opportunities to bargain effectively in pursuit of their own particular interests. Until this situation is changed, developing countries will remain highly vulnerable to the vagaries of international finance, to the pressures of footloose TNCs, to exogenous shocks and to perennial balance-of-payments constraints.

Global financial stability, as much as an international trade system that contributes to faster growth in its weakest and most vulnerable members, is still principally the responsibility of the advanced industrial economies and the major international financial institutions that they dominate. It is therefore a matter of concern for all, but particularly the poorest countries and communities, that those dominant economies have all too cynically promoted the idea that resource gaps can only be closed by leaving all economic decisions to the invisible hand of the global marketplace, that leadership qualities are best honed in corporate boardrooms or on the bond trading floor, and that an appropriate measure of human progress is how many interconnected devices can be put on a computer chip.

Throughout this book we have insisted that the current era of globalisation is not being driven by autonomous and irresistible forces like the weather and therefore, as UK Prime Minister Blair claimed, not worth debating; instead, it is the product of deliberate policy choices made, for the most part, by the most developed and most powerful members of the global economy. Policy choices are generally based on a mixture of value premises, facts and beliefs about how the economy works, and a general framework of ideas that shape the mindsets of policy makers and their advisers. The predominant ideas shaping policy in the leading market economies in the last 20 years or so are those of neo-liberal economics which argue essentially for giving the fullest possible rein to competitive market forces in determining the structure of an economy and the most efficient allocation of resources, and for keeping the role of government as small as possible. The extension of such ideas to the rest of the world in the pursuit of policy conformity is a central feature of what is loosely called globalisation. Working to a large extent through the IMF, the World Bank and the WTO – the United Nations is rarely trusted by the G7 with such matters – the developed countries have pushed through similar changes in the standard strategy for development and growth in the developing countries. By stabilising and liberalising their domestic economies – through freeing the price mechanism, privatisation, deregulation and downsizing the role of government – and opening them up to international trade and foreign capital, it is claimed that entrepreneurial energies will be released, economic growth will accelerate and incomes will start to catch up with those of Western Europe and North America.

The earlier chapters have shown that such policies have delivered much less than what was promised. The major forces presumed to deliver the benefits of globalisation, trade and foreign investment, have been less global in their distribution than is commonly presented by politicians and the media; the benefits have been much smaller than anticipated; and in many cases they have been accompanied by serious costs. In short, the prevailing policies have failed to establish the conditions that would produce a take-off to higher rates of investment and output growth and a transformation of the structure of production in the developing countries. This record alone might be considered sufficient to start governments thinking about a change of strategy, but this is resisted by market fundamentalists, who hold that there are no alternatives and who simply sweep aside the considerable uncertainty that surrounds many of the relationships on which current policies are based. This is not just about a conflict of ideas, of course, since ideas usually need the support of interests if they are to influence policy. Just as sponsored research by the pharmaceutical companies tends to favour the treatment they are selling to patients, so the neo-liberal recommendations to developing countries tend to favour corporate interests in the developed economies. The hollowness of the "win-win" rhetoric of neo-liberalism was highlighted in the Uruguay Round of trade negotiations, which was biased in favour of the interests of the EU and the US, and more recently in the current Doha Round, where the Hong Kong Ministerial meeting in December 2005 indicated that the development content of the so-called "development round" was likely to be minimal.

The problem is not so much with the market economy *per se* – following James Meade, we have made it clear that we are more than content to raise two cheers for it – but with the narrowness of vision of those economists and politicians who claim to be able to show developing countries how to create efficient economies and integrate with the global economy, an objective which most of them share.

Economists too often ignore the fact that the effectiveness of policies is conditioned by the political and social context in which they are implemented – history, initial conditions and society matter, and so there is no point in one-policy-for-all. Moreover, the neo-liberal emphasis on optimal resource allocation is not the most relevant for countries seeking to expand the available resources and industrialise. Politicians in the developed countries also tend to be narrowly focused on short-run political objectives and on the interests of their own corporate sectors. "Technical" economic issues tend to be left in the hands of specialist ministries, as in the case of the WTO negotiations, where the mercantilism of the trade negotiators is rarely if ever balanced against more strategic foreign-policy interests such as improving the prospects for peace and security, not to mention the longer-term prospects for economic development.

The combination of market fundamentalism and special interests is supporting a dangerous complacency on the part of G7 leaders who still fail to see any urgent need for a significant change in their approach to development policy. It is therefore hardly surprising to find that the growing popular perception is of a system that has become heavily biased in favour of a handful of giant corporations and favoured economies. Despite brave talk about the final triumph of market capitalism, the crude fact of life is that no social or economic order is safe if it fails to benefit those who live under it or to provide a fair distribution of its costs and benefits. This is a basic political truth that was clearly understood by a long line of statesmen from Bismarck through Roosevelt to the architects of the original Bretton Woods system: if it is ignored or forgotten, any social system, national or international, will be threatened with instability and possible collapse.

We have stressed the importance of the interaction of economic, social and political factors in this book and of the need to take it into account if economic policies are to be effective. The same considerations can also be brought to bear on the requirements that must be met for any system to preserve its stability and its capability of sustaining itself. Stability here does not mean conservatism or stagnation but rather the capacity of the system to develop and adapt to change without serious disruption or violent upheaval. Following Kolodziej (1991) and Schroeder (1994), there are three key demands that must be satisfied if a system is to endure: these are for legitimacy, order and welfare. These criteria for stability must be met by a nation state, but also by any international system that creates rules or systems of governance for cooperation between groups of states, be they sub-regional, regional or global.

The demand for *legitimacy* refers to the basic justification of a government's authority over its citizens (or of an international or supranational body over its members), the procedures by which that authority is created and exercised, and more generally the manner in which political, social and economic institutions are rooted in and reflect the values and traditions or, in the words of Adam Smith, the "moral sentiments" of the population or community concerned. The justification of authority has obviously changed over time and still varies among communities. Monarchy justified by divine right and aristocracy by ownership of land have largely had their day. For most member states of the United Nations legitimacy is now generally regarded as being derived from the constitutional principles and processes of representative democracy, albeit such principles are sometimes more honoured in the breach than in the observance. Although the democratic principle is core, there is still plenty of scope for variation in the ways in which it is put into practice and, indeed, for disagreement as to how far it should go in emphasising the principle of individual liberty and free choice (following Locke, for example) or those of equality and social justice (following Rousseau, for example). There is of course a continuum of intermediate positions which will have implications for economic policy and will in turn be influenced by economic developments, but nevertheless the dominant principle of modern politics is that legitimate authority is based in some way or another on discussion with and approval by those over whom it is exercised.

The demand for *order* concerns the agreed laws, rules, social norms and informal conventions that govern relations among the various members of a society, or independent states in their international relations whether within or outside of formal institutions. The structure of incentives embedded in these laws, norms and standards defines the acceptable forms of behaviour throughout the system and provides for sanctions against the unacceptable. Clearly, for laws to be observed and for citizens to be able to pursue their legitimate aims, appropriate and effective institutions of enforcement must be in place. Well-ordered and effectual legislative and judicial systems are crucial for meeting this requirement of stability. But, more fundamentally, laws and rules will only stand when a majority of those subject to them agree to observe them voluntarily because it is in their interest to do so, not because of the threat of being caught or sanctioned for breaking them.

Finally, *welfare* refers to the capacity of the system to meet the needs of all its members. It recognises that popular support for institutions and the system as a whole will not be sustained if economic performance fails to generate an adequate standard of living, if it falls persistently below expectations or if too many citizens are left behind in poverty or regard the distribution of the benefits and costs of economic change as unjust.

The relationships between these three components are complex, as indeed are the relations between economic, social and political variables in general. It is therefore often difficult to judge how stable a system is or to assess the seriousness of threats to its stability. The relationships are almost certainly non-linear and subject to processes of "circular causation". A short-run deterioration in economic well-being, for example, may not threaten the stability of the system if popular support for institutions remains strong and if policies and institutions are capable of responding to social distress. In contrast, a smaller deterioration in all three criteria might pose a much greater threat to stability, and one that may begin to escalate if institutions proved incapable of responding to a deteriorating economy for example. There are also possible offsets: rapid income growth may distract attention from institutional failings or, more ominously, nationalism may be used to distract attention from deficiencies in legitimacy and economic performance. But in the medium and longer run, all three requirements must be met – two will not be enough. With hindsight it can be seen that what had been happening in Eastern Europe and the Soviet Union over a long period was a simultaneous and inter-related deterioration in all three components of stability: governments and political elites were increasingly seen by the populations they governed to lack the legitimacy of public support; political and social order was undermined by disillusionment with the institutions of the state – enhanced in Central and Eastern Europe by resentment at interference by a foreign hegemony – which encouraged widespread corruption and a burgeoning "black economy"; and there was a longstanding deterioration in economic performance and welfare, which in turn fed back to weaken legitimacy and undermine order. Much of the developing world is labouring under a similar set of corrosive forces: slow growth, deindustrialisation and growing informalisation of the economy are producing a growing sense of alienation in many sections of the population, and spawning a degree of resentment unseen since they gained their political independence.

As far as the international economic order is concerned, a number of obvious concerns arise. First, on the issue of *legitimacy*, the system is clearly dominated by just a few western economic powers who exercise a dominant influence in the running and policies of the IMF and the World Bank: their weighted voting systems, a form of shareholder democracy, resemble the Prussian electoral system of 1848 more closely than anything in a G7 country. Although all countries have equal voting rights in the WTO, in practice decisions are taken by consensus, which emerges obscurely as a result of consultations held by the chairpersons of the three principal WTO bodies. The developed countries have so far continued to dominate the WTO agenda with their superior resources for negotiation and their manipulation of bureaucratic procedures, but the deadlock in the Doha Round during 2005 and 2006 suggests that their dominance was starting to be challenged. On the criterion of *order*, we have already noted the increasing frequency and severity of financial crises since the early 1980s and the unstable nature of the international financial system, if indeed it can still be called a system. Another major issue is that trust and confidence in the rules-based system of the WTO, for example, is being undermined by the bias in favour of rich-country interests and the tendency of the rich to make numerous exceptions for themselves, particularly as regards the import of labour-intensive and other products of interest to developing countries. And in terms of providing acceptable and equitable outcomes of economic *welfare*, the system, as we have shown in earlier chapters, has not performed very well at all; indeed, it is challenged by the fact that the countries which have been most successful in integrating with the global economy, those in

East Asia, are precisely the ones that did not follow – or were not forced to follow – the neo-liberal prescriptions in the crucial early stages of their economic development.

Signs of resistance to the current international order are already beginning to accumulate: the growing political strength of indigenous and more mainstream political movements in Latin America reflects to a large extent a backlash against the policies promoted by the international financial institutions, as do the pre-payments of debt to the IMF by several countries; the accumulation of massive foreign-exchange reserves by a number of countries in East Asia is partly an attempt to provide a form of "self-insurance" against setbacks and international financial instability and to avoid being forced to seek assistance from the IMF; and in Europe and North America there have been growing protectionist pressures against foreign takeovers of domestic firms as well as a range of imports of manufactured goods from developing countries, and increasing hostility against current levels of immigration from poorer countries. Predictably, these developments have been dismissed by officials, ministers and much of the media in the developed countries as signs of irrationality and unwillingness to embrace economic reforms. Superficially that may be true, but underlying these reactions is a more general policy failure to deal effectively with the problems of adjustment and equity, including in the G7 economies, and the continued weakness of much of the global economy to combine output growth with adequate levels of employment and reductions in inequality. In large numbers of developing and transition economies, high rates of structural unemployment and underemployment have been left largely untouched by recent high rates of output growth and unresolved by current policies.

These developments all point to emerging risks to the present structure of the international economic system and if they are not addressed the present era of globalisation will fail like its predecessors. To quote Bertolt Brecht (to whom, of course, we owe the title of this book), things are beginning to change because they have to change. Market fundamentalism is resistible and should be resisted, not least in the broader interests of the most developed economies. If the leaders of the G7 have a serious, strategic interest in the development of the poorer countries in the system and wish to preserve an orderly international economic system, they should start to change direction now – otherwise, the initiative will come from elsewhere. They would do well to recall the words of Adam Smith, who is mistakenly adopted as a father figure by market fundamentalists: "Society may subsist, though not in the most comfortable state, without beneficence; but the prevalence of injustice must utterly destroy it...Justice is the main pillar that upholds the whole edifice" (Smith, 1976:86).

Bibliography

Aaron, H. (1989). "Politics and the Professors Revisited", *American Economic Review,* Papers and Proceedings, vol. 79, no. 2: 1-15.

Acemoglu, D. et al. (2001). "The Colonial Origins of Comparative Development: An Empirical Investigation", *American Economic Review*, vol. 91, no. 5, December.

Ackerman, F. (2005). "The Shrinking Gains from Trade: A Critical Assessment of Doha Round Projections", Global Development and Environment Institute Working Paper no. 05-01, Tufts University.

ActionAid (2005). *Real Aid: An Agenda for Making Aid Work.* Johannesburg: ActionAid International.

Adelman, I. (2000). "The role of government in economic development", in F. Tarp (ed.), *Foreign Aid and Development*, London: Routledge.

Agell, J., T. Lindh and H. Ohlsson (1997). "Growth and the Public Sector: A Critical Review Essay", *European Journal of Political Economy,* vol. 13, no. 1.

Agosin, M. and R. Mayer (2000). "Foreign investment in developing countries: Does it crowd in domestic investment?", UNCTAD Discussion Papers, No. 146.

Ahluwalia, M. (1999). "The IMF and the World Bank: Are overlapping roles a problem?", *International Monetary and Financial Issues for the 1990s,* vol. XI, United Nations publication, New York and Geneva, UNCTAD.

Aitken, B. et al. (1996). "Wages and foreign ownership: A comparative study of Mexico, Venezuela, and the United States", *Journal of International Economics*, vol. 40, no. 3-4.

Akyüz, Y. (1998). "New Trends in Japanese Trade and FDI: Post-Industrial Transformation and Policy Challenges", in R. Kozul-Wright and R. Rowthorn (eds.), *Transnational Corporations and the Global Economy*, London: Macmillan.

— (2004). "Trade, Growth and Industrialisation in Developing Countries: Issues, Experience and Policy Challenges", paper presented at UNDP Asia-Pacific Conference on Trade, Penang, Malaysia, 22-24 November.

— (2005). "The WTO Negotiations on Industrial Tariffs: What is at Stake for Developing Countries?", Geneva, Third World Network.

— (2006). "Reforming the IMF: Back to the Drawing Board", G-24 Discussion Paper Series, no. 38, Geneva, UNCTAD.

Akyüz, Y. et al. (1999). "New Perspectives on East Asian Development", in Y. Akyüz (ed.), *East Asian Development – New Perspectives*, London: Frank Cass.

Albala-Bertrand, J.M. (1999). "Industrial interdependence and structural change in Chile, 1960-1990. A comparison with South Korea and Taiwan", *International Review of Applied Economics,* vol. 13, no. 2: 161-91.

Alfaro, L. et al. (2006). "Capital flows in a globalized world: The role of policies and institutions", paper prepared for NBER Conference on Capital Controls and Capital Flows in Emerging Economies: Policies, Practices and Consequences, February.

Amadeo, E. (1998). "International Trade, Outsourcing and Labour: A View from the Developing Countries", in R. Kozul-Wright and R. Rowthorn (eds.), *Transnational Corporations and the Global Economy*, London: Macmillan.

Amadeo, E. and V. Pero (2000). "Adjustment, Stabilization and the Structure of Employment in Brazil", *Journal of Development Studies,* special section on Structural Adjustment and the Labour Market, vol. 36, no. 4.

Amiti, M. and K. Wakelin (2003). "Investment liberalization and international trade", *Journal of International Economics*, vol. 61, no. 1.

Amsden, A. (1989). *Asia's Next Giant: South Korea and Late Industrialization.* Oxford: Oxford University Press.

— (2000). "Industrialization under new WTO law", paper presented at UNCTAD X High-Level Round Table on Trade and Development: Directions for the Twenty-first Century, Bangkok, 12 February.

— (2001). *The Rise of the "Rest": Challenges to the West from Late Industrializing Economies.* Oxford: Oxford University Press.

Anderson, B. (1991). *Imagined Communities: Reflections on the Origin and Spread of Nationalism.* Revised ed. London: Verso Books.

Arbache, J., A. Dickerson and F. Green (2004). "Trade Liberalisation and Wages in Developing Countries", *Economic Journal*, vol. 114, no. 493.

Arestis, P. (2004). "Financial liberalization and poverty: Channels and influences", The Levy Economics Institute, Working Paper no. 411, Bard College.

Armstrong, P., A. Glyn and J. Harrison (1984). *Capitalism Since World War II: The Making and Break-up of the Great Boom.* London: Fontana.

Arndt, H. (1987). *Economic Development: The History of an Idea.* Chicago: University of Chicago Press.

Asian Development Bank (2000). Asia Recovery report 2000: May Update, Manila, ADB.

— (2006). *Labor Markets in Asia: Promoting Full, Productive, and Decent Employment.* Manila: ADB.

Astier, H. (2005). "The World from France", *Times Literary Supplement,* 18 March.

Atkinson, A. (2001). "A critique of the transatlantic consensus on rising income inequality", *World Economy,* vol. 24, no. 4.

Auer, P. et al. (2005). *Active Labour Market Policies Around the World.* Geneva: ILO.

Aw, B.Y. et al. (1998). "Productivity and the Decision to Export: Micro Evidence from Taiwan and South Korea", NBER Working Paper No. 6558, National Bureau of Economic Research.

Aykut, D. and D. Ratha (2004). "South-South FDI flows: How big are they?", *Transnational Corporations*, vol. 13, no. 1.

Bairoch, P. (1976). *Commerce Exterieur et Developpement Economique de l'Europe au XIXe Siecle*. Mouton, Paris-La Haye.

— (1982). "International industrialisation levels from 1750 to 1980", *The Journal of European Economic History*, vol. 11, no. 2.

— (1989). "European Trade Policy, 1815-1914", in P. Mathias and S. Pollard (eds.), *The Cambridge Economic History of Europe, Vol. VIII*, Cambridge: Cambridge University Press.

— (1993). *Economics and World History: Myths and Paradoxes*. Chicago: University of Chicago Press.

Bairoch, P. and R. Kozul-Wright (1996). "Globalization Myths: Some Historical Reflections on Integration, Industrialization and Growth in the World Economy", UNCTAD Discussion Papers, No. 113, March.

Balasubramanyam, V.N. et al. (1996). "Foreign Direct Investment and Growth in EP and IS Countries", *Economic Journal*, vol. 106, no. 434.

Baldwin, R. and P. Martin (1999). "Two waves of globalisation: Superficial similarities, fundamental differences", NBER Working Paper No. 6904, National Bureau of Economic Research.

Bandeira de Mello (1935). *Politique Commerciale du Bresil*, Rio de Janeiro.

Barrell, R. and N. Pain (1999). "Trade restraints and Japanese direct investment flows", *European Economic Review*, vol. 43, no. 1.

Barro, J. and J.W. Lee (2002). "IMF programs: Who is chosen and what are the effects?", NBER Working Paper No. 8951, National Bureau of Economic Research.

Batou, J. (1990). *Cent Ans de Resistance du Sous-Developpement*. Geneva: Droz.

Baumol, W. (1990). "Entrepreneurship: productive, unproductive and destructive?", *Journal of Political Economy*, vol. 98, no. 5.

— (2000). "What Marshall *didn't* know: On the twentieth century's contributions to economics", *Quarterly Journal of Economics*, vol. 115, no. 1, February: 1-44.

Baumol, W. et al. (1991). *Productivity and American Leadership*. Cambridge: MIT Press.

Bayly, C.A. (2004). *The Birth of the Modern World 1780-1914*. Oxford: Blackwell.

Becker, G. et al. (1990). "Human capital, fertility and economic growth", *Journal of Political Economy*, vol. 98, no. 5.

Bekaert, G., C. Harvey and C. Lundblad (2001). "Does financial liberalization spur growth?", NBER Working Paper No. 8245, National Bureau of Economic Research.

Ben-David, D. and D. Papell (1995). "Slowdowns and meltdowns: Postwar growth evidence from 74 countries", CEPR Discussion Paper 1111, London, CEPR.

Berger, S. and R. Dore (1996). *National Diversity and Global Capitalism.* Ithaca: Cornell University Press.

Bergsten, F. and J. Schott (1997). "A preliminary evaluation of NAFTA", statement to Subcommittee on Trade Ways and Means Committee, US House of Representatives, 11 September.

Berlin, I. (1990). "The Bent Twig. On the Rise of Nationalism", in I. Berlin, *The Crooked Timber of Humanity* (editor: H. Hardy), London: John Murray: 238-61.

Bernard, A. and J. Jensen (1998). "Exporting and Productivity", paper presented at the 1998 Summer Institute, NBER, Cambridge, MA, August.

Berry, A. and J. Serieux (2004). "All About the Giants: Probing the Influences on World Growth and Income Inequality at the End of the 20th Century", *CESifo Economic Studies,* vol. 50, no. 1: 133-70.

Berthelemy, J.C. and L. Soderling (2001). "The role of capital accumulation, adjustment and structural change for economic take-off: Empirical evidence from African growth episodes", *World Development,* vol. 29, no. 2: 323-43.

Berthelot, Y. and P. Rayment (2004). "The ECE: A Bridge Between East and West", in Y. Berthelot (ed.), *Unity and Diversity in Development Ideas,* Bloomington: Indiana University Press.

Bhagwati, J. (1998). "The capital myth", *Foreign Affairs,* May/June: 7-12.

— (2003). *Free Trade Today.* Princeton: Princeton University Press.

— (2005). "From Seattle to Hong Kong", *Foreign Affairs,* December.

Bhagwati, J. and T. Srinivasan (1999). "Outward orientation and development: Are revisionists right?", Yale University Economic Growth Center Discussion Paper 806.

Bhaskar, V. and A. Glyn (1992). "Investment and Profitability: The Evidence from the Advanced Capitalist Countries", Economics Series Working Papers 99144, Department of Economics, University of Oxford.

Birdsall, N. (2005). "Rising Inequality in the New Global Economy", *WIDER Angle,* no. 2005/2.

Birdsall, N. and A. Hamoudi (2002). "Commodity dependence, trade and growth: When 'openness' is not enough", Center for Global Development Working Paper no. 7, Washington DC.

BIS (Bank for International Settlements) (1998). *68th Annual Report.* Basel: Bank for International Settlements.

Blackburn, R. (2006). "Finance and the Fourth Dimension", *New Left Review,* 39, May-June.

Blattman, C. et al. (2003). "The terms of trade and economic growth in the periphery, 1870-1983", NBER Working Paper No. 9940, National Bureau of Economic Research.

Blecker, R. and A. Razmi (2005). "Developing Country Exports of Manufactures: Moving Up the Ladder to Escape the Fallacy of Composition?", Working Paper no. 2, Department of Economics, University of Massachusetts, Amherst.

Blomström, M. and A. Kokko (2003). "Human Capital and Inward FDI", CEPR Working Paper, no. 167, London, CEPR.

Blomstrom, M. et al. (1994). "What Explains Developing Country Growth?", NBER Working Paper No. 4132, National Bureau of Economic Research.

Bloningen, B. and M. Wang (2004). "Inappropriate pooling of wealthy and poor countries in empirical FDI studies", NBER Working Paper No. 10378, National Bureau of Economic Research.

Bloomfield, A. (1968). *Patterns of Fluctuations in International Investment Before 1914*, Princeton Studies in International Finance No. 21, Princeton University.

Bohman, J. and W. Relig (1997). *Deliberative Democracy. Essays on Reason and Politics.* Cambridge: MIT Press.

Bond, S. et al. (2004). "Capital accumulation and growth: A new look at the evidence", IZA Discussion Paper no. 1174, Bonn, IZA.

Bordo, M. et al. (1999). "Is globalization today really different than globalization a hundred years ago?", NBER Working Paper No. 7195, National Bureau of Economic Research.

Borensztein E. et al. (1995). "How Does Foreign Direct Investment Affect Economic Growth?", NBER Working Paper No. 5057, National Bureau of Economic Research.

Bosworth, B. and S. Collins (2004). "The empirics of growth: an update", Washington DC, Brookings Institute.

Bradford, C. (2005). "Prioritizing economic growth: Enhancing macroeconomic policy choice", G-24 Discussion Paper Series, no. 37, Geneva, UNCTAD.

Braudel, F. (1984). *Civilization and Capitalism 15th-18th Century. Vol. III: The Perspective of the World.* London: Collins.

Braunstein, E. and G. Epstein (2004). "Bargaining Power and Foreign Direct Investment in China: Can 1.3 Billion Consumers Tame the Multinationals?", in W. Milberg (ed.), *Labor and the Globalization of Production: Causes and Consequences of Industrial Upgrading*, London: Palgrave Macmillan.

Brittan, S. (2004). "A dubious ideal", *Financial Times,* 2 July.

Britton, A. (1991). "Economic Growth in the Market Economies 1950-2000", *ECE Discussion Papers,* 1, no. 4.

Broadberry, S. and B. Gupta (2006). "The early modern great divergence: wages, prices and economic development in Europe and Asia, 1500-1800", *Economic History Review,* vol. 59, no. 1: 2-31.

Brooker Group, The (2002). "Foreign Direct Investment: Performance and Attraction – The Case of Thailand", Conference on Foreign Direct Investment: Opportunities and Challenges for Cambodia, Lao P.D.R. and Vietnam, Hanoi, 16-17 August.

Brooks, D. and H. Hill (2004). "Divergent views on Asian FDI and its governance", *Asian Development Review*, vol. 21, no. 1.

Brunetti, A. (1997). "Political variables in cross-country growth analysis", *Journal of Economic Surveys*, vol. 11, no. 2.

Bruno, M. and J. Sachs (1985). *The Economics of Worldwide Stagflation*. Cambridge: Harvard University Press.

Buffie, E. (2001). *Trade Policy in Developing Countries*. Cambridge: Cambridge University Press.

Buira, A. (2003). "An analysis of IMF conditionality", G-24 Discussion Paper Series, no. 22, Geneva, UNCTAD.

Burki, S. and S. Edwards (1996). *Dismantling the Populist State: The Unfinished Revolution in Latin America and the Caribbean*. Washington DC: World Bank.

Butterfield, H. (1931). *The Whig Interpretation of History*. London: G. Bell.

Camdessus, M. (1997). "Global capital flows: Raising the returns and reducing the risks", speech to Los Angeles World Affairs Council, 17 June.

Campbell, B. (ed.) (2004). *Regulating Mining in Africa: For Whose Benefit?*. Uppsala: Nordiska Afrikainstitutet.

Carkovic, M. and R. Levine (2002). "Does foreign direct investment accelerate economic growth?", mimeo, University of Minnesota, Minneapolis, May.

Cashin, P. and J. McDermott (2002). "The Long-Run Behavior of Commodity Prices: Small Trends and Big Variability", *IMF Staff Papers*, vol. 49, no. 2.

CEPR (Centre for Economic Policy Research) (2002). *Making Sense of Globalization*. London: Centre for Economic Policy Research.

Chang, H-J. (2001). *Joseph Stiglitz at the World Bank: The Rebel Within*. London: Anthem Press.

— (2002). *Kicking Away the Ladder. Development Strategy in Historical Perspective*. London: Anthem Press.

Chang, H-J. and R. Kozul-Wright (1994). "Comparing National Systems of Entrepreneurship in Sweden and South Korea", *Journal of Development Studies*, July.

Chang, H-J. et al. (1998). "Interpreting the Korean Crisis: Financial Liberalisation, Industrial Policy, and Corporate Governance", *Cambridge Journal of Economics*, vol. 22, no. 6.

Chang, H-J. et al. (eds.) (2001). *Financial Liberalization and the Asian Crisis*. London: Palgrave.

Chenery, H. et al. (1986). *Industrialization and Growth: A Comparative Study*. Oxford: Oxford University Press.

Cheng, T-J., S. Haggard and D. Kang (1998). "Institutions and growth in Korea and Taiwan: the bureaucracy", *Journal of Development Studies*, vol. 34, no. 6.

Chortareas, G. and T. Pelagidis (2004). "Trade flows: a facet of regionalism or globalisation?", *Cambridge Journal of Economics*, vol. 28, no. 2.

Chudnovsky, D. and A. Lopez (2002). "Estragias de las empresas transnacionales en la Argentina de los anos", *Revista de la Cepal*, no. 76.

Claessens, S. et al. (1995). "Portfolio capital flows: Hot or cold?", *World Bank Economic Review*, vol. 9, no. 1.

Clemens, M. and J. Williamson (2001). "A growth-tariff paradox? Protection's impact on the world around 1875-1997", NBER Working Paper No. 8459, National Bureau of Economic Research.

— (2002). "Closed Jaguar, Open Dragon: Comparing Tariffs in Latin America and Asia before World War II", NBER Working Paper No. 9401, National Bureau of Economic Research.

— (2004). "Wealth Bias in the First Global Capital Market Boom, 1870-1913", *Economic Journal*, vol. 114, no. 495.

Clemens, M. et al. (2004). "Counting chickens when they hatch: The short-term effects of aid on growth", CGD Working Paper No. 44, Washington DC, Center for Global Development.

Clerides, S. et al. (1998). "Is Learning by Exporting Important? Micro-Dynamic Evidence from Colombia, Mexico, and Morocco", *Quarterly Journal of Economics,* vol. 113, no. 3.

Cline, W. (2005). "Doha and Development", *Foreign Affairs*, December.

Cohen, S. (1977). *Modern Capitalist Planning: The French Model.* Berkeley: University of California Press.

Congressional Budget Office (1997). *The Role of Foreign Aid in Developing Countries.* Washington DC: The Congress of the United States.

Corden, W.M. (1974). *Trade Policy and Economic Welfare.* Oxford: Clarendon Press.

Cornford, A. (2005). "Enron and internationally agreed principles for corporate governance and the financial sector", G-24 Discussion Paper Series, no. 30, Geneva, UNCTAD.

Cornia, G. (ed.) (2003). *Inequality, Growth and Poverty in an Era of Liberalization and Globalization.* Oxford: Oxford University Press.

Cragg, M. and M. Epelbaum (1996). "Why has wage dispersion grown in Mexico? Is it the incidence of reforms or the growing demand for skills?", *Journal of Development Economics,* vol. 51, no. 1.

Crotty, J. (1990). "Owner-Manager Conflict and Financial Theories of Investment Instability: A Critical Assessment of Keynes, Tobin and Minsky", *Journal of Post Keynesian Economics,* Summer.

Dabrowski, M. (1996). "Different Strategies of Transition to a Market Economy. How Do They Work in Practice?", World Bank Policy Research Working Paper 1579, March.

Dagdeviren, H. et al. (2001). "Redistribution Matters: Growth for Poverty Reduction", ILO Employment Papers, no. 10.

Dangerfield, G. (1970). *The Strange Death of Liberal England.* St. Albans: Paladin.

Darity, W. and L. Davis (2005). "Growth, trade and uneven development", *Cambridge Journal of Economics*, vol. 29, no. 1.

Das, B.L. (2003). *The WTO and the Multilateral Trading System. Past, Present and Future.* London: Zed Books.

David, P. (2000). "Path dependence, its critics and the quest for 'historical economics'", mimeo, All Souls College, Oxford.

Davies, J., S. Sandstrom, A. Shorrocks and E. Wolff (2006). "The world distribution of household wealth", mimeo, December, WIDER, Helsinki.

Davis, C. and J. Foreman-Peck (2001). "The Russian Transition through the Historical Looking-Glass: Gradual versus Abrupt Decontrol of Economic Systems in Britain and Russia", in P.A. David and M. Thomas (eds.), *Economic Challenges of the 21st Century in Historical Perspective,* Oxford: Oxford University Press.

Davis, M. (2004). "Planet of Slums", *New Left Review*, 26, March-April.

De Grauwe, P. and F. Camerman (2002). *How Big are Multinational Corporations?* Research Report. University of Leuven and Belgian Senate. Leuven.

de Long, B. (1999). "Financial Crises in the 1890s and the 1990s: Must History Repeat?", *Brookings Papers on Economic Activity*, no. 2.

de Long, B. and L. Summers (1991). "Equipment Investment and Economic Growth", *Quarterly Journal of Economics*, vol. 106, no. 2.

de Mello, L. (1997). "Foreign direct investment in developing countries and growth: A selective survey", *Journal of Development Studies*, vol. 34, no. 1: 1-34.

— (1999). "Foreign direct investment-led growth: Evidence from time series and panel data", *Oxford Economic Papers,* 51.

Dew-Becker, I. and R. Gordon (2005). "Where did the productivity growth go? Inflation dynamics and the distribution of income", NBER Working Paper No. 11842, National Bureau of Economic Research.

Diaz-Alejandro, C. (1985). "Good-bye financial repression, hello financial crash", *Journal of Development Economics,* vol. 19, no. 1-2.

Dicken, P. (2003). *Global Shift: Transforming the World Economy.* Fourth ed. London: Paul Chapman.

Dijkstra, A. (2000). "Trade liberalization and industrial development in Latin America", *World Development*, vol. 28, no. 9.

Djilas, M. (1962). *Conversations with Stalin.* New York: Harcourt, Brace and World.

Dollar, D. and A. Kraay (2001). "Trade, growth and poverty", *Finance and Development,* vol. 38, no. 3, September.

Doner, R. (1991). *Driving a Bargain: Automobile Industrialization and Japanese Firms in Southeast Asia.* Berkeley: University of California Press.

Doremus, P. et al. (1998). *The Myth of the Global Corporation.* Princeton: Princeton University Press.

Dorman, P. (1997). "The free trade magic act", Economic Policy Institute Briefing Paper, Washington DC, EPI.

Dowrick, S. and J. Golley (2004). "Trade openness and growth: Who benefits?", *Oxford Review of Economic Policy*, vol. 20, Spring.

Dowrick, S. and M. Akmal (2003). "Contradictory trends in global income inequality: A tale of two biases", paper prepared for UNU/WIDER conference on Inequality, Poverty and Human Well-being, Helsinki, May.

Drèze, J. and A. Sen (1981). *Hunger and Public Action.* Oxford: Oxford University Press.

Driffield, N. and J. Love (2005). "Intra-industry foreign direct investment, uneven development and globalisation: The legacy of Stephen Hymer", *Contributions to Political Economy*, vol. 24, no. 1.

Dumenil, G. and D. Levy (2004). "Neo-liberal Income Trends: Wealth, Class and Ownership in the USA", *New Left Review*, 30, November-December.

Dunning, J. (1981). *International Production and the Multinational Enterprise.* London: George Allen and Unwin.

— (1984). "Changes in the level and structure of international production: The last 100 years", in M. Casson (ed.), *The Growth of International Business,* London: Allen and Unwin.

— (1997). "The advent of alliance capitalism", in J. Dunning and K. Hamdani (eds.), *The New Globalism and Developing Countries,* Tokyo and New York: United Nations University Press.

Durbin, E.F.M. (1945). "Professor Hayek on Economic Planning and Political Liberty", *Economic Journal,* vol. 55.

Easterly, W. (2001). "The effect of International Monetary Fund and World Bank programs on poverty", World Bank Policy Research Working Paper 2517.

— (2002). *The Elusive Quest for Growth: Economists' Adventures and Misadventures in the Tropics.* Cambridge: MIT Press.

— (2005). "What did structural adjustment adjust? The association of policies and growth with repeated IMF and World Bank adjustment loans", *Journal of Development Economics*, vol. 76, no. 1.

— (2006). *The White Man's Burden: Why the West's Efforts to Aid the Rest Have Done So Much Ill and So Little Good.* London: Penguin Books.

Eatwell, J. and L. Taylor (2000). *Global Finance at Risk: The Case for International Regulation.* New York: The New Press.

ECLAC (Economic Commission for Latin America and the Caribbean) (1997). *The Equity Gap. Latin America, the Caribbean and the Social Summit.* Santiago: United Nations.

— (2000). *Equity, Development and Citizenship.* New York: United Nations.

Edwards, S. (1998). "Openness, productivity and growth: What do we really know?", NBER Working Paper No. 5978, National Bureau of Economic Research.

Eichengreen, B. (1996). *Globalizing Capital*. Princeton: Princeton University Press.

— (2002). *Financial Crises: And What to Do About Them*. Oxford: Oxford University Press.

— (2004). "Global Imbalances and the Lessons of Bretton Woods", NBER Working Paper No. 10497, National Bureau of Economic Research.

Eichengreen, B. and M. Bordo (2002). "Crises now and then: What lessons from the last era of financial globalization?", NBER Working Paper No. 8716, National Bureau of Economic Research.

Eichengreen, B. and P. Temin (1997). "The Gold Standard and the Great Depression", NBER Working Paper No. 6060, National Bureau of Economic Research.

Ellman, M. (2000). "The Social Costs and Consequences of the Transformation Process", *Economic Survey of Europe*, no. 2/3.

Enrich, P. (2006). "Lining the pockets of big business", *Boston Globe,* 28 February.

Epstein, G. and D. Power (2002). "The Return of Finance and Finance's Returns: Recent Trends in Rentier Incomes in OECD Countries, 1960-2000", Research Brief 2002-2, Political Economy Research Institute, University of Massachusetts, Amherst.

Ernst, D. and D. O'Connor (1992). *Competing in the Electronics Industry: The Experience of the Newly Industrializing Economies*. Paris: OECD Development Centre.

Evans, P. (1979). *Dependent Development: The Alliance of Multinationals, State and Local Capital in Brazil*. Princeton: Princeton University Press.

— (1995). *Embedded Autonomy: States and Industrial Transformation*. Princeton: Princeton University Press.

— (1998). "Transnational Corporations and Third World States", in R. Kozul-Wright and R. Rowthorn (eds.), *Transnational Corporations and the Global Economy*, London: Macmillan.

— (1999). "Transferable Lessons? Re-examining the Institutional Prerequisites of East Asian Economic Policies", in Y. Akyüz (ed.), *East Asian Development – New Perspectives*, London: Frank Cass.

Everhart, S. and M. Sumlinski (2001). *Trends in Private Investment in Developing Countries: Statistics for 1970-2000 and the Impact on Private Investment of Corruption and the Quality of Public Investment*. Washington DC: International Finance Corporation.

Evrensel, A. (2005). "IMF programmes in emerging countries", *Comparative Economic Studies*, vol. 47, no. 1.

Fanelli, J. and R. Frenkel (1993). "On gradualism, shock therapy and sequencing", *International Monetary and Financial Issues for the 1990s*, vol. II, Geneva, UNCTAD.

FAO (Food and Agriculture Organisation) (2004). *The State of Agricultural Commodity Markets 2004*. Rome: FAO.

Feenstra, R. and G. Hanson (1996). "Globalization, Outsourcing, and Wage Inequality", *American Economic Review*, vol. 86, no. 2.

Felix, D. (1961). "An Alternative View of the 'Monetarist'-'Structuralist' Controversy", in A.O. Hirschman (ed.), *Latin American Issues,* New York: The Twentieth Century Fund.

— (1996). "Financial globalization versus free trade: The case for the Tobin Tax", *UNCTAD Review* (UNCTAD/SGO/10).

— (2003). "The past as future? The contribution of financial globalization to the current crisis of neo-liberalism as a development strategy", Working Paper Series, No. 69, Political Economy Research Institute, University of Massachusetts, Amherst.

Fernandez, R. and D. Rodrik (1991). "Resistance to Reform: Status Quo Bias in the Presence of Individual Specific Uncertainty", *American Economic Review,* vol. 81, no. 5, December: 1146-55.

Fields, G. (2001). *Distribution and Development: A New Look at the Developing World.* Cambridge: MIT Press.

Fields, K. (1995). *Enterprise and the State in Korea and Taiwan.* Ithaca: Cornell University Press.

Findlay, R. (1991). "Comparative advantage", in *Palgrave Economic Dictionary*, London: Macmillan.

Fine, B. (2000). "Endogenous growth theory: A critical assessment", *Cambridge Journal of Economics*, vol. 24, no. 2.

Finger, M. and J. Nogues (2001). "The unbalanced Uruguay Round outcome: The new areas in future WTO negotiations", World Bank Policy Research Working Paper 2732.

Firebaugh, G. (2003). *The New Geography of Global Income Inequality.* Cambridge: Harvard University Press.

Fischer, S. (1995). "Comments on 'Economic reform and the process of global integration' by Sachs and Warner", *Brookings Papers on Economic Activity,* no. 1.

— (2003). "Globalization and its challenges", *American Economic Review,* Papers and Proceedings, vol. 93, no. 2.

Fitzgerald, V. (2002). "The conflict of economic doctrines in Latin America", in V. Fitzgerald and R. Thorp (eds.), *Economic Doctrines in Latin America: Origins, Embedding and Evolution*, London: Palgrave Macmillan.

— (2006). "Financial development and economic growth: A critical view", background paper for World Economic and Social Survey, March, New York, UNDESA.

Fontaine, P. (1996). "The French Economists and Politics, 1750-1850: The Science and Art of Political Economy", *Canadian Journal of Economics,* XXIX, no. 2, May.

Francois, J. (2001). "General equilibrium studies of multilateral trade negotiations: Do they really help?", mimeo, Geneva, UNCTAD.

Frankel, J.A. (ed.) (1998). *The Regionalization of the World Economy.* Chicago and London: University of Chicago Press.

Frankel, J. and D. Romer (1999). "Does Trade Cause Growth?", *American Economic Review,* vol. 89, no. 3, June: 379-99.

Freeman, C. (1989a). "New technology and catching-up", *European Journal of Development Research*, vol. I, no. 1.

— (1989b). "The third Kondratieff wave: age of steel, electrification and imperialism", in Kihlstrom et al. (eds.), *Festschrift in Honour of Lars Herlitz*, Gothenburg.

Freeman, R. (2003). "Trade wars: The exaggerated impact of trade in economic debate", NBER Working Paper No. 10000, National Bureau of Economic Research.

— (2005). "What really ails Europe (and America): The doubling of the global workforce", *The Globalist*, 3 June.

Friedman, T. (2005). *The World is Flat: A Brief History of the Twenty-First Century.* New York: Farrar, Strauss and Giroux.

Froebel, F. et al. (1979). *The New International Division of Labor.* Cambridge: Cambridge University Press.

Fukasaku, K. et al. (2005). "Policy coherence towards East Asia: Development challenges for OECD countries", Policy Brief No. 26, Paris, OECD.

Furman, J. and J. Stiglitz (1998). "Economic crises: Evidence and insights from East Asia", *Brookings Papers on Economic Activity*, no. 2.

Galbraith, J.K. (2004). *The Economics of Innocent Fraud: Truth for Our Times.* London: Allen Lane.

Gallagher, K. (ed.) (2005). *Putting Development First: The Importance of Policy Space in the WTO and International Financial Institutions.* London: Zed Books.

Gallagher, K. and L. Zarsky (2003). *Sustainable Industrial Development? The Performance of Mexico's FDI-led Integration Strategy.* Medford: Global Development and Environment Institute, Tufts University.

Galli, R. and D. Kucera (2004). "Labour standards and informal employment in Latin America", *World Development*, vol. 32, no. 5.

Gamble, A. (2001). "Neo-Liberalism", *Capital and Class*, no. 79, Autumn.

Gardels, N. (1991). "Two Concepts of Nationalism: An Interview With Isaiah Berlin", *New York Review of Books,* vol. 38, no. 19, 21 November.

Gerschenkron, A. (1962). *Economic Backwardness in Historical Perspective.* Cambridge: Harvard University Belknap Press.

Ghosh, A. (2004). "Capital inflows and investment in developing countries", *Employment Strategy Papers*, November, Geneva, ILO.

Glaeser, E. and C. Goldin (eds.) (2006). *Corruption and Reform: Lessons from America's Economic History.* Chicago: University of Chicago Press for NBER.

Glass, A. et al. (1999). "Linkages, multinationals, and industrial development", Working Paper No. 99-16, August, Department of Economics, Ohio State University.

Glyn, A. (2004). "The Assessment: How Far has Globalization Gone?", *Oxford Review of Economic Policy*, vol. 20, no. 1.
— (2006). *Capitalism Unleashed. Finance, Globalization, and Welfare.* Oxford: Oxford University Press.
Goldstein, M. (2005). "What might the next emerging-market financial crisis look like?", IIE Working Paper Series no. 05-07, Washington DC.
Gomory, R. and W. Baumol (2000). *Global Trade and Conflicting National Interests.* Cambridge: MIT Press.
Gorg, H. and D. Greenaway (2001). "Foreign direct investment and intra-industry spillovers", paper prepared for the UNECE/EBRD Expert Meeting on Financing for Development, Geneva, 3 December.
Gourinchas, P.O. and O. Jeanne (2003). "The elusive gains from international financial integration", NBER Working Paper No. 9684, National Bureau of Economic Research.
Grabowski, R. (2003). "Promoting industrialization: The role of the traditional sector and the state in East Asia", *Journal of International Development*, vol. 15, no. 5.
Grafton, R., S. Knowles and P.D. Owen (2001). "Social Divergence and Economic Performance", CREDIT Research Paper No. 01/08, April.
Grahl, J. (2001). "Globalized finance", *New Left Review*, 8, March-April.
Gray, J. (1998). *False Dawn. The Delusions of Global Capitalism.* London: Granta Books.
Greenaway, D. (1993). "Liberalising Foreign Trade Through Rose-Tinted Glasses", *Economic Journal,* vol. 103, no. 416, January.
Greenfeld, E. (2000). *The Spirit of Capitalism.* Cambridge: Harvard University Press.
Greider, W. (1997). *One World Ready or Not: The Manic Logic of Global Capitalism.* New York: Simon & Schuster.
Habbakuk, H.J. (1962). *American and British Technology in the Nineteenth Century.* Cambridge: Cambridge University Press.
Hadass, Y. and J. Williamson (2001). "Terms of trade shocks and economic performance, 1870-1914: Prebisch and Singer revisited", NBER Working Paper No. 8188, National Bureau of Economic Research.
Haggard, S. (2004). "Institutions and Growth in East Asia", *Studies in Comparative International Development*, vol. 38, Winter.
Hamilton, G. (1991). *Business Networks and Economic Development in East and Southeast Asia.* Hong Kong: University of Hong Kong.
Hanson, G. (2001). "Should countries promote FDI?", G-24 Discussion Paper Series, no. 9, Geneva, UNCTAD.
Hanson, G. et al. (2002). "Expansion Strategies of US Multinational Firms", in S.M. Collins and D. Rodrik (eds.), *Brookings Trade Forum 2001*, Washington DC: Brookings Institution Press: 245-82.
Hanson, H. and F. Tarp (2000). "Aid effectiveness disputed", in F. Tarp (ed.), *Foreign Aid and Development*, London: Routledge.

Harcourt, G.C. (1972). *Some Cambridge Controversies in the Theory of Capital.* London: Cambridge University Press.

Hare, P. (1990). "From Central Planning to Market Economy: Some Microeconomic Issues", *Economic Journal,* vol. 100, no. 401: 581-95.

Harris, R. (2004). "Government and the Economy, 1688-1850", in R. Floud and P. Johnson (eds.), *The Cambridge Economic History of Modern Britain. Vol. I: Industrialisation 1700-1860,* Cambridge: Cambridge University Press.

Harrison, A. (1996). "Openness and growth: A time-series, cross-country analysis for developing countries", *Journal of Development Economics,* vol. 48, no. 2.

Harrison, A.E. and M.S. McMillan (2006). "Outsourcing jobs? Multinationals and US employment", NBER Working Paper No. 12372, National Bureau of Economic Research.

Harrod, R. (1948). *Towards a Dynamic Economics.* London: Macmillan.

Hart-Landsberg, M. (2002). "Challenging neo-liberal myths: A critical look at the Mexican experience", *Monthly Review,* December.

Hausmann, R. and D. Rodrik (2002). "Economic Development as Self-Discovery", NBER Working Paper No. 8952, National Bureau of Economic Research.

Hausmann, R. and E. Fernandez-Arias (2000). "Foreign direct investment: Good cholesterol?", paper prepared for the seminar The New Wave of Capital Flows: Sea Change or Just Another Tide?, New Orleans, 26 March.

Hausmann, R. et al. (2004). "Growth Accelerations", NBER Working Paper No. 10566, National Bureau of Economic Research.

Hayek, F.A. (ed.) (1935). *Collectivist Economic Planning: Critical Studies on the Possibilities of Socialism.* London: Routledge.

— (1944). *The Road to Serfdom.* London: Routledge and Kegan Paul.

Heilbroner, R. (1980). *The Worldly Philosophers: The Lives, Times and Ideas of the Great Economic Thinkers.* Harmondsworth: Penguin.

Heintz, J. (2003). "The new face of unequal exchange: Low-wage manufacturing, commodity chains and global inequality", Working Paper Series, No. 59, Political Economy Research Institute, University of Massachusetts, Amherst.

Held, D. (ed.) (2000). *A Globalizing World? Culture, Politics, Economics.* London: Taylor and Francis.

Helleiner, G. (1973). "Manufacturing Exports from Less Developed Countries and Multinational Firms", *Economic Journal,* vol. 83.

— (2000). "Markets, Politics and Globalisation: Can the Global Economy Be Civilised?", Tenth Raul Prebisch Lecture, Geneva, UNCTAD.

— (ed.) (2003). *Non-traditional Export Promotion in Africa: Experience and Issues.* London: Palgrave.

Henderson, J. (1991). *The Globalisation of High Technology Production.* London: Routledge.

Herrick, B. and C. Kindleberger (1983). *Economic Development.* Fourth ed. New York: McGraw-Hill.

Hertz, N. (2001). *The Silent Takeover: Global Capitalism and the Death of Democracy.* London: Arrow Books.

Hibbs, D. (2001). "The Politicization of Growth Theory", *Kyklos,* vol. 54, no. 2/3: 265-86.

Hicks, J.R. (1960). "Thoughts on the theory of capital", *Oxford Economic Papers.*

— (1973). "The mainspring of economic growth", Nobel Lecture, Oslo, April.

Hirschman, A.O. (1958). *The Strategy of Economic Development.* New Haven: Yale University Press.

— (1968). "The Political Economy of Import-Substituting Industrialization in Latin America", *Quarterly Journal of Economics,* vol. LXXXII, no. 1.

— (1987). "On the political economy of Latin America", in A.O. Hirschman (1995), *A Propensity to Self-Subversion,* Cambridge: Harvard University Press.

— (1989). "How the Keynesian Revolution was exported from the United States", in A.O. Hirschman (1995), *A Propensity to Self-Subversion,* Cambridge: Harvard University Press.

— (1994). "Social conflicts as pillars of democratic market societies", in A.O. Hirschman (1995), *A Propensity to Self-Subversion,* Cambridge: Harvard University Press.

— (1995). *A Propensity to Self-Subversion.* Cambridge: Harvard University Press.

Hirst, P. and G. Thompson (1999). *Globalization in Question. The International Economy and the Possibilities of Governance.* Cambridge: Polity Press.

Hobsbawm, E.J. (1977). *The Age of Capital.* London: Weidenfeld and Nicolson.

— (1994). *The Age of Empire 1875-1914.* London: Abacus.

Hobson, J.M. (2004). *The Eastern Origins of Western Civilisation.* Cambridge: Cambridge University Press.

Hoppen, K.T. (1998). *The Mid-Victorian Generation 1846-1886.* Oxford: Clarendon Press.

Hufbauer, G. et al. (1994). "Determinants of direct foreign investment and its connections to trade", *UNCTAD Review.*

Hymer, S. (1960). *The International Operations of National Firms: A Study of Direct Foreign Investment.* Cambridge: MIT Press (1976).

— (1979). Various papers, in R.B. Cohen et al. (eds.), *The Multinational Corporations: A Radical Approach. Papers by Stephen Herbert Hymer,* Cambridge: Cambridge University Press.

IDS (Institute of Development Studies) (2005). "Increased aid: Minimising problems, maximising gains", *IDS Bulletin*, vol. 36, no.3.

IIE (Institute for International Economics) (2006). *China: The Balance Sheet – What the World Needs to Know Now about the Emerging Superpower.* Washington DC: IIE.

ILO (International Labour Organisation) (1996). *World Employment Report 1996/97.* Geneva: ILO.

— (2001). *Trade Liberalization and Employment. Paper Prepared for the Working Party on the Social Dimension of Globalization.* Geneva: ILO.

— (2003). *A Fair Globalization. Creating Opportunities for All.* Geneva: ILO.

— (2004). *Changing Patterns in the World of Work.* Geneva: ILO.

Imbs, J. and R. Wacziarg (2000). "Stages of Diversification", CEPR Discussion Papers 2642, London, CEPR.

IMF (International Monetary Fund) (1997). *World Economic Outlook.* Washington DC: IMF.

— (2001). *Silent Revolution: The International Monetary Fund 1979-1989.* Washington DC: IMF.

— (2003). *World Economic Outlook.* Washington DC: IMF.

— (2005). "Review of Access Policy in the Credit Tranches, the Extended Fund Facility and the Poverty Reduction and Growth Facility, and Exceptional Access Policy", Washington DC.

Irwin, D. (2001). "Did import substitution industrialisation promote growth in the late 19th century?", mimeo, Department of Economics, Dartmouth College.

Isham, J., D. Kaufmann and L. Pritchett (1997). "Civil Liberties, Democracy and the Performance of Government Projects", *World Bank Economic Review,* vol. 11, no. 2.

Jacques, M. (2005). "It is national sovereignty that has given China and India their edge", *The Guardian,* 17 September.

James, H. (2001). *The End of Globalization. Lessons from the Great Depression.* Cambridge: Harvard University Press.

Jawara, F. and A. Kwa (2003). *The Real World of International Trade Negotiations.* London/Bangkok: Zed Books.

Johnson, C. (1982). *MITI and the Japanese Miracle.* Palo Alto: Stanford University Press.

Johnson, H.G. (1967). *Economic Policies Towards Less Developed Countries.* London: Allen & Unwin.

Jomo, K.S. (2003). "Capital accumulation, state intervention and privatisation", Initiative for Policy Dialogue Privatisation Task Force, Columbia University.

Jomo, K.S. et al. (1997). *Southeast Asia's Misunderstood Miracle: Industrial Policy and Economic Development in Thailand, Malaysia and Indonesia.* Boulder: Westview Press.

Jomo, K.S. with J. Baudot (eds.) (2007). *Flat World, Big Gaps: Economic Liberalization, Globalization, Poverty and Inequality.* London: Zed Books.

Kaldor, N. (1972). "The irrelevance of equilibrium economics", *Economic Journal*, vol. 82, no. 338.

Kamaly, A. (2003a). "Behind the surge of FDI to developing countries in the 1990s: An empirical investigation", mimeo, Department of Economics, University of Cairo, September.

— (2003b). "Mergers and acquisitions: The forgotten facet of FDI", mimeo, Department of Economics, University of Cairo, September.

Kaplinsky, R., M. Morris and J. Readman (2002). "The globalization of product markets and immiserizing growth: Lessons from the South African furniture industry", *World Development*, vol. 30, no. 7.

Kapur, D. (1997). "The new conditionalities of the international financial institutions", *International Monetary and Financial Issues for the 1990s*, vol. VIII, New York and Geneva, United Nations.

Kapur, D. and R. Webb (2000). "Governance-related conditionalities of the international financial institutions", G-24 Discussion Paper Series, no. 6, Geneva, UNCTAD.

Karshenas, M. (2001). "Agriculture and economic development in Sub-Saharan Africa", *Cambridge Journal of Economics*, vol. 25, no. 3.

Kaser, M. (1990). "The Technology of Decontrol: Some Macroeconomic Issues", *Economic Journal,* vol. 100, no. 401: 596-615.

Kay, J. (2004). *Culture and Prosperity: The Truth About Markets – Why Some Nations Are Rich But Most Remain Poor.* London: Penguin.

Kebbel, T.E. (1882). *Selected Speeches of the Late Right Honourable The Earl of Beaconsfield.* Two volumes. London: Longmans, Green.

Kennedy, P. (1988). *African Capitalism: The Struggle for Ascendency.* Cambridge: Cambridge University Press.

Kenny, C. and D. Williams (2001). "What Do We Know About Economic Growth? Or, Why Don't We Know Very Much?", *World Development*, vol. 29, no. 1.

Kenwood, A.G. and A.L. Lougheed (1994). *The Growth of the International Economy 1820-1980.* London: Unwin Hyman.

Kepel, G. (2005). *The Roots of Radical Islam.* London: Saqi Books.

Keynes, J.M. (1919). *The Economic Consequences of the Peace.* London: Macmillan.

— (1926). *The End of Laissez-Faire.* London: Macmillan.

— (1936). *The General Theory of Employment, Interest and Money.* London: Macmillan.

Khan, M. and K.S. Jomo (eds.) (2000). *Rents, Rent-seeking and Economic Development: Theory and Evidence in Asia.* New York: Cambridge University Press.

Killick, T. (1995). *IMF Programmes in Developing Countries: Design and Impact.* London: Routledge.

Kim, L. (1997). *Imitation to Innovation: The Dynamics of Korea's Technological Learning*. Boston: Harvard Business School Press.

Kindleberger, C. (1984). *Manias, Panics and Crashes*. New York: Basic Books.

— (1986). "International Public Goods without International Government", *American Economic Review*, vol. 76.

— (1989). *The German Economy 1945-1947*. Westport: Meckler.

Kindleberger, C. and P. Lindert (1978). *International Economics*. Homewood: Richard D. Irwin, Inc.

Kirkpatrick, C. (1994). "Regionalization, regionalism and East Asian economic cooperation", *World Economy,* vol. 17, no. 2, March.

Kissinger, H. (1999). "Globalization and World Order", lecture delivered at Trinity College, Dublin, 12 October.

Kobrin, S. (2005). "The determinants of liberalization of FDI policy in developing countries: A cross-sectional analysis, 1992-2001", *Transnational Corporations,* vol. 14, no. 1.

Kolodziej, E.A. (1991). "The Cold War as Cooperation", in R. Kanet and E.A. Kolodziej (eds.), *The Cold War as Cooperation,* Baltimore: Johns Hopkins University Press.

Kosack, S. and J. Tobin (2006). "Funding Self-Sustaining Development: The Role of Aid, FDI and Government in Economic Success", *International Organisation*, Winter.

Kostrzewa, W., P. Nunnenkamp and H. Schmieding (1990). "A Marshall Plan for Middle and Eastern Europe", *World Economy,* vol. 13, no. 1: 27-49.

Köves, A. (1992). "Shock Therapy Versus Gradual Change: Economic Problems and Policies in Central and Eastern Europe (1989-1991)", *Acta Oeconomica,* 44, no. 1.

Kozul-Wright, R. (1995). "The myth of Anglo-Saxon capitalism: Reconstructing the history of the American state", in H-J. Chang and R. Rowthorn (eds.), *The Role of the State in Economic Change*, Oxford: Clarendon Press.

— (2007). "Mind the gaps: Uneven development in an open world", in J.A. Ocampo et al. (eds.), *Growth Divergences: Explaining Differences in Economic Performance*, London: Zed Books.

Kozul-Wright, R. and P. Rayment (1997). "The institutional hiatus in economies in transition and its policy consequences", *Cambridge Journal of Economics,* vol. 21, no. 5, September: 641-61.

Kozul-Wright, R. and R. Rowthorn (1997). "Globalization and Economic Convergence: An Assessment", UNCTAD Discussion Papers, No. 131, Geneva, UNCTAD.

— (1998). "Spoilt for choice? Multinational corporations and the geography of international production", *Oxford Review of Economic Policy*, vol. 14, no. 2.

— (eds.) (1998). *Transnational Corporations and the Global Economy.* London: Macmillan.

Kraev, E. (2005). "Estimating GDP effects of trade liberalisation on developing countries", mimeo, Centre for Development, Policy and Research, School of Oriental and African Studies, London.

Kregel, J. (1994). "Capital flows: globalization of production and financing development", *UNCTAD Review.*

— (1996a). "Some risks and implications of financial globalization for national policy autonomy", *UNCTAD Review,* Geneva, UNCTAD.

— (1996b). "Germany and the creation of Universal Banks", Chapter 5 of *Origini e sviluppi dei mercati finanziari.* Arezzo, Banca Popolare dell'Etruria e del Lazio – studi e ricerche.

— (2004). "External financing for development and international financial instability", G-24 Discussion Paper Series, no. 32, Geneva, UNCTAD.

Kregel, J., E. Matzner and G. Grabher (1992). *The Market Shock. An Agenda for the Economic and Social Reconstruction of Central and Eastern Europe.* Vienna: Austrian Academy of Sciences, Research Unit for Socio-Economics.

Krueger, A. (1990). "Government Failures in Development", *Journal of Economic Perspectives,* vol. 4, no. 3, Summer.

— (1997). "Trade policy and economic development: How we learn", *American Economic Review,* vol. 87, no. 1, March.

— (2004). "Willful Ignorance: The Struggle to Convince the Free Trade Skeptics", address to the Graduate Institute of International Studies, Geneva, 18 May.

Krugman, P. (1987). "Is Free Trade Passe?", *Journal of Economic Perspectives,* Fall.

— (1994). "The Fall and Rise of Development Economics", in L. Rodwin and D. Schon (eds.), *Rethinking the Development Experience: Essays Provoked by the Work of Albert O. Hirschman,* Washington: Brookings Institution.

— (1995). "Growing World Trade: Causes and Consequences", *Brookings Papers on Economic Activity,* no. 1.

— (1998). "Fire-sale FDI", mimeo, prepared for NBER Conference on Capital Flows to Emerging Markets, MIT, Cambridge, MA, 20-21 February.

Krugman, P. and M. Obstfeld (1997). *International Economics: Theory and Policy.* Reading: Addison-Wesley.

Kuznets, S. (1971). "Modern economic growth: Findings and reflections", Nobel Lecture, Oslo, December.

Labour Party, The (2005). *Britain Forward Not Back. The Labour Party Manifesto 2005.* London: The Labour Party.

Lal, D. (2006). *Reviving the Invisible Hand: The Case for Classical Liberalism in the 21st Century.* Princeton: Princeton University Press.

Lall, S. (1995). "Structural adjustment and African industry", *World Development,* vol. 23, no. 12.

— (1996). *Learning from the Asian Tigers: Studies in Technology and Industrial Policy*. New York: St. Martin's Press.

— (2004). "Reinventing Industrial Strategy: The Role of Government Policy in Building Industrial Competitiveness", G-24 Discussion Paper Series, no. 28, Geneva, UNCTAD.

Lamy, P. (2006). "Humanizing globalization", speech, Santiago de Chile, Chile, 30 January.

Langford, P. (1989). *A Polite and Commercial People. England 1727-1783*. Oxford: Clarendon Press.

Lazear, E. (2000). "Economic Imperialism", *Quarterly Journal of Economics*, vol. 115, no. 1: 99-146.

Lazonick, W. (2001). "Public and Corporate Governance: The Institutional Foundations of the Market Economy", *Economic Survey of Europe*, no. 2: 59-72.

League of Nations (1945). *Industrialization and Foreign Trade*. Geneva: League of Nations.

Leblanc, D. (1997). "Political Democracy and Economic Growth: Pooled Cross-Sectional and Time Series Evidence", *British Journal of Political Science*, vol. 27, no. 3, July: 453-72.

Lee, C. and E. Ramstetter (1991). "Direct investment and structural change in Korean manufacturing", in E. Ramstetter (ed.), *Direct Foreign Investment in Asia's Developing Economies and Structural Change in the Asia-Pacific Region*, Boulder: Westview Press.

Levine, R. (1992). "Financial structures and economic development", World Bank Policy Research Working Paper 849.

Levine, R. and D. Renelt (1992). "A Sensitivity Analysis of Cross-Country Growth Regressions", *American Economic Review*, vol. 82, no. 4.

Levy Yeyati, E. et al. (2007). "A Re-appraisal of State-owned Banks", *Economia* (forthcoming).

Liebenstein, H. (1968). "Entrepreneurship and Development", *American Economic Review*, vol. 58.

Lipsey, R. and F. Sjoholm (2004). "Host Country Impacts of Inward FDI: Why Such Different Answers?", in M. Blomström, E. Graham and T. Moran (eds.), *The Impact of Foreign Direct Investment on Development: New Measurements, New Outcomes, New Policy Approaches*, Washington DC: Institute for International Economics.

Lipson, C. (2003). *Reliable Partners: How Democracies Have Made A Separate Peace*. Princeton: Princeton University Press.

List, F. (1983). *The National System of Political Economy*. London: Cass.

Liu, J-T. et al. (1999). "Export activity and productivity: Evidence from the Taiwan electronic industry", *Weltwirtschaftliches Archiv*, vol. 135.

Londoño, J. and M. Székely (1997). "Sopresas distributivas despues de una decada de reformas: America Latina en los Noventa", IDB, February.

Loungani, P. and A. Razin (2001). "How Beneficial is Foreign Direct Investment for Developing Countries?", *Finance and Development*, vol. 38, no. 2, June.

Lucas, R. (1990). "Why doesn't capital flow from rich to poor countries?", *American Economic Review,* vol. 80, no. 2.

Lukacs, J. (1999). *Five Days in London. May 1940.* New Haven: Yale University Press.

Machiavelli, N. (1961). *The Prince.* London: Penguin Books.

Maddison, A. (1995). *Monitoring the World Economy, 1820-1992.* Paris: OECD Development Centre.

— (2000). *The World Economy: Historical Statistics.* Paris: OECD Development Centre.

— (2001). *The World Economy: A Millennial Perspective.* Paris: OECD Development Centre.

Maizels, A. (1963). *Industrial Growth and World Trade.* Cambridge: Cambridge University Press.

— (2000). "The manufactures terms of trade of developing countries with the United States, 1981-1997", Working Paper 36, Queen Elizabeth House, Oxford University.

Maizels, A. et al. (1998). "The Prebisch-Singer hypothesis revisited", in D. Sapsford and J. Chen (eds.), *Development Economics and Policy,* London: Macmillan Press.

Mankiw, G. (1995). "The growth of nations", *Brookings Papers on Economic Activity,* no. 1.

Marichal, C. (1989). *A Century of Debt Crises in Latin America.* Princeton: Princeton University Press.

Markusen, J. (1995). "The boundaries of multinational enterprises and the theory of international trade", *Journal of Economic Perspectives,* vol. 9, no. 2.

Marshall, A. (1890). *Principles of Economics.* London: Macmillan.

Marx, K. and F. Engels (1967). *The Communist Manifesto.* 1888 ed. London: Penguin Books.

Matthews, J.A. and D. Cho (2000). *Tiger Technology: The Creation of a Semiconductor Industry in East Asia.* New York: Cambridge University Press.

Mauro, P. (1995). "Corruption and Growth", *Quarterly Journal of Economics,* vol. 110, no. 3.

May, R. (2005). *Threats to Tomorrow's World. Anniversary Address 2005.* London: The Royal Society.

Mayer, J. (1997). "Is having a rich natural-resource endowment detrimental to export diversification?", UNCTAD Discussion Papers, No. 124, March.

Mazower, M. (1998). *Dark Continent. Europe's Twentieth Century.* London: Allen Lane, The Penguin Press.

— (2005). "The west needs a new sense of self", *Financial Times,* 31 March.

McKinnon, R. (1973). *Money and Capital in Economic Development.* Washington DC: The Brookings Institute.

Meade, J. (1975). *The Intelligent Radical's Guide to Economic Policy.* London: Allen and Unwin.

Mende, T. (1955). *South-East Asia. Between Two Worlds.* London: Turnstile Press.

Micco, A. et al. (2007). "Bank ownership and performance: Does politics matter?", *Journal of Banking and Finance,* vol. 31, no. 1.

Middleton, R. (2004). "Government and the Economy, 1860-1939", in R. Floud and P. Johnson (eds.), *The Cambridge Economic History of Modern Britain. Vol. II: Economic Maturity, 1860-1939,* Cambridge: Cambridge University Press: 456-89.

Milanovic, B. (2002a). "True world income distribution, 1988 and 1993: First calculation based on household surveys alone", *Economic Journal,* vol. 112, no. 476.

— (2002b). "Ricardian vice: Why Sala-i-Martin's calculations of world income are wrong", mimeo, Washington DC, World Bank.

— (2005). "Why did the poorest countries fail to catch up?", Carnegie Papers no. 62, November, Washington DC, Carnegie Endowment for International Peace.

— (2006). "Global income inequality: what it is and why it matters", World Bank Policy Research Working Paper 3865.

Milanovic, B. and S. Yitzhaki (2001). "Decomposing World Income Distribution: Does the World Have a Middle Class?", World Bank Policy Research Working Paper 2562, February.

Milberg W. (1998). "Globalization and its Limits", in R. Kozul-Wright and R. Rowthorn (eds.), *Transnational Corporations and the Global Economy,* London: Macmillan.

— (1999). "Foreign direct investment and development: Balancing costs and benefits", *International Monetary and Financial Issues for the 1990s,* vol. XI, New York and Geneva, United Nations.

Milgate, M. (1987). "Equilibrium: development of the concept", in J. Eatwell, M. Milgate and P. Newman (eds.), *The New Palgrave – A Dictionary of Economics,* London: Macmillan.

Milward, A. (1992). *The European Rescue of the Nation-State.* London: Routledge.

Mishkin, F. (2006). "Promoting the next globalisation", *Financial Times,* 10 October.

Mitchie, J. and M. Kitson (1995). "Trade and growth: an historical perspective", in J. Mitchie and J.G. Smith (eds.), *Managing the Global Economy,* Oxford: Oxford University Press.

Mkandawire, T. (2001). "Thinking about developmental states in Africa", *Cambridge Journal of Economics,* vol. 25, no. 3.

Mody, A. (2004). "Is FDI Integrating the World Economy?", *World Economy,* vol. 27, no. 8.

Mody, A. and A. Murshid (2002). "Growing Up with Capital Flows", IMF Working Paper WP/02/75.

Moore, M. (2002). "How Trade Liberalisation Impacts Employment", speech to the International Labour Organisation, Geneva, March.

Moran, T. (2003). "FDI and development: what is the role of international rules and regulations?", *Transnational Corporations*, vol. 12, no. 2.

Mortimore, M. (1998). "Mexico's TNC-centric industrialization process", in R. Kozul-Wright and R. Rowthorn (eds.), *Transnational Corporations and the Global Economy*, London: Macmillan.

— (2000). "Corporate Strategies for FDI in the Context of Latin America's New Economic Model", *World Development*, vol. 28, no. 9.

Mosley, L. (2006). "Constraints, opportunities and information: Financial market-government relations around the world", in P. Bardhan et al. (eds.), *Globalization and Egalitarian Redistribution*, Princeton: Princeton University Press.

Mosley, P. (1999). "Globalization, economic policy and growth performance", *International Monetary and Financial Issues for the 1990s*, vol. X, New York and Geneva, United Nations.

Murshed, S. (2004). "When does natural resource abundance lead to a resource curse?", EEP Discussion Paper 04-01, London, International Institute for Environment and Development.

Myint, H. (1958). "The 'classical' theory of international trade and the underdeveloped countries", *Economic Journal*, vol. 68, June: 317-37.

Myrdal, G. (1944). *An American Dilemma*. New York: Harper.

— (1953). *The Political Element in the Development of Economic Theory.* London: Routledge and Kegan Paul.

— (1968). *Asian Drama. An Inquiry into the Poverty of Nations.* New York: Pantheon Books.

— (1969). *Objectivity in Social Research.* New York: Pantheon Books.

— (1970). *The Challenge of World Poverty. A World Anti-Poverty Programme in Outline.* Harmondsworth: Penguin Books.

— (1975). "The Equality Issue in World Development", Nobel Lecture, Oslo, 17 March.

Nagesh, N. and J. Pradhan (2002). "Foreign Direct Investment, Externalities and Economic Growth in Developing Countries: Some Empirical Explorations and Implications for WTO Negotiations on Investment", RIS Discussion Papers no. 27, New Delhi.

Nair-Reichert, U. and D. Weinhold (2001). "Causality tests for cross-country panels: A new look at FDI and economic growth in developing countries", *Oxford Bulletin of Economics and Statistics,* vol. 63, no. 2.

Nayyar, D. (ed.) (2002). *Governing Globalization: Issues and Institutions.* Oxford: Oxford University Press.

Nelson, M. and R. Singh (1998). "Democracy, Economic Freedom, Fiscal Policy and Growth in LDCs: A Fresh Look", *Economic Development and Cultural Change,* vol. 46, no. 4, July.

Niall, B. and J. Thompson (eds.) (1999). *The Oxford Book of Australian Letters.* Oxford: Oxford University Press.

Nolan, P. (2004). *Transforming China: Globalization, Transition and Development.* London: Anthem.

Nolan, P. and G. Yeung (2001). "Big business with Chinese characteristics: Two paths to growth of the firm in China under reform", *Cambridge Journal of Economics,* vol. 25, no. 4.

Noorbakhsh, F. and A. Paloni (1999). "The State of Industry in Sub-Saharan African Countries Undertaking Structural Adjustment Programmes", mimeo, Centre for Development Studies, Department of Economics, University of Glasgow.

North, D. (1990). *Institutions, Institutional Change and Economic Performance.* Cambridge: Cambridge University Press.

— (1994). "Economic Performance Through Time", *American Economic Review,* vol. 84, no. 3, June.

— (2003). "The Role of Institutions in Economic Development", UNECE Occasional Paper No. 1.

Nunnenkamp, P. and J. Spatz (2004). "FDI and economic growth in developing countries: how relevant are host-economy and industry characteristics?", *Transnational Corporations*, vol. 13, no. 3.

Nye, J. (1991). "The Myth of Free-Trade Britain and Fortress France: Tariffs and Trade in the Nineteenth Century", *Journal of Economic History,* vol. 51, no. 1.

Obstfeld, M. and A. Taylor (1997). "The Great Depression as a watershed: International capital mobility over the long run", NBER Working Paper No. 5960, National Bureau of Economic Research.

— (2002). "Global Capital Markets", in M.D. Bordo, A.M. Taylor and J.G. Williamson (eds.), *Globalization in Historical Perspective*, Chicago: University of Chicago Press.

Ocampo, J.A. (1993). "New Theories of International Trade and Trade Policy in Developing Countries", in M. Agosin and D. Tussie (eds.), *Trade and Growth: New Dilemmas in Trade Policy*, London: Macmillan.

— (2002a). "The lost half-decade", *WIDER Angle*, no. 2002/2, Helsinki, WIDER.

— (2002b). "Reforming the international financial architecture: consensus and divergence", in D. Nayyar (ed.), *Governing Globalization: Issues and Institutions,* Oxford: Oxford University Press.

— (2005). "A broad view of macroeconomic stability", DESA Working Paper No. 1, ST/ESA/2005/DWP/1, New York, United Nations.

— (ed.) (2006). *Regional Financial Cooperation.* Washington DC: Brookings Institution Press.

Ocampo, J.A. and M.A. Parra (2005). "Explaining the dual divergence: Successes and collapses in the developing world since 1980", background paper for World Economic and Social Survey, New York, UNDESA.

OECD (Organisation for Economic Cooperation and Development) (1978). *From Marshall Plan to Global Interdependence.* Paris: OECD.

Ogilvie, S. (2000). "The European Economy in the Eighteenth Century", in T.C.W. Blanning (ed.), *The Eighteenth Century,* Oxford: Oxford University Press.

Okun, A. (1975). *Equality and Efficiency: The Big Tradeoff.* Washington DC: Brookings.

Oman, C. (2000). *Policy Competition for Foreign Direct Investment: A Study of Competition among Governments to Attract FDI.* Paris: OECD Publications.

Orchard, L.O. and H. Streeten (1997). "Public choice", *Cambridge Journal of Economics,* vol. 21, no. 3.

Ormerod, P. (1994). *The Death of Economics.* London: Faber and Faber.

O'Rourke, K. and J. Williamson (1999a). *Globalization and History.* Cambridge: MIT Press.

— (1999b). "Around the European Periphery 1870-1913: Globalization, Schooling and Growth", NBER Working Paper No. 5392, National Bureau of Economic Research.

OTA (Office of Technology Assessment) (1993). *Multinationals and the National Interest.* Washington DC: Office of Technology Assessment, US Congress.

Owen, R. (2004). *Lord Cromer. Victorian Imperialist, Edwardian Proconsul.* Oxford: Oxford University Press.

Oxford Analytica (2003). "China: Round-tripping inflates FDI inflows", 29 July.

Palma, G. (2004). "Flying geese and waddling ducks: The different capabilities of East Asia and Latin America to demand-adapt and supply-upgrade their export productive capacity", mimeo, Faculty of Economics and Politics, University of Cambridge.

— (2006). "Growth after Globalisation: a 'Structuralist-Kaldorian' game of musical chairs?", mimeo, UNDESA, New York.

Panić, M. (1988). *National Management of the International Economy.* London: Macmillan.

— (1991). "Managing reforms in the East European countries: lessons from the post-war experience of Western Europe", *ECE Discussion Papers,* 1, no. 3.

— (1992). *European Monetary Union. Lessons from the Classical Gold Standard.* London: Macmillan.

Papageorgiou, D., M. Michaely and A. Choksi (eds.) (1991). *Liberalising Foreign Trade.* Washington DC: World Bank.

Pauly, L. and S. Reich (1997). "National Structures and Multinational Corporate Behavior: Enduring Differences in the Age of Globalization", *International Organization,* vol. 51, no. 1.

Pauly, M. (1997). *Who Elected the Bankers?.* Ithaca: Cornell University Press.

Peart, S. (2000). "Irrationality and intertemporal choice in early neo-classical thought", *Canadian Journal of Economics,* vol. 33, no. 1, February.

Penrose, E. (1975). "Ownership and control: Multinational firms in less developed countries", in G. Helleiner (ed.), *A World Divided: Less Developed Countries in the International Economy,* Cambridge: Cambridge University Press.

Persson, T. and G. Tabellini (1994). "Is Inequality Harmful for Growth?", *American Economic Review,* vol. 84, no. 3, June.

Petit, P. (1986). "Full-employment policies in stagnation: France in the 1980s", *Cambridge Journal of Economics*, vol. 10, no. 4.

Pieper, U. (2000). "Deindustrialisation and the Social and Economic Sustainability Nexus in Developing Countries: Cross-Country Evidence on Productivity and Employment", *Journal of Development Studies*, vol. 36, no. 4.

Piketty, T. and E. Saez (2003). "Income Inequality in the United States: 1913-1998", *Quarterly Journal of Economics,* vol. 118, no. 1.

Plender, J. (2003). *Going Off the Rails. Global Capital and the Crisis of Legitimacy.* Chichester: Wiley.

Pogge, T.W. and S. Reddy (2002). "Unknown: The extent, distribution, and trend of global income poverty", 26 July version. Available at www.columbia.edu/~sr793/povpop.pdf.

Polanyi, K. (1944). *The Great Transformation: The Political and Economic Origins of Our Time.* Boston: Beacon Press.

Pollard, S. (1964). "Fixed capital formation in the industrial revolution in Britain", *Journal of Economic History*, 3: 299-314.

Pomerantz, K. (2000). *The Great Divergence: China, Europe and the Making of the Modern World Economy.* Princeton: Princeton University Press.

Popper, K. (1966). *The Open Society and Its Enemies.* Fifth ed. London: Routledge and Kegan Paul.

Prasad, E., K. Rogoff, S-J. Wei and A. Kose (2004). "Financial globalization, growth and volatility in developing countries", NBER Working Paper No. 10942, National Bureau of Economic Research.

Pritchett, L. (1996). "Measuring Outward Orientation in LDCs: Can It be Done?", *Journal of Development Economics*, vol. 49, no. 2.

Przeworksi, A. and F. Limongi (1993). "Political Regimes and Economic Growth", *Journal of Economic Perspectives*, vol. 7, no. 3.

Przeworski, A. and J. Vreeland (2000). "The effect of IMF programs on economic growth", *Journal of Development Economics,* vol. 62, no. 2.

Przeworski, A. et al. (2000). *Democracy and Development.* Cambridge: Cambridge University Press.

Quah, D. (1996). "Twin Peaks: Growth and Convergence in Models of Distribution Dynamics", *Economic Journal*, vol. 106, no. 437.

Radelet, S. and J. Sachs (1998). "The East Asian Financial Crisis: Diagnosis, Remedies, Prospects", *Brookings Papers on Economic Activity*, no. 1.

Rajan, R. and L. Zingales (2001). "Financial Systems, Industrial Structure, and Growth", *Oxford Review of Economic Policy*, vol. 17, no. 4.

Ramirez, M. and N. Nazmi (2003). "Public investment and economic growth in Latin America: An empirical test", *Review of Development Economics*, vol. 17, no. 1.

Rand, J. and F. Tarp (2002). "Business cycles in developing countries: Are they different?", *World Development*, vol. 30, no. 12.

Rasiah, R. (1998). "The export manufacturing experience of Indonesia, Malaysia and Thailand: Lessons for Africa", UNCTAD Discussion Papers, No. 137, Geneva, UNCTAD.

Rawls, J. (2001). *Justice as Fairness: A Restatement.* Cambridge: Belknap Press of Harvard University Press.

Rayment, P.B.W. (1983). "Intra-industry Specialization and the Foreign Trade of Industrial Countries", in S.F. Frowen (ed.), *Controlling Industrial Economies,* London: Macmillan: 1-28.

Reiss, H. (ed.) (1970). *I. Kant. Political Writings.* Cambridge: Cambridge University Press.

Robbins, D. (1996). "HOS hits facts: Facts win; evidence on trade and wages in the developing world", Development Discussion Paper no. 557, Harvard Institute for International Development, Cambridge, MA.

Robbins, L.C. (1932). *An Essay on the Nature and Significance of Economic Science.* London: Macmillan.

Rodger, N.A.M. (2004). *The Command of the Ocean. A Naval History of Britain, 1649-1815.* London: Allen Lane.

Rodriguez, F. and D. Rodrik (1999). "Trade policy and economic growth: A skeptic's guide to the cross-national evidence", NBER Working Paper No. 7081, National Bureau of Economic Research.

Rodrik, D. (1998). "Why do more open governments have bigger governments?", *Journal of Political Economy,* vol. 106, no. 5: 997-1032.

— (1999). *The New Global Economy and Developing Countries: Making Openness Work.* Washington DC: Overseas Development Council.

— (2000). "Institutions for high-quality growth: What they are and how to acquire them", *Studies in Comparative International Development,* vol. 35, no. 3, Fall.

— (2002). "Feasible globalizations", mimeo, Harvard University.

— (2003). "Growth Strategies", NBER Working Paper No. 10050, National Bureau of Economic Research.

— (ed.) (2003). *In Search of Prosperity: Analytic Narratives on Economic Growth.* Princeton: Princeton University Press.

— (2004a). "Rethinking growth policies in the developing world", Luca D'Agliano Lecture in Development Economics, Turin, October.

— (2004b). "Industrial Policy for the Twenty-First Century", CEPR Discussion Paper Series, No. 4767.

— (2004c). "Getting institutions right", mimeo, John F Kennedy School of Government, Harvard University, April.

— (2006). "Goodbye Washington Consensus, hello Washington Confusion?", *Journal of Economic Literature,* vol. 44, no. 4.

Rodrik, D. and R. Wacziarg (2004). "Do democratic transitions produce bad economic outcomes?", mimeo, Harvard University, December.

Rogoff, K. (1999). "International institutions for reducing global financial instability", *Journal of Economic Perspectives,* vol. 13, Fall.

Rolt, L.T.C. (1970). *Isambard Kingdom Brunel.* Harmondsworth: Penguin Books.

Roodman, D. (2003). "The Anarchy of Numbers: Aid, Development and Cross-country Empirics", Working Paper Number 32, September, Washington DC, Center for Global Development.

Ros, J. (2000). *Development Theory and the Economics of Growth.* Ann Arbor: University of Michigan Press.

Rose, A. (2002). "Do We Really Know That the WTO Increases Trade?", CEPR Discussion Papers, No. 3538, CEPR.

Rose, S. (1997). *Lifelines: Biology, Freedom, Determinism.* London: Penguin.

Rosenberg, N. and L. Birdzell (1986). *How the West Grew Rich: The Economic Transformation of the Industrial World.* London: I.B. Tauris and Co.

Rowthorn, R. (1992). "Intra-industry trade and investment under oligopoly: the role of market size", *Economic Journal*, vol. 102, no. 411.

— (1999). "Where are the advanced economies going?", in G. Hodgson et al. (eds.), *Capitalism in Evolution*, Cheltenham: Edward Elgar.

— (2005). "The impact on advanced economies of North-South trade in manufacturing and services", in E. Hershberg and C. Thornton (eds.), *The Development Imperative: Toward a People-Centered Approach,* New York: Social Science Research Council.

— (2006). "The renaissance of China and India: Implications for the advanced economies", mimeo, Economics Faculty, Cambridge University.

Rowthorn, R. and J. Wells (1987). *Deindustrialization and Foreign Trade.* Cambridge: Cambridge University Press.

Rowthorn, R. and R. Ramaswamy (1999). "Growth, trade and deindustrialization", *IMF Staff Papers,* vol. 46, no. 1.

Sachs, J. (1997). "Ireland's growth strategy: lessons for economic development", in A. Gray (ed.), *International Perspectives on the Irish Economy,* Dublin: Indecon.

— (2005). *The End of Poverty.* London: Penguin Books.

Sachs, J. and A. Warner (1995). "Economic reform and the process of global integration", *Brookings Papers on Economic Activity,* no. 1.

Sachs, J. et al. (2004). "Ending Africa's Poverty Trap", *Brookings Papers on Economic Activity*, no. 1.

Safarian, E. (1999). "Host country policies towards inward foreign direct investment in the 1950s and 1990s", *Transnational Corporations*, vol. 8, no. 2.

Sakakibara, E. and S. Yamakawa (2003). *Regional Integration in East Asia: Challenges and Opportunities.* Washington DC: World Bank.

Sala-i-Martin, X. (1996). "The classical approach to convergence analysis", *Economic Journal,* vol. 106, no. 437: 1019-43.

— (2002a). "The disturbing rise in global income inequality", NBER Working Paper No. 8904, National Bureau of Economic Research.

— (2002b). "The world distribution of income (estimated from individual country estimations)", NBER Working Paper No. 8905, National Bureau of Economic Research.

Samuelson, P. (2004). "Where Ricardo and Mill Rebut and Confirm Arguments of Mainstream Economists Supporting Globalization", *Journal of Economic Perspectives,* vol. 18, no. 3, Summer.

Santos-Paulino, A. and A. Thirlwall (2004). "The impact of trade liberalisation on exports, imports and the balance of payments of developing countries", *Economic Journal,* vol. 114, no. 493.

Saul, J. (2005). *The Collapse of Globalism.* London: Atlantic Books.

Schein, E.C. (1996). *Strategic Pragmatism: The Culture of Singapore's Economic Development Board.* Cambridge: MIT Press.

Schive, C. and J-H. Tu (1991). "Foreign Firms and Structural Change in Taiwan", in E. Ramstetter (ed.), *Direct Foreign Investment in Asia's Developing Economies and Structural Change in the Asia-Pacific Region,* Boulder: Westview Press.

Schneider, F. (2002). "Size and measurement of the informal economy in 110 countries around the world", paper presented at an Australian National Tax Centre workshop, Canberra, 17 July.

Schroeder, P. (1994). *The Transformation of European Politics 1763-1848.* Oxford: Clarendon Press.

Schumpeter, J. (1935). "Analysis of Economic Change", *Review of Economic Statistics,* XVII, no. 4, May.

Scott, M. (1991). *A New View of Economic Growth.* Oxford: Clarendon Press.

Self, P. (1993). *Government by the Market?: The Politics of Public Choice.* London: Macmillan.

Sen, A. (1981). *Poverty and Famines.* Oxford: Oxford University Press.

— (1999). *Development as Freedom.* New York: Anchor Books.

— (2005). *The Argumentative Indian.* London: Allen Lane, Penguin Books.

— (2006). "The man without the plan", *Foreign Affairs,* March/April.

Senghaas, D. (1985). *The European Experience: A Historical Critique of Development Theory.* Leamington Spa: Berg Publishers.

Shaw, E. (1973). *Financial Deepening in Economic Development.* New York: Oxford University Press.

Shen, J-G. (2002). "Democracy and Economic Growth", BOFIT Discussion Papers, 2002/13.

Shonfield, A. (1965). *Modern Capitalism. The Changing Balance of Public and Private Power.* London: Oxford University Press.

Shukla, S. (2002). "From GATT to WTO and beyond", in D. Nayyar (ed.), *Governing Globalization: Issues and Institutions,* Oxford: Oxford University Press.

Siegle, J., M. Weinstein and M. Halperin (2004). "Why Democracies Excel", *Foreign Affairs,* September/October.

Singer, H. (1950). "The Distribution of Gains between Investing and Borrowing Countries", *American Economic Review,* vol. 40.

Singh, A. (1999). "Savings, Investment and the Corporation in the East Asian Miracle", in Y. Akyüz (ed.), *East Asian Development – New Perspectives,* London: Frank Cass.

— (2002). "Competition and competition policy in emerging markets: International and developmental dimensions", G-24 Discussion Paper Series, no. 18, Geneva, UNCTAD.

Sklair, L. (2001). *The Transnational Capitalist Class.* Oxford: Blackwell.

Slaughter, A-M. (2004). *A New World Order.* Princeton and Oxford: Princeton University Press.

Slaughter, M. (1998). "International trade and per capita income convergence: A difference-in-differences analysis", NBER Working Paper No. 6557, National Bureau of Economic Research.

Smith, A. (1976). *The Theory of Moral Sentiments.* Oxford: Clarendon Press.

Soueif, A. (2000). *The Map of Love.* London: Bloomsbury.

Stedman Jones, G. (2004). *An End to Poverty? A Historical Debate.* London: Profile Books.

Steele Gordon, J. (2005). *An Empire of Wealth: The Epic History of American Power.* New York: Harper.

Stein, H. (1992). "Deindustrialisation, Adjustment, the World Bank and the IMF in Africa", *World Development*, vol. 20, no. 1.

Stern, N. (2001). *Investment and Poverty: The Role of the International Financial Institutions.* London: EBRD.

Stewart, F. (1995). *Adjustment and Poverty: Options and Choices.* London: Routledge.

Stiglitz, J. (1982). "Ownership, Control and Efficient Markets: Some Paradoxes in the Theory of Capital Markets", in K.D. Boyer and W.G. Shepherd (eds.), *Economic Regulation: Essays in Honor of James R. Nelson*, East Lansing: Michigan State University Press.

— (1985). "Credit Markets and Control of Capital", *Journal of Money, Credit, and Banking,* May.

— (1993). "The role of the state in financial markets", paper contributed to the World Bank Annual Conference on Development Economics, May.

— (1998). "Redefining the role of the state – What should it do? How should it do it? And how should these decisions be made?", paper presented at the Tenth Anniversary of MITI Research Institute, Tokyo, March.

— (1999). "More instruments and broader goals: Moving towards the Post-Washington Consensus", in G. Kochendorfer-Lucius and B. Pleskovic (eds.), *Development Issues in the 21st Century,* Berlin: German Foundation for International Development: 11-39.

— (2001). "Towards a New Paradigm for Development: Strategies, Policies and Processes", the 9th Raul Prebisch Lecture 1998, Geneva, UNCTAD.

— (2002). *Globalization and Its Discontents.* London: Penguin Books.

— (2005). "The Ethical Economist", *Foreign Affairs*, November/December.

Stiglitz, J. and A. Weiss (1981). "Credit rationing in markets with imperfect information", *American Economic Review*, vol. 71, no. 3.

Streeten, P. (1975). "The multinational enterprise and the theory of development policy", reprinted in S. Lall (ed.) (1993), *Transnational Corporations and Economic Development*, London: Routledge.

Studart, R. (1995). *Investment Finance in Economic Development*, London: Routledge.

Subramanian, A. and D. Roy (2003). "Who can explain the Mauritian miracle? Meade, Romer, Sachs or Rodrik?", in D. Rodrik (ed.), *In Search of Prosperity: Analytic Narratives on Economic Growth*, Princeton: Princeton University Press.

Supiot, A. (2006). "The condition of France", *London Review of Books*, 8 June.

Supple, B. (1974). "The State and industrial revolution 1700-1914", in C. Cipolla (ed.), *The Fontana Economic History of Europe, Vol. III – The Industrial Revolution*, London: Fontana.

Sutcliffe, R. (1998). "Capitalism sans frontiere?", *South-North Development Monitor (SUNS)*, 11 November.

— (2003). "A more or less unequal world? World income distribution in the 20th century", Working Paper Series, No. 54, Political Economy Research Institute, University of Massachusetts, Amherst.

— (2007). "A converging or diverging world?", in K.S. Jomo with J. Baudot (eds.), *Flat World, Big Gaps: Economic Liberalization, Globalization, Poverty and Inequality*, London: Zed Books.

Svedberg, P. (2004). "World income distribution: which way?", *Journal of Development Studies*, vol. 40, no. 5.

Svennilson, I. (1954). *Growth and Stagnation in the European Economy*. Geneva: United Nations.

Tahari, A. et al. (2004). "Sources of growth in sub-Saharan Africa", IMF Working Paper 176, Washington DC, International Monetary Fund.

Tavares, J. and R. Wacziarg (2001). "How Democracy Affects Growth", *European Economic Review*, vol. 45, no. 8.

Taylor, A. (1972). *Laissez-faire and State Intervention in Nineteenth Century Britain*. London: Macmillan.

Taylor, L. (1994). "Hirschman's Strategy at Thirty-Five", in L. Rodwin and D. Schon (eds.), *Rethinking the Development Experience: Essays Provoked by the Work of Albert O. Hirschman*, Washington: Brookings Institution.

— (1996). "International capital mobility in history: The savings-investment relationship", NBER Working Paper No. 5743, National Bureau of Economic Research.

Taylor, L. and J.A. Ocampo (1998). "Trade Liberalisation in Developing Economies: Modest Benefits but Problems with Productivity Growth, Macro Prices, and Income Distribution", *Economic Journal*, vol. 108, no. 450.

Temple, J. (2003). "Growing into trouble: Indonesia since 1966", in D. Rodrik
    (ed.), *In Search of Prosperity: Analytic Narratives on Economic
    Growth*, Princeton: Princeton University Press.
Thirlwall, A. (2004). "The structure of production, the balance of payments
    and growth in developing countries", paper prepared for UNCTAD
    workshop on The Relationship Between Economic Growth,
    International Specialisation, and Structural and Technological Change,
    November.
Tiffen, M. (2003). "Transition in Sub-Saharan Africa: Agriculture,
    urbanization and income growth", *World Development*, vol. 31, no. 8.
Tinbergen, J. (1969). "The use of models: Experience and prospects", Nobel
    Lecture, Oslo, December.
Tobin, J. (1984). "On the efficiency of the financial system", *Lloyds Bank
    Review*, no. 153.
Todaro, M. (1983). *Economic Development in the Third World*. New York:
    Longman.
Tomlinson, J. (1990). *Hayek and the Market*. London: Pluto Press.
Toner, P. (1999). *Main Currents in Cumulative Causation: The Dynamics of
    Growth and Development*. London: Macmillan.
Toporowski, J. (2005). *Theories of Financial Disturbance: An Examination
    of Critical Theories of Finance from Adam Smith to the Present Day*.
    Cheltenham: Edward Elgar.
Toye, J. (1993). *Dilemmas of Development: Reflections on the Counter-
    Revolution in Development Theory and Policy*. Second ed. Oxford:
    Blackwell.
Toye, J. and R. Toye (2004). *The UN and Global Political Economy: Trade,
    Finance, and Development*. Bloomington: Indiana University Press.
Trefler, D. (1995). "The Case of the Missing Trade and Other Mysteries",
    American Economic Review, vol. 85, no. 5.
Twomby, M.J. (1998). "Patterns of Foreign Investment in the Third World in
    the Twentieth Century", mimeo, University of Michigan at Dearborn.
UNCTAD (United Nations Conference on Trade and Development) (1988).
    Trade and Development Report 1988. Geneva: United Nations.
— (1993). *World Investment Report 1993*. Geneva: United Nations.
— (1995). *Trade and Development Report 1995*. Geneva: United Nations.
— (1996). *Trade and Development Report 1996*. New York and Geneva:
    United Nations.
— (1997). *Trade and Development Report 1997*. New York and Geneva:
    United Nations.
— (1998). *Trade and Development Report 1998*. New York and Geneva:
    United Nations.
— (1999a). *Trade and Development Report 1999*. New York and Geneva:
    United Nations.
— (1999b). *World Investment Report 1999*. New York and Geneva: United
    Nations.

— (2000a). *Capital Flows and Growth in Africa.* New York and Geneva: United Nations.

— (2000b). *World Investment Report 2000.* New York and Geneva: United Nations.

— (2000c). *Trade and Development Report 2000.* New York and Geneva: United Nations.

— (2001a). *Economic Development in Africa: Performance, Prospects and Policy Issues.* New York and Geneva: United Nations.

— (2001b). *Trade and Development Report 2001.* New York and Geneva: United Nations.

— (2002a). *Trade and Development Report 2002.* New York and Geneva: United Nations.

— (2002b). *Economic Development in Africa: From Adjustment to Poverty Reduction – What is New?.* New York and Geneva: United Nations.

— (2003a). *Trade and Development Report 2003.* New York and Geneva: United Nations.

— (2003b). *Economic Development in Africa: Trade Performance and Commodity Dependence.* New York and Geneva: United Nations.

— (2004). *Economic Development in Africa: Debt Sustainability – Oasis or Mirage?.* New York and Geneva: United Nations.

— (2005a). *Trade and Development Report 2005.* New York and Geneva: United Nations.

— (2005b). *Economic Development in Africa: Rethinking the Role of FDI.* New York and Geneva: United Nations.

— (2005c). *World Investment Report 2005.* New York and Geneva: United Nations.

— (2006a). *Trade and Development Report 2006.* New York and Geneva: United Nations.

— (2006b). *Economic Development in Africa: Doubling Aid – Making the "Big Push" Work.* New York and Geneva: United Nations.

UNDESA (United Nations Department of Economic and Social Affairs) (2005). *World Economic and Social Survey 2005.* New York: United Nations.

— (2006). *World Economic and Social Survey 2006.* New York: United Nations.

UNDP (United Nations Development Programme) (2003). *Making Global Trade Work for People.* New York: UNDP.

UNECA (United Nations Economic Commission for Africa) (2004). *Economic Report on Africa.* New York and Addis Ababa: United Nations.

UNECE (United Nations Economic Commission for Europe) (1984). "Structural changes in North-South trade with emphasis on the trade of the ECE region, 1965-1983", *Economic Bulletin for Europe,* vol. 36, no. 4.

— (1990). "Economic Reform in the East: A Framework for Western Support", *Economic Survey of Europe*: 5-26.

— (2001). "Creating a Supportive Environment for Business Enterprise and Economic Growth: Institutional Reform and Governance", *Economic Survey of Europe*, no. 2.

UN-HABITAT (United Nations Human Settlements Programme) (2003). *The Challenge of the Slums: Global Report on Human Settlements*. London: United Nations.

UNIDO (United Nations Industrial Development Organisation) (2003). *World Industrial Development Report*. Vienna: UNIDO.

United Nations (1988). *Transnational Corporations in World Development: Trends and Prospects*. New York: United Nations Centre on Transnational Corporations.

— (2000). *We the Peoples: The Role of the United Nations in the 21st Century. The Millennium Report of the Secretary General*. New York: United Nations.

— (2005). *The Inequality Predicament*. New York: United Nations.

Vaggi, G. and P. Groenewegen (2003). *A Concise History of Economic Thought: From Mercantilism to Monetarism*. Houndmills: Palgrave.

Van Arkadie, B. (1995). "The state and economic change in Africa", in H-J. Chang and R. Rowthorn (eds.), *The Role of the State in Economic Change*, Oxford: Clarendon Press.

van der Hoeven, R. and M. Lubker (2006). "External Openness and Employment: The Need for Coherent International and National Policies", paper presented at the XXII G-24 Technical Group Meeting, Geneva, 16-17 March.

Van Pottelsberghe de la Potterie, B. and F. Lichtenberg (2001). "Does foreign direct investment transfer technology across borders?", *The Review of Economics and Statistics*, vol. 83, no. 3.

Vartianen, J. (1995). "The state and structural change: What can be learnt from successful late industrializers", in H-J. Chang and R. Rowthorn (eds.), *The Role of the State in Economic Change*, Oxford: Clarendon Press.

Venables, A. (1996). "Equilibrium locations of vertically linked industries", *International Economic Review*, vol. 37, no. 2.

Vernon, R. (1999). "Review of *World Investment Report 1997*", *Economic Development and Cultural Change*, vol. 47, no. 2.

Vreeland, J. (2003). *The IMF and Economic Development*. Cambridge: Cambridge University Press.

Wacziarg, R. and K. Welch (2003). "Trade Liberalization and Growth: New Evidence", NBER Working Paper No. 10152, National Bureau of Economic Research.

Wade, R. (1990). *Governing the Market*. Princeton: Princeton University Press.

— (1995). "Resolving the state-market dilemma in East Asia", in H-J. Chang and R. Rowthorn (eds.), *The Role of the State in Economic Change*, Oxford: Clarendon Press.

— (2001). "Is globalization making world income distribution more equal?", Working Paper Series 01-10, London, LSE Development Studies Institute.

Walsh, B. (1996). "Stabilization and Adjustment in a Small Open Economy: Ireland, 1979-1995", *Oxford Review of Economic Policy*, vol. 12, no. 3.

Wei, S-J. (1997). "Gradualism versus big bang: speed and sustainability of reforms", *Canadian Journal of Economics,* XXX, no. 4b: 1234-47.

— (2001). "Corruption in Economic Development: Grease or Sand?", *Economic Survey of Europe*, no. 2: 101-12.

Weiss, L. and J. Hobson (1995). *States and Economic Development.* Cambridge: Polity.

Williams, H. (2006). "How the City of London came to power", *Financial Times*, 21 March.

Williamson, J. (1990). "What Washington Means by Policy Reform", in J. Williamson (ed.), *Latin American Adjustment: How Much Has Happened?*, Washington: Institute for International Economics.

— (2000). "What should the World Bank think about the Washington Consensus?", *World Bank Research Observer,* vol. 15, no. 2, August: 251-64.

— (2002). "Did the Washington Consensus fail?", speech to Institute for International Economics, Washington DC, 6 November.

Winch, D. (1978). *Adam Smith's Politics.* Cambridge: Cambridge University Press.

Winchester, S. (2003). *Krakatoa.* London: Viking.

Winters, L.A. (2004). "Trade liberalization and economic performance: an overview", *Economic Journal,* vol. 114, no. 493: F4-F21.

Wolf, M. (2001). "Will the Nation-State Survive Globalization?", *Foreign Affairs*, January/February.

— (2003). "Is globalisation in danger?", *World Economy*, vol. 26, no. 4, April.

— (2005). *Why Globalization Works.* New Haven and London: Yale University Press.

— (2006). "A New Gilded Age", *Financial Times*, 25 April.

Woodward, D. (2001). *The Next Crisis? Direct and Equity Investment in Developing Countries.* London: Zed Books.

World Bank (1987). *World Development Report 1987.* Washington DC: World Bank.

— (1991). *World Development Report.* Washington DC: World Bank.

— (1993). *East Asian Miracle: Economic Growth and Public Policy.* Washington DC: World Bank.

— (1995). *Global Economic Prospects and the Developing Countries.* Washington DC: World Bank.

— (1997). *Global Economic Prospects.* Washington DC: World Bank.

— (1999). *Global Development Finance.* Washington DC: World Bank.

— (2000a). *East Asia: Recovery and Beyond.* Washington DC: World Bank.

— (2000b). *Global Economic Prospects and the Developing Countries.* Washington DC: World Bank.

— (2002a). *Global Economic Prospects.* Washington DC: World Bank.

— (2002b). *Globalization, Growth and Poverty: Building An Inclusive World Economy.* Oxford: Oxford University Press.

— (2003a). *Global Economic Prospects.* Washington DC: World Bank.

— (2003b). *Lessons from NAFTA for Latin America and the Caribbean Countries.* Washington DC: World Bank.

— (2004). *Global Economic Prospects.* Washington DC: World Bank.

— (2005a). *Economic Growth in the 1990s: Learning From a Decade of Reform.* Washington DC: World Bank.

— (2005b). *2004 Annual Review of Development Effectiveness: The Bank's Contributions to Poverty Reduction.* Washington DC: World Bank.

— (2006). *Poverty Reduction and Growth: Virtuous and Vicious Circles.* Washington DC: World Bank.

Wraith, R. and E. Simpkins (1963). *Corruption in Developing Countries.* New York: W.W. Norton and Co.

WTO (World Trade Organisation) (1998). *Annual Report.* Geneva: WTO.

— (2004). *World Trade Report 2004.* Geneva: WTO.

Yanikkaya, H. (2003). "Trade openness and economic growth: a cross-country empirical investigation", *Journal of Development Economics*, vol. 72, no. 1.

Young, A. (1928). "Increasing Returns and Economic Progress", *Economic Journal,* XXXVIII, December.

Younge, G. (2005). "We will pay for cheap bananas with prisons, fear and fragmentation", *The Guardian*, 12 December.

Zakaria, F. (1997). "The rise of illiberal democracies", *Foreign Affairs*, November.

Zevin, R. (1988). "Are World Financial Markets More Open? If So Why and With What Effect?", paper delivered at WIDER Conference on Financial Openness, Helsinki, July.